W9-CUO-521

THE FIRST INTERNATIONAL AND AFTER

KARL MARX

FOREWORD BY TARIQ ALI
INTRODUCTION BY DAVID FERNBACH

THE FIRST INTERNATIONAL
AND AFTER

Also available from Verso in the Marx's Political Writings series:

THE FIRST INTERNATIONAL AND AFTER

Political Writings Volume 3

KARL MARX

Edited and Introduced by David Fernbach

VERSO

London • New York

This edition published by Verso 2010
Introduction © David Fernbach 1973
Foreword © Tariq Ali 2010

Translations from the German: 'The Prussian Military Question', the letters on
Germany and on Ireland, 'Speech on the Hague Congress', 'Circular Letter to Bebel,
Liebknecht, Bracke et al.'and 'For Poland' © Paul Jackson 1974; 'Critique of the
Gotha Programme' © Joris de Bres 1974; 'Conspectus of Bakunin's *Statism
and Anarchy*' and 'Letter to the Brunswick Committee of the SDAP' © David
Fernbach 1974; Translations from the French: 'The General Council to the Federal
Council of French Switzerland' and 'The Alleged Splits in the International' ©
Rosemary Sheed 1974; 'Introduction to the Programme of the French Workers' Party'
© David Fernbach 1974
Translations from the Italian: 'Political Indifferentism' © Geoffrey
Nowell-Smith 1970 (reprinted here from the *Bulletin of the Society
for the Study of Labour History*, no. 20, spring 1970)

Contents

References to Marx and Engels's works in the most frequently quoted editions have been abbreviated as follows:

MECW 1–50   Marx and Engels, *Collected Works*, Lawrence & Wishart, 1975–2005.
MEW 1–39   *Marx-Engels-Werke*, Dietz Verlag, Berlin, 1956–64.

Foreword

The recession caused by the capitalist crisis of 2008 triggered a revival of interest in Marx's *Capital* and his other writings on the specific dynamics of the capitalist mode of production. That this system was the central subject of his work is indisputable, but he never thought of the economy in isolation. Capitalism was, for him and Engels, above all a socio-economic or social formation. 'Politics', as one of Marx's more gifted followers from a subsequent generation wrote, 'is concentrated economics'. What was true, if only partially visible during the first few decades of the twentieth century, can now be seen in full-frontal view. In the traditional capitalist states, democracy is being hollowed out by a process – 'globalization' – that systematically subordinates politics to economics, reducing the basic differences between centre-left and centre-right so that there is virtually no difference between existing mainstream political parties. For all practical purposes, the West is in the grip of a political system that has both the incentive and the means to become increasingly despotic. Whether it does so will depend on the degree and nature of the opposition that it encounters from below.

It is this relegation of politics and its Siamese twins, history and philosophy, which makes the republication of Marx's political and historical writings all the more necessary at this time. We are living in a period of historical transition that began with the overwhelming triumph of capitalism in the last decade of the preceding century. As a result Marx's interventionist essays have suffered in recent years, but not, as is sometimes stated on the right, because their premises have been exploded. Marx's political writings have been a casualty of the downgrading and dumbing-down of politics, sociology and history as scholarly disciplines on both a secondary and tertiary level, especially, but not exclusively in English-speaking cultures.

Many of the new radicals of the present generation find it sexy to read *Capital* while ignoring the politics underlying the project. This would have angered Marx, who regarded his work as a unity, which is how it was read by some of his most astute opponents a century later. Joseph Schumpeter, to take one example, wrote in his classic work *Capitalism, Socialism and Democracy* that:

> We have seen how in the Marxian argument sociology and economics pervade each other. In intent and to some degree also in actual practice, they are one. All the major concepts and propositions are hence both economic and sociological and carry the same meaning on both planes.

In other words, it is difficult to grasp the essence of *Capital* without understanding Marx's revolutionary approach to politics and the understanding of history. How could it be otherwise? He belonged to a generation that came of age in the historical period that followed the French Revolution. The cyclical pattern of victory–defeat–restoration–new revolutions–new defeats, and so on, taught him that every historical epoch is a period of transition, of ebb and flow, of crash and renewal, of annihilation and resurgence. The socialism he favoured was based on a society of abundance; its political institutions a reflection of radical, popular sovereignty on every level; its culture transcending the confines of a single nation and creating a world-view. Most importantly, Marx visualized a state that, far from becoming huge, unwieldy and authoritarian, would be pushed to near oblivion. The contrast between this and what became the reality of 'actually existing socialisms' needs little commentary.

Cosmopolitan by nature, revolutions have no respect for borders and can never remain the exclusive property of the country in which they first occurred. This fact also shapes the counterrevolution. Marx observed that this was certainly the case for Europe and, possibly, North America, where the rise of capitalism, he thought, would produce midwives impatient to drag out new children from the womb of the system. As David Fernbach points out in his introductory text, it didn't quite turn out like that; the 'the rock of Soviet civilization' proved to be hollow. Still, the universality of the revolution, or its originality, was never in doubt. It leapt over the heartlands of capital and moved eastwards: first Russia, then China, later Vietnam and, last of all, the American hemisphere. Ignoring the mainland, it alighted on a small Caribbean island, which, at time of writing, remains the only space where capitalism has not yet been permitted to return.

The collapse of 'communism' resulted in passivity, a loss of hope and a new common sense of the age, according to which no alternatives to the new system were possible. Even the agency that

Marx had hoped would lead to revolutionary change in the West had been dismantled. Fordism lay dead, its founding factory in Detroit covered in cobwebs. Production moved east and China is today the workshop of the world, whose impact it is still far too early to predict.

In times like these, when reaction reigned supreme, Marx and Engels did not attempt to mask reality with false optimism. They had written the *Manifesto* while insurrections and civil war had erupted throughout continental Europe, but the 'spectre of communism' was defeated everywhere. The two authors now argued that the rise of a new revolutionary wave was impossible in the short to medium term and that communists should use the period of defeat to study, educate and work hard to develop theories that explained the mechanics of the world to future generations.

Engels retreated to Manchester to work for the family firm; Marx retired to the British Library to study economics. Their erstwhile comrades in the Communist League resorted to character assassination, denounced Marx and Engels as traitors and referred to them as 'counter-revolutionaries', 'hostile to the proletariat' and isolated 'literati'. Never one to ignore an insult, Marx responded in kind just as he had done earlier to Proudhon's intemperate assaults on Babeuf and his socialists. Like some latter-day unconscious mimics, Proudhon too believed that the world could be changed without taking power, a notion that won him the support of many a charlatan. The violent anti-communist language he used in *System of Economic Contradictions* found few defenders even in his own ranks. Marx responded that 'he (Proudhon) bursts into violent explosions of rage, vociferation and righteous wrath (*irae hominis probi*), foams at the mouth, curses, denounces, cries shame and murder, beats his breast and boasts before man and God that he is not defiled by socialist infamies.' Whatever else it was, the cut and thrust of political debate on the left was never a polite conversation, then or later. Nor were the results of this style of debate always positive.

Some of the writing contained in these volumes is the product of financial necessity. Compelled by poverty and the misery of everyday life in Soho to write regularly for the New York *Tribune*, Marx often cut corners and pronounced on subjects of which he could possess only limited information. This did not apply to his essays on Europe. The brilliant imagery contained in his texts on France remains striking to this day, and *The Eighteenth Brumaire of Louis Bonaparte* still inspires admiration from many non-Marxist writers. Unsurprisingly, he got things wrong, which is why his transformation into a secular icon after 1917 did Marx few favours. It was as if everything he wrote was scripture; memories of communist militants in different parts of the world repeating his phrases parrot-like still make one wince.

The idea of a new Marx Library, which originated on the Editorial Committee of *New Left Review* in 1968, was partly designed to challenge this doctrinal approach. It was a year before the magazine launched New Left Books (NLB), which was, in any case, intended to be a quality hardback publisher producing a limited number of books each year. The NLR was of the opinion that given the political and intellectual turbulence then sweeping the globe, a carefully selected and edited Marx Library with new translations from the German was best suited to a mass paperback imprint. Penguin Books and one of its more gifted publishers, Neil Middleton, appeared to be the perfect match at the time, and so it proved. The general editor of the series was Quintin Hoare, and his choices were happily vindicated by the sales figures. The fact that Penguin keeps most of the Library in print is a unique tribute in these times when commerce dominates all. Ernest Mandel introduced the three volumes of Marx's *Capital*, Lucio Colletti the *Early Writings*, and the *Grundrisse* was translated (for the first time in English) and introduced by the American scholar Martin Nicolaus. The political writings were edited and introduced by David Fernbach, who has helped to update this reissue.

The intellectual and commercial success of New Left Books led to the launch of its paperback imprint, Verso, in 1970. It is therefore only appropriate that as Verso marks its fortieth anniversary (and *New Left Review* its fiftieth), the political writings of the thinker who inspired the founders of both are made available once again. There is, of course, another reason. As the century moves forward it is likely that history will have a few pleasant surprises in store for Europe, Asia and Africa. Few predicted the turn of events in South America, where a combination of mass struggles produced social movements and a new-style social democracy that challenged the neo-liberal form of capitalism and reasserted the social responsibilities of the state. Future generations might thus be grateful to have these political texts available once again.

TARIQ ALI
MAY 2010

Introduction

The International Working Men's Association

After an interval of twelve years, Marx returned to organized politics when the International Working Men's Association was founded in 1864. The setting for this second major phase of his political work had changed considerably since the days of 1848, and Marx had to face new problems of political theory and tactics. The Communist Manifesto, in which Marx had formulated the principles of scientific communism, had been far in advance of the actual development of the proletarian movement at the time, and this disparity led to problems which were discussed in the Introduction to *The Revolutions of 1848*. In this period Marx had had to deal first and foremost with the tactics that the proletariat should pursue during a bourgeois revolution, when the industrial working class was a small fraction of the population on the European continent, and only a tiny minority of advanced workers were conscious of the historical tasks that faced them.

By the 1860s, however, modern industry had begun to make substantial headway throughout western Europe. The industrial workers were increasing rapidly in numbers, and had in many parts overshadowed the ranks of pre-industrial artisans and journeymen. Whereas in the 1840s English Chartism was the only mass movement specifically characteristic of the modern proletariat, during the 1860s such movements began to develop in several countries of western and central Europe, as well as in the United States. The theory of scientific communism could now find for the first time a substantial material base. But while the Communist League of the 1840s could easily be very principled in its practice, as a small theoretical vanguard with little effect on the historical process, the broad workers' movements that developed in the 1860s had slowly to undergo the difficult development of theoretical consciousness, each starting from ideologies that reflected their different national experience of economic and political struggle. Working with such movements, Marx found himself called on to apply the tactic he had laid down in the Manifesto: to point out from within the developing proletarian movement its own international and long-term interests, attempting to educate it step by step to the positions of scientific communism.

The organizational initiative that founded the International was taken jointly by representatives of the English and French working classes. On the English side the protagonists were the trade-union leaders involved in the London Trades Council formed in 1860. These trade-unionists were by no means revolutionary or even socialist, and they represented not the broad mass of the English working class but the skilled and relatively privileged 'labour aristocracy' that comprised around ten to fifteen per cent of the English workers. Their chief political aim was to win the suffrage, and on most questions they tended to follow the lead of the bourgeois Radicals. But as workers they had their own specific interests that extended into the international arena, in particular preventing the import of foreign workers to break strikes, which was a quite common practice in the mid nineteenth century. And when a series of strikes in the building trades over the demand for a nine-hour day signalled an upsurge of working-class militancy, the London Trades Council felt its strength and began to extend its activity into political agitation, filling the vacuum in working-class politics left by the demise of Chartism in 1858.

Three events in the international arena helped focus the political consciousness of the English workers in the early 1860s and prepared the way for the formation of the First International. If the Italian Risorgimento aroused the sympathy of the Radical lower-middle class in England, it was followed yet more keenly by the politicized workers. When the exiled Garibaldi arrived in England in 1864 he was fêted by the London Working Men's Garibaldi Committee, and when the British government forced him to leave the country after a short stay, a workers' demonstration in London led to clashes with the police. More crucial was the political question raised by the American civil war, which impinged directly on a large section of the English working class through the cotton famine. At first both major working-class newspapers, *Reynolds'* and the *Beehive*, followed the bourgeois parties in support for the South, but after much controversy Lincoln's abolition of slavery in January 1863 finally swung working-class opinion to override immediate economic considerations, and a campaign of pro-Northern mass meetings helped deter the British government from intervening on the Southern side. Finally, the Polish insurrection of 1863 once more brought into prominence this old touchstone of democratic allegiance, and here again the increasingly confident skilled workers organized their own rallies in support of Poland, and a trade-union deputation called on Palmerston to press for British intervention against Russia.[1]

The actions over Italy, America and Poland were all led by the London Trades Council, in particular by Odger, Cremer and Howell, who were to play important roles in the International.[2] At the same time the suffrage movement gathered steam with the formation of the Trade Union Manhood Suffrage Association in November 1862, and a campaign of mass meetings during 1863. Even though this agitation lacked the revolutionary overtones of Chartism and was carried out in conjunction with the bourgeois Radicals, it marked a definite political renascence.

The campaign of solidarity with Poland was instrumental in forging the link between English and French workers that led to the founding of the International. Under the repression of the Bonapartist regime, the French workers' movement was slow to recover from its defeats of 1848. Blanqui[3] had been released from prison in 1859, but soon went into exile in Belgium; although he left some small groups of followers, they were perforce deep underground and had very little foothold in the growing industrial working class. But although there was at this time no right of

1. For Marx's views on these international developments, see the Introduction to *Surveys from Exile*, pp. 29–33.

2. George Odger was a shoemaker, one of the founders of the London Trades Council and its secretary from 1862 to 1872. He was a member of the International's General Council from its foundation until 1871, and its president until 1867, when the office was abolished. William Cremer, a carpenter, was a member of the International's General Council and its general secretary from 1864 to 1866. He later became a Liberal MP. George Howell, a mason, was secretary of the London Trades Council from 1861 to 1862, and a member of the International's General Council from 1864 to 1869.

3. Auguste Blanqui was the outstanding French workers' leader of the nineteenth century, but still believed that the overthrow of the bourgeois state could be accomplished simply by conspiratorial means (see the Introduction to *The Revolutions of 1848*, p. 24). Blanqui's Société des Saisons organized the uprising of May 1839, and he and his followers played an important role in the revolutions of 1848 and 1870–1. In all, Blanqui spent thirty-six years of his life in prison.

association or assembly, and no freedom of the press, Louis Napoleon tolerated cooperatives and mutual benefit societies as a safety valve for working-class discontent, and in these conditions Proudhon's ideas of social transformation through 'mutualism' took firm root.[4] In 1862 the emperor subsidized the visit of an elected delegation of Parisian workers to the London International Exhibition, and despite the rather compromising circumstances the Proudhonist leaders Tolain and Fribourg[5] made contact for the first time with the English workers' movement. By the following year Bonaparte had inaugurated the 'liberal empire' policy, attempting to stave off the danger of revolution by tolerating a constitutional opposition. In the new political climate the first workers' candidates stood for election to the legislature, and in February 1864, when strikes were legalized, the Proudhonists issued the 'Manifesto of Sixty', which spoke of the conflict between labour and capital. In July 1863 Tolain and four other delegates again travelled to London, this time to speak at a meeting in support of Poland organized by the London Trades Council. At this meeting Odger took the opportunity to raise the question of the import of lower-paid workers into England from the Continent to break strikes, and proposed 'regular and systematic communication between the industrious classes of all countries' as the solution to this problem.[6] From now on this communication was established at least between English and French workers, and on 28 September 1864 a further Anglo-French public meeting was held at St Martin's Hall, where it was agreed to form an international association.

The foundation of the International caught Marx at a transitional stage in his life. In 1862, thanks to a legacy, he became able for the first time since his arrival in England to support his family at a tolerable standard of comfort, and no longer had to undertake journalistic work. Marx had spent the greater part of the years

4. On Pierre-Joseph-Proudhon and his ideas, see the Introduction to *The Revolutions of 1848*, p. 23, and below, pp. 16–19 and 330–2.

5. Henri Tolain, an engraver, became the leading figure of the International's Paris Federation. During the Paris Commune, however, he sat in the Versailles National Assembly and was expelled from the International. E. Fribourg, also an engraver, was his close collaborator.

6. H. J. Collins and C. Abramsky, *Karl Marx and the British Labour Movement*, London, 1965, p. 24.

1861–3 writing the immense manuscript of one and a half million words out of which the great bulk of all four volumes of *Capital* (i.e. including *Theories of Surplus-Value*) was constructed. During this period Marx was frequently ill, and withdrew into almost complete isolation. From the beginning of 1863 to the foundation of the International he published nothing, and only nine letters of his have been found other than those to his family and Engels. When the International was founded in September 1864, Marx's health was still poor, but his economic circumstances and the progress of his theoretical work permitted him to engage once more in organizational activity, and the circumstances in which the International was founded encouraged him to do so. Marx realized that the long night of reaction was now over and that a new upsurge of working-class struggle had finally begun. After the founding meeting he wrote to Engels that he had departed from his usual custom and involved himself in the new organization as 'I knew on this occasion "people who really count" were appearing, both from London and Paris'.[7]

The International was founded without Marx, but it would not have held together had it not been for the leadership he provided. Not only were the European workers' movements at very different stages of ideological development, but the General Council in London, consisting of English trade-unionists on the one hand and Continental émigrés on the other, needed Marx's unifying perspective in order to speak for the international proletariat. For instance, the French representatives elected at the St Martin's Hall meeting were republican democrats, and the Italians were followers of Mazzini; both groups actively opposed an independent workers' movement. Marx was able by skilful manoeuvring to force the resignation of these explicitly non-working-class tendencies, but he realized that to build a united international organization, and to maintain his own position, he would have to tread extremely carefully. The English trade-unionists, though politicized, were indifferent to socialism and hostile to revolution, and the French Proudhonists, who professed a form of socialism, were hostile not only to revolution but to all forms of politics. The Proudhonists also, in their reaction against the rhetorical revolutionism of the republican democrats, were hostile to the presence of intellectuals in a workers' organization. As Marx wrote to Engels, 'It will take time before the revival of the movement

7. Marx to Engels, 4 November 1864; *MECW* 42, p. 16.

allows the old boldness of language to be used. We must be *fortiter in re, suaviter in modo*.'[8]

In line with this tactic, Marx drew up for the General Council the Inaugural Address and Provisional Rules. These were particularly designed to present at least a part of the ideas of scientific communism in a form acceptable to the pragmatic English trade-unionists, from which base Marx hoped to win over the Proudhonists of the French-speaking countries and the German Lassalleans.[9] The Address was privately described by Marx as 'a sort of review of the adventures of the Working Classes since 1845',[10] and he took as his starting-point the uncontentious thesis of the ever widening gap between the wealth produced by modern industry and the poverty of the working class that had characterized the previous two decades, and the 'solidarity of defeat' that united the English and Continental working classes after the failures of 1848.

The programmatic formulations of the Inaugural Address read rather tamely beside the declamatory language of the Manifesto, and although the essential thesis of Marxian communism is hinted at in the Address, it is couched in veiled and cautious terms. Thus after referring to the Ten Hours Act passed in 1846 as 'the victory of a principle . . . the first time that in broad daylight the political economy of the middle class succumbed to the political economy of the working class', and to the producers' cooperative movement as 'a still greater victory',[11] Marx goes on to argue that capitalism cannot be transformed by purely economic means. 'National means' are necessary to develop cooperative labour to national dimensions, 'yet the lords of land and the lords of capital will always use their political privileges for the defence and perpetuation of their economical monopolies . . . To conquer political power has therefore become the great duty of the working classes.'[12] Marx's insistence on conquering political power may seem decisive in our hindsight, but in the context of the Address it was ambiguous enough, and the majority of the International's English supporters undoubtedly interpreted it simply as winning

8. 'Strong in deed, gentle in style'; ibid., p. 17.

9. On Ferdinand Lassalle and the movement he founded, see below, pp. 20–3.

10. Marx to Engels, 4 November 1864; *MECW* 42, p. 18.

11. 'Inaugural Address of the International Working Men's Association', below, p. 79.

12. Ibid., p. 80.

the suffrage. Although Marx had once written, in the days of the Chartist movement, that 'universal suffrage is the equivalent for political power for the working class in England',[13] he certainly did not see the Second Reform Bill of 1867, which satisfied present trade-union aspirations, as 'equivalent for political power', especially in the circumstances in which it was carried. However, Marx was convinced that the commitment of the working class to political activity would necessarily lead it onto the road of communist revolution, and he was certainly correct in counting it a significant advance to bring the working classes of Europe together into a common political organization. Marx ended the Address by stressing the importance of the 'heroic resistance' of the English working class to the government's aspirations for war with the Northern states of America, and asserted that the indifference with which the upper classes of Europe had allowed the assassination of the Polish insurrection had 'taught the working classes the duty to master themselves the mysteries of international politics'.[14]

As Marx had anticipated, the Address struck a particularly favourable chord in the ranks of the English trade-unionists. They were proud of the internationalist record they had built up over the past few years, they were once more engaged in struggle for the suffrage, and they expected the International they had set up to provide the material benefits of international cooperation. With the Address Marx proved himself a friend of the English workers, and this alliance provided the political centre of the International up to the split of 1871–2.

Following the General Council's acceptance of the Address and the Provisional Rules, Marx set to work to build up the International's organization. He was able to use the General Council's power of cooption to bring on some former members of the Communist League and other exiles more or less under his influence, and a particularly valuable role was played in the International's early years by Eccarius,[15] a German exile and former League member who had integrated himself into the English trade-union movement.

13. 'The Chartists', *Surveys from Exile*, p. 264.
14. 'Inaugural Address . . .', below, p. 81.
15. Johann Georg Eccarius, a tailor and writer, was at the time one of Marx's closest followers, but in the later 1860s fell into the reformism of his English colleagues.

Two more of Marx's supporters, Jung and Dupont,[16] became the corresponding secretaries for Switzerland and France, while Marx himself acted as corresponding secretary for Germany. As one of his first initiatives on the General Council, Marx drew up an 'Address to President Lincoln',[17] congratulating Lincoln on his re-election, which gave the International its first burst of publicity when a cordial reply sent via the US legation was published in *The Times*. Marx intervened consistently to stress the importance of solidarity with Poland, and began to conduct some basic educational work among the General Council members, notably producing in spring 1865 his paper *Value, Price and Profit*,[18] in which he presented for the first time his theory of surplus-value.

The main ideological struggle during the first four years of the International's life was between the ideas of Marx and those of Proudhon. Proudhon's characteristic doctrine of mutualism envisaged the transformation of capitalism by means of producer cooperatives financed by a 'people's bank'. The Proudhonists rejected strikes as a 'forcible' interference into economic relations, and they rejected *a fortiori* all political struggle. Despite the working-class social base of Proudhonism, Marx had already characterized it in 1847 as a petty-bourgeois ideological tendency,[19] and in the 1860s it continued to express the outlook of a proletariat that still had a strong artisanal consciousness, not least in its insistence on relegating women to their 'proper' place in the home.[20]

16. Hermann Jung was a Swiss watchmaker, Eugène Dupont a French musical instrument maker; both were political exiles.

17. In *MECW* 20, pp. 19–21. For Marx's attitude to Lincoln, see also the Introduction to *Surveys from Exile*, p. 32.

18. In *MECW* 20, pp. 101–48.

19. In *The Poverty of Philosophy*. After Proudhon's death, Marx wrote a shorter critique of his ideas in a letter to Schweitzer of 24 January 1865; *MECW* 20, pp. 26–33.

20. The International, based as it was on an alliance between the exclusively male 'labour aristocracy' in England and the militantly anti-feminist Proudhonists of the French-speaking countries, was essentially male in its outlook, as its very name implies. But this was not unchallenged. A women's section of the International was founded in Paris in April 1871, during the Commune, and in August 1871 Victoria Woodhull and Tennessee Claflin founded a section of the International in New York on an explicitly feminist programme. Marx responded to the French development by moving a resolution at the London Conference of 1871 recommending the formation of working women's branches, which was not to 'interfere with the existence or formation of branches composed of both sexes' (*IWMA* IV, p. 442). However, he would have no truck with the American feminists, noting Victoria Woodhull as a 'banker's

The first round in this battle was prepared at the London Conference of the International in September 1865, and fought out at its first Congress, held in Geneva a year later. For the Geneva Congress Marx drafted a set of instructions for the delegates of the General Council, on the basis of a series of preliminary discussions. This document amounts to a concrete programme of action for the International. It emphasizes the importance of the struggle to win reforms from the existing bourgeois state, with particular regard to labour legislation (the eight-hour day, etc.), and the role of the trade unions in this struggle. Marx argued against the Proudhonists that the working class could win valuable reforms before it could bring about socialism, and that there was no other method at present of achieving these than through '*general laws*, enforced by the power of the state'. He stressed that 'in enforcing such laws, the working class do not fortify governmental power. On the contrary, they transform that power, now used against them, into their own agency.'[21] However, although Marx was to be historically vindicated in his insistence that the working class could win concessions from the capitalist state, these formulations, if taken in isolation, lay themselves open to a reformist interpretation. Marx did not make clear here to what extent the workers could transform the existing governmental power into their own agency, and what the limits of this transformation were. The revisionist Social-Democrats were later to use texts such as these to justify their claim that the working class could gradually take over the existing state and wield it to its own purposes. As we shall see, Marx rejected this possibility in the two most important political texts of this later period, *The Civil War in France* and the 'Critique of the Gotha Programme'. In the International's early years, however, Marx was forced to operate '*suaviter in modo*', and this fact must be taken into account in interpreting the documents he wrote for the International.

In the 'Instructions for Delegates' Marx went on to argue that trade unions were legitimate and necessary, while simultaneously insisting with an eye to his English audience that the present trade unions had

---

woman, free-lover, and general humbug' (*MECW* 23, p. 636). Marx's general attitude towards the nineteenth-century women's movement is difficult to discover, as it emerges only in asides such as this; Victoria Woodhull's section did undoubtedly have a definite middle-class character.

21. 'Instructions for Delegates to the Geneva Conference', below, p. 89.

'not yet fully understood their power of acting against the system of wage slavery itself', and 'must now learn to act deliberately as organizing centres of the working class in the broad interest of its *complete emancipation*. They must aid every social and political movement tending in that direction.'[22] Marx certainly had no illusion that the English trade-unionists of this time represented more than a minority of relatively privileged skilled workers, and he specifically stressed that they had to learn to 'consider themselves and act as the champions and representatives of the whole working class', to 'enlist the non-society men in their ranks' and 'convince the world at large that their efforts, far from being narrow and selfish, aim at the emancipation of the downtrodden millions'.[23] However, Marx was to be deceived in the expectations he held out for the English 'new model unions'. At this time these were the only working-class organizations in England, and therefore the only working-class representatives with whom Marx could make contact, but the stake that the labour aristocracy's privilege gave it in bourgeois society was to lead the trade unions into firm alliance with the Liberal party once the 1867 Reform Bill had been won.

Marx's struggle against Proudhonism carried over from the Geneva Congress of 1866 to the Congresses of Lausanne in 1867 and Brussels in 1868. At Geneva Marx's alliance of English trade-unionists, German Social-Democrats and his personal supporters among the London exiles carried through most of his resolutions, with certain minor concessions to the Proudhonists; but at Lausanne, where only a few English delegates attended, the Proudhonists were in a majority and easily dominated the Congress. However, the Brussels Congress of 1868, the largest and most representative of the International's Congresses to date, marked Marx's decisive victory. Although lip-service was still paid to 'mutual credit', the capitalist tendencies of existing cooperative experiments were denounced, and for the first time the Congress went on record in favour of the public ownership of land, including mines, railways, forests, canals, roads and telegraphs. This resolution was passed by a considerable majority, though in view of its importance, the subject was tabled for further discussion the following year. The International had thus developed a long way from its original conception as simply a workers' defence society.

22. Ibid., pp. 91–2.
23. Ibid., p. 92.

During the late 1860s the International gradually extended its organization. The structure it adopted was one of branches that corresponded with the General Council in London either directly, or via a national federal council. The General Council itself filled the function of a federal council for England. Besides individual membership, trade unions and other workers' societies that endorsed the aims of the International could affiliate. Even at its peak, the individual membership of the International does not seem to have run into more than a few thousands, although affiliated membership in England, where this was most important, reached over 50,000. However, the International steadily acquired influence and support well beyond the limits of its formal adherents. It did this in large measure through the support it was able to provide for strikes in different countries, both financially and, more important, by preventing the import of foreign blacklegs and by mobilizing international solidarity. In 1866 the Sheffield Conference of trade unions, forerunner of the TUC, called on its member societies to support the International, and the General Council steadily gained affiliations. It is noteworthy, however, that the English affiliations to the International came almost entirely from the craft unions in small-scale traditional industries and the building trades, and scarcely at all from unions engaged in mining, engineering and heavy industry, where the threat of foreign competition was at this time minimal.

On the Continent the International was at first slower to gain ground, but began to make rapid headway from 1867 onwards, when an upsurge of strike activity across most of western Europe followed in the wake of economic recession. In France, Switzerland and Belgium, successful intervention by the International in local strikes led to the building of strong sections, and these strikes also dealt a severe blow to Proudhonist ideology, as became visible at the Brussels Congress. In turn, the French Internationalists' involvement in successful strikes brought down on them severe repression from the Bonapartist regime, and the Paris Federation was crippled by three trials and the imprisonment of most of its leaders. This led to a section of left-wing Proudhonists taking a further step towards understanding the need for political action, and this group, led by Varlin,[24] was to play an important role in the Paris Commune of 1871.

24. Eugène Varlin, a bookbinder and the leader of the left-wing Proudhonists, played a prominent role in the organization of the Commune's defence, and was captured and shot by the Versailles forces.

German Social-Democracy

A major weakness of the International was the relative indifference it met with in Germany. Although the 1860s saw the development in Germany of a political workers' movement stronger in numbers and possibly more advanced in its ideology than elsewhere in Europe, Marx's influence on German Social-Democracy remained minimal, although this movement was later to present itself as the paradigm of a Marxist workers' party. German Social-Democracy arose in a political conjuncture dominated by the struggle between Prussia and Austria for German hegemony, and was at first strongly marked by its Prussian origins. After the defeat of the 1848 revolution, heavy political reaction had reigned in Prussia until 1859, when the regency of Prince William (later William I) inaugurated the 'New Era'. Opposition activity was once more tolerated, and in 1861 the liberal bourgeoisie formed the Progressive party, which demanded parliamentary government, though not universal suffrage. The German working class was slow to develop any political consciousness after the period of reaction, and the first workers' organizations were only a tail of the liberal bourgeoisie. However, German politics were polarized in October 1862, when the Prussian Diet refused Bismarck, the newly appointed Chancellor, the army credits he requested. Bismarck then announced his intention to unify Germany by 'blood and iron', and proceeded for the next four years to levy taxation unconstitutionally.

It was against this background that Ferdinand Lassalle conducted his agitation. Lassalle had taken part in the 1848 revolution, but, less compromised than most, he remained in Germany during the 1850s and was Marx and Engels's most regular correspondent there. Although he claimed to accept the Communist Manifesto, Lassalle was personally ambitious and lapsed into opportunism, seeing himself in the role of heroic saviour of the working class. However, Lassalle had already shown, in the international crisis of 1859, that he understood earlier than Marx and Engels the changed balance of forces within Germany.[25] Realizing that a renewed attempt at a democratic revolution of the 1848 type was no longer possible, he premised his campaign on the acceptance of German unification from

---

25. See the Introduction to *Surveys from Exile*, pp. 30–1.

above by Prussian arms. In May 1863 Lassalle founded the General Association of German Workers (ADAV) and conducted a series of mass meetings calling for universal suffrage and state-financed 'cooperative factories'. Lassalle's historic merit, as Marx recognized, was to have reawakened the German working class and formed the first socialist workers' party,[26] but in the circumstances of the time and under Lassalle's leadership this took a highly distorted form. Lassalle was even in secret correspondence with Bismarck, and hoped to secure working-class support for Bismarck's annexationist plans in return for universal suffrage and state-supported cooperatives – a deal that Bismarck rejected, realizing that Lassalle could not deliver the goods. Soon after, in August 1864, Lassalle was killed in a duel.

As far as perspectives for German development were concerned, Marx was most probably mistaken in holding that the liberal bourgeoisie could not be dismissed as a revolutionary force, and that the working class could successfully spur it onwards in the constitutional struggle against Bismarck. However, Marx was unquestionably right in insisting that the workers' party should attack as its main enemy the feudal and absolutist state, and not hedge this fundamental issue as Lassalle did by concentrating simply on the workers' exploitation by capital. Marx saw Lassalle's failure to demand the repeal of the anti-combination laws as particularly pernicious, since this did not just follow from Lassalle's mistaken theory of the 'iron law of wages', but expressed his refusal to accept and encourage the direct expression of working-class self-activity. The right of combination was 'a means of breaking the rule of the police and bureaucracy, and of smashing the "*Gesindeordnung*" and the rule of the aristocracy on the land'.[27]

Marx did not attack Lassalle publicly during his agitation, which took place while he had completely withdrawn from political activity. But the International brought Marx back into political life only one month after Lassalle's death. The ADAV was thrown into crisis by the loss of its charismatic leader, and Marx took the opportunity to attempt to counteract the pernicious legacy of the 'workers' dictator'.[28] As a first step, Marx allowed himself to be

26. Marx to Schweitzer, 13 October 1868; below, p. 154.
27. Marx to Schweitzer, 13 February 1865; below, p. 147. The *Gesindeordnung* (farm servants' code) was the semi-feudal legal code in force in east-Elbian Prussia.
28. Marx to Kugelmann, 23 February 1865; below, p. 148.

nominated for the ADAV presidency in December 1864, though only for propaganda purposes, as he had no intention of returning to Prussia. However this move failed, and only signalled the fact that Marx was virtually unknown to the new generation of German working-class militants. Secondly, Marx attempted to obtain ADAV affiliation to the International, but this also drew a blank, as the party would not risk contravening the law that prohibited such international affiliation. Marx's final attempt to influence the ADAV was to accept an offer that he and Engels should collaborate with the Lassallean newspaper *Social-Demokrat*, making the one condition that the paper should follow an uncompromising line towards the Prussian government, and attack the feudal-absolutist regime at least as strongly as it attacked the bourgeoisie. However it was not long before J. B. von Schweitzer, who now led the Lassallean party, openly expressed ADAV support for Bismarck's national policy in the columns of the paper, whereupon Marx and Engels publicly broke off all relations with the Lassallean organization.[29]

In February 1865, therefore, Marx had to abandon for the time being his hopes of winning the ADAV for the International, and for the next three years he had only a minimal entry into the German workers' movement, through the work of Wilhelm Liebknecht and Johann Philipp Becker. Liebknecht, later the leader of the German Social-Democratic Party, had been a protégé of Marx in London during the 1850s. Back in Germany in the 1860s, he worked with the Union of German Workers' Societies, although this was composed primarily of artisans rather than industrial workers, had been formed as a loose federation on a specifically non-socialist programme, and was allied to the petty-bourgeois People's Party of south Germany. Marx corresponded regularly with Liebknecht, and attempted to guide his work. It cannot be denied that Liebknecht and his comrade August Bebel[30] did valuable work in drawing sections of the working class outside of Prussia towards the International, and in 1868 their Union adopted the preamble to the International's

29. See Marx and Engels's letter 'To the Editor of the *Social-Demokrat*', 23 February 1865; *MECW* 20, p. 80.

30. August Bebel, a manual worker by origin, first proved himself as a workers' leader in this period. He later became both the leading tactician of the German Social-Democratic Party and a socialist theorist, publishing in particular *Woman and Socialism* (1883).

Rules[31] as its own statement of principles. However, in the face of the unresolved problem of German unification, Liebknecht acted as a 'great German' and anti-Prussian first, and a workers' leader second. Marx had frequent occasion to criticize him for his uncritical attitude towards the south German petty bourgeoisie, and his inability to attack simultaneously both the pro-Prussian and pro-Austrian bourgeois fractions. Throughout this period the International could not exist as a public organization in Germany, and J. P. Becker coordinated the German-speaking sections from Geneva, where he published *Die Vorbote* [*The Herald*]. It was largely Becker's work that prepared the Union of German Workers' Societies to adopt the International's programme, and his influence was also felt within the ADAV. However, Becker, despite the advice he received from Marx, was considerably more confused ideologically than Liebknecht – in 1868 he temporarily switched his allegiance to Bakunin – and could not hope to provide an effective leadership from outside Germany.

During the critical years of German unification, Marx thus had no real influence on the growing German workers' movement. However, after Prussian hegemony became a *fait accompli* with the defeat of Austria in 1866, the ADAV was no longer imprisoned by its position on the national question and began to function far more independently. When Liebknecht, along with his petty-bourgeois friends in the People's Party, refused to recognize the irreversible character of the Prussian victory, Marx established friendly relations with Schweitzer, advising him in particular on the formation of trade unions.[32] In 1869 the ADAV split (Schweitzer remaining with the dogmatic Lassalleans), and the ADAV opposition joined forces with Liebknecht and Bebel's Union to form the Social-Democratic Workers' Party (SDAP) on a programme that rather confusedly amalgamated Marxist, Lassallean and democratic ideas. However, the SDAP, although it now affiliated formally to the International, maintained what Engels called a 'purely platonic relationship'[33] to it. It thus showed itself, even before the Franco-Prussian war of 1870, to be the new strictly national type of workers' party that was to characterize the period between the Franco-Prussian war and the First World War.

---

31. I.e. the first six paragraphs of the Rules; below, p. 82.
32. Marx to Schweitzer, 13 October 1868; below, pp. 156–7.
33. Engels to Cuno, 7–8 May 1872; *MECW* 44, p. 371.

England and Ireland

After Marx's failure to influence the German workers' movement, he turned his attention primarily to England. On the General Council Marx had the ear of a considerable section of influential English trade-unionists, and over the years he led them through a series of discussions which included the theory of surplus-value, the role of trade unions, the Polish question, suffrage reform, land nationalization, cooperatives, etc. However, despite his initial optimism, Marx failed to make any real progress in winning the English workers' leaders towards the ideas of scientific communism. His first setback with the English was the course taken by the Reform League. This organization was formed in spring 1865 by the same trade-unionists who were involved in the International, and based itself on the principle of manhood suffrage as opposed to the Radical platform of household suffrage. Marx was highly enthusiastic, and wrote to Engels on 1 May 1865, 'The great success of the International Association is this: the Reform League is our work . . . We have baffled all attempts of the middle class to mislead the working class.'[34]

In the summer of 1866 the Reform League led militant demonstrations in Trafalgar Square and Hyde Park, and on 6 May 1867 a Reform League meeting in Hyde Park, which with 150,000 participants was the most massive workers' demonstration in Britain since 1848, ended in a riot. Certainly in the 1860s the English workers had not entirely lost the revolutionary potential they had shown in the 1840s. However, the Reform League was never the independent working-class organization that Marx at first believed. It was financed by the same sources as the middle-class Reform Union (i.e. far-sighted industrial capitalists) and it qualified its demand for manhood suffrage with the phrase 'registered and residential', thus deliberately excluding the large 'dangerous class' of casual workers and unemployed. By May 1867 the Reform League leaders had already accepted household suffrage as a compromise for the time being, and worked in conjunction with Walpole, the Home Secretary, to contain the 6 May demonstration. The Hyde Park riot led nevertheless to Walpole's resignation and forced Disraeli to insert the 'lodger clause' in his Reform Bill as a

34. *MECW* 42, p. 150.

concession, and the Reform League now counted its members in six figures. But Howell, Cremer and Applegarth[35] had quite literally 'sold out' to the bourgeoisie,[36] and after the passage of the 1867 Reform Act they worked secretly and successfully – in exchange for Home Office bribes – to mobilize the working class behind the Liberal party in the 1868 general election. During this period Applegarth, for example, was still actively involved in the General Council, and Marx saw him as a promising workers' leader. This contradiction illustrates the fact that the English trade-unionists basically used the International as a surrogate international department of the newly formed TUC. They were already well set on a reformist course, and thus were *a priori* unsusceptible to Marx's ideological influence.

From the time of the 'Fenian outrages'[37] in 1867 Marx and Engels took an increased interest in the Irish question, which was acquiring an ever greater importance in English politics. The General Council of the International discussed Ireland on several occasions in the late 1860s, and the evolution of Marx's position is of particular interest here. In November 1867, when Marx first introduced a discussion on Ireland at a meeting of the General Council, he explained his position to Engels in the following terms: the repeal of the Corn Laws (1846) marked the beginning of a new phase of English rule, characterized by Ireland's transition from a privileged position as England's corn supplier to the production of wool and meat. The 'sole significance of English rule' in Ireland was now 'Clearing of the Estate of Ireland', and it was because of this that Fenianism was 'characterized by a socialistic tendency' and 'a lower orders movement'. What the Irish needed, therefore, was self-government, an agrarian revolution, and protective tariffs against England, and Marx would advise the English workers to 'make the *repeal of the Union* . . . an article of their *pronunziamento*',[38] for English landlordism was the common

35. Robert Applegarth, a cabinet-maker, was a member of the London Trades Council and of the General Council of the International (1865, then 1868–72).

36. Marx created a stir by denouncing the reformist trade-union leaders in these terms at the Hague Congress of 1872. (See H. Gerth, ed., *The First International*, Madison, 1958, p. 186.) The truth of this allegation is conclusively proved by Rodney Harrison in *Before the Socialists*, London, 1965, Chapter IV.

37. The Fenians, or Irish Republican Brotherhood, were a conspiratorial organization with little explicit ideology, but reflecting the agrarian and national aspirations of the Irish peasantry. They attempted an armed uprising against the British in February –March 1867.

38. Marx to Engels, 30 November 1867; below, pp. 160–1.

enemy of both English workers and Irish peasants. However, by 1869 Marx gave the Irish struggle a far more fundamental place in the English revolution, a change no doubt related to the political experience of the intervening years – in particular the unwillingness of most English trade-unionists to solidarize with the Irish Fenian movement, and the defection of the Reform League leaders to the Liberal party.

Now disaffected with his former allies in the English trade unions, Marx was led to attribute partial responsibility for their betrayals to the national antagonism between England and Ireland. Thus on 29 November 1869, while he was mobilizing the General Council of the International in support of the Irish amnesty movement (to free a group of Fenians condemned for terrorist activities), Marx wrote to his German correspondent Kugelmann that, without dissolution of the Union,

the English people will be kept in tether by the ruling classes, because they will have to establish a common front with them against Ireland. Every one of its movements in England itself remains paralysed by the quarrel with the Irish, who form a very considerable section of the working class in England itself.[39]

This had a striking strategic implication, which Marx spelled out in a letter to Engels a few days later:

I long believed it was possible to overthrow the Irish regime by way of English working-class ascendancy . . . A deeper study has now convinced me of the opposite. The English working class will never achieve anything before it has got rid of Ireland. The lever must be applied in Ireland. This is why the Irish question is so important for the social movement in general.[40]

Marx elaborated this new position in the General Council's letter to the Federal Council of French Switzerland of January 1870, and in a letter to the German-Americans Meyer and Vogt some three months later. His argument in these texts falls into two parts. Firstly, Marx presents Ireland as the weak link of the English ruling classes. 'Ireland is the bulwark of the *English landed aristocracy*', and

---

39. Below, p. 165.
40. Marx to Engels, 10 December 1869; below, pp. 166–7.

the overthrow of the English aristocracy in Ireland involves and would necessarily be followed by its overthrow in England. Thus one prerequisite for the proletarian revolution in England would be fulfilled . . . the destruction of the English landed aristocracy in Ireland is an infinitely easier operation than in England itself, because in Ireland the *land question* has up till now been the *exclusive form* which the social question has taken, because it is a question of existence, a *question of life and death* for the majority of the Irish people, because at the same time it is inseparable from the *national* question.[41]

On top of this:

Ireland is the only excuse the English government has for keeping up a large regular army which can, as we have seen, in case of need attack the English workers after having done its basic training in Ireland.[42]

But the English ruling classes were not merely more vulnerable in Ireland. Most important of all, according to Marx, was the privileged position that the national oppression of Ireland gave the English workers vis-à-vis their Irish brothers. This was why 'the English working class will never achieve anything before it has got rid of Ireland'. In England, the English and the Irish workers formed 'two *hostile* camps'. This division had an economic basis, as 'the ordinary English worker hates the Irish worker because he sees in him a competitor who lowers his standard of life,' but Marx also laid particular stress on ideological factors:

Compared with the Irish worker [the English worker] feels himself a member of the *ruling nation*, and for this very reason he makes himself into a tool of the aristocrats and capitalists *against Ireland* and thus strengthens their domination *over himself*.

The English worker also 'cherishes religious, social and national prejudices against the Irish worker', which are 'artificially sustained and intensified by the press, the pulpit, the comic papers, in short, by all the means at the disposal of the ruling classes'.

The antagonism between English and Irish workers, Marx claimed, was '*the secret of the impotence of the English working class*, despite

41. Marx to Meyer and Vogt, 9 April 1870; below, p. 168.
42. 'The General Council to the Federal Council of French Switzerland', below, p. 118.

its organization. It is the secret which enables the capitalist class to maintain its power, as this class is perfectly aware.' In this situation, and given the special importance of England as the 'metropolis of capital', the International had 'to bring the conflict between England and Ireland into the foreground, and everywhere to side openly with Ireland.'[43]

Marx's writings on the relationship between England and Ireland mark a significant new departure for his political theory. Marx and Engels had previously seen the exploitation of the colonies as invariably a secondary feature of capitalism's international dimension. Capitalism, despite its barbarous side-effects, was the only means of bringing the more backward countries into 'civilization', and so colonization was in the last instance progressive. When Engels first put forward a position on the Irish question, in 1848, he presented Irish liberation as a by-product of the English revolution. The future of the Irish people lay in their alliance with the English Chartists, whose victory would transform the association between England and Ireland from an exploitative to an egalitarian one.[44] But twenty years later, Marx came to ascribe to the Irish national struggle a determining role in the English revolution. The 'lever' had to be applied in Ireland, and the English workers would be tied to the leading-strings of their own ruling class until Irish national liberation was achieved.

This seems to presage the theory of imperialism founded by Lenin half a century later. However, there is a crucial difference. Lenin's innovation was to argue from a general economic relationship between metropolises and colonies to general political effects, including the corruption of a section of the metropolitan working class that benefited from colonial exploitation. Even though Marx's assertion that national liberation in Ireland had actually to precede proletarian revolution in England appears to go further than Lenin, Marx presented this relation between metropolis and colony as a particular case, the product of specific local circumstances. Marx certainly never held that the 'lever' of the revolution had as a general rule to be applied in the colonies. On the contrary, he was never to revise his initial assumption that the non-European colonies would have to follow the historical trajectory of the exploiting nations.[45]

43. Marx to Meyer and Vogt, 9 April 1870; below, pp. 169–70.

44. See Engels's articles of January 1848, 'The Coercion Bill for Ireland and the Chartists' and 'Feargus O'Connor and the Irish People', in *MECW* 6, pp. 445–9.

45. See the Introduction to *Surveys from Exile*, pp. 24–8, and below, p. 68.

Lacking an adequate theory of capitalism's international dimension, Marx did not satisfactorily account for the failure of the English working class to fulfil the expectations he had entertained in the mid 1860s. The role Marx attributed to Ireland in 1869–70 was almost certainly too great, and after 1870 he never again adduced this as an explanation of English reformism. Indeed, even in 1870 Marx would seem not to have ruled out altogether the beginnings, at least, of a revolutionary workers' movement in England before Irish emancipation was achieved. Furthermore, in the section of the letter to the Federal Council of French Switzerland that discusses perspectives for the English working class, Marx's argument is vitiated by a highly untypical voluntarism. Marx claimed here, 'The English have all that is needed *materially* for social revolution', and lacked only *'the sense of generalization and revolutionary passion'*.[46] Marx saw this spiritual lack as remediable by the efforts of the General Council of the International, ascribing to it powers far beyond any feasible attainment. The General Council could take initiatives, such as the foundation of the Land and Labour League,[47] 'which as they develop further appear to the public to be spontaneous movements of the English working class',[48] and by this sleight of hand the English workers would allegedly be imbued with the revolutionary passion in which they were deficient. Marx's resort to such an implausible explanation is clearly a sign of uncertainty, and signals the fact that he had not developed – and indeed was never to develop – a satisfactory theory of imperialism and working-class reformism.

46. Below, p. 116.
47. The Land and Labour League was formed in November 1869 by the more left-wing English members of the General Council. It based itself on the demand for land nationalization which had recently been ratified by the Basle Congress, and on republicanism, and campaigned in solidarity with the Irish movement and on issues such as unemployment. Its significance was that it did reach down to organize sections of the working class outside the labour aristocracy, particularly in east London, where several branches of the International were also formed in 1870–1. However, the League was split by the Paris Commune, and subsequently went into decline, with its left wing falling for the sectarian panacea of currency reform. Its experience suggests that the conditions for a new independent political movement of the English proletariat, which was to come into existence in the 1890s with the formation of the independent Labour Party, were not yet present at this stage.
48. Below, p. 116.

The Paris Commune

On 19 July 1870 Louis Napoleon declared war on the North German
Confederation, set up under Prussian hegemony after the defeat of
Austria in 1966. It is now known that Bismarck lured Bonaparte
into war with the Ems telegram. At the time, however, Marx, in
common with democratic and socialist opinion generally, saw
Bonaparte as the aggressor, and justified the Prussian campaign
in its first stage as a war of defence.[49] However, Marx certainly
did not succumb to German chauvinism, and in the 'First Address
of the General Council on the Franco-Prussian War', written only
four days after the war was declared, he specifically put the onus
on the German working class to prevent the war from losing its
initial defensive character and degenerating into a war against the
French people. Marx equally insisted that the German workers
must counter the annexation of Alsace and Lorraine, as soon as
such a plan became evident.[50]

On 1 September the French army capitulated at Sedan and Louis
Napoleon was himself taken prisoner. Three days later the republic
was proclaimed in Paris, and a Government of National Defence set
up. On 9 September Marx wrote for the General Council a Second
Address, which called on the workers of Europe and North America
to agitate for the recognition of the French republic, and exposed
Prussian annexationist plans. The SDAP, which had been temporarily
split by the war, now rallied to the anti-annexationist position taken
by Liebknecht and Bebel in the Reichstag, and conducted a campaign
which brought down on it severe repression.

The Paris Commune of spring 1871 was the product of a patriotic
movement of the workers and petty bourgeoisie against the ruling
classes' capitulation to the Prussians. It took its title from the
elected municipal council of Paris first established in 1792, whose
revolutionary and patriotic role was of crucial importance in the
first French revolution. With the fall of the Second Empire, the

49. Engels, in his manuscript 'The Role of Force in History', written in 1887–8,
accepted that Louis Napoleon had attempted to avert the war, but had 'walked into a
trap'; *MECW* 26, p. 487.

50. See Marx's letter to the Brunswick Committee of the SDAP, c. 1 September
1870; below, pp. 177–9. In this letter Marx forecast, with striking clarity, that the
German annexationist policy of 1870 would necessarily lead to a war of France and
Russia against Germany.

question of a revolutionary working-class initiative was inevitably raised. In Lyon, Bakunin and Cluseret[51] seized the town hall and proclaimed the 'abolition of the state'. They were soon rebuffed, though insurrectionary attempts also took place in Marseilles and Toulouse. At first the Government of National Defence succeeded in organizing new armies from its base in Tours, but the balance of forces soon shifted decisively in the Prussians' favour. From the end of September the Prussian army occupied all France north and east of Orleans, and laid siege to Paris. Two attempts were made in Paris during the siege to set up a revolutionary government, the first on 31 October, and the second on 22 January, both after unsuccessful attempts to break the siege. The initiative in both these attempts, as in the successful revolution of 18 March, was taken by the Blanquists, in alliance with the petty-bourgeois democrats or 'Jacobins'.

By the end of January the Government of National Defence recognized defeat, and on 8 February elections were held to a National Assembly, entrusted with making peace with the Prussians. The siege of Paris was now lifted, but the Assembly preferred to sit under Prussian protection in Versailles. The remaining obstacle in the way of a peace treaty was the disarmament of Paris, and Thiers's[52] attempt to effect this led to the seizure of power by the Central Committee of the National Guard,[53] the evacuation of all government bodies from Paris, and the election of the Commune. The second siege of Paris now began, and on 21 May the Versailles forces, strengthened by prisoners of war released for the purpose by the Prussians, began their invasion, defeating the last resistance after eight days of bitter fighting. The massacre of prisoners perpetrated by the Thiers government followed in the tradition of June 1848, but on a larger scale. Altogether, several tens of thousands of victims were killed, wounded or deported.

From September 1870 to the fall of the Commune eight months later, Marx's activity was oriented to events in France. After Sedan Marx roused the General Council to campaign for recognition of

51. Gustave Cluseret, a French officer influenced by Bakunin, was later chief of staff of the Paris Conmunard forces. On Bakunin see below, pp. 43–53.

52. Adolphe Thiers, a historian and Orleanist politician, and twice Prime Minister under Louis Philippe, headed the Government of National Defence, supervised the bloody repression of the Commune, and was President of the French Republic from 1871 to 1873.

53. The citizens' militia, formed in Paris on a district basis.

the French republic, and in this he worked closely with the English Positivists (intellectual followers of Comte). Up to the Communard revolution of March 1871, Marx had to steer a difficult course on the General Council against Odger, who identified recognition of the French republic with support for the government of Thiers and Favre, and against the Land and Labour League, who called for British intervention against Germany. Marx's attitude towards the demand for a Commune government, raised by the Blanquists immediately after Sedan, was quite unambiguous. He realized that the Paris workers did not have the strength to defeat the combined forces of the bourgeoisie and the Prussians, and bent himself to forestalling a revolutionary attempt. The General Council's Second Address specifically stated, 'Any attempt at upsetting the new government in the present crisis, when the enemy is almost knocking at the doors of Paris, would be a desperate folly,' and called on the French workers to 'calmly and resolutely improve the opportunities of republican liberty, for the work of their own class organization.'[54]

Contrary to the legend later propagated by the French government, the Communard revolution was not the work of the International. The fall of the Second Empire found the International's Paris Federation severely weakened after three successive prosecutions; it was now also divided by the issues raised by the war. The right-wing Proudhonists supported the republic, and their leader Tolain was to sit in the Versailles Assembly right through the rise and fall of the Commune. The left-wing Proudhonists still opposed revolutionary action in principle, although under Varlin's leadership they served on the Commune when this was set up, and fought valiantly in its defence. From September through to May, the revolutionary initiative remained in the hands of the Blanquists and their middle-class allies, and in the last stage of the Commune these two parties were to take political power into their own hands with a Committee of Public Safety. Blanquists and Jacobins formed a substantial majority on the elected Commune, with fifty-seven members against the Proudhonist minority of twenty-two, seventeen of whom were members of the International.[55]

The Paris Commune roused considerable support from the

54. Below, p. 185.
55. Only one member of the Commune was in any sense a Marxist, the Hungarian Leo Frankel, a protégé of Marx's in London, who served as the Commune's Minister of Labour, and later founded the Hungarian Social-Democratic party.

European working classes, and meetings and demonstrations of solidarity were held across the Continent and in England. Yet the General Council of the International, while participating in solidarity actions, issued no statement on the Commune during its two-month life. This fact is probably attributable to Marx's realization that the heroic attempt of the Communards to 'storm heaven'[56] was doomed in advance to failure. Marx wrote *The Civil War in France* while the Commune was fighting its losing battle against the Versailles army. It was approved by the Council on 30 May, two days after the Commune's defeat, and immediately printed.

The Civil War in France is the most crucial political text of Marx's later years, and contains his most substantial addition to the theory of the proletarian revolution worked out more than two decades previously. Like Marx's earlier writings, *The Class Struggles in France* and *The Eighteenth Brumaire of Louis Bonaparte*,[57] *The Civil War in France* presents an analysis of contemporary history. In this text, however, Marx's theoretical conclusions are less deeply embedded in the historical analysis. In the third section, Marx explains quite straightforwardly why the Commune was such an important revolutionary model, and what its essential features were. A valuable supplement to the published text of *The Civil War in France* is provided by two manuscript drafts[58] in which Marx elaborated at greater length some of the key theoretical questions raised by the Commune.

The starting point of Marx's analysis of the Commune is where *The Eighteenth Brumaire* left off – with the executive power and its 'immense bureaucratic and military organization'.[59] Now, more clearly than in 1852, Marx explained that the subjugation of bourgeois society by its own executive power was the inevitable result of the development of capitalism and the ever increasing threat presented by the working class. The thesis that the Empire was 'the only form of government possible at a time when the bourgeoisie had already lost, and the working class had not yet acquired, the faculty of ruling the nation',[60] does not imply that it was in any

56. Marx to Kugelmann, 12 April 1871; *MECW* 44, p. 132.

57. Both of these are printed in *Surveys from Exile*.

58. An extract from the first of these drafts is printed below, pp. 236–68. For the complete texts, see *MECW* 22, pp. 435–551.

59. *Surveys from Exile*, p. 237.

60. *The Civil War in France*: 'Address of the General Council', below, p. 208.

way neutral between bourgeoisie and proletariat. Although Marx presented the Bonapartist state as endowed with a certain measure of autonomy, he insisted more clearly than he had in *The Eighteenth Brumaire* that Bonapartism was a variety of the bourgeois state, defined by its function in maintaining the exploitation of labour by capital:

At the same pace at which the progress of modem industry developed, widened, intensified the class antagonism between capital and labour, the state power assumed more and more the character of the national power of capital over labour, of a public force organized for social enslavement, of an engine of class despotism.[61]

Imperialism is, at the same time, the most prostitute and the ultimate form of the state power ... which full-grown bourgeois society had finally transformed into a means for the enslavement of labour by capital.[62]

In *The Eighteenth Brumaire* Marx had predicted that the next act of the French revolution would be 'to concentrate all its forces of destruction' against the executive power, and to smash the bureaucratic and military apparatus.[63] What is new in 1871 is Marx's theoretical development, on the basis of the experience of the Commune, of the 'governmental machinery' with which the proletariat must replace the bourgeois state in order to carry out its own aims, i.e. the expropriation of the capitalist class.[64]

Marx introduces his analysis of the Commune with a quotation from the National Guard Central Committee's Manifesto of 18 March, that 'the proletarians of Paris' were herewith 'seizing upon the governmental power'.[65] In his first draft of *The Civil War in France*, Marx elaborated on this signal fact, implicitly seeing the Commune as embodying the tactical recommendations he had laid down in the March Address of 1850, i.e. that the workers, after the overthrow of the existing governments, must not lay down their arms:[66]

61. Ibid., p. 207.
62. Ibid., p. 208. Here, and in general, Marx uses the term 'Imperialist' not in its later sense, but as an adjective for the Bonapartist Empire.
63. *Surveys from Exile*, p. 237.
64. Below, p. 261.
65. Below, p. 206.
66. *The Revolutions of 1848*, p. 325.

That the workmen of Paris have taken the initiative of the present revolution and in heroic self-sacrifice bear the brunt of this battle, is nothing new . . . That the revolution is made in *the name of* and confessedly *for* the popular masses, that is the producing masses, is a feature this revolution has in common with all its predecessors. The new feature is that the people, after the first rise, have not disarmed themselves and surrendered their power into the hands of the republican mountebanks of the ruling classes, that, by the constitution of the *Commune*, they have taken the actual management of their revolution into their own hands and found at the same time, in the case of success, the means to hold it in the hands of the people itself, displacing the state machinery, the governmental machinery of the ruling classes by a governmental machinery of their own.[67]

According to Marx, the 'true secret' of the Commune was:

It was essentially a working-class government, the produce of the struggle of the producing against the appropriating class, the political form at last discovered under which to work out the economical emancipation of labour.[68]

Marx's presentation of the basic structural features of the Commune can be summarized as follows:

1. The abolition of an armed force separate from and hence opposed to the people. 'The first decree of the Commune, therefore, was the suppression of the standing army, and the substitution for it of the armed people.'[69]

2. The vesting of all political functions not in representatives but in recallable delegates. 'The Commune was formed of the municipal councillors, chosen by universal suffrage in the various wards of the town, responsible and revocable at short terms.' 'The police was at once stripped of its political attributes, and turned into the responsible and at all times revocable agent of the Commune. So were the officials of all other branches of the administration.' 'Instead of deciding once in three or six years which member of the ruling class was to misrepresent the people in parliament, universal suffrage was to serve the people, constituted in communes, as individual

67. 'First Draft of *The Civil War in France*', below, p. 261.
68. *The Civil War* . . . : 'Address', below, p. 212.
69. Ibid., p. 209. All the quotations under these five headings are from pp. 209–11 below.

suffrage serves every other employer in the search for the workmen and managers in his business.'

3. The absence of all material privileges for the delegated officials. 'From the members of the Commune downwards, the public service had to be done at *workmen's wages*. The vested interests and the representation allowances of the high dignitaries of state disappeared along with the high dignitaries themselves.'

4. The union of executive, legislative and judicial power in the same organs. 'The Commune was to be a working, not a parliamentary body, executive and legislative at the same time.' 'The judicial functionaries were to be divested of that sham independence which had but served to mask their abject subserviency to all succeeding governments . . . Like the rest of public servants, magistrates and judges were to be elective, responsible and revocable.'

5. The organization of national unity from the base upwards. 'The commune was to be the political form of even the smallest country hamlet . . . The rural communes of every district were to administer their common affairs by an assembly of delegates in the central town, and these district assemblies were again to send deputies to the national delegation in Paris . . . The few but important functions which still would remain for a central government were not to be suppressed . . . but were to be organized by Communal, and therefore strictly responsible agents.' 'While the merely repressive organs of the old governmental power were to be amputated, its legitimate functions were to be wrested from an authority usurping pre-eminence over society itself, and restored to the responsible agents of society.'

It is important to note that these structural features of the Commune do not explicitly demarcate a privileged position for the industrial working class, any more than the corresponding features of the bourgeois state, in either its parliamentary, Bonapartist or fascist variants, do for the bourgeoisie. But just as the maintenance of the power of capital over labour requires a state machinery which is divorced from the mass of the people and uncontrollable by them, so the working class, in order to expropriate the bourgeoisie and set up a communist order, requires a form of government through which the political power of the mass of the people can be directly expressed. And this is what all the institutions of the Commune were designed to do, backed in the last instance by the armed people themselves. Marx makes this distinction between ruling class and form of state in the following terms:

As the state machinery and parliamentarism are not the real life of the ruling classes, but only the organized general organs of their dominion, the political guarantees and forms and expressions of the old order of things, so the Commune is not the social movement of the working class and therefore of a general regeneration of mankind, but the organized means of action.[70]

The distinction is an important one, as throughout his life Marx always held that a new class, including the working class, could only come to power and transform society to its design if it represented, not merely its own particular interest, but a universal interest of historical development, so that only those with a vested interest in the old order would stand in its way. The Commune was thus 'a thoroughly expansive political form, while all previous forms of government had been emphatically repressive',[71] although by this Marx does not mean that the Commune government did not need to repress the minority who resisted the progress it represented. Indeed, Marx specifically states:

The Communal organization once firmly established on a national scale, the catastrophes it might still have to undergo would be sporadic slaveholders' insurrections, which, while for a moment interrupting the work of peaceful progress, would only accelerate the movement, by putting the sword into the hand of the social revolution.[72]

In the 'political form' of the Commune, Marx found the historical experience necessary to develop and concretize his theory of proletarian political power. The theory of scientific communism, as formulated in the Communist Manifesto, presents the proletarian revolution as passing through a sequence of stages: seizure of political power, expropriation of the bourgeoisie, disappearance of the political state. In the 1848 period, for lack of a concrete model of proletarian political power, Marx left it unclear what relation there is between the dictatorship of the proletariat and the disappearance of the state. In 1871, however, using the model of the Commune, Marx developed more clearly

70. 'First Draft . . .', below, pp. 252–3.
71. *The Civil War* . . . : 'Address', below, p. 212.
72. 'First Draft . . .', below, p. 253. 'Slaveholders' insurrection' refers to the recent North American Civil War. (See the Introduction to *Surveys from Exile*, pp. 31–2.)

the concept of the transient nature of the proletarian dictatorship. The substantive change in his position is that he no longer presented the inauguration of the proletarian dictatorship and the 'withering away' of the state as two discrete and unrelated stages. Throughout his writing on the Commune, Marx stresses that the political power which the proletariat puts in place of the smashed bourgeois state machine is a power of a fundamentally different kind to that of the bourgeois state. The Commune form of government, which mediates the class rule of the proletariat, is already no longer a state in the former sense of the term, because it is no longer separate from and antagonistic to civil society. This is why Marx deliberately refrains from calling the Commune a state, and precisely uses the terms 'Commune' and 'state' as opposites, e.g. 'this new Commune, which breaks the modern state power'.[73] While the Second Empire represented for Marx the highest level of absorption of civil functions by the state, the Commune, as its 'direct antithesis', 'would have restored to the social body all the forces hitherto absorbed by the state parasite feeding upon, and clogging the free movement of, society'.[74]

In his manuscript draft, Marx is even more explicit on the opposition between Commune and state. Here he describes the Commune as 'a revolution against the *state* itself, this supernaturalist abortion of society, a resumption by the people for the people of its own social life'.[75] It is this attribute of the Commune, its restoration to civil society of the social functions usurped by the state, and its delegation of political functions, including the 'few but important functions which would still remain for a central government' to 'strictly responsible agents', that differentiates it from the bourgeois state machine with its drive to dominate and control civil society, a drive that Marx had explained as the product of the class struggle. The working class still needs political power to overcome the bourgeoisie's resistance to its expropriation, but the repressive role of this power gradually disappears of itself with the cessation of the bourgeoisie's resistance, as it is not entrusted to a power separate from and uncontrolled by the mass of the people. Thus Marx saw the dictatorship of the proletariat as, right from the start, a political form that tends to wither away of itself, and the Paris Commune

73. *The Civil War* . . . : 'Address', below, p. 211.
74. Ibid., pp. 208 and 211.
75. 'First Draft of . . .', below, p. 249.

which first institutionalized this political form was henceforth to serve Marx and Engels, and the Marxist movement after them, as a basic reference point.

If the Commune was 'essentially a working-class government', and provided a general model for the proletarian dictatorship, Marx also recognized that, in a country in which the industrial working class was still a minority of the population, the Commune depended for its survival on the workers maintaining alliances with other classes – particularly a section of the middle class, and the peasantry. Part of the middle class in fact spontaneously rallied to the side of the proletariat, and Marx presents this as a sign of the Commune's strength and the workers' historical mission. The peasantry was never more than a potential ally, although Marx believed that the Commune would have won over the peasants if it had been given time. In his manuscript draft, Marx elaborated in greater detail the character of these alliances, actual and hypothetical, bringing the same kind of analysis to bear on the proletarian revolution itself, in terms of a ruling class bloc and a dominant class or class fraction within it, as he had employed in *The Class Struggles in France* to analyse the state of the exploiting classes.[76]

Marx summarizes this analysis under a very significant heading, 'The Communal Revolution as the Representative of all Classes of Society not Living on Foreign Labour'.[77] This category clearly includes the great majority of the peasantry, and divides the middle class between its 'true vital elements'[78] who played a necessary role in production, and the 'wealthy capitalists'[79] who had fled to Versailles. Working class, peasantry and petty bourgeoisie thus formed the ruling class bloc that would have come into existence if the Commune revolution had been able to survive and spread across France as a whole. Towards the peasantry, the Commune's relationship was in the circumstances a completely hypothetical one. The Commune had no chance to develop any real relationship with the peasants, although Marx believed that it could soon have won them over on the basis of its ability to stave off a war indemnity, abolish conscription, provide cheap government and local self-government. Marx was in fact too optimistic in holding that 'being immediately benefited by

76. See the Introduction to *Surveys from Exile*, pp. 10–14.
77. 'First Draft . . .', below, p. 258.
78. Ibid., p. 257.
79. *The Civil War* . . . : 'Address', below, p. 214.

the Communal republic, [the peasant] would soon confide in it',[80] and that three months of rule by the Versailles government would provoke a peasant rebellion. In the event, it was the peasantry that defeated the Commune, passively, since this greater part of the French nation did not mobilize in its defence, and actively, as soldiers in the army that overran Paris at the end of May. However, Marx's theoretical model of a worker-peasant alliance remains an important one, and was later to be developed and put into practice by Lenin.[81]

In contrast to the projected alliance with the peasantry, the Commune did establish a working alliance between working class and petty bourgeoisie, partly on the basis of patriotism, but above all on the question of the war indemnity of five billion francs demanded by the Prussians, which the Commune insisted should be paid primarily by the upper classes responsible for the war.[82] This gave the petty bourgeoisie a direct material incentive for 'rallying round the working class'.[83] It is clear from Marx's drafts that he saw this alliance as an intimate one. The workers did not just pacify the lower middle class with economic concessions, but actually gave them a share in the Communal government proportional to their numbers:

For the first time in history the petty and middling middle class has openly rallied round the workmen's revolution, and proclaimed it as the only means of their own salvation and that of France! It forms with them the bulk of the National Guard, it sits with them in the Commune, it mediates for them in the Union Républicaine![84]

80. 'First Draft of. . .', below, p. 257.

81. Although Marx certainly maintained that the communist revolution could only be led by the proletariat, he was far from ruling out the possibility of proletarian revolutions in countries where the majority of the population were still peasants – as was evidently the case in the France of 1871 – and consistently stressed that the success of such revolutions depended on peasant participation. Besides Marx's formulations on the peasant problem in *The Civil War in France* and particularly in the first draft, see also *The Eighteenth Brumaire*, in *Surveys from Exile*, p. 245, n. 53, and 'Conspectus of Bakunin's *Statism and Anarchy*', below, pp. 333–5. Regarding Russia, Marx even maintained in his last years that the peasantry could in certain special circumstances be the main force of a communist revolution; see below, p. 67.

82. 'First Draft . . .', below, p. 254.

83. *The Civil War* . . . : 'Address', below, p. 214.

84. 'First Draft . . .', below, p. 258. On the 'Union Républicaine', see below, p. 214, n. 63.

But within the ruling bloc of workers and lower middle class, with potential space for the peasants, Marx leaves no doubt that the dominant class, that which determines the character of the ruling bloc as a whole, is the industrial proletariat. It is the 'workmen's revolution' that the middle class rallies around, and, as Marx writes in *The Civil War in France* itself, 'The working class was openly acknowledged as the only class capable of social initiative, even by the great bulk of the Paris middle class – shopkeepers, tradesmen, merchants – the wealthy capitalists alone excepted.'[85]

Had the Commune survived, i.e. had it been able to win peasant support, Marx believed that the working class could have gone on to build socialism in France.[86] Naturally this would eventually have broken its alliance with the urban and rural petty bourgeoisie, and Marx refers to this obliquely when he writes, 'The Commune does not do away with the class struggles, through which the working classes strive to the abolition of all classes . . . It could start violent reactions and as violent revolutions.' Yet Marx held that the Commune 'affords the rational medium in which that class struggle can run through its different phases in the most rational and humane way'.[87] Class struggle of this kind arose in a highly acute form in Russia after a proletarian revolution had been made in alliance with the peasantry, but where, despite Marx's warning that the proletariat 'must not hit the peasant over the head',[88] the working class did not manage to ease the peasants' transition to socialism by economic incentives, but forcibly appropriated the peasants' surplus in order to obtain the funds for industrial development. In these circumstances, the ensuing class struggle was far from conducted in 'the most rational and humane way' that Marx had hoped for.

In the conditions prevailing in spring 1871, the Commune had little time to carry out measures of a socialist character. Marx himself noted that 'the principal measures taken by the Commune

85. Below, p. 214.

86. In conformity with modern usage, 'socialism' is used here for the 'lower stage of communism', i.e. the collectivized economy constructed by the expropriation of the capitalist class, but still dominated by material scarcity. See 'Critique of the Gotha Programme', below, pp. 346–7.

87. 'First Draft . . .', below, p. 253.

88. 'Conspectus of Bakunin's *Statism and Anarchy*', below, pp. 334.

are taken for the salvation of the middle class'.[89] The measures that the Commune took in the particular interest of the working class were limited to such things as the prohibition on employers levying fines and the abolition of night work for bakers. Workshops and factories closed by renegade employers were indeed handed over to workers' self-management, but as a temporary measure and with the proviso of compensation. The Commune's two working-class parties, Blanquists and Proudhonists, were both highly confused in their economic theories, and would no doubt have made many errors in the course of building socialism. But for Marx, the fundamental premise of this development had already been achieved in the Commune. 'The great social measure of the Commune was its own working existence.'[90] If it had been able to develop, Marx held that the Commune government would necessarily tend towards communism, as

The political rule of the producer cannot coexist with the perpetuation of his social slavery. The Commune was therefore to serve as a lever for uprooting the economical foundations upon which rests the existence of classes, and therefore of class rule.[91]

In the style of much of *The Civil War in France*, Marx's phrase here – 'was therefore to serve' – does not simply refer to the subjective intent of the Communards, but to the objective tendency within the Communal form of government, which the working class, having political power in its hands, could not avoid furthering. Throughout this text and the preliminary drafts for it, Marx constantly moves from present actuality to theoretical conclusions. As in his earlier works on France, analysis of contemporary history was always for Marx the raw material of theoretical development.

In Lenin's influential commentary on Marx's writings on the state, he stressed that Marx in no sense 'made up or invented a "new" society', but that

he studied the birth of the new society out of the old, and the forms of transition from the latter to the former, as a natural-historical process. He examined the actual experience of a mass proletarian movement and tried to draw practical lessons from it. He 'learned' from the Commune, just as all

89. 'First Draft . . .', below, p. 258.
90. *The Civil War* . . . : 'Address', below, p. 217.
91. Ibid., p. 212.

the great revolutionary thinkers learned unhesitatingly from the experience of great movements of the oppressed classes.[92]

In the Manifesto Marx and Engels had not been able to see what formal political transformation would be needed in order for the proletariat to constitute itself as the ruling class. When the Manifesto was reprinted in 1872, Marx and Engels added a Preface in which they found it necessary to make only one significant qualification: 'One thing especially was proved by the Commune, viz. that "the working class cannot simply lay hold of the ready-made state machinery, and wield it for its own purposes"', and they refer to the section of *The Civil War in France* from which this quote is taken.[93]

If Marx had warned the Paris workers before the revolution of 18 March that any attempt to seize power in one isolated city was doomed to defeat, the Commune government of Blanquists, Proudhonists and Jacobins certainly made many mistakes that worsened its position. It failed to take the offensive against Versailles when this was still possible, and even to seize the Bank of France, which Marx believed would have put it in a position where it could have forced a compromise settlement on the Versaillais.[94] By the end of May 1871 the Paris Commune, 'glorious harbinger of a new society',[95] had been ruthlessly crushed, with the massacre of some 14,000 workers and the imprisonment or deportation of more than 10,000 others.

Marx and Bakunin

The vicious reaction triumphant in France found an echo in the persecution of the Commune's supporters in almost all Continental countries. Marx's brilliant vindication of the Commune led to the International being identified as its instigator, and its strength was ludicrously inflated by the hysterical propagandists of reaction. Martial law was declared throughout France, and in March 1872 Thiers passed through the French Assembly a special bill that made membership in the International a crime punishable

92. *The State and Revolution*, in Lenin, *Selected Works*; online at www.marxists.org/archive/lenin/works/sw/index.htm

93. *The Revolutions of 1848*, p. 66.

94. See Marx's letter to Ferdinand Domela-Nieuwenhuis, 22 February 1881; *MECW* 46, p. 65.

95. *The Civil War in France*, below, p. 233.

by imprisonment. In June 1872 Jules Favre, the French foreign minister, circularized the European governments calling for joint action to stamp out the International, and Bismarck proposed a European alliance against the International a month later. The following year not only the chancellors of Austria and Germany, but the two emperors themselves, discussed the threat of the International at two conferences, and the same theme was taken up by the Pope. In the prevailing conditions of repression, the International had to forgo holding its annual Congress for the second year running, but the General Council called instead, as in 1865, a Conference in London with the explicit aim of consolidating the International's organization in this difficult period. The London Conference marks the beginning of the International's internal crisis, and this cannot be discussed without returning to the period before the Franco-Prussian war and the entry of Michael Bakunin into the ranks of the International.

Bakunin's political career had been interwoven with that of Marx from the days of the Young Hegelian movement in the 1840s. He had been a member of the *Deutsche-Französische Jahrbücher* circle in 1844,[96] and had taken an active part in the German revolution of 1848. Despite Bakunin's differences with Marx and Engels over the Slav question, they disputed with him in 1849 as a friend, and respected the revolutionary militancy which led him to sacrifice himself in the Dresden insurrection during the Reich Constitution Campaign.[97] From 1849 to 1863 Bakunin was imprisoned, passing from Prussia through Austria to Russia, and spending years in solitary confinement in the Schüsselberg fortress before being exiled to Siberia. In 1863 Bakunin made a dramatic escape, and soon after arrived in London. At first he worked with Alexander Herzen, the then leader of the Russian emigration, whom Marx detested as a liberal with an ambiguous attitude towards tsarism, but in 1865 Bakunin broke with Herzen and left for Italy. Before leaving London he re-established friendly relations with Marx, and agreed to work in Italy for the International.

Once installed in Italy, however, Bakunin did not devote himself to the workers' movement, which was in its earliest stage of development there, and about which Bakunin still understood very

96. See the Introduction to *The Revolutions of 1848*, pp. 13–14.
97. Ibid., pp. 48–9, and 'Democratic Pan-Slavism', ibid., p. 227.

little. Instead, he bent his efforts to conspiratorial organization among the young Italian intelligentsia who had rallied to the cause of the Risorgimento and been subsequently disaffected by its anti-democratic outcome. The aims of Bakunin's secret International Brotherhood were vague, but it worked publicly not within the workers' International, but within the bourgeois-democratic organization known as the League of Peace and Freedom. At the League's Congress in September 1868, however, when its anti-working-class nature became evident, Bakunin organized some of the more left-wing elements of the League into the Alliance of Socialist Democracy, and as such wrote to the General Council applying for affiliation.

The starting-point of Bakunin's political practice was not commitment to the proletariat in its struggle against capital, but opposition to the state as such. Bakunin only rallied to the proletarian movement when he realized that the single class with an interest in the overthrow of the modern bourgeois state was the industrial working class. This realization coincided with the first stirrings of an independent workers' movement in Italy, and Bakunin went on to establish the doctrine of anarcho-communism which he is historically remembered as a tendency within the workers' movement, and attempted to dominate the International from his Italian base.

Bakunin's essential thesis was that the proletariat, while it must overthrow the existing state apparatus in order to liberate itself, must not set up in its place its own political power, as by doing so it necessarily substitutes a new authoritarian apparatus which will perpetuate its oppression. The workers' movement must therefore refrain from organizing as a political party, and from activity that involves it in working through the existing political state (e.g. the struggle for reforms, participation in parliament). The only permissible relationship to the state is the revolution that overthrows all political authority once and for all. Instead of the proletariat becoming the ruling class (which for Bakunin was almost a contradiction in terms), and using its political power to transform society, it must build the organization of the new society within the old in the form of the International. This must therefore be based on the principle of complete local autonomy, and Bakunin launched his attack on Marx over the question of the International's organization, thereby managing to unite behind his banner of 'anti-authoritarianism' all those elements, including English trade-unionists, who for their own reasons resented the 'authoritarian' interference of the General Council into their affairs.

Despite Bakunin's attack on the General Council's 'authoritarianism', he recognized as clearly as did Marx the need for revolutionary leadership. The inevitable counterpart of Bakunin's insistence that the working class organize not an 'authoritarian' party but an embryonic new society was his construction of a hidden leadership, immune to democratic control, to carry out the insurrectionary overthrow of the state. Bakunin's network of secret societies, the greater part of which existed only in his scheming brain, is legendary. When Bakunin first attempted to take over the International, he formed the Alliance as a public front, arrogating to it 'the special mission of studying political and philosophical questions on the basis of the great principle of equality'.[98] However, when the General Council refused affiliation to the Alliance on the grounds that an 'International within the International' was not permissible, Bakunin was quite happy to abandon this paper organization, reducing the Alliance to a 'central section' in Geneva, as his real concern was to organize his supporters into secret societies, and infiltrate the International in this way.

Bakunin and Marx first came into conflict at the time of the Basle Congress, over the 'abolition of the right of inheritance', the means proposed by Bakunin to transform capitalism into socialism. This was opposed by Marx, firstly because it was bound to antagonize the peasantry, and secondly because it reflected Bakunin's mistaken notion that the state, and not the economy, was the fundamental social structure and the basis of proletarian oppression. Bakunin carried the day at Basle, although this was in itself a relatively minor defeat for the Marxists. But shortly after the Basle Congress, Bakunin launched a general offensive against the General Council on several points, and it is these attacks, made in the Swiss papers *Égalité* and *Progrès* which he controlled, that Marx replied to in January 1870 with a 'Circular' to the Federal Council of French Switzerland. In the following months Bakunin succeeded in winning over a section of the Federal Council of French Switzerland, which then split. The overthrow of Louis Bonaparte provided Bakunin's followers with the

98. *Programme and Rules of the International Alliance of Socialist Democracy*, printed in *IWMA* III, pp. 273–8, together with Marx's marginal comments. See also 'The Alleged Splits in the International', below, pp. 272–314.

opportunity to work in the southern part of France, and in the wake of the Commune the Bakuninists' revolutionary militancy attracted the growing numbers of workers that joined the International's sections in Spain and Italy.

The internal crisis of the International, leading up to the Hague Congress and the subsequent split, is one of the most important periods of Marx's political activity, and, as Engels later wrote, 'the least amenable to accurate portrayal from printed sources'.[99] Marx was not merely fighting a defensive struggle against Bakunin's attempt to take over the International. It is evident that he had his own plans for its further development, and although these are not explicitly formulated in any written document, it seems that Marx hoped to transform the International's organizations in the various countries into political parties centred on London. Already in 1867, when the International first began to develop into a significant force on the Continent, Marx had written to Engels, 'And when the next revolution comes, and that will perhaps be sooner than might appear, we (i.e. you and I) will have this mighty Engine *at our disposal*',[1] and in the Circular of January 1870 Marx again emphasized, indeed overemphasized,[2] the role that the General Council could play. Meanwhile, as Marx wrote in the General Council's 'Report to the Brussels Congress':

The year 1867–8 will mark an epoch in the history of the Association. After a period of peaceable development it has assumed dimensions powerful enough to provoke the bitter denunciations of the ruling classes and the hostile demonstrations of governments. It has entered upon the phases of strife.[3]

Marx thus probably intended the International to become, in the event of revolution, a tactical weapon, and by 1868 he already saw a new revolutionary crisis on the horizon. The remaining condition for transforming the International into a more centralized and disciplined

99. Engels to Kautsky, 25 March 1895; *MECW* 50, p. 481. In September 1870 Engels sold his share in his family's business and moved from Manchester to London, where he became an active member of the General Council. During the critical period of 1870–72, Marx and Engels were thus able to work directly together for the first time since 1850.
1. Marx to Engels, 11 September 1867; *MECW* 42, pp. 423–4.
2. See above, p. 29.
3. Below, p. 94.

body was a certain degree of ideological homogeneity, and the Brussels Congress marked a great victory for Marx in this regard, in that he succeeded in winning over a section of the Proudhonists to his own positions and defeating the Proudhonist diehards. The stage was now set for Marx's organizational plans: at the Basle Congress of 1869, held before Bakunin's operations became evident, Marx obtained passage of a resolution that considerably increased the powers of the General Council, in particular giving it the right to suspend, pending the decision of the Congress, branches of the International that contravened its principles and decisions. Marx did not in fact make use of this power vis-à-vis the Bakuninists, although the General Council did use it against the London French branch of the International, which was in Blanquist hands, and compromised the International by calling for terrorist actions such as the assassination of Bonaparte.

After the Basle Congress, the Bakuninist campaign against the General Council got under way, and by the time the London Conference met in September 1871 Marx responded by obtaining a further increase in the powers of the Council, giving it the right to appoint delegates to attend any branch or committee of the International, prohibiting groups of the International to call themselves by other than geographical titles, or to 'pretend to accomplish special missions within the International', and specifically excluding secret societies.[4] Marx thus hoped to block both the secret and the public activity of Bakunin's Alliance. However, the battle between Bakunin and Marx was no mere personal struggle for power, but a struggle of principles. The key issue at stake was that of working-class political action, and on this vital question Bakunin was diametrically opposed to the direction in which Marx was attempting to move the International. The most important result of the London Conference was therefore the passage of Marx's resolution on 'Working-Class Political Action'. This resolution reminded the International of the preamble to its own Rules which Marx had drafted in 1864 and which had spoken of the need to conquer political power, and went on to define this in more concrete terms. It argued from the 'presence of an unbridled reaction which . . . pretends to maintain by brute force the distinction of classes and the political domination of the propertied classes resulting from it',

4. The Resolutions of the London Conference are printed in *IWMA* IV, pp. 440–50.

that 'the working class cannot act, as a class, except by constituting itself into a political party, distinct from, and opposed to, all old parties formed by the propertied classes,' and that 'this constitution of the working class into a political party is indispensable in order to ensure the triumph of the social revolution and its ultimate end – the abolition of classes'.[5]

From the London Conference resolutions Marx evidently hoped to go forward to defeat Bakunin both organizationally and ideologically. But the growth of the International in southern Europe, and the accumulated minor grievances of other sections against the General Council, made it possible for Bakunin to rally a considerable force behind his 'anti-authoritarian' banner. At the Hague Congress in September 1872, which both sides prepared for by rather dubious means, and the greater part of which was spent in challenging credentials, Marx won a paper victory, but also a Pyrrhic one. The Hague Congress ratified the decisions of the London Conference and expelled Bakunin and Guillaume[6] from the International on the grounds that they had attempted to organize a secret society within it. Bakunin's expulsion is unlikely to have been passed had not Marx and Engels presented circumstantial evidence that appeared to implicate Bakunin in the 'Nechayev affair'; they were certainly not above using foul means when political necessity demanded.[7]

By the time the Hague Congress met, however, it was already obvious to Marx that, despite formal majorities, he had failed to win sufficient support to make his envisaged transformation of the International possible, or even to guarantee that Bakunin would

5. Below, p. 270.

6. James Guillaume, a Swiss schoolteacher, was the organizer of Bakunin's faction within the International.

7. Sergei Nechayev, a leading figure in the St Petersburg student movement of 1868–9, travelled to Switzerland in 1869 and established contact with Bakunin. In Nechayev Bakunin found a fellow-conspirator in whose mind fantasy and reality merged even more intimately than in his own. On the basis of the secret societies that he concocted with Bakunin, on returning to Russia Nechayev claimed to represent the International while he made himself notorious for his unscrupulous manipulation of revolutionary comrades, a practice he justified in his *Catechism of the Revolutionist*. Nechayev's arrest in 1871, and the exposure of his activities, threatened to discredit the International, and the London Conference therefore declared, 'Netschajeff has never been a member or an agent of the International Working Men's Association' (*IWMA* IV, p. 434). At the Hague Congress, Marx and Engels successfully used against Bakunin his connections with Nechayev, although they knew that Bakunin was guilty of nothing worse than crass misjudgement and gullibility. See p. 282 below, n. 34.

not take over the International at a future date. As Marx wrote to Kugelmann, the Hague Congress was 'a matter of life and death for the International; and before I retire I want at least to protect it from disintegrating elements'.[8] For this reason, Marx travelled in person to The Hague, his only attendance at one of the International's Congresses. Marx's majority at The Hague was composed chiefly of Germans, the exiled French Blanquists and a part of the English delegates, as well as his personal supporters on the General Council. Against Marx were ranged forces that counted for at least as much in real terms: the Spanish, the Belgians, the French-Swiss, and some of the English. The Italians, although Bakunin's most loyal disciples, refused to attend the Hague Congress in the same company as the 'authoritarians'. In order to prevent the General Council from falling into Bakuninist hands, Marx played his master-stroke: Engels proposed its removal to New York, which was carried by a narrow majority against both Bakuninist and Blanquist opposition. In New York the General Council was in the safe hands of Marx's German-American followers, until it died a natural death. The 'anti-authoritarians' called their own conference a week later, but they set up no executive body and, although their International nominally survived until 1881, it never developed a coherent unity. The Marxist International was finally wound up at the Philadelphia Congress of 1876.

Marx held an extremely poor opinion of Bakunin as a theorist, which was abundantly justified by Bakunin's muddled ideas. Thus in the programme of the Alliance of Socialist Democracy Bakunin demanded the 'social and economic equality of classes',[9] a nonsensical phrase which Marx made great play with. He also declared the Alliance atheist, which Marx saw as archaic and ridiculous posturing, as he had held ever since the 1840s that religion could only disappear when society was transformed. In one crucial respect, however, Marx underrated Bakunin, classing his theory together with Proudhonism as a variety of 'political indifferentism'. It is true that Bakunin inherited from Proudhon his view of political authority as an unmitigated evil; Marx saw this as an ideological position that reflected the recent artisanal background of the Latin working classes. However, Marx failed to make the significant

8. Marx to Kugelmann, 29 July 1872; *MECW* 44, p. 413.
9. *IWMA* III, p. 273.

distinction that while Proudhon's abstentionism was a purely passive one, Bakunin, for all his errors, was a socialist revolutionary who aimed, like Marx (and like Blanqui whom Marx always respected), at the overthrow of the bourgeois state and the abolition of private property. Bakunin's abstentionism, however mistaken, reflected his almost instinctive fear of reformist diversion from the revolutionary goal, and of bureaucratic authority in the post-revolutionary society.

In their articles 'Political Indifferentism' and 'On Authority', Marx and Engels made short work of Bakunin's politics. Marx wrote ironically that

if the workers replace the dictatorship of the bourgeois class with their own revolutionary dictatorship, then they are guilty of the terrible crime of *lèse-principe*; for, in order to satisfy their miserable profane daily needs and to crush the resistance of the bourgeois class, they, instead of laying down their arms and abolishing the state, give to the state a revolutionary and transitory form.[10]

And Engels asked the anarchists:

Have these gentlemen ever seen a revolution? A revolution is certainly the most authoritarian thing there is; it is the act whereby one part of the population imposes its will on the other part by means of rifles, bayonets and cannons . . . [and] it must maintain this rule by means of the terror which its arms inspire in the reactionaries.[11]

The mistake of the anti-authoritarians was that they 'demand that the authoritarian political state be abolished at one stroke even before the social conditions that gave birth to it have been destroyed'.[12] But however correct Marx was to insist that the working class can only expropriate the bourgeoisie and establish socialism by itself becoming the ruling class, and that political authority can only disappear consequent on the abolition of classes, Bakunin's rejection of working-class participation in the bourgeois political system, and his warning of the dangers involved in the proletarian seizure of political power, raise questions that Marx did not solve altogether satisfactorily. The former leads on to the question of reformism, which is the subject of the next section of this Introduction. As

10. 'Political Indifferentism', below, p. 328.
11. 'On Authority', in *MECW* 23, p. 425.
12. Ibid.

for Bakunin's criticisms of his alleged 'state communism', Marx countered this charge in his 'Conspectus of Bakunin's *Statism and Anarchy*', with a series of comments interspersed between excerpts of Bakunin's book that he copied out.

Bakunin's key attack on Marx is a classic anarchist formulation:

> The election of people's representatives and rulers of the state . . . [is] a lie, behind which is concealed the despotism of the *governing minority*, and only the more dangerously in so far as it appears as expression of the so-called people's will.

No matter that the workers may elect representatives from their own number, Bakunin claims that such representatives, once elected, '*cease to be workers* . . . and look down on the whole common workers' world from the height of the state . . . Anyone who can doubt this knows nothing of the nature of men.'[13] On the contrary, Marx claims that the relation between electors and elected depends on the 'economic foundation, the economic situation of the voters'. In communist society, Marx holds, 'the distribution of the general functions has become a business matter, that gives no one domination', and 'election has nothing of its present political character'.[14] Marx gives the examples of a trade-union executive committee, the manager of a cooperative factory, and the Russian village commune and *artel* to show how in the absence of antagonistic interests there is no domination involved in the election of representatives, which is always necessary in order to carry out the 'general functions'.

Marx was certainly not oblivious of the dangers of political bureaucracy. In the context of the International he had attacked the dictatorial leadership of Lassalle and Schweitzer, and stressed the importance of trade unions as a school for proletarian self-government. He saw the form of direct democracy adopted by the Paris Commune, with its revocability of representatives, the absence of material privileges and the unity of executive and legislative powers, as important precisely because it made possible political control by the direct producers. Bakunin was certainly misguided in seeing a workers' government as necessarily leading to the formation of a new governing caste, and

13. Below, pp. 336–7.
14. Ibid., p. 336.

in founding the equation of political coercion and governing caste in 'human nature'. Indeed, from Bakunin's standpoint, a classless society would never be possible at all; at least Bakunin gives no adequate answer as to how the revolutionary proletariat is to overcome the resistance of the old ruling classes without using political coercion. But Bakunin, for all his errors, was conscious in advance of the revolution, albeit in a defective way, that there is a real problem of bureaucracy in the post-revolutionary period, a problem which the Marxist movement was only to begin seriously to deal with in Lenin's last writings on the bureaucratic deformations of the Soviet Russian state. Although the problems that the Russian revolution later posed could not have been solved in advance, it remains true that only through the solution of these problems can the withering away of the state that Marxism looks forward to become a reality.[15]

The Problem of Reformism

The defeat of the Second Empire marked the transition between two eras of working-class history. Up to 1870 European politics in general, and the workers' movement in particular, had been dominated by the Bonapartist regime in France and the unresolved problem of national unification in Germany and Italy. The French defeat consolidated the system of national states, and Marx realized even before Sedan that, *'This war has shifted the centre of gravity of the Continental workers' movement from France to Germany.'*[16] Despite the defeat of the Commune, the European proletariat of the 1870s found new opportunities open to it, and even in France the workers' movement recovered within a decade from this terrible blow. With the rapid growth of industry, it was no longer possible for the ruling classes of more advanced countries to contain the workers' movement by simple repression. Manhood suffrage had been granted in Bismarck's North German Confederation of 1867,

15. In this 'Conspectus', Marx accepted Bakunin's attribution to him of the concept of a 'workers' state, if he wants to call it that' (p. 337). As Marx implies, it is not the word used that is important, but the concept it denotes. It is clear from this context, as also in the 'Critique of the Gotha Programme' (below, p. 355), that where Marx does sometimes use the term 'state' to refer to the political form of workers' power, this represents no departure from his position in *The Civil War in France*, except at the level of terminology.

16. Marx to the Brunswick Committee of the SDAP, c. 1 September 1870; below, pp. 178–9.

and was extended to the German Reich established in 1871. The French Third Republic could also not avoid giving the working class freedom to organize politically within the legal framework of the bourgeois-democratic state. In those countries where democratic reforms were slower in coming, their attainment, proved possible by the German and French examples, provided the immediate goal of the socialist workers.

The tactics that Marx laid down for the workers' movement in the 1870s, and which Engels maintained until his death in 1895, were to provide the mass parties of the Second International (founded 1889) with their guiding principles. These parties, however, subordinated these tactical positions to an essentially reformist strategy, and failed completely to come to grips with the new problems and tasks that arose after Marx and Engels were dead, in the era of monopoly capitalism and modern imperialism. As Marx's dicta on the use of parliament, the peaceful road to socialism, and the proletarian party have been interpreted in a reformist as well as a revolutionary sense, it is necessary to examine his precise formulations and the contexts in which they arose, in order to judge the disputes over the Marxist legacy that have been fought now for over a century.

For Marx, the use that the working class could make of the suffrage and parliament, and the question of the peaceful road to socialism, were distinct and separate issues. Marx held that the working class should always make use of the representative institutions of bourgeois democracy, which, as a majority of the population, it could turn against the bourgeoisie itself. The franchise was to be 'transformed from the instrument of fraud that it has been up till now into an instrument of emancipation'.[17] The resolution of the London Conference on working-class political action referred to precisely this. Marx's insistence there, so infuriating to the anarchists, that the working class had to constitute itself 'into a political party, distinct from, and opposed to, all old parties formed by the propertied classes . . . in order to ensure the triumph of the social revolution',[18] implied that although the aims of the working class lay beyond the bourgeois state (as Marx had explained only a few months earlier in *The Civil War in France*), the way for the advanced workers to build up their strength and rally to them their class as a whole was through the

17. 'Introduction to the Programme of the French Workers' Party', below, p. 377.
18. Below, p. 270.

electoral arena. The prototype of such a party was the German SDAP, which had been formed two years before the London Conference, and which served Marx as a living example. After the defeat of the Commune, the SDAP decisively emerged as the 'centre of gravity' of the European workers' movement. It had successfully used the parliamentary tribune as a forum for agitation, built up a disciplined mass membership, and survived undamaged the imprisonment of its leaders, Liebknecht and Bebel, for their campaign against the annexation of Alsace and Lorraine. The socialist workers' parties that grew up in almost every European country in the 1880s formed themselves more or less on the German example. Marx, and Engels after him, were to give every encouragement to the formation of these parties, and saw in them the organizational form through which to prepare the socialist revolution.

The theme of the 'peaceful road to socialism', on the other hand, emerges in Marx's work only in a strictly limited context. There were specific countries where Marx believed that the proletarian revolution could be carried out by peaceful means, but he presented these as exceptional cases. The key formulation of this 'peaceful road' position is in the speech Marx gave at a public meeting in Amsterdam after the Hague Congress, where he said:

We know that heed must be paid to the institutions, customs and traditions of the various countries, and we do not deny that there are countries, such as America and England, and if I was familiar with its institutions I might include Holland, where the workers may attain their goal by peaceful means.[19]

Marx also expressed this position, in rather stronger form, in a letter to his English friend and would-be disciple Henry Mayers Hyndman,[20] in 1880, claiming that, 'If the unavoidable evolution [i.e. to socialism in England] turn into a revolution, it would not only be the fault of the ruling classes, but also of the working class.'[21] However, Marx

19. 'Speech on the Hague Congress', below, p. 324.
20. Shortly after Marx's death, Hyndman founded the first British Marxist organization, the Social Democratic Federation. However Hyndman led this group onto a highly sectarian course, and the SDF was repudiated by Engels. Hyndman himself, a former Tory, never relinquished either his high bourgeois lifestyle or his jingoism.
21. Marx to Hyndman, 8 December 1880; *MECW* 46, p. 49. Cf. however 'The Curtain Raised', below, p. 400, for an example of Marx's thesis that, even if the working class in countries like England should take the parliamentary road to socialism, it would still be faced with a 'slave-owners' war'.

consistently contrasted these exceptional cases with the general rule. In this Amsterdam speech he stressed, 'We must recognize that in most continental countries the lever of the revolution will have to be force; a resort to force will be necessary one day in order to set up the rule of labour,'[22] and in the letter to Hyndman quoted above Marx contrasted the position in England with that of Germany, where 'military despotism' made a 'revolution' necessary. There are even occasional formulations of Marx's to the effect that 'the working classes would have to conquer the right to emancipate themselves on the battlefield',[23] unqualified by these exceptions; and there are no general statements whatever affirming the normal possibility of a 'peaceful road'.

Marx's basic determinant of the ability of the working class to make a non-violent revolution seems to be the absence of a bureaucratic-military state apparatus of the kind he had analysed for the French case in *The Eighteenth Brumaire*. Thus Marx wrote to Kugelmann in 1871, 'No longer, as before, to transfer the bureaucratic-military machine from one hand to another, but to *smash* it . . . is essential for every real people's revolution on the Continent.'[24] In the 1870s England and the USA evidently appeared to Marx as the two major countries where there was no bureaucratic-military machine to enforce the power of capital over labour, and thus where the transformation from capitalism to communism could be achieved without having violently to smash the army and civil bureaucracy. Marx's position regarding England and America was therefore far from an ahistorical absolute. And as Lenin pointed out in *The State and Revolution*, the development of monopoly capitalism 'has clearly shown an extraordinary strengthening of the "state machine" and an unprecedented growth in its bureaucratic and military apparatus.'[25]

22. Below, p. 324.
23. 'Speech on the Seventh Anniversary of the International', below, p. 272.
24. Marx to Kugelmann 12 April 1871; *MECW* 44, p. 131.
25. Lenin, *The State and Revolution*, loc. cit. Lenin's conclusion from this, which would most likely have been Marx's also, rings particularly true today for the USA, now that Britain has long since sunk to a minor power: 'Both Britain and America, the biggest and the last representatives – in the whole world – of Anglo-Saxon "liberty", in the sense that they had no militarist cliques and bureaucracy, have completely sunk into the all-European filthy, bloody morass of bureaucratic–military institutions which subordinate everything to themselves, and suppress everything. Today, in Britain and America too, the "precondition for every real people's revolution" is the smashing, the destruction of the "ready-made state machinery".'

The question that Marx never did deal with, however, and which became vitally important as international capitalism moved towards a cataclysmic crisis with the First World War, is how, in those countries which combine a bureaucratic-military machine with institutions of universal suffrage and parliamentary government, the working class is to make the transition from electoral politics to insurrection. In Marx's lifetime, to be sure, the workers' parties, even in Germany, were far from being immediately faced with this problem. In his letter to Hyndman of 1880, he typically combines an assertion of the eventual need for violent revolution in Germany with a vindication of the German party's present adherence to electoral politics as the means to build up its strength. The classic Marxist formulation on the transition from electoral politics to insurrection is in Engels's 1895 Introduction to *The Class Struggles in France*, where he argues the position (as Marx himself seems to have done) that the working class should wait for the ruling classes to break the rules of representative democracy and not take the initiative in a test of strength.[26] The reasons behind Engels's argument are evident: the working class will then enjoy the benefits of moral superiority, and it will be easier for it to win over sections of the intermediate classes and subvert the armed forces. However, this tactic has the drawback that it deprives the workers of the offensive, a vital advantage in insurrection. This question invariably presents a dilemma to revolutionary Marxists in bourgeois-democratic countries. But whatever choice is made, one essential precondition, if insurrection will or even may be necessary, is that the workers' party should carry out work well in advance to prepare for this contingency. Lenin therefore made the combination of legal and illegal work a condition for all parties wishing to join the Third International. The parties of the Second International, on the other hand, and the German Social-Democrats in particular, managed to combine a verbal orthodoxy that held to the letter of Marx's doctrines with a practical reformism quite alien to their spirit. (The classic representative of this tendency was the German Social-Democratic theorist Karl Kautsky, the 'pope of Marxism' after Engels's death.) It was possible, in other words, for these parties to claim, and even to believe, that they were moving to supersede capitalism and the bourgeois state, while the real direction of

26. *MECW* 27, pp. 506–24.

their practice led towards taking government office within it. Not one of the parties of the Second International that operated in a parliamentary democracy was to escape this degeneration.

With historical hindsight, we can see the failure of the Second International as already prepared by the circumstances in which the First International split. The International Working Men's Association did not split between revolutionaries and reformists, but between proponents of working-class political action and 'political indifferentists', as Marx referred to them. In the former camp, as also in the latter, there was a definite space for reformism, as revolutionary Marxists and 'political' reformists were united by agreement on the immediate tactical priority – the need to build up the workers' movement in the electoral arena. The label of 'Social-Democracy' thus concealed from the start the crucial question that divided revolutionaries from reformists, and neither Marx nor Engels ever fully realized the nature of the parties to which they gave their blessing.

Despite Marx's steadfast attack on all visible reformist manifestations, he seriously underestimated the strength of reformism and its underlying roots. In the Communist Manifesto Marx had presented the development of the proletarian movement as a two-stage process. In the first stage the proletariat develops from an unorganized mass, through local struggle against its immediate capitalist antagonists and the formation of 'combinations', into a constituted class subject; in the second stage it struggles as a class to overthrow capital on a national scale. Historical experience has certainly borne out the first part of Marx's model. In all countries where capitalist production has developed, the industrial proletariat has formed class organizations to defend its interests against capital: trade-union federations and political parties. But in by no means all cases has the whole organized working class struggled politically to overthrow capital. In general, a greater or smaller part of the working class, depending on specific conditions, has taken a revolutionary anti-capitalist path, while another part has struggled only for reforms within the capitalist system.

Marx's basic attitude towards working-class reformism is summed up in his aphorism 'The working class is revolutionary or it is nothing'.[27] What Marx meant by this emerges clearly from a letter he wrote in 1871 to his German-American follower Bolte,

27. Marx to Schweitzer, 13 February 1865; below, p. 148.

which provides an interesting gloss on the Communist Manifesto from more than two decades later. It is surprising how firmly Marx maintains in this letter the position on the development of the proletarian movement put forward in the Manifesto, despite the experience of the intervening years. On the one hand, 'the political movement of the working class has as its ultimate object, of course, the conquest of political power for this class', but in his definition, 'every movement in which the working class comes out as a *class* against the ruling classes and tries to coerce them by pressure from without is a political movement.'[28] No more than in the Manifesto does Marx leave a theoretical space for the possibility of a workers' movement that is organized politically as a class and yet struggles solely for reforms within capitalism. Marx's sureness that the political movement that 'has as its ultimate object, of course, the conquest of political power', and the political movement that is 'every movement in which the working class comes out as a *class* against the ruling classes', are one and the same may well be true in the long run. Marx believed on the basis of his analysis of capitalism that the imprisonment of the ever expanding productive forces within the straitjacket of capitalist relations was bound to become more and more intolerable to all but a small minority of big capitalists. Yet while outlying portions of the capitalist world have broken free, capitalism's imperialist trajectory has delayed the second, revolutionary stage of the proletarian movement in the heartlands for a whole historical epoch. In this era of imperialism, it has been possible for vast numbers of workers in the advanced capitalist countries to follow a reformist course continuously reinforced by the material gains it has brought – the losses, from world war to ecological crisis, being not self-evidently attributable to capitalist relations of production.

The Gotha Programme on which Marx wrote his critical marginal notes was drawn up in 1875 as the basis of the unification of the SDAP with the Lassallean ADAV.[29] Marx, and the SDAP leaders themselves, only countenanced this merger because the ADAV had succeeded in throwing off the worst features of Lassalleanism. After the settlement of the German national question, the ADAV

28. Marx to Bolte, 23 November 1871; *MECW* 44, p. 258.
29. The new party's name was for a while the German Socialist Workers' Party (SAPD), later changed to the German Social-Democratic Party (SPD) by which it is generally known.

proved its independence from Bismarckian manipulation by its anti-annexationist position in the Franco-Prussian war and its support for the Paris Commune, by its purchase on the everyday struggles of the German working class and its consequent quantitative growth. However, Marx was far from satisfied with the unity programme prepared for the Gotha Congress, which he considered 'thoroughly reprehensible and demoralizing for the party'.[30]

Of the Gotha Programme's Lassallean formulations, Marx singles out for his most bitter criticism the diagnosis 'in relation to [the working class,] all other classes are a *single reactionary mass*,' and the thesis 'the working class must initially work for its emancipation within the framework of the present-day national state'. The first of these only served, according to Marx, 'to extenuate [Lassalle's] alliance with the absolutist and feudal opponents of the bourgeoisie'. The Manifesto had never claimed that all other classes were 'a single reactionary mass', but only that 'of all the classes that stand face to face with the bourgeoisie today, the proletariat alone is a *really revolutionary class*', since 'the other classes decay and finally disappear in the face of modern industry; the proletariat is its special and essential product.' Marx reminds his German comrades that the 'Manifesto adds . . . that the lower middle class is becoming revolutionary "in view of (its) impending transfer into the proletariat"'. Conscious as always of the need to make alliances appropriate to each stage of the proletarian movement, Marx asks, 'At the last elections, did we proclaim to the artisans, small manufacturers, etc. and *peasants*: In relation to us you, together with the bourgeoisie and the feudal lords, form a single reactionary mass?'[31] As for the formulation that 'the working class must initially work for its emancipation *within the framework of the present-day national state*', Marx pointed out that the 'present-day national state' was in fact the German Reich. Even though the Gotha Programme proclaimed that 'the result of their efforts "will be *the international brotherhood of peoples*"', its damning omission was that there was 'not a word . . . of the *international role* of the German working class', i.e. how it was 'to challenge . . . Herr Bismarck's international policy of conspiracy'. Running through the whole of Marx's Critique is the suspicion that the Gotha Programme tends, not to revolution, but to reformist

30. Marx to Bracke, 5 May 1875; below, p. 340.
31. Below, pp. 348–9.

accommodation with the German Empire, 'a state which is no more than a military despotism and a police state, bureaucratically carpentered, embellished with parliamentary forms and disguised by an admixture of feudalism although already under the influence of the bourgeoisie'.[32]

However, the 'Critique of the Gotha Programme' is not simply directed against the Lassallean elements of German Social-Democratic ideology, but equally against the 'vulgar democratic' tendencies that the new party inherited from the SDAP. Perhaps the most crucial of all Marx's critical remarks, therefore, are that 'there is nothing in its political demands beyond the old and generally familiar democratic litany: universal suffrage, direct legislation, popular justice, a people's army, etc.'; and that it does not ask what transformation the state will undergo in the transition period between capitalist and communist society, when 'the state can only take the form of a *revolutionary dictatorship of the proletariat*'.[33]

This is the best known instance of Marx's use of the phrase 'dictatorship of the proletariat', but this key concept, which has always marked the division between revolutionaries and reformists,[34] recurs at several places in Marx's political writings. In *The Class Struggles in France*, written in 1850, Marx had lauded the Blanquists of 1848 for raising the slogan *'Dictatorship of the working class!'*[35] In his letter to Weydemeyer of 5 March 1852, Marx claimed as one of his chief discoveries that 'the class struggle necessarily leads to the dictatorship of the proletariat'.[36] Referring to the Paris Commune in his speech on the seventh anniversary of the International, Marx spoke of the need for a 'proletarian dictature'[37] (in the original English), and in his article on 'Political Indifferentism' of 1873 he referred again to the workers' 'revolutionary dictatorship'.[38] What is important, as always, is not the words used but the concept involved. For Marx, the proletarian dictatorship means simply the unrestrained political power of the working class, expressed through whatever political

32. Ibid., pp. 349–50 and 356.

33. Ibid., p. 355.

34. See Lenin's 'The Proletarian Revolution and the Renegade Kautsky', in *Selected Works*; online at www.marxists.org/archive/lenin/works/sw/index.htm

35. *Surveys from Exile*, p. 61.

36. *MECW* 39, pp. 62–3.

37. Below, p. 272.

38. Below, p. 328.

forms it may need to suppress the opposition of the former ruling classes and to expropriate the owners of capital. Marx himself saw the Commune as the prototype of this political form, although the Commune model may not be applicable in all cases. It was to insist that, in general, the working class must replace the bourgeois state by its own form of political power, that Marx used the term 'dictatorship of the proletariat'.

Marx and Engels came near to breaking with their German comrades over the Gotha Programme, but held back from this ultimate step. When their threat to 'publish a short statement dissociating ourselves from the said programme of principles and stating that we have had nothing to do with it'[39] was ignored, they backed down and collaborated after all with the new party. However, in 1879 they had further occasion to return to the attack, as the reformist tendency of the Gotha Programme invaded the Social-Democratic Party's practice when Bismarck introduced the Anti-Socialist Law. This move to repress the party was induced by its growing strength and electoral support (it had polled almost half a million votes in the 1878 elections), and Bismarck found a pretext in two attempts by anarchists on the life of the emperor. The crisis highlighted the predominant reformist orientation of the party. When a 'minor state of siege' was declared in Berlin, as a preliminary to the deportation from the capital of dozens of Socialist leaders, Liebknecht declared in the Reichstag that the SAPD was a party of reform, was opposed to 'revolution-mongering', and would obey the Anti-Socialist Law. The SAPD parliamentary group began to follow a policy of conciliation, even giving opportunist support to Bismarck's protectionist tariff policy, and Marx declared, 'They are already so far affected by parliamentary idiotism that they think they are *above criticism.*'[40]

When the party leadership grudgingly accepted the need for a party organ to be published abroad and smuggled into Germany, the three comrades it appointed to produce this in Switzerland, who included Bernstein,[41] came out instead with a 'Yearbook for Social

39. Marx to Bracke, 5 May 1875; below, p. 339.

40. Marx to Sorge, 19 September 1879; *MECW* 45, pp. 410–14.

41. Eduard Bernstein, later the grand doyen of revisionism, was already at this time a prominent figure in the SAPD. In the 1880s he became a close friend of Engels, who appointed him his literary executor. From 1881 until 1890, when the Anti-Socialist Law was repealed, Bernstein edited from exile the *Social-Demokrat*, the clandestinely distributed SAPD organ.

Science and Social Policy' which commenced with a criticism of the party's record from a bourgeois-democratic position, attacking it not, as Marx had done, for its reformism, but for its '*one-sided*' class character.[42]

In their 'Circular Letter' to the SAPD leadership written in response to this, Marx and Engels reiterated their basic theses on the class struggle as laid down in the Manifesto thirty years earlier. They stressed more clearly, however, in the light of the experience of the German party, the danger of the workers' party becoming contaminated by bourgeois ideology. Marx accepts, as always, that 'people from the hitherto ruling class [will] join the struggling proletariat and supply it with educative elements', but he insists that 'when such people from other classes join the proletarian party the first requirement is that they do not bring any remnants of bourgeois, petty-bourgeois etc. prejudices with them, but that they adopt the proletarian outlook without prevarication.'[43] Marx ascribes the party's errors to the presence in its ranks of bourgeois ideologists, and implies that alien elements may have to be purged from the party in order to keep it to its revolutionary course. In a letter written some two years earlier he had also made it clear that it is not merely from those of bourgeois social origin that this danger comes: 'The workers themselves, when . . . they give up work and become *professional literary men*, always breed "theoretical" mischief and are always ready to join muddleheads from the allegedly "learned" caste.'[44]

However, lacking a structural explanation of working-class reformism, Marx and Engels continued to see this simply as the product of external bourgeois influence, and to believe that these false ideas could be rectified by ideological struggle within a united party, at most by excluding a few bourgeois intellectuals. In the last analysis, they did not believe that reformism could take serious and systematic root in the working class.

Poland and Russia

A constant element in Marx and Engels's politics, from 1846 through to the 1880s, was support for Polish national liberation. This was neither a merely sentimental solidarity nor an absolute general principle, but held an important place in their conception of the

42. 'Circular Letter to Bebel, Liebknecht, Bracke, et al.', below, p. 368.
43. Ibid., pp. 373–4.
44. Marx to Sorge, 19 October 1877; *MECW* 45, p. 282.

proletarian revolution, as this developed in the context of specific relations of international politics. As these relations changed, and Marx and Engels had to recommend new tactics to the proletarian movement, the significance they gave the Polish struggle shifted, but its overall importance remained.

As discussed in the Introduction to *The Revolutions of 1848*, the cardinal plank of Marx and Engels's foreign policy in 1848 was 'war with Russia, including the restoration of Poland'.[45] In the 1870s and after, however, the unification of Germany and the development of capitalism in eastern Europe substantially altered the terms of the Polish question.

In the mid 1860s, Marx and Engels still held to their line of 1848. In 1863 Marx argued that 'without an independent Poland there can be no independent and united Germany',[46] but this thesis was soon to be disproved in practice. Engels's articles of 1866 recapitulate those of 1849, including the differentiation between the 'great historic nations' and the minor nationalities, only directed against the Proudhonists instead of against Bakunin. However, there is already the hint of change to come, when Engels refers to the contingency that 'the working classes of Russia . . . form a political programme'.[47] Previously Marx and Engels had seen Russia purely as a monolithic barbarian presence in Europe. But after the emancipation of the serfs in 1861, the beginnings of capitalism and the development of the radical-democratic opposition represented at this time above all by Chernyshevsky,[48] whom Marx greatly admired, they took an ever greater interest in Russian developments. Both learned the Russian language, and Marx spent a great part of his energies in the last decade of his life on Russian studies. In the 1870s the tsarist regime, as reactionary as ever at home, could no longer arbitrate central European affairs as it had done in the past. Above all, it was the establishment of the German Reich that had changed things, but also of increasing importance was the intensification of contradictions within Russia.

45. Engels, 'Marx and the *Neue Rheinische Zeitung*', *MECW* 26, p. 124. See the Introduction to *The Revolutions of 1848*, pp. 49–52.

46. 'Proclamation on Poland', *Surveys from Exile*, p. 354.

47. 'What Have the Working Class To Do with Poland?', below, p. 381.

48. In the Afterword to the second German edition of *Capital* (1873), Marx pays an unparalleled tribute to Chernyshevsky for his critical *Outline of Political Economy according to Mill*; this, more than anything, indicates Marx's awareness of the rapid development of revolutionary socialist ideas in Russia.

As early as 1875 Engels could write, if too optimistically, 'Russia undoubtedly is on the eve of a revolution',[49] in which he saw the main force in overthrowing feudalism and absolutism as the peasantry. In 1882, a year after the assassination of Alexander II, Marx and Engels explicitly contrasted the contemporary state of affairs with that of 1848:

During the revolution of 1848–9 ... the tsar was proclaimed the chief of European reaction. Today he is a prisoner of war of the revolution, in Gatchina, and Russia forms the vanguard of revolutionary action in Europe.[50]

By the 1870s, then, the Polish struggle was no longer necessarily linked with the German revolution, as it had been in the past. Marx and Engels, as representatives of the international workers' party, continued to support the Poles, but the reasons that they adduced for this support gradually changed. In this period of transition, three out of four points that appear in Marx's and Engels's speeches of 1875 are of dubious validity.

Marx now presents, as 'the main reason for the sympathy felt by the working class for Poland', the participation of Poles in an essentially individual way as '*cosmopolitan soldier[s] of the revolution*'. Whatever the sympathy this evokes, it is highly uncharacteristic of Marx to argue a case like this, in no way based on an objective assessment of the Polish struggle. Seemingly more substantial is the argument that 'as long as the independent life of a nation is suppressed by a foreign conqueror it inevitably directs all its strength, all its efforts and all its energy against the external enemy',[51] and that therefore the social revolution in Poland can only proceed when the national question has been settled. But however correct the principle behind this, the assumption is still made, as in 1848, that unlike the other oppressed nationalities of eastern Europe, Poland belonged to a privileged category of 'great historic nations', an assumption which history has proved false. Indeed, Polish nationalism was sufficiently weak among the industrial proletariat that developed in the cities of Russian Poland towards the end of the century that the workers' party founded by

49. 'Social Relations in Russia', *MECW* 24, p. 50.
50. 'Preface to the Second Russian Edition of the Communist Manifesto', *MECW* 24, p. 426.
51. 'For Poland', below, p. 391.

Rosa Luxemburg could reject the national question entirely and challenge the nationalism it considered petty-bourgeois by styling itself the Social-Democratic Party of the Kingdom of Poland and Lithuania – the official title of Russian Poland.

The 'particular geographic, military, and historical position' of Poland, so important in the 1848 period and after, is now relegated to merely 'another reason'. But even the weight that Marx gives this, as 'the cement which holds together the three great military despots: Russia, Prussia and Austria', is less than convincing. The previous significance given to the partition of Poland was precisely its role in keeping Germany weak and divided, with a restored Poland being needed as a bastion between Germany and Russia.[52] But after the foundation of the German Reich, there was no essential reason why the partition of Poland necessarily held the three partitioners together. Indeed, Marx had already predicted in 1870 that the very circumstances in which the Reich was founded were 'pregnant with a *war between Germany and Russia*'.[53]

But besides these less cogent justifications of their support for Poland, which should perhaps be seen as residues from a previous position, the genuine new objective significance of the Polish struggle in the 1870s and after is also present. Just as Polish liberation in 1848 was a vital interest of the German revolution, so in this later period it was a vital interest, for very different reasons, of the Russian revolution. Engels noted in his 1875 speech that, in 1863, 'Russian chauvinism . . . poured over Poland once the preservation of Russian rule in Poland was at stake'.[54] Polish liberation would therefore now more than anything weaken the tsarist empire. It was for this reason that Lenin was to take issue with Rosa Luxemburg on the national question, and uphold the right of self-determination for all national groups, a position that acquired a greater significance in the era of twentieth-century imperialism. The Bolshevik national policy towards Poland and other nationalities oppressed by tsarism contributed in no small way to the victory of the socialist revolution of 1917.[55]

When Marx and Engels recognized in 1882 that 'Russia forms

---

52. See Engels's 'Speech on Poland', *The Revolutions of 1848*, pp. 105–8.

53. See 'Letter to the Brunswick Committee of the SDAP', below, p. 178.

54. 'For Poland', below, p. 390.

55. See Lenin's article 'The Right of Nations to Self-Determination', in *Selected Works*, loc. cit.

the vanguard of revolutionary action in Europe', the form of the Russian revolution was already a point of debate among Russian revolutionaries, as it was to be for a long time ahead. In 1874 Engels took issue with the petty-bourgeois writer Tkachov, who derived his views on Russian exceptionalism from Bakunin, and believed that Russia could step over capitalism and build a socialist society on the basis of the peasant commune – the *obshchina*. Engels stressed that capitalist development was well under way in Russia and was already undermining this collective form of property. It was to be the position of the Russian Marxists, in particular of Plekhanov's Emancipation of Labour group founded in 1881, that Russia would have to go through a similar process of capitalist development as had western Europe, before it could make the transition to socialism. They were to be proved at least partly right; but in Marx's last years, neither he nor Engels saw this question as already closed. Engels wrote in 1875:

The possibility undeniably exists of raising this form of society [Russian communal ownership] to a higher one, if [among other factors] . . . before the complete break-up of communal ownership, a proletarian revolution is successfully carried out in western Europe, creating for the Russian peasant . . . the material conditions which he needs, if only to carry through the revolution necessarily connected therewith of his whole agricultural system.[56]

In a manuscript of 1881,[57] Marx investigated this possibility in great detail, and finally he and Engels set down their view in the Preface to the 1882 Russian edition of the Communist Manifesto:

If the Russian Revolution becomes the signal for a proletarian revolution in the West, so that the two complement each other, the present Russian common ownership of land may serve as the starting-point for communist development.[58]

The elaboration of his position towards Russia was to be the final milestone in Marx's political development. The last decade of his life had been one of incessant illness, and on 14 March 1883 Marx died at his home in Hampstead.

56. 'Social Relations in Russia', op. cit.
57. 'Drafts of the letter to Vera Zasulich', *MECW* 24, pp. 346–69.
58. *MECW* 24, pp. 425–6.

Conclusion

In his speech at Marx's funeral, Engels said that Marx was 'before all else a revolutionist'.[59] Marx's political work, backed up by his critique of bourgeois economics, was devoted to the liberation of the proletariat – the working class of capitalist society.

The great service that Marx had performed was rapidly demonstrated after his death, as mass working-class parties arose across the capitalist world, following Marx in their aim to take over the state and transform the economic system in a socialist direction. But their fatal weakness was shown in 1914, when the parties of the Second International, with very few exceptions, reneged on their commitment to proletarian internationalism and followed their respective governments into the First World War.

If this can be traced to a flaw in Marx's own thinking, it would be his inadequate appreciation of capitalism's international dimension. Marx was certainly aware that capitalism, from its very origins, involved the exploitation of some countries by others, and he described in *Capital* the role of colonialism in 'primitive accumulation'.[60] Where Marx was wrong was in holding that despite this exploitation, and even through it, metropolitan capitalism would develop the productive forces of the colonies and satellites essentially as it had done in the west European heartlands; and that socialism would have to spread from metropolis to colony in the wake of capitalism.[61] In fact, capitalist imperialism radically differentiated the historical trajectories of metropolis and colony, keeping the lands of the 'third world' as underdeveloped suppliers of raw materials and cheap labour from which the whole population of the advanced countries could benefit, including their working classes. In this context, the first successful proletarian revolution took place in Russia, on the fringe of European capitalism, and the direction of the process this set in motion was eastward to Asia rather than back to the heartlands of the west.

Marx believed that a mass workers' party would necessarily become increasingly conscious of its long-term interest and follow a revolutionary course. In the context of the advanced capitalist

59. 'Karl Marx's Funeral', in *MECW* 24, p. 467.

60. See in particular *Capital* Volume 1, chapter XXXI, and Volume 3, chapter XX.

61. See the Introduction to *Surveys from Exile*, pp. 24–8.

countries, however, this meant greatly underestimating a reformism fuelled by the privileges derived from imperialism. On this basis, the ruling classes in Europe and North America were able to concede demands for universal suffrage and a welfare state, and steadily integrate the working class into a consumer society. Remaining references in these parties' programmes to Marx or even socialism were eventually dropped altogether.

If Marx's ideas seemed for many decades to have triumphed in Russia and China, this was due to the distinctive development of Marx's politics that Lenin had undertaken in the Russian context. Lenin held that the proletarian party should be a much more unified and disciplined body, confined to those prepared to work both legally and illegally along an agreed tactical line. This was certainly the precondition for the success of the Bolshevik revolution in 1917, which opened a new phase of 'Marxism-Leninism'. Yet in the harsh conditions of civil war and foreign intervention, the proclaimed 'dictatorship of the proletariat' fell too easily into the dictatorship of a party, of its leadership, and even of an individual. Despite raising Russia to an industrial power with high standards of health and education, and despite the immense achievement of defeating European fascism, the Soviet Union degenerated into an unwieldy bureaucracy running an inefficient economy. And while China sought to escape this dynamic with the Cultural Revolution of the 1960s, after Mao's death the Communist leaders opted for a capitalist road of development as their preferred form of modernization.

When this edition of Marx's Political Writings was first published in the 1970s, it was tempting to succumb to surface appearance. For all their failings, governments from Prague to Hanoi still claimed to be Marxist, as did the mass workers' parties of France and Italy, revolutionary movements across Latin America, and a number of newly independent African states. Twenty years later, this illusion had been fatally punctured, with the collapse of the Soviet Union, the wave of neoliberal globalization, and the brutal reassertion of United States hegemony.

Re-issuing these volumes in 2010, however, the resurgent interest in Marxism is readily understandable. The world economy is experiencing a crisis unprecedented since the 1930s, making a mockery of the claim that capitalism can provide a decent life for all. Still more seriously, capitalist patterns of production threaten a planetary disaster triggered by global warming. Though working-class politics has still to recover from the setbacks of the late twentieth century, the transformation required to set the world on a sustainable course is increasingly urgent. For all the progress of the last hundred years, the situation today has similarities to the alternative that Rosa Luxemburg posed in the First World War – between socialism and barbarism. It is all too clear that the ecological crisis cannot be solved from the side of capital; only a movement from the side of labour can undertake the changes needed. If the first shoots of this movement are visible here and there, its precise form is still impossible to foresee, and will no doubt vary from one region of the world to another. But the reformist path of social-democracy seems inadequate to the task in hand, and the Leninist path too narrowly based. We rather need what Marx in the Communist Manifesto called a 'self-conscious, independent movement of the immense majority, in the interest of the immense majority',[62] today as an imperative of human survival. And however unprecedented the task we confront, Marx's Political Writings will remain a lasting point of reference.

*

Besides certain texts that Marx and Engels co-authored, a few articles written by Engels alone have been included in this volume where these are necessary to the understanding of Marx's own politics. Although Engels's positions sometimes diverged slightly from Marx's, the two did operate a very close division of labour from 1846 through to Marx's death, in which Marx generally left Engels the fields of international politics and military affairs. Not only did Marx and Engels invariably consult together before publishing any significant political statement, but Engels often wrote pieces at Marx's express request. Although Engels's individual work, these are nevertheless an essential dimension of Marx and Engels's joint political practice.

62. The Communist Manifesto, in *The Revolutions of 1848*, p. 78.

In the Introduction and Notes to this volume 'Marx' is sometimes used for 'Marx and Engels' in this sense, and when Marx alone is involved and it is necessary to avoid ambiguity, this is made explicit.

All texts written by Marx and Engels in German and French have been newly translated for this edition.

DAVID FERNBACH

1973 AND 2010

Documents of the First International: 1864–70

INAUGURAL ADDRESS OF THE INTERNATIONAL
WORKING MEN'S ASSOCIATION[1]

Fellow working men,

It is a great fact that the misery of the working masses has not diminished from 1848 to 1864, and yet this period is unrivalled for the development of its industry and the growth of its commerce. In 1850, a moderate organ of the British middle class, of more than average information, predicted that if the exports and imports of England were to rise fifty per cent, English pauperism would sink to zero. Alas! On 7 April 1864[2] the Chancellor of the Exchequer delighted his parliamentary audience by the statement that the total import and export trade of England had grown in 1863 'to £443,955,000, that astonishing sum about three times the trade of the comparatively recent epoch of 1843'. With all that, he was eloquent upon 'poverty'. 'Think,' he exclaimed, 'of those who are on the border of that region,' upon 'wages . . . not increased'; upon 'human life . . . in nine cases out of ten but a struggle of existence'. He did not speak of the people of Ireland, gradually replaced by machinery in the north, and by sheep-walks in the south, though even the sheep in that unhappy country are decreasing, it is true, not at so rapid a rate as the men. He did not repeat what then had been just betrayed by the highest representatives of the upper ten thousand in a sudden fit of terror. When the garotte[3] panic had reached a certain height, the House of Lords

---

1. Marx drafted the Inaugural Address and the Provisional Rules of the International during the last week of October 1864. They were adopted by the General Council on 1 November, and published as a pamphlet: *Address and Provisional Rules of the Working Men's International Association*, London, 1864. In this and other texts originally published in English, printers' errors and archaic orthography have been corrected where necessary.

2. The day of Gladstone's budget speech for 1864.

3. The garotte panic was over a series of violent street robberies, some involving murder, which led to a parliamentary inquiry. The resulting blue book was the *Report of the Commissioners . . . relating to Transportation and Penal Servitude*, vol. 1, London, 1863.

caused an inquiry to be made into, and a report to be published upon, transportation and penal servitude. Out came the murder in the bulky blue book of 1863, and proved it was, by official facts and figures, that the worst of the convicted criminals, the penal serfs of England and Scotland, toiled much less and fared far better than the agricultural labourers of England and Scotland. But this was not all. When, consequent upon the civil war in America, the operatives of Lancashire and Cheshire were thrown upon the streets, the same House of Lords sent to the manufacturing districts a physician commissioned to investigate into the smallest possible amount of carbon and nitrogen, to be administered in the cheapest and plainest form, which on an average might just suffice to 'avert starvation diseases'. Dr Smith, the medical deputy, ascertained that 28,000 grains of carbon and 1,330 grains of nitrogen were the weekly allowance that would keep an average adult just over the level of starvation diseases, and he found furthermore that quantity pretty nearly to agree with the scanty nourishment to which the pressure of extreme distress had actually reduced the cotton operatives.[4] But now mark! The same learned doctor was later on again deputed by the Medical Officer of the Privy Council to inquire into the nourishment of the poorer labouring classes. The results of his researches are embodied in the *Sixth Report on Public Health*, published by order of Parliament in the course of the present year. What did the doctor discover? That the silk weavers, the needle women, the kid glovers, the stocking weavers, and so forth, received, on an average, not even the distress pittance of the cotton operatives, not even the amount of carbon and nitrogen 'just sufficient to avert starvation diseases'. 'Moreover,' we quote from the report,

as regards the examined families of the agricultural population, it appeared that more than a fifth were with less than the estimated sufficiency of carbonaceous food, that more than one-third were with less than the estimated sufficiency of nitrogenous food, and that in three counties (Berkshire, Oxfordshire, and Somersetshire) insufficiency of nitrogenous food was the average local diet.

4. We need hardly remind the reader that, apart from the elements of water and certain inorganic substances, carbon and nitrogen form the raw materials of human food. However, to nourish the human system, those simple chemical constituents must be supplied in the form of vegetable or animal substances. Potatoes, for instance, contain mainly carbon, while wheaten bread contains carbonaceous and nitrogenous substances in a due proportion [Marx].

'It must be remembered,' adds the official report,

that privation of food is very reluctantly borne, and that, as a rule, great poorness of diet will only come when other privations have preceded it . . . Even cleanliness will have been found costly or difficult, and if there still be self-respectful endeavours to maintain it, every such endeavour will represent additional pangs of hunger . . . These are painful reflections, especially when it is remembered that the poverty to which they advert is not the deserved poverty of idleness; in all cases it is the poverty of working populations. Indeed, the work which obtains the scanty pittance of food is for the most part excessively prolonged.

The report brings out the strange, and rather unexpected fact, 'that of the divisions of the United Kingdom', England, Wales, Scotland, and Ireland, 'the agricultural population of England', the richest division, 'is considerably the worst fed'; but that even the agricultural labourers of Berkshire, Oxfordshire, and Somersetshire, fare better than great numbers of skilled indoor operatives of the east of London.

Such are the official statements published by order of Parliament in 1864, during the millennium of free trade, at a time when the Chancellor of the Exchequer[5] told the House of Commons that: 'The average condition of the British labourer has improved in a degree we know to be extraordinary and unexampled in the history of any country or any age.'

Upon these official congratulations jars the dry remark of the official *Public Health Report*: 'The public health of a country means the health of its masses, and the masses will scarcely be healthy unless, to their very base, they be at least moderately prosperous.'

Dazzled by the 'Progress of the Nation' statistics dancing before his eyes, the Chancellor of the Exchequer exclaims in wild ecstasy: 'From 1842 to 1852 the taxable income of the country increased by 6 per cent; in the eight years from 1853 to 1861, it has increased from the basis taken in 1853 20 per cent. The fact is so astonishing to be almost incredible . . . This intoxicating augmentation of wealth and power,' adds Mr Gladstone, 'is entirely confined to classes of property'.[6]

---

5. Gladstone, in his 1864 budget speech.

6. This quotation is from Gladstone's budget speech of 16 April 1863. Marx was at one time accused of having invented the last sentence of this quotation, which he also cites in *Capital*. But although the sentence in question is not to be found in *Hansard*, whether by accident, or, as Marx believed,

If you want to know under what conditions of broken health, tainted morals, and mental ruin, that 'intoxicating augmentation of wealth and power entirely confined to classes of property' was, and is being, produced by the classes of labour, look to the picture hung up in the last *Public Health Report* of the workshops of tailors, printers, and dressmakers! Compare the *Report of the Children's Employment Commission* of 1863, where it is stated, for instance, that:

> The potters as a class, both men and women, represent a much degenerated population, both physically and mentally . . . The unhealthy child is an unhealthy parent in his turn . . . A progressive deterioration of the race must go on . . . The degenerescence of the population of Staffordshire would be even greater were it not for the constant recruiting from the adjacent country, and the intermarriages with more healthy races.

Glance at Mr Tremenheere's blue book on *The Grievances complained of by the Journeymen Bakers!*[7] And who has not shuddered at the paradoxical statement made by the inspectors of factories, and illustrated by the Registrar General, that the Lancashire operatives, while put upon the distress pittance of food, were actually improving in health because of their temporary exclusion by the cotton famine from the cotton factory, and that the mortality of the children was decreasing, because their mothers were now at last allowed to give them, instead of Godfrey's cordial, their own breasts.[8]

Again reverse the medal! The Income and Property Tax Returns laid before the House of Commons on 20 July 1864 teach us that the persons with yearly incomes valued by the tax-gatherer at £50,000 and upwards, had, from 5 April 1862 to 5 April 1863, been joined by a dozen and one, their number having increased in that single year from 67 to 80. The same returns disclose the fact that about 3,000 persons divide amongst themselves a yearly income of about £25,000,000 sterling, rather more than the total revenue doled out annually to the whole mass of the agricultural labourers of England and Wales. Open the Census of 1861, and

by Gladstone's censorship, it appears in the parliamentary reports of both *The Times* and the *Morning Star*, and Marx was thus able to vindicate himself. See Engels's Preface to the fourth German edition of *Capital*, Volume 1, Harmondsworth 1976, pp. 115–20.

7. London, 1862.

8. *Report of the Inspectors of Factories . . . for the half-year ending 31 October 1863*, London, 1864.

you will find that the number of the male landed proprietors of England and Wales had decreased from 16,934 in 1851, to 15,066 in 1861, so that the concentration of land had grown in 10 years 11 per cent. If the concentration of the soil of the country in a few hands proceeds at the same rate, the land question will become singularly simplified, as it had become in the Roman empire, when Nero grinned at the discovery that half the province of Africa was owned by six gentlemen.

We have dwelt so long upon these 'facts so astonishing to be almost incredible', because England heads the Europe of commerce and industry.[9] It will be remembered that some months ago one of the refugee sons of Louis Philippe publicly congratulated the English agricultural labourer on the superiority of his lot over that of his less florid comrade on the other side of the Channel. Indeed, with local colours changed, and on a scale somewhat contracted, the English facts reproduce themselves in all the industrious and progressive countries of the Continent. In all of them there has taken place, since 1848, an unheard-of development of industry, and an undreamed-of expansion of imports and exports. In all of them 'the augmentation of wealth and power entirely confined to classes of property' was truly 'intoxicating'. In all of them, as in England, a minority of the working classes got their real wages somewhat advanced; while in most cases the monetary rise of wages denoted no more a real access of comforts than the inmate of the metropolitan poor-house or orphan asylum, for instance, was in the least benefited by his first necessaries costing £9 15s. 8d. in 1861 against £7 7s. 4d. in 1852. Everywhere the great mass of the working classes were sinking down to a lower depth, at the same rate, at least, that those above them were rising in the social scale. In all countries of Europe it has now become a truth demonstrable to every unprejudiced mind, and only denied by those whose interest it is to hedge other people in a fool's paradise, that no improvement of machinery, no appliance of science to production, no contrivances of communication, no new colonies, no emigration, no opening of markets, no free trade, nor all these things put together, will do away with the miseries of the industrious masses; but that, on the present false base, every fresh development of the productive powers of labour must tend to deepen social contrasts and point

9. Marx's own German translation adds here: '. . . and in fact represents it on the world market'.

social antagonisms. Death of starvation rose almost to the rank of an institution, during this intoxicating epoch of economical progress, in the metropolis of the British empire. That epoch is marked in the annals of the world by the quickened return, the widening compass, and the deadlier effects of the social pest called a commercial and industrial crisis.

After the failure of the revolutions of 1848, all party organizations and party journals of the working classes were, on the Continent, crushed by the iron hand of force, the most advanced sons of labour fled in despair to the transatlantic republic, and the short-lived dreams of emancipation vanished before an epoch of industrial fever, moral marasmus, and political reaction. The defeat of the continental working classes, partly owed to the diplomacy of the English government, acting then as now in fraternal solidarity with the cabinet of St Petersburg, soon spread its contagious effects on this side of the Channel. While the rout of their continental brethren unmanned the English working classes, and broke their faith in their own cause, it restored to the landlord and the money-lord their somewhat shaken confidence. They insolently withdrew concessions already advertised. The discoveries of new goldlands led to an immense exodus, leaving an irreparable void in the ranks of the British proletariat. Others of its formerly active members were caught by the temporary bribe of greater work and wages, and turned into 'political blacks'. All the efforts made at keeping up, or remodelling, the Chartist movement, failed signally; the press organs of the working class died one by one of the apathy of the masses, and, in point of fact, never before seemed the English working class so thoroughly reconciled to a state of political nullity. If, then, there had been no solidarity of action between the British and the continental working classes, there was, at all events, a solidarity of defeat.

And yet the period passed since the revolutions of 1848 has not been without its compensating features. We shall here only point to two great facts.

After a thirty years' struggle, fought with most admirable perseverance, the English working classes, improving a momentaneous split between the landlords and money-lords, succeeded in carrying the Ten Hours Bill.[10] The immense physical, moral, and intellectual benefits hence accruing to the factory operatives,

---

10. Lord Shaftesbury's Act instituting the ten-hours limitation for women and children in textile factories was passed in June 1847.

half-yearly chronicled in the reports of the inspectors of factories, are now acknowledged on all sides. Most of the continental governments had to accept the English Factory Act in more or less modified forms, and the English Parliament itself is every year compelled to enlarge its sphere of action. But besides its practical import, there was something else to exalt the marvellous success of this working men's measure. Through their most notorious organs of science, such as Dr Ure, Professor Senior,[11] and other sages of that stamp, the middle class had predicted, and to their heart's content proved, that any legal restriction of the hours of labour must sound the death knell of British industry, which vampire-like, could but live by sucking blood, and children's blood, too. In olden times, child murder was a mysterious rite of the religion of Moloch, but it was practised on some very solemn occasions only, once a year perhaps, and then Moloch had no exclusive bias for the children of the poor. This struggle about the legal restriction of the hours of labour raged the more fiercely since, apart from frightened avarice, it told indeed upon the great contest between the blind rule of the supply and demand laws which form the political economy of the middle class, and social production controlled by social foresight, which forms the political economy of the working class. Hence the Ten Hours Bill was not only a great practical success; it was the victory of a principle; it was the first time that in broad daylight the political economy of the middle class succumbed to the political economy of the working class.

But there was in store a still greater victory of the political economy of labour over the political economy of property. We speak of the cooperative movement, especially the cooperative factories raised by the unassisted efforts of a few bold 'hands'. The value of these great social experiments cannot be overrated. By deed, instead of by argument, they have shown that production on a large scale, and in accord with the behests of modern science, may be carried on without the existence of a class of masters employing a class of hands; that to bear fruit, the means of labour need not be monopolized as a means of dominion over, and of

11. Dr Andrew Ure and Professor Nassau Senior were characteristic representatives of what Marx termed 'vulgar economy', the degenerate form of bourgeois political economy that, after 1830, abandoned the attempt of scientific explanation for mere apologetics, as a result of the development of the class struggle between capital and labour. See *Capital*, Volume 1, pp. 96–7.

extortion against, the labouring man himself; and that, like slave labour, like serf labour, hired labour is but a transitory and inferior form, destined to disappear before associated labour plying its toil with a willing hand, a ready mind, and a joyous heart. In England, the seeds of the cooperative system were sown by Robert Owen; the working men's experiments, tried on the Continent, were, in fact, the practical upshot of the theories, not invented, but loudly proclaimed, in 1848.

At the same time, the experience of the period from 1848 to 1864 has proved beyond doubt[12] that, however excellent in principle, and however useful in practice, cooperative labour, if kept within the narrow circle of the casual efforts of private workmen, will never be able to arrest the growth in geometrical progression of monopoly, to free the masses, nor even to perceptibly lighten the burden of their miseries. It is perhaps for this very reason that plausible noblemen, philanthropic middle-class spouters, and even keen political economists, have all at once turned nauseously complimentary to the very cooperative labour system they had vainly tried to nip in the bud by deriding it as the utopia of the dreamer, or stigmatizing it as the sacrilege of the socialist. To save the industrious masses, cooperative labour ought to be developed to national dimensions, and, consequently, to be fostered by national means. Yet the lords of land and the lords of capital will always use their political privileges for the defence and perpetuation of their economical monopolies. So far from promoting, they will continue to lay every possible impediment in the way of the emancipation of labour. Remember the sneer with which, last session, Lord Palmerston put down the advocates of the Irish Tenants' Right Bill. The House of Commons, cried he, is a house of landed proprietors.[13]

To conquer political power has therefore become the great duty of the working classes. They seem to have comprehended this, for in England, Germany, Italy and France there have taken place simultaneous revivals, and simultaneous efforts are being made at the political reorganization of the working men's party.

---

12. Marx's German translation adds: '– what the most intelligent leaders of the English working class already maintained in 1851–2, regarding the cooperative movement –'.

13. This refers to Palmerston's speech of 23 June 1863, in which he described the moderate reforms in the land tenure system proposed by Maguire and the Irish MPs, designed to guarantee an outgoing tenant compensation for the value of improvements made, as 'communist doctrines'.

One element of success they possess – numbers; but numbers weigh only in the balance, if united by combination and led by knowledge. Past experience has shown how disregard of that bond of brotherhood which ought to exist between the workmen of different countries, and incite them to stand firmly by each other in all their struggles for emancipation, will be chastised by the common discomfiture of their incoherent efforts. This thought prompted the working men of different countries assembled on 28 September 1864, in public meeting at St Martin's Hall, to found the International Association.

Another conviction swayed that meeting.

If the emancipation of the working classes requires their fraternal concurrence, how are they to fulfil that great mission with a foreign policy in pursuit of criminal designs, playing upon national prejudices, and squandering in piratical wars the people's blood and treasure? It was not the wisdom of the ruling classes, but the heroic resistance to their criminal folly by the working classes of England, that saved the west of Europe from plunging headlong into an infamous crusade for the perpetuation and propagation of slavery on the other side of the Atlantic. The shameless approval, mock sympathy, or idiotic indifference, with which the upper classes of Europe have witnessed the mountain fortress of the Caucasus falling a prey to, and heroic Poland being assassinated by, Russia;[14] the immense and unresisted encroachments of that barbarous power, whose head is at St Petersburg, and whose hands are in every cabinet of Europe, have taught the working classes the duty to master themselves the mysteries of international politics; to watch the diplomatic acts of their respective governments; to counteract them, if necessary, by all means in their power; when unable to prevent, to combine in simultaneous denunciations, and to vindicate the simple laws of morals and justice, which ought to govern the relations of private individuals, as the rules paramount of the intercourse of nations.

The fight for such a foreign policy forms part of the general struggle for the emancipation of the working classes.

Proletarians of all countries, unite!

14. In January 1863 a new national uprising broke out in Poland. It was crushed within two months by Russian forces, in alliance with Prussia. See 'Proclamation of Poland', *Surveys from Exile*, pp. 354–6.

Considering,

That the emancipation of the working classes must be conquered by the working classes themselves; that the struggle for the emancipation of the working classes means not a struggle for class privileges and monopolies, but for equal rights and duties, and the abolition of all class rule;

That the economical subjection of the man of labour to the monopolizer of the means of labour, that is, the sources of life, lies at the bottom of servitude in all its forms, of all social misery, mental degradation, and political dependence;

That the economical emancipation of the working classes is therefore the great end to which every political movement ought to be subordinate as a means;

That all efforts aiming at that great end have hitherto failed from the want of solidarity between the manifold divisions of labour in each country, and from the absence of a fraternal bond of union between the working classes of different countries;

That the emancipation of labour is neither a local nor a national, but a social problem, embracing all countries in which modern society exists, and depending for its solution on the concurrence, practical and theoretical, of the most advanced countries;

That the present revival of the working classes in the most industrious countries of Europe, while it raises a new hope, gives solemn warning against a relapse into the old errors and calls for the immediate combination of the still disconnected movements;

For these reasons –

The undersigned members of the committee, holding its powers by resolution of the public meeting held on 28 September 1864, at St Martin's Hall, London, have taken the steps necessary for founding the Working Men's International Association;

They declare that this International Association and all societies and individuals adhering to it, will acknowledge truth, justice,

---

15. The Provisional Rules of the International were ratified by the Geneva Congress of September 1866, and were later supplemented by the resolutions of the successive Congresses. The most significant amendment in the final General Rules published in November 1871 was the insertion of a paragraph 7a, which paraphrased Resolution IX of the London Conference of September 1871 (see below, pp. 269–70).

and morality, as the basis of their conduct towards each other, and towards all men, without regard to colour, creed, or nationality;

They hold it the duty of a man to claim the rights of a man and a citizen, not only for himself, but for every man who does his duty. No rights without duties, no duties without rights;

And in this spirit they have drawn up the following provisional rules of the International Association:

1. This association is established to afford a central medium of communication and cooperation between working men's societies existing in different countries, and aiming at the same end, viz., the protection, advancement, and complete emancipation of the working classes.

2. The name of the society shall be: 'The Working Men's International Association'.

3. In 1865 there shall meet in Belgium a general working men's Congress,[16] consisting of representatives of such working men's societies as may have joined the International Association. The Congress will have to proclaim before Europe the common aspirations of the working classes, decide on the definitive rules of the International Association, consider the means required for its successful working, and appoint the Central Council[17] of the Association. The General Congress is to meet once a year.

4. The Central Council shall sit in London, and consist of working men belonging to the different countries represented in the International Association. It shall from its own members elect the officers necessary for the transaction of business, such as a president, a treasurer, a general secretary, corresponding secretaries for the different countries, etc.

5. On its annual meetings, the General Congress shall receive a public account of the annual transactions of the Central Council. The Central Council, yearly appointed by the Congress, shall have power to add to the number of its members. In cases of urgency, it may convoke the General Congress before the regular yearly term.

6. The Central Council shall form an international agency be-

16. The first Congress of the International did not in fact meet until September 1866, in Geneva. In 1865 the General Council, on Marx's advice, judged it premature to hold a Congress, and called instead a private conference in London.

17. As from the Geneva Congress, the 'Central Council' was officially referred to as the General Council, the designation by which it is now more commonly known.

tween the different cooperating associations, so that the working men in one country be constantly informed of the movements of their class in every other country; that an inquiry into the social state of the different countries of Europe be made simultaneously, and under a common direction; that the questions of general interest mooted in one society be ventilated by all; and that when immediate practical steps should be needed, as, for instance, in case of international quarrels, the action of the associated societies be simultaneous and uniform. Whenever it seems opportune, the Central Council shall take the initiative of proposals to be laid before the different national or local societies.

7. Since the success of the working men's movement in each country cannot be secured but by the power of union and combination, while, on the other hand, the usefulness of the International Central Council must greatly depend on the circumstance whether it has to deal with a few national centres of working men's associations, or with a great number of small and disconnected local societies, the members of the International Association shall use their utmost efforts to combine the disconnected working men's societies of their respective countries into national bodies, represented by central national organs. It is self-understood, however, that the appliance of this rule will depend upon the peculiar laws of each country, and that, apart from legal obstacles, no independent local society shall be precluded from directly corresponding with the London Central Council.

8. Until the meeting of the first Congress, the committee chosen on 28 September 1864 will act as a Provisional Central Council, try to connect the different national working men's associations, enlist members in the United Kingdom, take the steps preparatory to the convocation of the General Congress, and discuss with the national and local societies the main questions to be laid before that Congress.

9. Each member of the International Association, on removing his domicile from one country to another, will receive the fraternal support of the associated working men.

10. While united in a perpetual bond of fraternal cooperation, the working men's societies, joining the International Association, will preserve their existent organizations intact.

INSTRUCTIONS FOR DELEGATES TO THE
GENEVA CONGRESS[18]

1. Organization of the International Association

Upon the whole, the Provisional Central Council recommend the *plan of organization* as traced in the Provisional Statutes.[19] Its soundness and facilities of adaptation to different countries without prejudice to unity of action have been proved by two years' experience. For the next year we recommend London as the seat of the Central Council, the continental situation looking unfavourable for change.

The members of the Central Council will of course be elected by Congress (5 of the Provisional Statutes) with power to add to their number.

The *General Secretary* to be chosen by Congress for one year and to be the only paid officer of the Association. We propose £2 for his weekly salary.

The *uniform annual contribution of each individual member of the Association* to be *one half penny* (perhaps one penny). The cost price of cards of membership (*carnets*) to be charged extra.

While calling upon the members of the Association to form benefit societies and connect them by an international link, we leave the initiation of this question (*établissement des sociétés de secours mutuels. Appui moral et matériel accordé aux orphelins de l'association*)[20] to the Swiss who originally proposed it at the conference of September last.[21]

18. Marx wrote these Instructions for the General Council's own delegates to the Geneva Congress of September 1866, following from discussion at the Council's meetings on the different questions. The 'Instructions' were read out at the Congress as the General Council's report, and published in the *International Courier*, the General Council's official organ, on 20 February and 13 March 1867. The full title given in the newspaper text is: 'Instructions for the Delegates of the Provisional General Council. The Different Questions'.

19. I.e. the Provisional Rules.

20. Setting up of benefit societies. Moral and material support for orphans of the association.

21. The London Conference of the International, September 1865.

2. International Combination of Efforts, by the Agency of the Association, in the Struggle between Labour and Capital

(*a*) From a general point of view, this question embraces the whole activity of the International Association which aims at combining and generalizing the till now disconnected efforts for emancipation by the working classes in different countries.

(*b*) To counteract the intrigues of capitalists always ready, in cases of strikes and lock-outs, to misuse the foreign workman as a tool against the native workman, is one of the particular functions which our society has hitherto performed with success. It is one of the great purposes of the Association to make the workmen of different countries not only *feel* but *act* as brethren and comrades in the army of emancipation.

(*c*) One great 'international combination of efforts' which we suggest is a *statistical inquiry into the situation of the working classes of all countries to be instituted by the working classes themselves*. To act with any success, the materials to be acted upon must be known. By initiating so great a work, the workmen will prove their ability to take their own fate into their own hands. We propose therefore:

That in each locality, where branches of our Association exist, the work be immediately commenced, and evidence collected on the different points specified in the subjoined scheme of inquiry.

That the Congress invite all workmen of Europe and the United States of America to collaborate in gathering the elements of the statistics of the working class; that reports and evidence be forwarded to the Central Council. That the Central Council elaborate them into a general report, adding the evidence as an appendix.

That this report together with its appendix be laid before the next annual Congress, and after having received its sanction, be printed at the expense of the Association.

General Scheme of Inquiry, which may of course be modified by each locality:

1. Industry, name of.
2. Age and sex of the employed.
3. Number of the employed.
4. Salaries and wages: (*a*) apprentices; (*b*) wages by the day or piece work; scale paid by middlemen. Weekly, yearly average.

5. (*a*) Hours of work in factories. (*b*) The hours of work with small employers and in homework, if the business be carried on in those different modes. (*c*) Nightwork and daywork.

6. Mealtimes and treatment.

7. Sort of workshop and work: overcrowding, defective ventilation, want of sunlight, use of gaslight. Cleanliness, etc.

8. Nature of occupation.

9. Effect of employment upon the physical condition.

10. Moral condition. Education.

11. State of trade: whether season trade, or more or less uniformly distributed over year, whether greatly fluctuating, whether exposed to foreign competition, whether destined principally for home or foreign competition, etc.

3. Limitation of the Working Day

A preliminary condition, without which all further attempts at improvement and emancipation must prove abortive, is the *limitation of the working day*.

It is needed to restore the health and physical energies of the working class, that is, the great body of every nation, as well as to secure them the possibility of intellectual development, sociable intercourse, social and political action.

We propose *eight hours' work* as the *legal limit* of the working day. This limitation being generally claimed by the workmen of the United States of America,[22] the vote of the Congress will raise it to the common platform of the working classes all over the world.

For the information of continental members, whose experience of factory law is comparatively short-dated, we add that all legal restrictions will fail and be broken through by capital if the *period of the day* during which the eight working hours must be taken, be not fixed. The length of that period ought to be determined by the eight working hours and the additional pauses for meals. For instance, if the different interruptions for meals amount to *one hour*, the legal period of the day ought to embrace nine hours, say from 7 a.m. to 4 p.m., or from 8 a.m. to 5 p.m., etc. Nightwork to be but exceptionally permitted, in trades or branches of trades specified by law. The tendency must be to suppress all nightwork.

22. The demand for the eight-hour day was first put forward by the National Labour Union at its Baltimore convention in August 1866.

This paragraph refers only to adult persons, male or female, the latter, however, to be rigorously excluded from all *nightwork whatever*, and all sort of work hurtful to the delicacy of the sex, or exposing their bodies to poisonous and otherwise deleterious agencies. By adult persons we understand all persons having reached or passed the age of eighteen years.

4. Juvenile and Children's Labour (Both Sexes)

We consider the tendency of modern industry to make children and juvenile persons of both sexes cooperate in the great work of social production, as a progressive, sound and legitimate tendency, although under capital it was distorted into an abomination. In a rational state of society *every child whatever*, from the age of nine years, ought to become a productive labourer in the same way that no able-bodied adult person ought to be exempted from the general law of nature, viz.: to work in order to be able to eat, and work not only with the brain but with the hands too.

However, for the present, we have only to deal with the children and young persons of both sexes [belonging to the working people. They ought to be divided][23] into three *classes*, to be treated differently; the first class to range from nine to twelve; the second, from thirteen to fifteen years; and the third, to comprise the ages of sixteen and seventeen years. We propose that the employment of the first class in any workshop or housework be legally restricted to *two*; that of the second, to *four*; and that of the third, to *six* hours. For the third class, there must be a break of at least one hour for meals or relaxation.

It may be desirable to begin elementary school instruction before the age of nine years; but we deal here only with the most indispensable antidotes against the tendencies of a social system which degrades the working man into a mere instrument for the accumulation of capital, and transforms parents by their necessities into slaveholders, sellers of their own children. The *right* of children and juvenile persons must be vindicated. They are unable to act for themselves. It is, therefore, the duty of society to act on their behalf.

23. The words in brackets were omitted in the original version of this text, apparently by printer's error. They are reinstated here after the pamphlet *The International Working Men's Association. Resolutions of the Congress of Geneva, 1866, and the Congress of Brussels, 1868*, London [1869].

If the middle and higher classes neglect their duties toward their offspring, it is their own fault. Sharing the privileges of these classes, the child is condemned to suffer from their prejudices.

The case of the working class stands quite different. The working man is no free agent. In too many cases, he is even too ignorant to understand the true interest of his child, or the normal conditions of human development. However, the more enlightened part of the working class fully understands that the future of its class, and, therefore, of mankind, altogether depends upon the formation of the rising working generation. They know that, before everything else, the children and juvenile workers must be saved from the crushing effects of the present system. This can only be effected by converting *social reason* into *social force*, and, under given circumstances, there exists no other method of doing so, than through *general laws*, enforced by the power of the state. In enforcing such laws, the working class do not fortify governmental power. On the contrary, they transform that power, now used against them, into their own agency. They effect by a general act what they would vainly attempt by a multitude of isolated individual efforts.

Proceeding from this standpoint, we say that no parent and no employer ought to be allowed to use juvenile labour, except when combined with education.

By education we understand three things.

Firstly: *Mental education*.

Secondly: *Bodily education*, such as is given in schools of gymnastics, and by military exercise.

Thirdly: *Technological training*, which imparts the general principles of all processes of production, and simultaneously initiates the child and young person in the practical use and handling of the elementary instruments of all trades.

A gradual and progressive course of mental, gymnastic, and technological training ought to correspond to the classification of the juvenile labourers. The costs of the technological schools ought to be partly met by the sale of their products.

The combination of paid productive labour, mental education, bodily exercise and polytechnic training, will raise the working class far above the level of the higher and middle classes.

It is self-understood that the employment of all persons from [nine] and to seventeen years (inclusively) in nightwork and all health-injuring trades must be strictly prohibited by law.

5. Cooperative Labour

It is the business of the International Working Men's Association to combine and generalize the *spontaneous movements* of the working classes, but not to dictate or impose any doctrinary system whatever. The Congress should, therefore, proclaim no *special system* of cooperation, but limit itself to the enunciation of a few general principles.

(*a*) We acknowledge the cooperative movement as one of the transforming forces of the present society based upon class antagonism. Its great merit is to practically show, that the present pauperizing and despotic system of the *subordination of labour* to capital can be superseded by the republican and beneficent system of *the association of free and equal producers*.

(*b*) Restricted, however, to the dwarfish forms into which individual wage slaves can elaborate it by their private efforts, the cooperative system will never transform capitalistic society. To convert social production into one large and harmonious system of free and cooperative labour, *general social changes* are wanted, *changes of the general conditions of society*, never to be realized save by the transfer of the organized forces of society, viz., the state power, from capitalists and landlords to the producers themselves.

(*c*) We recommend to the working men to embark in *cooperative production* rather than in *cooperative stores*. The latter touch but the surface of the present economical system, the former attacks its groundwork.

(*d*) We recommend to all cooperative societies to convert one part of their joint income into a fund for propagating their principles by example as well as by precept, in other words, by promoting the establishment of new cooperative fabrics, as well as by teaching and preaching.

(*e*) In order to prevent cooperative societies from degenerating into ordinary middle-class joint-stock companies (*sociétés par actions*), all workmen employed, whether shareholders or not, ought to share alike. As a mere temporary expedient, we are willing to allow shareholders a low rate of interest.

6. Trade Unions. Their Past, Present and Future

(A) Their Past

Capital is concentrated social force, while the workman has only to dispose of his working force. The *contract* between capital and labour can therefore never be struck on equitable terms, equitable even in the sense of a society which places the ownership of the material means of life and labour on one side and the vital productive energies on the opposite side. The only social power of the workmen is their number. The force of numbers, however, is broken by disunion. The disunion of the workmen is created and perpetuated by their *unavoidable competition amongst themselves*.

Trade unions originally sprang up from the *spontaneous* attempts of workmen at removing or at least checking that competition, in order to conquer such terms of contract as might raise them at least above the condition of mere slaves. The immediate object of trade unions was therefore confined to everyday necessities, to expediencies for the obstruction of the incessant encroachments of capital, in one word, to questions of wages and time of labour. This activity of the trade unions is not only legitimate, it is necessary. It cannot be dispensed with so long as the present system of production lasts. On the contrary, it must be generalized by the formation and the combination of trade unions throughout all countries. On the other hand, unconsciously to themselves, the trade unions were forming *centres of organization* of the working class, as the medieval municipalities and communes did for the middle class. If the trade unions are required for the guerrilla fights between capital and labour, they are still more important as *organized agencies for superseding the very system of wage labour and capital rule*.

(B) Their Present

Too exclusively bent upon the local and immediate struggles with capital, the trade unions have not yet fully understood their power of acting against the system of wage slavery itself. They therefore kept too much aloof from general social and political movements. Of late, however, they seem to awaken to some sense of their great historical mission, as appears, for instance, from their participation, in England, in the recent political movement, from the enlarged views taken of their function in the United States, and from the following resolution passed at the recent great conference of trade-union delegates at Sheffield:[24]

> That this conference, fully appreciating the efforts made by the International Association to unite in one common bond of brotherhood the working men of all countries, most earnestly recommend to the various societies here represented, the advisability of becoming affiliated to that body, believing that it is essential to the progress and prosperity of the entire working community.

(c) Their Future

Apart from their original purposes, they must now learn to act deliberately as organizing centres of the working class in the broad interest of its *complete emancipation*. They must aid every social and political movement tending in that direction. Considering themselves and acting as the champions and representatives of the whole working class, they cannot fail to enlist the non-society men into their ranks. They must look carefully after the interests of the worst paid trades, such as the agricultural labourers, rendered powerless by exceptional circumstances. They must convince the world at large that their efforts, far from being narrow and selfish, aim at the emancipation of the downtrodden millions.

7. Direct and Indirect Taxation

(a) No modification of the form of taxation can produce any important change in the relations of labour and capital.

(b) Nevertheless, having to choose between two systems of taxation, we recommend the *total abolition of indirect taxes*, and the *general substitution of direct taxes*.

Because indirect taxes enhance the prices of commodities, the tradesmen adding to those prices not only the amount of the indirect taxes, but the interest and profit upon the capital advanced in their payment;

Because indirect taxes conceal from an individual what he is paying to the state, whereas a direct tax is undisguised, unsophisticated, and not to be misunderstood by the meanest capacity. Direct taxation prompts therefore every individual to

---

24. This conference was the forerunner of the TUC, which first met in 1869.

control the governing powers while indirect taxation destroys all tendency to self-government.

8. *International Credit*

Initiative to be left to the French.[25]

9. *Polish Question*[26]

(*a*) Why do the workmen of Europe take up this question? In the first instance, because the middle-class writers and agitators conspire to suppress it, although they patronize all sorts of nationalities on the Continent, [and] even Ireland. Whence this reticence? Because both, aristocrats and bourgeois, look upon the dark Asiatic power in the background as a last resource against the advancing tide of working-class ascendancy. That power can only be effectually put down by the restoration of Poland upon a democratic basis.

(*b*) In the present changed state of central Europe, and especially Germany, it is more than ever necessary to have a democratic Poland. Without it, Germany will become the outwork of the Holy Alliance, with it, the cooperator with republican France.[27] The working-class movement will continuously be interrupted, checked, and retarded, until this great European question be set at rest.

(*c*) It is especially the duty of the German working class to take

25. It was the French Proudhonists who had proposed this subject for discussion.

26. In the French translation of this text, made by Paul Lafargue (who later married Marx's daughter Laura) on Marx's authorization, and published in *Le Courrier International* of 16 March 1867, this section is headed, 'On the Need to Destroy Russian Influence in Europe in order to Apply the Right of Peoples to Self-Determination and to Reconstruct Poland on a Democratic and Social Basis.' This is taken from a resolution drafted by Marx and passed by the 1865 London Conference; see *IWMA* I, pp. 246–7.

27. Central Europe had recently been changed by the defeat of Austria in the Austro-Prussian war of June–July 1866, and the formation of the North German Confederation under Prussian hegemony. The Holy Alliance existed at this period only in a figurative sense; Marx's point is that Prussia/Germany was still tied to Austria and Russia by the partition of Poland. (See Engels's article, 'What Have the Working Classes To Do with Poland?', below, pp. 380–81.)

the initiative in this matter, because Germany is one of the partitioners of Poland.

10. Armies[28]

(a) The deleterious influence of large standing armies upon *production* has been sufficiently exposed at middle-class congresses of all denominations, at peace congresses, economical congresses, statistical congresses, philanthropical congresses, sociological congresses. We think it, therefore, quite superfluous to expatiate upon this point.

(b) We propose the general armament of the people and their general instruction in the use of arms.

(c) We accept as a transitory necessity small standing armies to form schools for the officers of the militia; every male citizen to serve for a very limited time in those armies.

11. Religious Question[29]

To be left to the initiative of the French.

REPORT TO THE BRUSSELS CONGRESS[30]

The year 1867–8 will mark an epoch in the history of the Association. After a period of peaceable development it has assumed dimensions powerful enough to provoke the bitter denunciations of the ruling classes and the hostile demonstrations of governments. It has entered upon the phases of strife.

The French government took, of course, the lead in the reactionary proceedings against the working classes. Already last year we had to signalize some of its underhand manoeuvres. It meddled with our correspondence, seized our Statutes [Rules] and the Congress documents. After many fruitless steps to get them

28. In the French translation, this section is headed, 'Standing Armies: Their Relationship to Production.'

29. In the French translation, this section is headed, 'Religious Ideas: Their Influence on the Social, Political and Intellectual Movement.' This also had been proposed for discussion by the anti-clerical Proudhonists.

30. The General Council's report to the September 1868 Brussels Congress was drafted by Marx in English and approved by the General Council on 1 September 1868. It was published in *The Times*, 9 September 1868.

back, they were at last given up only under the official pressure of
Lord Stanley, the English Minister of Foreign Affairs.[31]

But the Empire has this year thrown off the mask and tried to
directly annihilate the International Association by *coups de police*
and judiciary prosecution. Begot by the struggle of classes, of
which the days of June 1848 are the grandest expression, it could
not but assume alternately the attitudes of the official saviour of
the bourgeoisie and of the paternal protector of the proletariat.
The growing power of the International having manifested itself
in the strikes of Roubaix, Amiens, Paris, Geneva, etc., reduced our
would-be patron to the necessity of turning our society to his own
account or of destroying it. In the beginning he was ready enough
to strike a bargain on very moderate terms. The manifesto of the
Parisians read at the Congress of Geneva[32] having been seized at
the French frontier, our Paris executive demanded of the Minister of
the Interior the reasons of this seizure. M. Rouher then invited one
of the members of the Committee to an interview, in the course of
which he declared himself ready to authorize the entry of the manifesto on the condition of some modifications being inserted. On the
refusal of the delegate of the Paris executive, he added, 'Still, if you
would introduce some words of gratitude to the emperor, who has
done so much for the working classes, one might see what could
be done.'

M. Rouher's, the sub-emperor's, insinuation was met by a blank
rebuff. From that moment the Imperial government looked out
for a pretext to suppress the Association. Its anger was height-
ened by the anti-chauvinist agitation on the part of our French
members after the German war.[33] Soon after, when the Fenian
panic had reached its climax, the General Council addressed to
the English government a petition demanding the commutation
of the sentence on the three victims of Manchester, and

31. The case referred to here involved the interception by French government
agents, in September 1866, of printed matter and correspondence being carried by a
Swiss, Jules Gottraux, from Geneva to London following the Geneva Congress. See
'The French Government and the International Association of Working Men', *IWMA*
II, pp. 271–6.

32. This document, which set out the views of the French Proudhonists
on the issues discussed at the Geneva Congress, was published in Brussels in
1866 under the title *Congrès de Genève, Mémoire des délégués français*. (It is
printed in J. Freymond (ed.), *La Première Internationale*, vol. I, Droz, Geneva,
1962.)

33. The Austro-Prussian war of 1866.

qualifying their hanging as an act of political revenge.[34] At the same time it held public meetings in London for the defence of the rights of Ireland. The Empire, always anxious to deserve the good graces of the British government, thought the moment propitious for laying hands upon the International. It caused nocturnal perquisitions to be made, eagerly rummaged the private correspondence, and announced with much noise that it had discovered the centre of the Fenian conspiracy, of which the International was denounced as one of the principal organs. All its laborious researches, however, ended in nothing. The public prosecutor himself threw down his brief in disgust. The attempt at converting the International Association into a secret society of conspirators having miserably broken down, the next best thing was to prosecute our Paris branch as a non-authorized society of more than twenty members. The French judges, trained by the Imperialist[35] discipline, hastened, of course, to order the dissolution of the Association and the imprisonment of its Paris executive. The tribunal had the *naïveté* to declare in the preamble of its judgement that the existence of the French Empire was incompatible with a working men's association that dared to proclaim truth, justice, and morality as its leading principles.[36] The consequences of these prosecutions made themselves felt in the departments, where paltry vexations on the part of the prefects succeeded to the condemnations of Paris. This governmental chicanery, however, so far from annihilating the Association, has given it a fresh impulse by forcing the Empire to drop its patronizing airs to the working classes.

In Belgium the International Association has made immense strides. The coal lords of the basin of Charleroi, having driven their miners to riots by incessant exactions, let loose upon those unarmed men the armed force which massacred many of them.[37] It was in the midst of the panic thus created that our Belgian branch took up the cause of the miners, disclosed their miserable economical condition, rushed to the rescue of the families of the

34. See below, pp. 158–9.

35. See p. 34, n. 62.

36. The first trial of the Paris Committee of the International took place in March 1868. Its fifteen members were fined, and the Paris sections declared dissolved. Meanwhile, a new Committee was elected, whose nine members were tried in May, and sentenced to three months' imprisonment and a fine.

37. In March 1868.

dead and wounded, and procured legal counsel for the prisoners, who were finally all of them acquitted by the jury. After the affair of Charleroi the success of the International in Belgium was assured. The Belgian Minister of Justice, Jules Bara, denounced the International Association in the Chamber of Deputies and made of its existence the principal pretext for the renewal of the law against foreigners. He even dared to threaten he should prevent the Brussels Congress from being held. The Belgium government ought at last to understand that petty states have no longer any *raison d'être* in Europe except they be the asylums of liberty.

In Italy, the progress of the Association has been impeded by the reaction following close upon the ambuscade of Mentana;[38] one of the first consequences was the restriction put upon the right of association and public meeting. But the numerous letters which have come to our hands fully prove that the Italian working class is more and more asserting its individuality quite independently of the old parties.

In Prussia, the International cannot exist legally, on account of a law which forbids all relations with foreign societies. Moreover, in regard to the General Union of the German Working Men,[39] the Prussian government has imitated Bonapartism on a shabby scale. Always ready to fall foul of each other, the military governments are cheek by jowl when entering upon a crusade against their common enemy, the working classes. In spite, however, of all these petty tribulations, small groups spread over the whole surface of Germany have long since rallied round our Geneva centre.[40] The General Union of the German Working Men, whose branches are mostly confined to northern Germany, have in their recent Congress held at Hamburg[41] decided to act in concert with the International Working Men's Association, although debarred from joining it officially. In the programme of the Nuremberg Congress, representing upwards of 100 working men's societies, which mostly belong to middle and southern Germany, the direct adhesion to the International has been put on the order

38. Garibaldi's expedition to secure Rome and the Papal State for the Kingdom of Italy was defeated at Mentana on 3 November 1867 by Papal guards backed by French forces.

39. I.e. the General Association of German Workers (ADAV); see the Introduction to this volume, pp. 21–3.

40. See the Introduction to this volume, p. 23.

41. The Hamburg Congress of the ADAV was held in August 1868.

of the day. At the request of their leading committee we have sent a delegate to Nuremberg.[42]

In Austria the working-class movement assumes a more and more revolutionary aspect. In the beginning of September a congress was to meet at Vienna, aiming at the fraternization of the working men of the different races of the empire. They had also sent an address to the English and French working men, in which they declared for the principles of the International. Your General Council had already appointed a delegate to Vienna[43] when the liberal government of Austria, on the very point of succumbing to the blows of the feudal reaction, had the shrewdness to stir the anger of the working men by prohibiting their congress.

In the struggle maintained by the building trades of Geneva the very existence of the International in Switzerland was put on its trial. The employers made it a preliminary condition of coming to any terms with their workmen that the latter should forsake the International. The working men indignantly refused to comply with this dictate. Thanks to the aid received from France, England, Germany, etc., through the medium of the International, they have finally obtained a diminution of one hour of labour and ten per cent increase of wages. Already deeply rooted in Switzerland, the International has witnessed since that event a rapid increase in the number of its members. In the month of August last the German working men residing in Switzerland (about fifty societies) passed at their Congress in Neuenburg [Neuchâtel] a unanimous vote of adhesion to the International.

In England the unsettled state of politics, the dissolution of the old parties, and the preparations for the coming electoral campaign have absorbed many of our most active members, and, to some degree, retarded our propaganda. Nevertheless, we have entered into correspondence with numerous provincial trade unions, many of which have sent in their adhesion. Among the more recent London affiliations those of the Curriers' Society and the City Men's Shoemakers are the most considerable as regards numbers.

Your General Council is in constant communication with the National Labour Union of the United States. On its last Congress

42. The Nuremberg Congress of the Union of German Workers' Societies was held in September 1868; see the Introduction to this volume, pp. 22–3. The General Council's delegate was J. G. Eccarius.

43. Peter Fox.

of August 1867, the American Union had resolved to send a delegate to the Brussels Congress, but, pressed for time, was unable to take the special measures necessary for carrying out the vote.

The latent power of the working classes of the United States has recently manifested itself in the legal establishment of a working day of eight hours in all the workshops of the federal government, and in the passing of laws to the same effect by many state legislatures. However, at this very moment the working men of New York, for example, are engaged in a fierce struggle for enforcing the eight hours' law, against the resistance of rebellious capital. This fact proves that even under the most favourable political conditions all serious success of the proletariat depends upon an organization that unites and concentrates its forces; and even its national organization is still exposed to split on the disorganization of the working classes in other countries, which one and all compete in the market of the world, acting and reacting the one upon the other. Nothing but an international bond of the working classes can ever ensure their definitive triumph. This want has given birth to the International Working Men's Association. That Association has not been hatched by a sect or a theory. It is the spontaneous growth of the proletarian movement, which itself is the offspring of the natural and irrepressible tendencies of modern society. Profoundly convinced of the greatness of its mission, the International Working Men's Association will allow itself neither to be intimidated nor misled. Its destiny, henceforward, coalesces with the historical progress of the class that bear in their hands the regeneration of mankind.

REPORT TO THE BASLE CONGRESS[44]

Citizens,

The delegates of the different sections will give you detailed reports on the progress of our Association in their respective countries. The report of your General Council will mainly relate to the guerrilla fights between capital and labour – we mean the strikes which during the last year have perturbed the continent of

44. The General Council's report to the September 1869 Basle Congress was drafted by Marx on the mandate of the General Council meeting of 31 August. It was published in the pamphlet *Report of the Fourth Annual Congress of the International Working Men's Association*, London, 1869.

Europe, and were said to have sprung neither from the misery of the labourer nor from the despotism of the capitalist, but from the secret intrigues of our Association.

A few weeks after the meeting of our last Congress, a memorable strike on the part of the ribbon-weavers and silk-dyers occurred in Basle, a place which to our days has conserved much of the features of a medieval town with its local traditions, its narrow prejudices, its purse-proud patricians, and its patriarchal rule of the employer over the employed. Still, a few years ago, a Basle manufacturer boasted to an English secretary of embassy, that 'the position of the master and the man was on a better footing here than in England', that 'in Switzerland the operative who leaves a good master for better wages would be *despised* by his own *fellow-workmen*', and that 'our advantage lies principally in the length of the working time and the moderation of the wages'. You see, *patriarchalism*, as modified by modern influences, comes to this – that the master is good, and that his wages are bad, that the labourer feels like a medieval vassal, and is exploited like a modern wage slave.

That patriarchalism may further be appreciated from an official Swiss inquiry into the factory employment of children and the state of the primary public schools. It was ascertained that 'the Basle school atmosphere is the worst in the world, that while in the free air carbonic acid forms only 4 parts of 10,000, and in closed rooms should not exceed 10 parts, it rose in Basle common schools to 20–81 parts in the forenoon, and to 53–94 in the afternoon'. Thereupon a member of the Basle Great Council, Mr Thurneysen, coolly replied, 'Don't allow yourselves to be frightened. The parents have passed through schoolrooms as bad as the present ones, and yet they have escaped with their skins safe.'

It will now be understood that an economical revolt on the part of the Basle workmen could not but mark an epoch in the social history of Switzerland. Nothing more characteristic than the starting-point of the movement. There existed an old custom for the ribbon-weavers to have a few hours' holiday on Michaelmas. The weavers claiming this small privilege at the usual time in the factory of Messrs Dubary & Sons, one of the masters declared, in a harsh voice and with imperious gesticulation, 'Whoever leaves the factory will be dismissed at once and for ever.' Finding their protestations in vain, 104 out of 172 weavers left the workshop without, however, believing in their definite dismissal, since master and men were bound by written contract to give a fourteen days' notice to quit. On their return the next morning they found the factory surrounded by gendarmes, keeping off the yesterday's rebels, with whom all their comrades now made common cause. Being thus suddenly thrown out of work, the weavers with their families were simultaneously ejected from the cottages they rented from their employers, who, into the bargain, sent circular letters round to the shopkeepers to debar the houseless ones from all credit for victuals. The struggle thus begun lasted from 9 November 1868 to the spring of 1869. The limits of our report do not allow us to enter upon its details. It suffices to state that it originated in a capricious and spiteful act of capitalist despotism, in a cruel lock-out, which led to strikes, from time to time interrupted by compromises, again and again broken on the part of the masters, and that it culminated in the vain attempt of the Basle 'High and Honourable State Council' to intimidate the working people by military measures and a quasi state of siege.

During their sedition the workmen were supported by the International Working Men's Association. But that was not all. That society, the masters said, had first smuggled the modern spirit of rebellion into the good old town of Basle. To again expel that mischievous intruder from Basle became, therefore, their great preoccupation. Hard they tried, though in vain, to enforce the withdrawal from it, as a condition of peace, upon their subjects. Getting generally worsted in their war with the International they vented their spleen in strange pranks. Owning some industrial branch establishments at Lörrach, in Baden, these republicans induced the grand-ducal official to suppress the International section at that place, a measure which, however, was soon after rescinded by the Baden government. The Augsburg *Allgemeine Zeitung*, a paper of world-wide circulation, presuming to report on the Basle events in an impartial spirit, the angry worthies threatened it in foolish letters with the withdrawal of their subscriptions. To London they expressly sent a messenger on the fantastic errand of ascertaining the dimensions of the International general 'treasury-box'. Orthodox Christians as they are, if they had lived at the time of nascent Christianity, they would, above all things, have spied into St Paul's banking accounts at Rome.

Their clumsily savage proceedings brought down upon them some ironical lessons of worldly wisdom on the part of the Geneva capitalist organs. Yet, a few months later, the uncouth

Basle vestrymen might have returned the compliment with usurious interest to the Geneva men of the world.

In the month of March there broke out in Geneva a building trades strike, and a compositors' strike, both bodies being affiliated to the International. The builders' strike was provoked by the masters setting aside a convention solemnly entered upon with their workmen a year ago. The compositors' strike was but the winding-up of a ten year quarrel which the men had during all that time in vain tried to settle by five consecutive commissions. As in Basle, the masters transformed at once their private feuds with their men into a state crusade against the International Working Men's Association.

The Geneva State Council dispatched policemen to receive at the railway stations, and sequestrate from all contact with the strikers, such foreign workmen as the masters might contrive to inveigle from abroad. It allowed the *'jeunesse dorée'*, the hopeful loafers of *'la jeune Suisse'*, armed with revolvers, to assault, in the streets and places of public resort, workmen and workwomen. It launched its own police ruffians on the working people on different occasions, and signally on 24 May, when it enacted at Geneva, on a small scale, the Paris scenes which Raspail has branded as *'les orgies infernales des casse-têtes'*.[45] When the Geneva workmen passed in public meeting an address to the State Council, calling upon it to inquire into these infernal police orgies, the State Council replied by a sneering rebuke. It evidently wanted, at the behest of its capitalist superiors, to madden the Geneva people into an *émeute*, to stamp that *émeute* out by the armed force, to sweep the International from the Swiss soil, and to subject the workmen to a Decembrist regime.[46] This scheme was baffled by the energetic action and moderating influence of our Geneva Federal Committee. The masters had at last to give way.

And now listen to some of the invectives of the Geneva capitalists and their press-gang against the International. In public meeting they passed an address to the State Council, where the following phrase occurs: 'The International Committee at Geneva ruins the Canton of Geneva *by decrees sent from London*

45. 'Hellish orgies with truncheons.' Thus François Raspail, a former associate of Blanqui, and at this time a republican deputy, referred to Bonapartist police violence in the elections of May–June 1869.

46. I.e. Bonapartist; Louis Napoleon's coup d'état was on 2 December 1851.

and Paris; it wants here to suppress all industry and all labour.'

One of their journals stated, 'The leaders of the International were secret agents of the emperor, who, at the opportune moment, were very likely to turn out public accusers against this little Switzerland of ours.'

And this on the part of the men who had just shown themselves so eager to transplant at a moment's notice the Decembrist regime to the Swiss soil, on the part of financial magnates, the real rulers of Geneva and other Swiss towns, whom all Europe knows to have long since been converted from citizens of the Swiss republic into mere feudatories of the French Crédit Mobilier[47] and other international swindling associations.

The massacres by which the Belgian government did answer in April last to the strikes of the puddlers at Seraing and the coal-miners of Borinage, have been fully exposed in the address of the General Council to the workmen of Europe and the United States.[48] We considered this address the more urgent since, with that constitutional model government, such working men's massacres are not an accident, but an institution. The horrid military drama was succeeded by a judicial farce. In the proceedings against our Belgian General Committee at Brussels, whose domiciles were brutally broken into by the police, and many of whose members were placed under secret arrest, the judge of instruction finds the letter of a workman, asking for 500 *'Internationales'*, and he at once jumps to the conclusion that 500 fighting-men were to be dispatched to the scene of action. The 500 *'Internationales'* were 500 copies of the *Internationale*, the weekly organ of our Brussels Committee.

A telegram to Paris by a member of the International, ordering a certain quantity of powder, is raked up. After a prolonged research, the dangerous substance is really laid hand on at Brussels. It is powder for killing vermin. Last, not least, the Belgian police flattered itself, in one of its domiciliary visits, to have got at that phantom treasure which haunts the great mind of the continental capitalist, viz.: the International treasure, the main stock of which is safely hoarded at London, but whose offsets travel con-

47. A government-sponsored bank set up in 1852, exposed by Marx in several articles in the *New York Daily Tribune* (e.g. 21 June, 24 June and 11 July 1856; 30 May and 1 June 1857).

48. 'The Belgian Massacres. To the Workmen of Europe and the United States', written by Marx; *IWMA* III, pp. 312–18.

tinually to all the continental seats of the Association. The Belgian official inquirer thought it buried in a certain strong box, hidden in a dark place. He gets at it, opens it forcibly, and there was found – some pieces of coal. Perhaps, if touched by the hand of the police, the pure International gold turns at once into coal.

Of the strikes that, in December 1868, infested several French cotton districts, the most important was that at Sotteville-lès-Rouen. The manufacturers of the department of the Somme had not long ago met at Amiens, in order to consult how they might undersell the English manufacturers in the English market itself. Having made sure that, besides protective duties, the comparative lowness of French wages had till now mainly enabled them to defend France from English cottons, they naturally inferred that a still further lowering of French wages would allow them to invade England with French cottons. The French cotton-workers, they did not doubt, would feel proud at the idea of defraying the expenses of a war of conquest which their masters had so patriotically resolved to wage on the other side of the Channel. Soon after it was bruited about that the cotton manufacturers of Rouen and its environs had, in secret conclave, agreed upon the same line of policy. Then an important reduction of wages was suddenly proclaimed at Sotteville-lès-Rouen, and then for the first time the Norman weavers rose against the encroachments of capital. They acted under the stir of the moment. Neither had they before formed a trade union nor provided for any means of resistance. In their distress they appealed to the International committee at Rouen, which found for them some immediate aid from the workmen of Rouen, the neighbouring districts, and Paris. Towards the end of December 1868, the General Council was applied to by the Rouen committee, at a moment of utmost distress throughout the English cotton districts, of unparalleled misery in London, and a general depression in all branches of British industry. This state of things has continued in England to this moment. Despite such highly unfavourable circumstances, the General Council thought that the peculiar character of the Rouen conflict would stir the English workmen to action. This was a great opportunity to show the capitalists that their international industrial warfare, carried on by screwing wages down now in this country, now in that, would be checked at last by the international union of the working classes. To our appeal the English workmen replied at once by a first contribution to Rouen, and the London Trades Council resolved to summon, in unison with the General Council, a metropolitan monster meeting on behalf of their Norman brethren. These proceedings were stopped by the news of the sudden cessation of the Sotteville strike. The miscarriage of that economical revolt was largely compensated for by its moral results. It enlisted the Norman cotton-workers into the revolutionary army of labour, it gave rise to the birth of trade unions at Rouen, Elboeuf, Darnétal, and the environs; and it sealed anew the bond of fraternity between the English and French working classes.

During the winter and spring of 1869 the propaganda of our Association in France was paralysed, consequent upon the violent dissolution of our Paris section in 1868,[49] the police chicaneries in the departments, and the absorbing interest of the French general elections.

The elections once over, numerous strikes exploded in the Loire mining districts, at Lyons, and many other places. The economical facts revealed during these struggles between masters and men struck the public eye like so many dissolving views of the high-coloured fancy pictures of working-class prosperity under the auspices of the Second Empire. The claims of redress on the part of the workmen were of so moderate a character and so urgent a nature that, after some show of angry resistance, they had to be conceded, one and all. The only strange feature about those strikes was their sudden explosion after a seeming lull, and the rapid succession in which they followed each other. Still, the reason of all this was simple and palpable. Having, during the elections, successfully tried their hands against their public despot, the workmen were naturally led to try them after the elections against their private despots. In one word, the elections had stirred their animal spirits. The governmental press, of course, paid as it is to misstate and misinterpret unpleasant facts, traced these events to a secret *mot d'ordre* from the London General Council, which, they said, sent their emissaries, from place to place, to teach the otherwise highly satisfied French workmen that it was a bad thing to be overworked, underpaid, and brutally treated. A French police organ, published at London, the *'International'* – (see its number of 3 August) – has condescended to reveal to the world the secret motives of our deleterious activity.

49. See above, p. 96.

The strangest feature is that the strikes were ordered to break out in such countries where misery is far from making itself felt. These unexpected explosions, occurring so opportunely for certain neighbours of ours, who had first had to apprehend war, make many people ask themselves whether these strikes took place on the request of some foreign Machiavelli, who had known how to win the good graces of this all-powerful Association.

At the very moment when this French police print impeached us of embarrassing the French government by strikes at home, in order to disembarrass Count Bismarck from war abroad, a Prussian paper accused us of embarrassing the North German Confederation with strikes, in order to crush German industry for the benefit of foreign manufactures.

The relations of the International to the French strikes we shall illustrate by two cases of a typical character. In the one case, the strike of Saint-Étienne and the following massacre at Ricamarie, the French government itself will no longer dare to pretend that the International had anything whatever to do with it. In the Lyons case, it was not the International that threw the workmen into strikes, but, on the contrary, it was the strikes that threw the workmen into the International.

The miners of Saint-Étienne, Rive-de-Giers, and Firminy had calmly, but firmly, requested the managers of the mining companies to reduce the working day, numbering twelve hours' hard underground labour, and revise the wages tariff. Failing in their attempt at a conciliatory settlement, they struck on 11 June. For them it was of course a vital question to secure the cooperation of the miners that had not yet turned out to combine with them. To prevent this, the managers of the mining companies requested and got from the prefect of the Loire a forest of bayonets. On 12 June, the strikers found the coal pits under strong military guard. To make sure of the zeal of the soldiers thus lent to them by the government, the mining companies paid each soldier a franc daily. The soldiers paid the companies back by catching, on 16 June, about sixty miners eager to get at a conversation with their brethren in the coal pits. These prisoners were in the afternoon of the same day escorted to Saint-Étienne by a detachment (150 men) of the fourth regiment of the line. Before these stout warriors set out, an engineer of the Dorian mines distributed them sixty bottles of brandy, telling them at the same time, they ought to have a sharp eye on their gang of prisoners, these miners being savages, barbarians, ticket-of-leave men. What with the brandy, and what with the sermon, a bloody collision was thus prepared for. Followed on their march by a crowd of miners, with their wives and children, surrounded by them on a narrow defile on the heights of the Moncel, Quartier Ricamarie, requested to surrender the prisoners, and, on their refusal, attacked by a volley of stones, the soldiers, without any preliminary warning, fired with their *chassepots* pell-mell into the crowd, killing fifteen persons, amongst whom were two women and an infant, and dangerously wounding a considerable number. The tortures of the wounded were horrible. One of the sufferers was a poor girl of twelve years, Jenny Petit, whose name will live immortal in the annals of the working-class martyrology. Struck by two balls from behind, one of which lodged in her leg, while the other passed through her back, broke her arm, and escaped through her right shoulder. '*Les chassepots avaient encore fait merveille.*'[50]

This time, however, the government was not long in finding out that it had committed not only a crime, but a blunder. It was not hailed as the saviour of society by the middle class. The whole municipal council of Saint-Étienne tendered its resignation in a document denouncing the scoundrelism of the troops and insisting upon their removal from the town. The French press rang with cries of horror! Even such conservative prints as the *Moniteur universel*[51] opened subscriptions for the victims. The government *had* to remove the odious regiment from Saint-Étienne.

Under such difficult circumstances, it was a luminous idea to sacrifice on the altar of public indignation a scapegoat always at hand, the International Working Men's Association. At the judicial trial of the so-called rioters, the act of accusation divided them into ten categories, very ingeniously shading their respective darkness of guilt. The first class, the most deeply tinged, consisted of workmen more particularly suspected to have obeyed some secret *mot d'ordre* from abroad, given out by the International. The evidence was, of course, overwhelming, as the following short extract from a French paper will show:

The interrogatory of the witnesses did not allow '*neatly*' to establish

50. '*Chassepots* [the French military rifle] had again worked wonders.'
51. The *Moniteur* had recently ceased to be the official organ of the French government.

the participation of the International Association. The witnesses affirm *only* the presence, at the head of the bands, of some *unknown* people, wearing white frocks and caps. *None of the unknown ones have been arrested, or appear in the dock.* To the question: do you *believe* in the intervention of the International Association? a witness replies: I *believe* it, but *without any proofs whatever!*

Shortly after the Ricamarie massacres, the dance of economical revolts was opened at Lyons by the silk-winders, most of them females. In their distress they appealed to the International, which, mainly by its members in France and Switzerland, helped them to carry the day. Despite all attempts at police intimidation, they publicly proclaimed their adhesion to our society, and entered it formally by paying the statutory contributions to the General Council. At Lyons, as before at Rouen, the female workers played a noble and prominent part in the movement. Other Lyons trades have since followed in the track of the silk-winders. Some 10,000 new members were thus gained for us in a few weeks amongst that heroic population which more than thirty years ago inscribed upon its banner the watchword of the modern proletariat: *'Vivre en travaillant ou mourir en combattant!'*[52]

Meanwhile the French government continues its petty tribulations against the International. At Marseilles our members were forbidden meeting for the election of a delegate to Basle. The same paltry trick was played in other towns. But the workmen on the Continent, as elsewhere, begin at last to understand that the surest way to get one's natural rights is to exercise them at one's personal risk.

The Austrian workmen, and especially those of Vienna, although entering their class movement only after the events of 1866,[53] have at once occupied a vantage-ground. They marched at once under the banners of socialism and the International, which, by their delegates at the recent Eisenach Congress,[54] they have now joined *en masse*.

If anywhere, the liberal middle class has exhibited in Austria its selfish instincts, its mental inferiority, and its petty spite

52. 'Live working or die fighting!' This slogan was raised by the Lyons silk workers in their revolt of 1831.

53. The Austro-Prussian war.

54. At the Eisenach Congress of August 1869 the dissident Lassalleans joined with Liebknecht and Bebel's group to form the Social-Democratic Workers's Party (SDAP); see the Introduction to this volume, pp. 23–4.

against the working class. Their ministry, seeing the empire distracted and threatened by an internecine struggle of races and nationalities, pounces upon the workmen who alone proclaim the fraternity of all races and nationalities. The middle class itself, which has won its new position not by any heroism of its own, but only by the signal disaster of the Austrian army, hardly able as it is, and knows itself to be, to defend its new conquests from the attacks of the dynasty, the aristocracy, and the clerical party, nevertheless wastes its best energies in the mean attempt to debar the working class from the rights of combination, public meeting, free press and free thought. In Austria, as in all other states of continental Europe, the International has supplanted the *ci-devant spectre rouge*.[55] When, on 13 July, a workmen's massacre on a small scale was enacted at Brünn [Brno], the cottonopolis of Moravia, the event was traced to the secret instigations of the International, whose agents, however, were unfortunately invested with the rare gift of rendering themselves invisible. When some leaders of the Vienna work-people figured before the judicial bench, the public accuser stigmatized them as tools of the foreigner. Only, to show how conscientiously he had studied the matter, he committed the little error of confounding the middle-class League of Peace and Freedom with the working man's International Association.

If the workmen's movement was thus harassed in Cis-Leithanian Austria, it has been recklessly prosecuted in Hungary. On this point the most reliable reports from Pest [Budapest] and Pressburg [Bratislava] have reached the General Council. One example of the treatment of the Hungarian workmen by the public authorities may suffice. Herr von Wenckheim, the Hungarian Home Minister, was just staying at Vienna on public business. Having for months been interdicted from public meetings and even from entertainments destined for the collection of the funds of a sick club, the Bratislava workmen sent at last delegates to Vienna, then and there to lay their grievances before the illustrious Herr von Wenckheim. Puffing and blowing his cigar, the illustrious one received them with the bullying apostrophe, 'Are you workmen? Do you work hard? For nothing else you have to care. You do not want public clubs; and if you dabble in politics, we shall know what measures to take against you. I shall do nothing for you. Let the workmen grumble to their hearts' content!' To the question of the workmen,

55. The former red spectre.

whether the good pleasure of the police was still to rule uppermost, the liberal minister replied: 'Yes, under my responsibility.' After a somewhat prolonged but useless explanation the workmen left the minister, telling him, 'Since state matters influence the workmen's condition, the workmen must occupy themselves with politics, and they will certainly do so.'

In Prussia and the rest of Germany, the past year was distinguished by the formation of trade unions all over the country. At the recent Eisenach Congress the delegates of 150,000 German workmen, from Germany proper, Austria and Switzerland, have organized a new democratic social party, with a programme literally embodying the leading principles of our Statutes. Debarred by law from forming sections of our Association, they have, nevertheless, formally entered it by resolving to take individual cards of membership from the General Council. At its congress at Barmen, the General Association of German Workers has also reaffirmed its adhesion to the principles of our Association, but simultaneously declared the Prussian law forbade them joining us.

New branches of our Association have sprung up at Naples, in Spain, and in Holland.

At Barcelona a Spanish, and at Amsterdam a Dutch organ of our Association is now being issued.[56]

The laurels plucked by the Belgian government on the glorious battlefields of Seraing and Frameries seem really to have roused the angry jealousy of the great powers. No wonder, then, that England also had this year to boast a workmen's massacre of its own. The Welsh coal-miners, at Leeswood Great Pit, near Mold, in Denbighshire, had received sudden notice of a reduction of wages by the manager of those works, whom, long since, they had reason to consider a most incorrigible petty oppressor. Consequently, they collected aid from the neighbouring collieries, and, besides assaulting him, attacked his house, and carried all his furniture to the railway station, these wretched men fancying in their childish ignorance thus to get rid of him for good and all. Proceedings were of course taken against the rioters; but one of them was rescued by a mob of 1,000 men, and conveyed out of the town. On 28 May, two of the ringleaders were to be taken before the magistrates of Mold by policemen under the escort of a detachment of the 4th Regiment of the line, 'The King's Own'.

56. *La Federación* and *De Werkman*.

A crowd of miners, trying to rescue the prisoners, and, on the resistance of the police and the soldiers, showering stones at them, the soldiers – without any previous warning – returned the shower of stones by a shower of bullets from their breachloaders (Snider fusils). Five persons, two of them females, were killed, and a great many wounded. So far there is much analogy between the Mold and the Ricamarie massacres, but here it ceases. In France, the soldiers were only responsible to their commander. In England, they had to pass through a coroner's jury inquest; but this coroner was a deaf and daft old fool, who had to receive the witnesses' evidence through an ear trumpet, and the Welsh jury, who backed him, were a narrowly prejudiced class jury. They declared the massacre 'justifiable homicide'.

In France, the rioters were sentenced to from three to eighteen months' imprisonment, and soon after, amnestied. In England, they were condemned to ten years' penal servitude! In France, the whole press resounded with cries of indignation against the troops. In England, the press was all smiles for the soldiers, and all frowns for their victims! Still, the English workmen have gained much by losing a great and dangerous illusion. Till now they fancied to have their lives protected by the formality of the Riot Act, and the subordination of the military to the civil authorities. They know now, from the official declaration of Mr Bruce, the Liberal Home Secretary, in the House of Commons – firstly, that without going through the premonitory process of reading the Riot Act, any country magistrate, some fox-hunter or parson, has the right to order the troops to fire on what he may please to consider a riotous mob; and, secondly, that the soldier may give fire on his own book, on the plea of self-defence. The Liberal minister forgot to add that, under these circumstances, every man ought to be armed, at public expense, with a breachloader, in self-defence against the soldier.

The following resolution was passed at the recent General Congress of the English trade unions at Birmingham:[57]

That as local organizations of labour have almost disappeared before organizations of a national character, so we believe the extension of the principle of free trade, which induces between nations such a competition that the interest of the workman is liable to be lost sight of and sacrificed in the fierce international race between capitalists, demands that such organizations should be still further extended and made inter-

57. The first TUC Congress.

national. And as the International Working Men's Association endeavours to consolidate and extend the interests of the toiling masses, which are everywhere identical, this Congress heartily recommends that Association to the support of the working men of the United Kingdom, especially of all organized bodies, and strongly urges them to become affiliated to that body, believing that the realization of its principles would also conclude to lasting peace between the nations of the earth.

During last May, a war between the United States and England seemed imminent. Your General Council, therefore, sent an address to Mr Sylvis, the President of the American National Labour Union, calling on the United States' working class to command peace where their would-be masters shouted war.[58]

The sudden death of Mr Sylvis, that valiant champion of our cause, will justify us in concluding this report, as an homage to his memory, by his reply to our letter:

Your favour of the 12th instant, with address enclosed, reached me yesterday. I am very happy to receive such kindly words from our fellow working men across the water: our cause is a common one. It is war between poverty and wealth: labour occupies the same low condition, and capital is the same tyrant in all parts of the world. Therefore I say our cause is a common one. I, in behalf of the working people of the United States, extend to you, and through you to those you represent, and to all the downtrodden and oppressed sons and daughters of toil in Europe, the right hand of fellowship. Go ahead in the good work you have undertaken, until the most glorious success crowns your efforts. That is our determination. Our late war resulted in the building up of the most infamous monied aristocracy on the face of the earth. This monied power is fast eating up the substance of the people. We have made war upon it, and we mean to win. If we can, we will win through the ballot-box; if not, then we will resort to sterner means. A little blood-letting is sometimes necessary in desperate cases.

58. This crisis followed the speech of the Republican Congressional leader Charles Summer on 13 April 1869, claiming 2 billion dollars compensation for the damage to US interests caused by English privateers during the civil war. In 1872 the dispute between England and the US was settled by an international tribunal, with England agreeing to pay 15½ million dollars. The General Council's 'Address to the National Labor Union of the United States', written by Marx, is printed in *IWMA* III, pp. 319–21.

THE GENERAL COUNCIL TO THE FEDERAL COUNCIL OF
FRENCH SWITZERLAND[59]

At its extraordinary meeting of 1 January 1870 the General Council resolved:

1. We read in *Égalité*,[60] 11 December 1869:

> It is *certain* that the General Council is neglecting matters of great importance. We would remind it of its obligations under Regulation II/2:[61] 'The General Council is *bound* to execute the Congress resolutions, etc. . . .' We could ask the General Council enough questions for its answers to make a somewhat lengthy document. These will come later . . . Meanwhile, etc. etc. . . .

The General Council knows of no article, either in the Rules or in the Regulations, which would oblige it to enter into correspondence or debate with *Égalité*, or provide any 'answers to questions' from newspapers. Only the Federal Committee in Geneva represents the branches of French Switzerland to the General Council. Whenever the Federal Committee addresses requests or objections to us by the one and only legitimate channel, i.e. through its secretary, the General Council will always be ready to reply. But the Federal Committee has no right either to hand over its functions to the editors of *Égalité* and *Progrès*,[62] or to permit those journals to usurp its functions.

59. This circular, sometimes known as the 'Confidential Communication', was written by Marx in French after the General Council's meeting of 1 January 1870, and distributed privately in hand-written copies. Marx's original text is not extant, and it is translated here from a manuscript copy made by Marx's wife and corrected by Marx himself, as reproduced in *IWMA* III, pp. 354–63.

60. *L'Égalité* was the official organ of the French-Swiss (*Romand*) Federal Council or Committee of the International, which was taken over by Bakunin's faction in autumn 1869. Marx replies to the allegations in question point by point in the present circular.

61. The Administrative Regulations of the International, adopted by the Geneva Congress of 1866 as a supplement to the Rules, and modified by subsequent Congress decisions. This reference is to the 1871 English edition, printed in *IWMA* IV, pp. 451–69.

62. *Le Progrès* was a Bakuninist paper, edited by James Guillaume in Le Locle, Switzerland.

Generally speaking, administrative correspondence between the General Council and the national and local committees cannot be made public without doing considerable damage to the general interests of the Association. Therefore, if other organs of the International were to imitate *Progrès* and *Égalité*, the General Council would be forced either to remain silent and thus earn the discredit of the public, or to violate its obligations by making a public reply. *Égalité* has combined with *Progrès* in urging *Le Travail*[63] (a Paris newspaper) also to attack the General Council. This is virtually a *ligue du bien public*.[64]

2. Accepting that the questions posed by *Égalité* originate from the French-Swiss Federal Council, we shall reply to them, on condition that in future such questions do not reach us by the same route.

3. Question of the Bulletin

According to the resolutions of the Geneva Congress, inserted into the Administrative Regulations, the national committees are supposed to send the General Council *documents* relating to the proletarian movement, and '*as often as its means permit*, the General Council shall publish a report, etc.'[65] in the various languages.

The General Council's obligation is thus dependent on *conditions* which have never been fulfilled; even the statistical inquiry, provided for in the Rules, decided on by successive General Congresses, annually requested by the General Council, has never been carried out. No document has been sent to the General Council. As for *means*, the General Council would have long since ceased to exist without the English 'regional' contributions and the personal sacrifice of its own members.

Thus the regulation in question adopted at the Geneva Congress has remained a dead letter.

The Brussels Congress, for its part, never discussed the *execution* of this regulation; it discussed the possibility of a bulletin in due

---

63. *Le Travail* was the newspaper of the Paris sections of the International.

64. The original Ligue du Bien Public (League of Public Welfare) was an association of French barons founded in 1464 to resist Louis XI's centralizing policy.

65. *IWMA* II, p. 269.

time but *it adopted no resolution*. (See the *German report* printed at Basle under the eyes of the Congress.)[66]

For the rest, the General Council believes that the original aim of the bulletin is at the moment perfectly well served by the different organs of the International published in the various languages and mutually exchanged. It would be absurd to produce costly bulletins to do what is already done without expense. On the other hand, a bulletin which published things which are not said in the International's organs would only serve to admit our enemies behind the scenes.

4. *Question of the Separation of the General Council and the Regional Council for England*[67]

Long before the founding of *Égalité* this proposal arose from time to time in the General Council itself, put forward by one or two of its English members. It was always rejected almost unanimously.

Although the revolutionary *initiative* will probably start from France, only England can act as a *lever* in any seriously *economic* revolution. It is the only country where there are no longer any peasants, and where land ownership is concentrated in very few hands. It is the only country where almost all production has been taken over by the *capitalist form*, in other words with work combined on a vast scale under capitalist bosses. It is the only country *where the large majority of the population consists of wage-labourers*. It is the only country where the class struggle and the organization of the working class into *trade unions* have actually reached a considerable degree of maturity and universality. Because of its domination of the world market, it is the only country where any revolution in the economic system will have immediate repercussions on the rest of the world. Though landlordism and capitalism are most traditionally established in this country, on the other hand the *material conditions* for *getting rid of them* are also most ripe here. Given that the General Council is now in the happy position of *having its hand directly*

66. The corresponding English account is *Report of the Fourth Annual Congress of the International Working Men's Association*, London [1869].

67. From the foundation of the International the General Council also fulfilled the role of the leading body for Britain, until an English Federal Council was set up by decision of the London Conference of 1871.

upon this tremendous lever for proletarian revolution, what lunacy, we would almost say what a crime, to let it fall into purely English hands!

The English have all that is needed *materially* for social revolution. What they lack is *the sense of generalization and revolutionary passion*. These are things that only the General Council can supply, and it can thus speed up the genuinely revolutionary movement in this country, and consequently *everywhere else*. The tremendous results we have already achieved in this direction are attested to by the most intelligent and authoritative newspapers of the ruling class – as for instance the *Pall Mall Gazette*, the *Saturday Review*, the *Spectator* and the *Fortnightly Review* – to say nothing of the so-called Radical members of both Houses of Parliament who, not long ago, still exercised enormous influence over the English workers' leaders. They are publicly accusing us of having poisoned and almost extinguished the *English spirit* of the working class, and having thrust the workers into revolutionary socialism.

The only way we could have produced this change was to act as the General Council of the International Association. As the General Council we can initiate moves (such as the foundation of the Land and Labour League)[68] which as they develop further appear to the public to be spontaneous movements of the English working class.

If a Regional Council were to be formed as distinct from the General Council, what would be the immediate effects?

Caught between the General Council and the TUC, the Regional Council would lack authority. On the other hand, the General Council of the International would lose its present control of the great lever I have described. If we wanted to replace our important underground activity with the publicity of the theatre, then we would perhaps have made the mistake of publicly answering the question put in *Égalité* as to why the General Council submits to fulfilling such an inconvenient plurality of functions!

England can not be considered simply as one country among many others. It must be treated as the metropolis of capital.

68. See p. 29, n. 47.

5. *Question of the General Council's Resolutions on the Irish Amnesty*

If England is the bulwark of European landlordism and capitalism, the only point at which one can strike a major blow against official England is *Ireland*.

In the first place, Ireland is the bulwark of English landlordism. If it collapsed in Ireland, it would collapse in England. The whole operation is a hundred times easier in Ireland, because there the economic struggle is concentrated exclusively on landed property, because that struggle is at the same time a national one, and because the people have reached a more revolutionary and exasperated pitch there than in England. Landlordism in Ireland is kept in being solely by the *English army*. If the enforced union between the two countries were to cease, a social revolution would immediately break out in Ireland – even if of a somewhat backward kind. English landlordism would lose not only a major source of its wealth, but also its greatest moral force – the fact of *representing England's domination over Ireland*. On the other hand, by preserving the power of its landlords in Ireland, the English proletariat makes them invulnerable in England itself.

In the second place, in dragging down the working class in England still further by the forced immigration of poor Irish people, the English bourgeoisie has not merely exploited Irish poverty. It has also divided the proletariat into two hostile camps. The fiery rebelliousness of the Celtic worker does not mingle well with the steady slow nature of the Anglo-Saxon; in fact in all *the major industrial centres of England* there is a profound antagonism between the Irish and the English proletarians. The ordinary English worker hates the Irish worker as a competitor who brings down his wages and standard of living. He also feels national and religious antipathies for him; it is rather the same attitude that the poor whites of the Southern states of North America had for the Negro slaves. This antagonism between the two groups of proletarians within England itself is artificially kept in being and fostered by the bourgeoisie, who know well that this split is the real secret of preserving their own power.

This antagonism is reproduced once again on the other side of the Atlantic. The Irish, driven from their native soil by cattle and sheep, have landed in North America where they form a considerable, and increasing, proportion of the population. Their sole thought, their sole passion, is their hatred for England. The English and American governments (in other words, the classes they represent) nourish that passion so as to keep permanently alive the underground struggle between the United States and England; in that way they can prevent the sincere and worthwhile alliance between the working classes on the two sides of the Atlantic which would lead to their emancipation.

Furthermore, Ireland is the only excuse the English government has for keeping up a large regular army which can, as we have seen, in case of need attack the English workers after having done its basic training in Ireland.

Finally, what ancient Rome demonstrated on a gigantic scale can be seen in the England of today. A people which subjugates another people forges its own chains.

Therefore the International Association's attitude to the Irish question is absolutely clear. Its first need is to press on with the social revolution in England, and to that end, the major blow must be struck in Ireland.

The General Council's resolutions on the Irish Amnesty[69] are designed simply to lead into other resolutions which will declare that, quite apart from the demands of international justice, it is an essential precondition for the emancipation of the English working class to transform the present enforced union (in other words, the enslavement of Ireland) into a free and equal confederation, if possible, and into a total separation, if necessary.

In any case, the hyper-naive pronouncements of *Égalité* and *Progrès* as to the connection, or rather lack of connection, between the social movement and the political movement have never, as far as we know, been approved by any of our International Congresses. They are in fact contrary to our Rules, which state: 'The *economical emancipation* of the working classes is therefore the great end to which every *political movement ought* to be subordinate *as a means*'.[70]

The phrase 'as a means' was left out in the French translation made by the Paris Committee in 1864.[71] When taxed with this

---

69. These resolutions, adopted by the General Council on 16 November 1869, are reproduced by Marx in his letter to Engels of 18 November; below, p. 163.

70. Above, p. 82.

71. *Congrès Ouvrier. Association Internationale des Travailleurs. Règlement Provisoire* [Paris, 1864] (printed in Freymond, op. cit., vol. I).

by the General Council, the Paris Committee gave as its excuse the wretchedness of its political situation.

There are other distortions of the text. The first consideration of the Rules is framed thus: 'The struggle for the emancipation of the working classes means . . . a struggle . . . for equal rights and duties, and *the abolition of all class rule.*'

The Paris translation mentions the 'equal rights and duties', in other words, the general phrase which exists in nearly all the democratic manifestoes of the past hundred years, and which means something quite different to different classes; but it leaves out the concrete phrase, 'the abolition of all class rule'.

Again, in the second consideration of the Rules we read: '. . . the economical subjection of the *man of labour* to the *monopolizer of the means of labour*, that is, the *sources of life*, etc.'

The Paris translation has 'capital' instead of 'the means of labour, that is, the sources of life', an expression which includes the land as well as the other means of labour.

However, the original and authentic text has been restored in the French translation published in Brussels by *La Rive gauche* (in 1866), and printed in pamphlet form.[72]

6. *The Liebknecht–Schweitzer Problem*

Égalité says: 'These two groups belong to the International.'

That is not true. The Eisenach group[73] (which *Progrès* and *Égalité* are trying to turn into 'citizen Liebknecht's group') belongs to the International. *Schweitzer's group*[74] *does not belong to it.*

Schweitzer has even explained at length in his newspaper (*Social-Demokrat*) why the Lassallean organization could not be united with the International without destroying itself;[75] un-

72. This translation (*Manifeste de l'Association Internationale des Travailleurs suivi du Règlement Provisoire*) was made by Charles Longuet, who later married Marx's daughter Jenny.

73. The Social-Democratic Workers' Party (SDAP); see p. 23.

74. The General Association of German Workers (ADAV), founded by Lassalle; see pp. 21–3.

75. On 16 July 1869. After nominally moving closer to the International in 1868, Schweitzer swung the ADAV onto an ultra-sectarian course in June 1869, effecting a reconciliation with Countess Hatzfeld's splinter group (see below, p. 148, n. 29). This led to a large section of the ADAV breaking away, and uniting with Liebknecht and Bebel's group in September 1869 to form the Social-Democratic Workers' Party.

knowingly, he was speaking the truth. His artificial and sectarian organization is wholly opposed to the historic and spontaneous organization of the working class.

Progrès and *Égalité* have demanded that the General Council give a public statement of 'opinion' as to the personal differences between Liebknecht and Schweitzer. Since citizen Johann Philipp Becker (who is slandered along with Liebknecht in Schweitzer's paper) is one of the editorial committee of *Égalité*, it seems curious that its editors are not better informed as to the facts. They should know that Liebknecht, in the *Demokratisches Wochenblatt*,[76] publicly invited Schweitzer to accept the General Council as arbiter of their differences, and that Schweitzer equally publicly rejected the General Council's authority.[77]

On its side, the General Council has done everything in its power to bring this scandal to an end. It asked its secretary for Germany[78] to correspond with Schweitzer, which he did for two years, but all the Council's attempts have failed, thanks to Schweitzer's firm resolution to preserve at all costs his autocratic power over his own sectarian organization. It is for the General Council to decide at what moment its public intervention in the dispute will be of more value than harm.

7. Since *Égalité*'s accusations have been public, and might be thought to come from the Geneva (French-Swiss) Committee, the General Council will communicate this reply to all the committees with which it is in correspondence.

BY ORDER OF THE GENERAL COUNCIL

76. On 20 February 1869. The *Demokratisches Wochenblatt* had been the organ of Liebknecht's Union of German Workers' Societies. Marx erroneously referred here to the *Volksstaat*, the organ of the SDAP, which Liebknecht edited at the time of Marx's writing.

77. *Social-Demokrat*, 24 February 1869.

78. I.e. Marx.

On Germany

THE PRUSSIAN MILITARY QUESTION AND
THE GERMAN WORKERS' PARTY[1] [*Extract*]

Frederick Engels

II

The political existence of the Prussian bourgeoisie – the most advanced section and, as such, the representative of the whole German bourgeoisie – is characterized by a lack of courage which is unparalleled even in the history of this, not exactly bold, class and which can only be partially excused by what has been happening abroad. In March and April 1848 it was master of the situa-

1. Engels wrote this pamphlet at Marx's request early in February 1865, and it was published in Hamburg at the end of the month. It is translated here from the text printed in *MEW* 16. The first section of Engels's pamphlet, omitted here, is chiefly technical in character, and presents the details of the army reorganization along with a military critique of the measures involved. The aim of the army reorganization was to expand Prussian military strength as required by the Prussian regime's aspirations to German hegemony. It involved a large increase in the officer corps, the expansion of the peacetime army to a strength of 200,000, and the transformation of the Landwehr (territorial army) into an army reserve or a second field army.

Universal military service had been introduced in Prussia in 1814, although it was by no means consistently applied. Although the Prussian government presented the army reorganization as a more consistent application of universal military service, its real tendency was towards the French and Austrian system of a large regular army based on selective long-term military service. Engels held that the Prussian government could be forced, by dint of its own requirements, to make concessions to the bourgeois opposition that would give the reorganized army a more democratic character: the thorough application of the principle of universal military service, with a duration of two years in the colours followed by a period in the reserve and Landwehr duty, and the institution of non-professional Landwehr officers.

The proposed army reorganization marked the start of the constitutional conflict between the Prussian government and the liberal bourgeois majority in the Lower House of the Prussian Assembly. When the 'New Era' government had refused to make significant concessions to the bourgeoisie, the Progressive party deputies refused to vote for the military budget, in March

tion; but with the first independent stirrings on the part of the working class it immediately took fright and fled back to the protection of the very bureaucracy and feudal aristocracy which, with the help of the workers, it had just defeated. The Manteuffel period[2] was the inevitable consequence. At length the 'New Era'[3] began – without any assistance from the bourgeois opposition. This unhoped-for piece of luck turned the heads of the bourgeoisie. It completely forgot the position into which it had got itself as a result of its continual withdrawal from one position back to the next, its repeated revisions of the constitution and its surrender to the bureaucracy and feudalism – in which it even went so far as to accept the reinstitution of the feudal provincial and district diets. It believed itself once again master of the situation; it completely forgot that it had itself reinstated all the forces hostile to it, which, having gathered their strength, now controlled the real power in the state just as they had before 1848. The reorganization of the army thus hit the bourgeoisie as if a bomb had been tossed into its midst.

There are only two ways for the bourgeoisie to obtain political power. Since it is an army of officers, and can only recruit its troops from among the workers, it must either ensure the support of the workers or it must buy political power piecemeal from those forces confronting it from above, in particular, from the monarchy. The history of the English and French bourgeoisies shows that there is no other way.

1862. After new elections failed to break the deadlock, Bismarck was appointed chancellor, in October 1862, and proceeded with the military reform, levying taxation in defiance of the constitution. This situation still obtained when Engels wrote his pamphlet, but the conflict was resolved in August 1866, when, following the Prussian defeat of Austria and the formation of the North German Confederation, the Progressive party split, and the majority converted themselves into National Liberals and capitulated to Bismarck.

2. Otto, Freiherr von Manteuffel, was Prime Minister and Foreign Minister from 1850 to 1858. The Manteuffel period was a dictatorship of the junkers and the court camarilla, and even the reactionary 1850 constitution was repeatedly 'revised' from above.

3. In October 1858 Prince William became the prince regent, and succeeded to the throne when mad Frederick William IV died in 1861. His first act was to dismiss Manteuffel and appoint a moderate liberal government, which the bourgeois press optimistically saw as inaugurating a 'New Era'. However, William's aim was solely to contain bourgeois demands, and the 'New Era' brought no real reforms. It came to an end with the appointment of Bismarck in October 1862.

The Prussian bourgeoisie – for no reason at all – had lost all desire to enter into an honest alliance with the workers. In 1848 the German workers' party, at that time still at the beginning of its development and organization, was ready to do the bourgeoisie's work on very cheap terms; the bourgeoisie, however, feared the least independent activity on the part of the proletariat more than it feared the feudal lords and the bureaucracy.[4] Peace bought at the price of servitude seemed to the bourgeoisie more desirable than freedom with even the mere *prospect* of a struggle. This holy fear of the workers subsequently became traditional among the bourgeoisie until Herr Schulze-Delitzsch began his 'savings-box' agitation.[5] This was designed to prove to the workers that they could know no greater happiness than to devote their lives and even those of their offspring to industrial exploitation by the bourgeoisie, indeed that they must themselves contribute to this exploitation by creating a subsidiary source of income from industrial cooperatives of all kinds, thus giving the capitalists an opportunity of lowering their wages. Now, although the industrial bourgeoisie, together with cavalry lieutenants, are without doubt the least educated class in the German nation, such agitation was from the very beginning without the least prospect of lasting success among so intellectually advanced a people as the Germans. The more intelligent members of the bourgeoisie could not help but realize that nothing would come of their plans, and their alliance with the workers collapsed again.

All that was left was to haggle with the government over political power, which had to be paid for in ready cash – from the people's pocket, of course. The only *real* power which the bourgeoisie had in the state consisted in the right to vote taxes, although even this right was hedged by a great many provisos. This, at any rate, was where the pressure had to be applied, and a class so skilled in haggling over prices was bound to be at an advantage in such matters.

But no. The Prussian bourgeois opposition – in complete contrast to the classical English bourgeoisie of the seventeenth and

4. See 'The Bourgeoisie and the Counter-Revolution', *The Revolutions of 1848*, pp. 186–212.

5. Franz Hermann Schulze-Delitzsch was a petty-bourgeois economist and a leading figure in the Progressive party. At the turn of the sixties he attempted to take the newly awakening workers' movement in tow by propagating harmless schemes for 'credit associations'.

eighteenth centuries – thought that it could get power on the cheap, *without* paying money for it.

What then was the correct policy for the bourgeois opposition, seen from a purely bourgeois standpoint and taking full account of the conditions under which the reorganization of the army was proposed? If it had been at all capable of judging its own strength it could not have failed to realize that, as a class which had just been raised up from the degradation it had suffered under Manteuffel – and without the least assistance from itself – it certainly did not have the power to prevent the actual *implementation* of the plan; this, indeed, was put into operation. It had to realize that the actual existence of the new institution was becoming increasingly difficult to reject with every fruitless session which passed; that is, it became more obvious from year to year that the government would offer less and less in order to gain the consent of the Chamber. It had also to realize that it was still far from having the power to appoint and dismiss ministers and that therefore the longer the conflict lasted the fewer ministers there would be who would be ready to compromise. Lastly it had to realize that it lay in its own interests not to bring matters to a head, for in view of the stage of development of the German working class, a serious conflict between the bourgeois opposition and the government was bound to give rise to an independent workers' movement. If the worst came to the worst, such a conflict would present the bourgeoisie with the old dilemma: either an alliance with the workers, but this time under much less favourable conditions than in 1848, or down on its knees before the government with a *pater, peccavi!*[6]

Accordingly, the bourgeois liberals and Progressives[7] ought to have subjected the reorganization of the army, together with the inevitable rise in its peacetime size, to an unbiased and objective examination, in which it would probably have reached conclusions much the same as ours. It was important not to forget that the changes already made could not be prevented and that in view of the many correct and valuable elements contained in the plan its final implementation could at best be delayed. Above all, the

6. 'Father, I have sinned', the opening words of a Catholic prayer.

7. The Progressive party in Prussia stood for German unity under Prussian hegemony, an all-German parliament, to which the ministry should be responsible, and liberal economic reforms. It did not demand universal suffrage, or the unrestricted freedom of association, assembly and the press.

bourgeoisie should have been on its guard against taking up, right from the start, a position opposed to the reorganization; on the contrary, it should have made use of this reorganization and the money to be voted for it in order to purchase from the 'New Era' as many equivalent concessions as possible and to convert the nine or ten million thalers of new taxation into as much political power for itself as possible.

And there was no shortage of things still to be done! There was all the legislation passed under Manteuffel restricting the press and the freedom of association; the whole power structure of the police and bureaucracy, which had been taken over unchanged from the absolute monarchy; the ineffectiveness of the courts due to jurisdictional conflicts; the provincial and district diets; there was, above all, the interpretation of the constitution which had prevailed under Manteuffel and which now had to be challenged by a new constitutional practice; there was the atrophy of municipal self-government caused by the bureaucracy and a hundred other things, which any other bourgeoisie under similar circumstances would have willingly paid for with a tax increase of a half thaler *per capita* and all of which were within reach if the business were conducted with any degree of skill. But the bourgeois opposition did not think this way. As far as freedom of the press, association and assembly were concerned, Manteuffel's laws had given them just enough to make them feel comfortable. They were allowed moderate demonstrations against the government without hindrance; any increase in freedom would have brought less advantage to them than to the workers, and before the bourgeoisie would give the workers freedom to form an independent movement they preferred to put up with more pressure from the government. It was the same story with the restrictions imposed by the power of the police and bureaucracy. The bourgeoisie believed that, thanks to the government of the 'New Era', the bureaucracy had been subdued; but it was glad to see that this bureaucracy was still allowed to have a free hand against the workers. It completely forgot that the bureaucracy was much stronger and more vigorous than a government which happened to be well-disposed towards the bourgeoisie. It also imagined that with Manteuffel's fall the bourgeois millennium had begun and that it was now only a question of reaping the rich harvest of bourgeois hegemony without paying a penny in return.

But all the money which had to be voted, after the few years since 1848 had already cost so much, after the national debt had increased to such a size and taxes had risen so steeply! Gentlemen, you are the deputies of the most recent constitutional state in the world and you do not know that constitutionalism is the world's costliest form of government? It is almost costlier than Bonapartism, which, in the spirit of *après moi le déluge*[8] tries repeatedly to meet old debts with new ones and thus in the course of ten years consumes the financial resources of a century. The golden age of an absolutism kept within bounds, which you are still dreaming of, will never return.

But what about the constitutional provisos covering the continued raising of taxes already approved? Everyone knows how bashful the 'New Era' was in its demands for money. Little would have been lost by including the supplies for the army reorganization in the official budget in return for guaranteed concessions. It was a question of voting new taxes to cover this expenditure. It was possible for the bourgeoisie to be tight-fisted on fiscal matters; and, anyway, a better government than that of the 'New Era' could not have been wished for. The bourgeoisie was surely as much master of the situation as it had ever been, and it had won new power in other areas.

But could it then strengthen the forces of reaction by doubling the size of their main instrument of power, the army? This is an area in which the bourgeois Progressive party has become caught in an irresolvable contradiction. It demanded that Prussia play the part of a German Piedmont,[9] and to do this Prussia needs a powerful and well-organized army. It had the 'New Era' government, which secretly cherished the same hopes – the best government which, under the circumstances, it could have – but it *refuses* this government a stronger army. Day in day out, from morning till night the bourgeoisie talks of Prussia's glory, Prussia's greatness and the development of Prussian power; but it *refuses* to grant Prussia an increase in the size of its army which would even be comparable with that introduced by the other great powers since 1814. What is the reason for all this? The reason is that the bourgeois opposition fears that such an increase would only be to the advantage of the forces of reaction, that it would revitalize the

8. 'After me the deluge', a motto attributed to Louis XV.
9. Cavour, as Prime Minister of Piedmont/Sardinia, had successfully pioneered in Italy the tactic of national unification from above that was Bismarck's model in Germany.

decrepit aristocratic officers' corps and give the feudal and bureau-cratic–absolutist party in general the power to bury constitutionalism in its entirety by means of a coup d'état.

Admittedly, the bourgeois Progressives were right not to strengthen the reaction and they were correct in regarding the army as the securest stronghold from which this party could launch a coup. But was there ever a better opportunity of bringing the army under parliamentary control than that presented by this reorganization, proposed, as it had been, by the most pro-bourgeois government which Prussia had ever experienced in peacetime? As soon as the bourgeoisie declared its readiness to approve the expansion of the army on certain conditions, was that not just the time to settle the problem of the military academies, the preference given to the aristocracy in the officers' corps and all the other grievances; was that not the time to obtain guarantees which would give the officers' corps a more bourgeois character? The 'New Era' was sure of only one thing: that the army had to be strengthened. The devious ways it took to smuggle through the reorganization demonstrated most clearly its guilty conscience and its fear of the deputies. The bourgeoisie should have seized the opportunity with both hands, for such a chance could not be expected again in a hundred years. Detailed concessions could have been wrung from this government if the Progressives had approached the matter, not in a niggardly spirit, but as great speculators!

And now the practical consequences resulting from the reor-ganization of the officers' corps itself! Officers had to be found for twice the number of battalions. The military academies were then nowhere near adequate. Recruitment policy was liberal as never before in peacetime; lieutenancies were offered almost as awards to students, young lawyers and all young people with an education. Anyone who saw the Prussian army after its reorgan-ization could not have recognized the officers' corps anymore. Our remarks are based not on hearsay but on our own observa-tions. The characteristic lieutenants' jargon was submerged and the younger officers spoke their natural mother tongue; they did not in the least belong to an exclusive caste but represented to a greater extent than ever since 1815 all educated classes and all provinces of the state. This position had been won as a result of the necessity imposed by events themselves; it was only a ques-tion of holding it and making use of it. Instead the whole thing was ignored and dismissed by the bourgeois Progressives, as if all these officers were aristocratic cadets. And yet since 1815 there had never been so many bourgeois officers in Prussia as just at this time.

We must mention incidentally that we attribute the efficient conduct of the Prussian officers in the face of the enemy in the Schleswig-Holstein war[10] largely to this infusion of new blood. By themselves, the old class of subalterns would never have dared to act so often on their own initiative. In this respect the government is right in attributing to the military reorganization a considerable influence on the 'elegance' of the military successes; we are not in a position to judge whether the reorganization contributed in any other way to the defeat of the Danes.

Finally, the main point: could a coup d'état be more easily carried out if the peacetime army were strengthened? It is perfectly true that armies are the instruments with which coups are executed and that therefore every increase in the strength of an army also increases the practicability of a coup. But for a major country the military strength required by a great state depends not on the prospects – large or small – of a coup, but on the size of the armies of the other major states. In for a penny, in for a pound. If a Prussian deputy accepts his mandate, and takes Prussian greatness and Prussian power in Europe as his motto, then he must agree to make the means available without which there can be no talk of Prussian greatness and Prussian power. If the means cannot be provided without facilitating a coup, all the worse for the gentlemen of the Progressive party. If they had not conducted themselves in such a ludicrously craven and clumsy fashion in 1848, the period of coups d'état would probably be long past by now. Under the present circumstances nothing remains for them but to acknowledge the reorganization of the army in one form or another and to keep their reservations about coups to themselves.

However, there is another side to the matter. Firstly, it would have been more advisable to negotiate the approval of this instrument for a potential coup with a government of the 'New Era' than with a government under Bismarck. Secondly, it goes without saying that every further step towards a real implementation of universal military service makes the Prussian army less suitable as a tool for a coup d'état. Since the masses took up the demand

10. In spring 1864 Bismarck, in a short-lived alliance with Austria, went to war with Denmark and secured for Germany the duchies of Schleswig and Holstein.

for self-government and recognized the need for a struggle against all elements opposing this demand, the twenty- and twenty-one-year-olds have become part of the movement and, even under feudal and absolutist officers, it must have become increasingly difficult to use them to execute a coup. The further political education progresses in Prussia, the more recalcitrant will the mood of the recruits become. Even the present struggle between the government and the bourgeoisie must have demonstrated this.

Thirdly, the two-year period of military service is an adequate counterweight to the expansion of the army. The strengthening of the army increases the material capability of the government to carry out coups but, in the same degree, the two-year conscription period decreases its moral capability. In the third year of military service the incessant drumming of absolutist doctrines and habits of obedience into the soldiers' heads may bear fruit temporarily, as long as their military service lasts. In this third year, during which, militarily, the individual soldier has almost nothing more to learn, our conscript approaches, to a certain extent, the character of the soldier in the French and Austrian systems, who is trained for long years of service. He acquires something of the character of the professional soldier and, as such, he can be more easily used than the younger soldier. From the point of view of a military coup the distance of soldiers from civilian life in their third year of service would certainly more than balance out the recruitment of an additional 60,000 to 80,000 men over a period of two years.

But now we come to another point, the most decisive of all. It cannot be denied – we know our bourgeoisie too well – that a situation could arise in which, even without mobilization, even with an army at its peacetime level, a coup would be possible. However, it would still not be probable. In order to carry out a full-scale military coup an army mobilization would almost always be necessary. But when this happens a great change takes place. In peacetime the Prussian army may under certain circumstances become a mere tool which the government can use internally, but this can never happen in time of war! Anyone who has ever had an opportunity of seeing a battalion first in peacetime and then under war conditions knows the tremendous difference in the attitude of the military, in the character of the rank and file. People who joined the army as half-grown lads return to it as men;

they bring with them a store of self-respect, self-confidence, resolve and character, which benefits the whole battalion. The relationship of the ranks to the officers and of the officers to the ranks is transformed immediately. Militarily the battalion profits considerably; but politically it becomes – for absolutist purposes – completely unreliable. This was evident even during the invasion of Schleswig-Holstein, when, to the great surprise of the English newspaper correspondents, the Prussian soldiers openly took part in political demonstrations and expressed their by no means orthodox views without fear. And we owe the political corruption of the mobilized army, that is, its unreliability as an instrument of absolutist plans, mainly to the Manteuffel period and to the latest 'new' era. In 1848 things were quite different.

One of the best aspects of the Prussian military system both before and since the reorganization has been the fact that with *this* military system Prussia can neither conduct an unpopular war, nor can it carry out a coup d'état with any prospect of permanence. For, even if the peacetime army lent itself to a little coup, the first mobilization and the first threat of war would suffice to endanger all that had been 'achieved'. Without the ratification of the wartime army the heroic deeds of a peacetime army – a Battle of Düppel,[11] as it were, on the home front – would only be of passing significance; and the longer this ratification is needed the more difficult it will be to obtain. Some reactionary newspapers have declared the 'army' rather than the Chambers to be the true representative of the people. By this they meant, of course, only the officers. Should it happen one day that the gentlemen of the *Kreuz-Zeitung*[12] carry out a coup, and require for this a *mobilized* army, these representatives of the people will give them the shock of their lives, they can depend on it.

In the last instance, however, this is not the main guarantee against a coup. The main guarantee lies in that firstly, no government can assemble, by means of a coup, a Chamber of Deputies which will vote it new taxes and loans; secondly, even if it managed to produce such a compliant Chamber, no banker in Europe would grant it credit on the strength of that Chamber's resolutions. It would be a different case in most other European states. But

11. The battle of Düppel in April 1864 was the decisive defeat of Denmark in the Schleswig-Holstein war.

12. A nickname for the *Neue Preussische Zeitung*, the semi-official organ of the Prussian government, after the Prussian cross it used as its emblem.

since the promises of 1815 and all the vain manoeuvrings to obtain money up until 1848 Prussia happens to have a reputation such that no one would lend it a penny without a legally binding and unimpeachable resolution from the Chambers. Even Herr Raphael von Erlanger, who lent money to the American Confederates, would hardly entrust a Prussian government with ready cash if it had come to power by means of a coup. Prussia owes this state of affairs quite simply to the stupidity of absolutism.

The strength of the bourgeoisie lies in the fact that when the government gets into financial difficulties – as it must, sooner or later – it will be obliged to *turn to the bourgeoisie for money* and this time not to the political representatives of the bourgeoisie, who, in the last analysis, are quite aware that they are there to pay, but to the bourgeoisie of high finance, which is interested in doing good business with the government. The financial bourgeoisie measures the creditworthiness of a government by the same standards which it uses to measure the creditworthiness of a private individual and it is completely indifferent as to whether the Prussian state needs many soldiers or only a few. These gentlemen only grant credit against three signatures. If only the Upper Chamber has signed next to the government, and not the Chamber of Deputies, or if they only have the signature of a Chamber of Deputies full of government puppets, then they will regard the matter as kite-flying and decline with thanks.

At this point the military question becomes a constitutional question. It is immaterial which mistakes and complications have forced the bourgeois opposition into its present position; it must fight out the military question to the end or else it will lose what political power it still possesses. The government has already called its whole power of budgetary appropriation into question. But if the government will be *forced*, sooner or later, to make its peace with the Chamber, is it not the best policy simply to hold out until this moment arrives?

Since the conflict has gone so far, the answer must be an unqualified 'Yes'. It is more than doubtful whether an acceptable basis can be found for an agreement with this government. By overestimating its own strength the bourgeoisie has put itself in the position of having to discover by means of this military question whether it is the decisive power in the state or no power at all. If it wins the struggle, it will also win the power to appoint and dismiss ministers that the English House of Commons has. If it loses the struggle, it will no longer be able to achieve any position of importance by constitutional means.

But anyone who expects such powers of endurance does not know our bourgeoisie. In political matters the courage of the bourgeoisie is always in direct proportion to its importance in society. In Germany the social power of the bourgeoisie is far less than in England or even France; it has neither allied itself with the old aristocracy, as in England, nor has it destroyed the aristocracy with the help of the peasants and the workers, as in France. In Germany the feudal aristocracy is still hostile to the bourgeoisie, as well as being allied with the government. For all the enormous progress which it has made since 1848, industry, the basis of all the social power of the modern bourgeoisie, is still not as highly developed in Germany as in France and England. The colossal accumulation of capital in particular social strata, which can frequently be found in England and even in France, is much rarer in Germany. Hence the petty-bourgeois character of our whole bourgeoisie. The spheres of its activity and the mental horizons within which it operates are of a petty nature: it is no wonder that its whole mentality is equally petty! Where is it to find the courage to fight an issue out to the bitter end? The Prussian bourgeoisie knows only too well how dependent its industrial activity is upon the government. Industrial concessions[13] and administrative supervision weigh on it like a mountain. The government can put obstacles in the way of every new business project, and this is now true in the political sphere as well. During the conflict over the military question the bourgeois Chamber can only adopt a negative position; it is obliged to stay on the defensive. Meanwhile, the government assumes the offensive, interprets the Constitution in its own fashion, disciplines liberal officials, declares the liberal municipal elections null and void, employs all the machinery of bureaucratic power to make the bourgeoisie fully conscious of their position as Prussian subjects, in fact, captures one vantage point after another and thus occupies a position such as Manteuffel himself did not have. In the meantime expenditure and taxation continue their steady course without a budget and the army reorganization is consolidated with every year that passes. In short, while the government's victories in matters of detail accumulate daily in all fronts and assume the form of accomplished

13. At this time, bureaucratic regulation of industry in Prussia still required prospective entrepreneurs to obtain state concessions.

facts, the prospect of the final victory of the bourgeoisie assumes from year to year an increasingly revolutionary character. In addition, there is a workers' movement which is completely independent of both bourgeoisie and government and which forces the bourgeoisie either to make very awkward concessions to the workers or to be prepared to act without the workers at the decisive moment. Will the Prussian bourgeoisie have the courage to hold out until the bitter end under these circumstances? To do so it will have to have changed miraculously since 1848. The longing for a compromise daily audible in the sighs of the Progressive party since the beginning of this session is hardly evidence of such a change. We fear that this time, too, the bourgeoisie will not hesitate to betray itself.

III

'What is the proper attitude of the workers' party to this army reorganization and to the resulting conflict between the government and the bourgeois opposition?'

To develop their political activity fully the working class needs a much wider arena than that provided by the individual states of Germany in its present fragmented form. The multiplicity of states may be an obstacle to the proletarian movement, but it will never be regarded as justified and it will never be the object of serious concern. The German proletariat will never concern itself with Reich Constitutions, 'Prussian leadership', *Trias*[14] and such things, except when the time comes to make a clean sweep; it is completely indifferent as to how many soldiers the Prussian state needs in order to continue to survive as a great power. Whether the reorganization increases the military burden or not will not make much difference to the working class *as a class*. On the other hand, it is by no means indifferent as to whether universal military service is fully introduced. The more workers who are trained in the use of weapons, the better. Universal conscription is the necessary and natural extension of universal suffrage; it enables the electorate to carry out its resolutions arms in hand against any coup that might be attempted.

14. These references are to the Reich Constitution drawn up by the Frankfurt Assembly of 1848–9 (see the Introduction to *The Revolutions of 1848*, p. 24), the Prussian scheme for German hegemony first formulated by Frederick William IV on 20 March 1848, and the plan to reorganize the German Confederation into Austria, Prussia and a league of small and middle states, particularly canvassed by Bavaria and Saxony in the 1850s and 1860s.

The ever more complete introduction of military service is the only aspect of the Prussian army reorganization which interests the German working class.

But more important is the question of the position the workers' party should take with regard to the conflict between government and Chamber which this reorganization has produced.

The modern worker, the proletarian, is a product of the great industrial revolution, which, particularly during the last hundred years, has totally transformed all modes of production in all civilized countries, first in industry and afterwards in agriculture too, and as a result of which only two classes remain involved in production: the capitalists, who own means of production, raw materials and provisions, and the workers, who own neither means of production, nor raw materials nor provisions, but first have to buy their provisions from the capitalists with their labour. The modern proletarian, then, is only directly faced with *one* hostile and exploiting social class: the capitalist class, the bourgeoisie. In countries where this industrial revolution has been completely carried out, such as in England, *all* workers are faced only with capitalists, because on the land, too, the large tenant farmer is nothing but a capitalist; the aristocrat, who only consumes the ground rent from his properties, has absolutely no point of social contact with the worker.

It is a different matter in countries like Germany where the industrial revolution is still taking place. Here many elements have been left over from earlier feudal and post-feudal conditions, which, so to speak, cloud the social medium and rob the social situation of that simple, clear and classical character which typifies England's present stage of development. We find in Germany, in an atmosphere growing daily more modern and amidst highly modern capitalists and workers, the most amazing antediluvian fossils still alive and roaming society: feudal lords, patrimonial courts of justice, country squires, flogging, aristocratic government officials, district magistrates, jurisdictional disputes, executive power to issue punishment, and so on. We find that in the struggle for political power all these living fossils band together against the bourgeoisie; the latter, which, as a result of its property, is the most powerful class in the new epoch, demands, in the name of the new epoch, that they hand over political power.

Apart from the bourgeoisie and the proletariat modern large-scale industry produces a kind of intermediate class between the two others: the petty bourgeoisie. This class consists partly of the remnants of the earlier semi-medieval citizenry (*Pfahlbürgertum*), and partly of workers who to a certain extent have come up in the world. Its role is less in production than in the distribution of goods; its main line of business is the retail trade. While the old citizenry was the most stable social class, the modern petty bourgeoisie is the most unstable; among this class bankruptcy has become an institution. With its small capital it shares in the life of the bourgeoisie; with the insecurity of its existence it shares that of the proletariat. Its political position is as contradictory as its social existence; in general, however, its most adequate political expression is the demand for 'pure democracy'. Its political mission is to spur the bourgeoisie on in its struggle against the remnants of the old society and, in particular, against its own weaknesses and cowardice, as well as to help win those liberties – freedom of the press, association and assembly, universal suffrage, local self-government – without which, despite their bourgeois character, a timid bourgeoisie can probably manage, but without which the workers can never achieve emancipation.

At some time or another during the course of the struggle between the remnants of the old, antediluvian society and the bourgeoisie there always comes a point at which both combatants turn to the proletariat and seek its support. This moment usually coincides with the first stirrings of the working class itself. The feudal and bureaucratic representatives of the doomed society call upon the workers to join with them in attacking the capitalist parasites, the only enemies of the worker; the bourgeoisie points out to the workers that, both together, they represent the new social epoch and that therefore they at least share the same interests in their opposition to the *old* moribund form of society. At this point the working class gradually becomes conscious of the fact that it is a class in its own right, with its own interests and its own independent future. Hence the question arises which has been asked successively in England, France and Germany: what should be the attitude of the workers' party towards the combatants?

This will depend, above all, upon the particular aims which the workers' party, i.e. that section of the working class which has become conscious of the common class interest, strives for in the interest of its class.

As far as is known,[15] the most advanced workers in Germany demand the emancipation of the workers from the capitalists by the transfer of state capital to workers' associations, so that production can be carried on, without capitalists, on common account; and as a means of achieving this aim they seek to conquer political power by way of universal and direct suffrage.

This much is now clear: neither the feudal–bureaucratic party, generally simply referred to as the '*reaction*', nor the liberal–radical bourgeois party will be inclined to concede these demands voluntarily. But the proletariat will become a political force the moment an autonomous workers' party is formed and becomes a power to be reckoned with. The two hostile parties are aware of this and at the right moment, therefore, they will be disposed to make apparent or actual concessions to the workers. From which side can the workers exact the greatest concessions?

The existence of both bourgeoisie and proletariat is already a thorn in the flesh of the reactionary party. Its power depends on its ability to stop, or at least slow down modern social development. Otherwise all the property-owning classes will gradually become capitalists and all the oppressed classes proletarians and thus the reactionary party will disappear automatically. If it is consistent, the party of reaction certainly wants to do away with the proletariat, however not by moving forward to workers' associations but by transforming the modern proletariat back into journeymen and by reducing them partially or completely to the status of peasant bondsmen. Would such a transformation be in the interests of our proletarians? Do they wish themselves back under the patriarchal discipline of the guild master and the 'noble lord', even if such a thing were possible? Definitely not! It is precisely the release of the working class from the whole false system of property and all illusory privileges of earlier times, and the development of the naked conflict between capital and labour, which have made possible the existence of a single huge working class with common interests, the existence of a workers' movement and a workers' party. Such a reversal of history is, moreover, simply impossible. The steam engines, the mechanical spinning frames and weaving looms, the steam ploughs and threshing machines, the railways, the electric telegraph and the steam

15. This circumlocution follows Marx's advice to Engels in a letter of 11 February 1865 (*MECW* 42, p. 86–8), and was designed to avoid committing Engels to accepting the Lassallean demands.

presses of the present day totally exclude the possibility of such an absurd retrogression; indeed these developments are gradually but implacably destroying all residues left over from a feudal, guild-ridden society; they are dissolving all the petty social conflicts handed down from an earlier age into the one historic antagonism between capital and labour.

The bourgeoisie, on the other hand, has no historical function in modern society other than to increase on all fronts the gigantic forces of production and means of transport mentioned above and to put them to their fullest possible use; to lay its hands too – by way of its credit associations – on the means of production passed on from earlier times, in particular, on landed property; to introduce modern means of production into all branches of industry; to destroy all remnants of feudal production and feudal society and hence to reduce the whole of society to the simple opposition between a class of capitalists and a class of propertyless workers. This simplification of class antagonisms is accompanied to the same degree by a growth in the strength of the bourgeoisie, but to an even greater degree by the growth in the strength, class consciousness and potential for victory of the working class. Only as a result of this increase in the strength of the bourgeoisie will the proletariat gradually succeed in becoming the majority, the overwhelming majority in the state. This is already the case in England, but by no means so in Germany where, on the land, peasants of all kinds, and, in the towns, small craftsmen and shopkeepers etc. exist side by side with the proletariat.

Thus every victory gained by the forces of reaction obstructs social development and inevitably delays the day on which the workers will win the struggle. Every victory gained by the bourgeoisie over the reaction, however, is in one respect also a victory for the workers; it contributes to the final overthrow of capitalist rule and brings nearer the day when the workers will defeat the bourgeoisie.

Let us compare the present position of the German workers' party with that of 1848. There are still plenty of veterans in Germany who worked for the foundation of an embryonic German workers' party before 1848 and who helped to extend it after the revolution as long as conditions allowed. You all know what an effort it cost, even in those turbulent days, to create a workers' movement, to keep it going and to free it from reactionary guild elements, and how the whole movement became dormant again after a few years. If a workers' movement has now come into being, as it were, of its own accord, what is the reason for this? The reason is that since 1848 large-scale bourgeois industry in Germany has made tremendous progress, that it has destroyed a mass of small craftsmen and other people located between the worker and the capitalist, and that it has driven a mass of workers into direct opposition to the capitalist; in short, it has created a significant proletariat where no proletariat, or only one of limited size, existed. As a result of this industrial development a workers' party and a workers' movement has become a necessity.

This is not to say that there may not be moments when the forces of reaction find it advisable to make concessions to the workers. These concessions, however, are always of a specific kind. They are never political concessions. The forces of feudal–bureaucratic reaction will neither extend the suffrage nor tolerate the freedom of the press, association and assembly, nor will they curb the power of the bureaucracy. The concessions which they make are always directed against the bourgeoisie, but under no circumstances in such a way that they increase the political power of the workers. Thus, for instance, in England, the Ten Hours Act was passed for the factory workers against the will of the manufacturers.[16] The workers, therefore, could demand and possibly obtain from the Prussian government the strict observance of the regulations covering working hours in the factories – which, at present, only exist on paper – together with the right for workers to form combinations, etc. But in the event of the forces of reaction granting these concessions, their acceptance must not lead to any reciprocal concessions on the part of the workers. This must be made clear, and rightly so, for by making life uncomfortable for the bourgeoisie the party of reaction will have achieved its aim. The workers are not obliged to thank them, as indeed they never do.

There is another sort of reaction, which has met with great success in recent times and which has become very fashionable among certain people: the brand of reaction known as Bonapartism. Bonapartism is the necessary form of government in a country where the working class – highly developed in the towns but outnumbered by the small peasants on the land – has been defeated in a great revolutionary struggle by the capitalist class,

16. See Engels's article 'The Ten Hours Bill', *MECW* 10, pp. 288–301.

the petty bourgeoisie and the army. When the Parisian workers were defeated in the tremendous struggle of June 1848 the bourgeoisie, too, completely exhausted itself in achieving its victory. It was aware that it could not survive a second such victory. It ruled only in name; it was too weak to rule in reality. Leadership was assumed by the army, the actual victor in the struggle; it was supported by the class from which it chiefly recruited its strength, the small farmers, who wanted peace and protection from the town rowdies. It goes without saying that the form which this rule took was military despotism; its natural head was the ancestral heir of military despotism, Louis Bonaparte.

The characteristic role of Bonapartism *vis-à-vis* workers and capitalists is to prevent these two classes from engaging in open struggle. It protects the bourgeoisie from violent attack by the workers while encouraging minor skirmishes of a peaceful nature between them, and it robs both of all trace of political power. It does not tolerate free association, free assembly or a free press; it allows universal suffrage, but under such bureaucratic pressures that it is almost impossible to vote for an opposition candidate; it rules by means of a police system which is hitherto unprecedented even in police-ridden France. Moreover, a part of the bourgeoisie and a part of the workers are nothing short of *bought*; the former by colossal credit frauds, in which the money of small capitalists is lured into the pockets of large capitalists; the latter by colossal public works which lead to the creation of an artificial, Imperialist[17] proletariat, which is dependent upon the state and which exists side by side with the natural, independent proletariat in the large towns. Lastly, national pride is flattered by apparently heroic wars, which however are always sanctioned by higher European authority; they are waged against the general scapegoat of the day and only under conditions which guarantee victory from the outset.

The only advantage of such a government for the workers and the bourgeoisie is that they can rest from the struggle and that industry can develop vigorously under favourable conditions. The result is that the elements of a new and more violent struggle are now accumulating, a struggle which will break out as soon as there is no further need for this period of recovery. It would be the very height of folly to expect any more for the workers from

17. See p. 34, n. 62.

a government which exists merely to hold in check their struggle against the bourgeoisie.

Let us return now to the particular case which we are examining. What do the reactionary forces in Prussia have to offer the workers' party?

Can the reaction offer the working class a real share in political power? Not the slightest! Firstly, neither in the recent history of England nor France has a reactionary government ever done such a thing. Secondly, in the present struggle in Prussia the problem is precisely whether the government should concentrate all real power in its own hands or whether it should share it with parliament. One thing is certain: the government will never summon up all its strength and seize power from the bourgeoisie merely to hand over this power to the proletariat!

The feudal aristocracy and the bureaucracy can keep their real power in Prussia even without parliamentary representation. Their traditional position at court, in the army and in the civil service guarantees it to them. Indeed they would not wish for any particular form of representation because the Peers' and Civil Servants' Chambers such as Manteuffel had are absolutely impossible in Prussia in the long run. Thus, they want to be rid of the whole representative system.

On the other hand, both the bourgeoisie and the workers can only function as a really organized political force through parliamentary representation; and this parliamentary representation is only of value if they can have their say and make decisions, in other words, if they can 'keep the purse strings tight'. But this is precisely what Bismarck wants to prevent, as he himself admits. The question must arise whether it lies in the workers' interests for this parliament to be robbed of all political power, this parliament which they themselves hope to enter by gaining universal and direct suffrage and in which they hope to form a majority one day. Is it in their interests to set all the machinery of agitation in motion in order to elect their representatives to an assembly which, in the final analysis, has no say in matters anyway? Hardly.

But what if the government upset the existing electoral law and imposed by *octroi*[18] a system based on universal and direct suffrage? Yes, *if*! If the government played such a Bonapartist

18. A French term, denoting an act performed by the monarch out of the plenitude of his own power, and therefore reversible at will.

trick and the workers fell for it, they would acknowledge from the very outset the government's right to repeal universal and direct suffrage by a new *octroi* as soon as it suited its purpose. What would the fullest universal and direct suffrage be worth then?

If the government imposed a system based on universal and direct suffrage it would, from the very outset, so hedge it with clauses and provisos that it would no longer be universal and direct suffrage.

And even with regard to universal and direct suffrage, one need only go to France to be convinced of the harmless elections it is possible to hold on this basis in a country with a large and stupid rural population, a well organized bureaucracy and a tightly controlled press, in a country where there are absolutely no political meetings and where associations are satisfactorily suppressed by the police. How many workers' representatives have been elected into the French parliament despite the existence of universal and direct suffrage? And yet compared with Germany the French proletariat is a much more concentrated class and has a longer experience of struggle and organization.

This brings us to another point. In Germany the rural population is twice as large as the urban; that is, two thirds of the people live from farming and one third from industry. And as the large estate is the rule in Germany and the smallholding peasant the exception, this means, in other words, that a third of the workers are controlled by the capitalists, while two thirds are *controlled by the feudal lords*. Let those who continuously attack the capitalists but utter not the least angry word against feudalism take this to heart. The feudalists exploit twice as many workers in Germany as does the bourgeoisie; they are no less the direct enemy of the workers than are the capitalists. But that is by no means the whole story. Patriarchal rule on the old feudal estates has made the landless day-labourer hereditarily dependent upon his 'noble lord', and this makes it exceedingly difficult for the agricultural proletarian to join the movement of the urban workers. The priests, the systematic stupefaction of the countryside, bad schooling and isolation from the outside world do the rest. The agricultural proletariat is that section of the working class which is the last to become aware of its interests and social position and has the most difficulty in understanding them. In other words, it is that section of the working class which remains longest the unconscious tool of an exploiting and privileged class.

And which class is this? In Germany, not the bourgeoisie but the *feudal aristocracy*. Even in France, where, of course, almost only free peasant proprietors exist on the land, and where the feudal aristocracy has long since been robbed of all political power, universal suffrage has not brought the workers into parliament, but has almost totally excluded them. What would be the result of universal suffrage in Germany, where the feudal aristocracy still has real social and political power and where there are two landless agricultural labourers for every one industrial worker? The struggle against feudal and bureaucratic reaction – the two are inseparable in Germany – is synonymous with the struggle for the mental and political emancipation of the rural proletariat. For as long as the rural proletariat is not carried along in the movement, the urban proletariat in Germany will not achieve anything; universal and direct suffrage will not be a weapon for the proletariat but a *trap*.

Perhaps this very candid but necessary explanation will encourage the feudalists to support universal and direct suffrage. So much the better.

Or is the government only curtailing the bourgeois opposition press, its freedom of association and assembly (as though there were much left to curtail) in order to make the workers a gift of these basic rights? Indeed, is the workers' movement not being allowed to develop peacefully and without hindrance?

But there's the rub! The government *knows* and the bourgeoisie knows too that at the present the whole German workers' movement is only *tolerated* and will only survive as long as the government *wishes*. The government will tolerate the movement as long as its existence suits it, as long as it is in its interests for the bourgeois opposition to be confronted by new and independent opponents. As soon as the workers develop through this movement into an independent power, as soon as this movement poses a danger for the government, the matter will come to an end immediately. The way in which the government put an end to the agitation of the Progressives in the press, to their associations and meetings, may serve as a warning to the workers. The same laws, decrees and measures which were applied there can be used at any time against the workers to deal a death-blow to their agitation; this will happen as soon as this agitation becomes dangerous. It is crucially important for the workers to be clear on this point and not to become victims of the same illusions as the bourgeoisie in the New Era, who were likewise merely *tolerated* although they thought themselves in complete control of the situation. And anyone who imagines that the present government will lift the present restrictions on the freedom of the press, association and assembly, places himself outside the arena of rational discussion. But without the freedom of the press, and the freedom of association and assembly, no workers' movement is possible.

The present Prussian government is not so stupid as to cut its own throat. Should it happen that the forces of reaction toss a few sham political concessions to the German proletariat as a bait – then, it is to be hoped, the German proletariat will answer with the proud words of the old *Hildebrandslied*:[19]

> *Mit gêrû scal man geba infâhân, ort widar orte.*
> Gifts shall be accepted with the spear, point against point.

As for the *social* concessions which the reaction might make to the workers – shorter working hours in the factories, a better implementation of the factory laws, the right to form combinations, etc. – the experience of all countries shows that the reactionaries introduce such legislative proposals without the workers having to offer the least in return. The reactionaries need the workers but the workers do not need them. Thus, as long as the workers insist on these points in their own agitation they can count on the moment coming when reactionary elements will present these same demands merely in order to annoy the bourgeoisie; and as a result the workers will achieve a victory over the bourgeoisie without owing the reactionaries any thanks.

But if the workers' party has nothing to expect from the reactionaries except minor concessions, which they would gain anyway, without having to go begging – what can it expect, then, from the bourgeois opposition?

We have seen that both the bourgeoisie and the proletariat are children of a new epoch; that in their social activity both aim at clearing away the outmoded trappings which have survived from an earlier age. They have, it is true, a very serious struggle to settle between themselves, but this struggle can only be fought out when they are left to face each other alone. Only by throwing the old lumber overboard will they be able to 'clear the decks for battle'. But this time the battle will not be conducted between

19. An eighth-century Old High German heroic saga.

two ships but on board one and the same ship – between officers and crew.

The bourgeoisie cannot gain political supremacy and express this in the form of a constitution and laws without, at the same time, arming the proletariat. On its banner it must inscribe human rights in place of the old system of social position based on birth, freedom to pursue trades and commerce in place of the guild system, freedom and self-government in place of bureaucratic authoritarianism. Therefore, for consistency's sake, it must demand universal and direct suffrage, freedom of the press, association and assembly, and the repeal of all emergency laws directed against particular social classes. But this is all that the proletariat need demand from the bourgeoisie. It can not expect the bourgeoisie to stop being the bourgeoisie, but it can demand that it apply its own principles consistently. The result will be that the proletariat will lay its hands on all the weapons which it needs for its final victory. With the help of the freedom of the press and the right of association and assembly it will win universal suffrage, and by way of universal and direct suffrage, together with the means of agitation mentioned above, it will achieve everything else.

It is in the interests of the workers, therefore, to support the bourgeoisie in its struggle against all reactionary elements, *on condition that it remain true to itself*. Every victory gained by the bourgeoisie over the forces of reaction will ultimately benefit the working class. The instinct of the German workers has been correct. In all the German states they have quite rightly voted for the most radical candidates who have had a prospect of winning.

But what if the bourgeoisie is untrue to itself and betrays its own class interests and the principles arising from these interests?

Then there are two courses of action left to the workers!

On the one hand the workers can push the bourgeoisie against its will and force it, as far as possible, to extend the suffrage, to fight for a free press, free association and assembly so as to create a space in which the proletariat can freely move and organize itself. The English workers have been doing this since the Reform Bill of 1832, as have the French workers since the July revolution of 1830; they have furthered their own development and organization by using and acting within this movement, whose most immediate aims were of a purely bourgeois character, rather than by any other means. This will always happen, because the bourgeoisie, with its lack of political courage, is in all countries untrue to itself at some time or another.

Alternatively the workers can withdraw completely from the bourgeois movement and leave the bourgeoisie to its fate. This is what happened in England, France and Germany after the failure of the European workers' movement of 1840 to 1850. This course of action is only possible following violent and temporarily fruitless efforts, after which the class needs peace and quiet. As long as the working class is in a healthy condition such a situation is impossible; it would amount to a complete political abdication, and in the long run a naturally courageous class, a class which has nothing to lose and everything to gain, is incapable of this.

Even at the worst, if the bourgeoisie creeps under the skirts of the reactionary party for fear of the workers, appealing to the enemy for protection, even then the workers' party will have no choice but to continue the agitation, betrayed by the bourgeoisie, for bourgeois freedom – freedom of the press, association and assembly – despite the bourgeoisie. Without these freedoms the workers' party cannot move freely; in this struggle it is fighting for its own vital element, for the air it needs to breathe.

It goes without saying that in all these situations the workers' party will not merely act as the tail of the bourgeoisie, but as a completely separate and independent party. At every opportunity it will remind the bourgeoisie that the class interests of the workers are directly opposed to those of the capitalists and that the workers are conscious of this fact. It will retain and develop its own organization quite separately from the party organization of the bourgeoisie, and will only treat with the latter as one force with another. In this way it will assure itself of a position which commands respect and it will educate the individual workers as to their class interests. With the outbreak of the next revolutionary storm – and these storms now recur as regularly as commercial crises and equinoctial gales – it will be ready for action.

The policy of the workers' party in the Prussian constitutional conflict follows automatically from what has been said:

The workers' party must above all remain organized, as far as present circumstances allow.

It must press the Progressive party to campaign for *real* progress, as far as that is possible; force it to radicalize its own programme and to stick to it; pitilessly chastise and ridicule all inconsistencies and weaknesses.

The workers' party should allow the actual military question to take its own course, remembering that one day it will conduct its own *German* 'military reorganization'.

But the hypocritical temptations of the forces of reaction must be answered thus:

> Gifts shall be accepted with the spear, point against point.

MARX TO SCHWEITZER[20]

London, 13 February 1865

... As our statement is partly out of date following what M. Hess has written in no. 21 (received today), we shall leave the matter at that.[21] However, our statement contained another point: praise for the anti-Bonapartist stand of the Paris proletariat and a call to the German workers to follow this example. This was more important for us than the attack on Hess. However, we shall elsewhere elaborate in detail our views on the relation of the workers to the Prussian government.[22]

In your letter of 4 February you say that I myself warned Liebknecht against kicking over the traces so as not to be hounded by the authorities. Quite right. But at the same time I wrote that it is possible to say *anything* if one finds the right form.[23] Even a form of anti-government polemic which is possible by Berlin standards is certainly quite a different matter from a flirtation

20. The letter actually sent to Johann von Schweitzer in Berlin has not survived, and the text published here is an excerpt of Marx's draft, as quoted by him in a letter to Engels of 18 February 1865.

21. This refers to Marx and Engels's 'Statement to the Editorial Board of *Social-Demokrat*' of 6 February 1865 (*MECW* 20, p. 36), complaining at the insinuations of Moses Hess, the Paris correspondent of the paper, that the French members of the General Council, and the International's members in Paris, contained Bonapartist agents.

22. Engels had just finished writing 'The Prussian Military Question', which was published a few weeks later.

23. During Marx and Engels's short-lived collaboration with the Lassallean *Social-Demokrat*, Wilhelm Liebknecht served as the paper's acting editor. As the *Social-Demokrat* was produced in Berlin, and Liebknecht was not a Prussian citizen, he faced the constant threat of deportation, and he was in fact banned from Berlin shortly after this time. Marx refers here to his letter to Liebknecht of 2 February 1865 (see *MECW* 42, p. 75), which seems not to have survived.

with the government, let alone an apparent compromise. I wrote to you myself that the *Social-Demokrat* must avoid creating such appearances.[24]

I see from your paper that the government is equivocating and procrastinating on the matter of the abolition of the combination laws. On the other hand a *Times* report indicates that government plans holding out the prospect of state patronage for cooperatives have been abandoned.[25] I would be not in the least surprised if *The Times* had reported correctly for once!

Combinations, together with trade unions, which develop out of these, are not only of the greatest importance for the working class as a means of organization in its struggle against the bourgeoisie, although this importance is demonstrated, among other things, by the fact that even the workers of the United States cannot do without them, despite the franchise and the republic. In Prussia and in Germany in general the right of combination is also a means of breaking the rule of the police and bureaucracy, and of smashing the *'Gesindeordnung'*[26] and the rule of the aristocracy on the land; in short, it is a measure which will release the 'subjects' from state tutelage. It is something which the Progressive party or any bourgeois opposition party in Prussia, unless it is mad, would be a hundred times more likely to allow than the Prussian government, let alone a government led by Bismarck! On the other hand, support from the Royal Prussian Government for the cooperatives – and anyone who knows the situation in Prussia knows in advance the dwarf-like proportions of these cooperatives – is worthless as an economic measure and serves, furthermore, to extend the system of state tutelage, to bribe a section of the working class and to emasculate the movement. In the same way that the bourgeois party in Prussia made a singular fool of itself and brought about its present predicament by believing that with the advent of the 'New Era', government power had fallen into their hands by the grace of the prince regent, the workers' party will make an even greater fool of itself if it imagines that the Bismarck era or any other era will cause golden apples to drop into its mouth by the

24. Here again Marx refers to a letter that has not survived.

25. Marx refers to a speech by Count Itzenplitz, the Prussian Minister of Commerce, of 11 February, reported in *The Times* on the 13th.

26. The Prussian feudal code which gave the aristocracy almost absolute power over farm servants (*Gesinde*) on their estates.

grace of the king. There is not the least doubt that disappointment will follow Lassalle's wretched illusions of a socialist intervention by a Prussian government. The logic of things will tell. But the *honour* of the workers' party demands the rejection of such illusions even before they are burst by experience and their emptiness proved. The working class is revolutionary or it is nothing . . .

MARX TO KUGELMANN[27]

London, 23 February 1865
1, Modena Villas, Maitland Park,
Haverstock Hill

Dear Kugelmann,

I received your very interesting letter yesterday and I shall now reply to the individual points you make.

First of all I shall briefly describe my attitude to Lassalle. During his agitation our relations were suspended, 1) because of his self-opinionated bragging, compounded with the most shameless plagiarism from my writings etc.; 2) because I *condemned* his *political* tactics; 3) because I had explained and 'proved' to him here in London even *before* he began his agitation that to hope for *socialist* measures from a 'Prussian *state*' was nonsense. In his letters to me (1848–63), as in our personal meetings, he had always declared himself a supporter of the party which I represent.[28] As soon as he had become convinced in London (at the end of 1862) that he could not play his games *with* me, he decided to set himself up as the 'workers' dictator' *against* me and the old party. In spite of everything I recognized his merit as an agitator, although towards the end of his short career I found that even his agitation appeared in an increasingly ambiguous light. His sudden death, old friendship, grief-stricken letters from Countess Hatzfeld,[29]

27. Ludwig Kugelmann, a doctor in Hanover, was a personal friend of Marx and a regular correspondent.

28. After the dissolution of the Communist League in 1852, Marx and Engels belonged to no formal political organization. They nevertheless considered themselves the true representatives of the workers' party. 'Party' (*Partei*) was a rather loose word in mid-nineteenth-century usage, both German and English.

29. Sophie, Countess Hatzfeld, was Lassalle's lover and disciple, and led an ultra-sectarian splinter group from the Lassallean party from 1867 to 1869.

indignation at the *craven impudence* shown by the bourgeois press towards one whom they had feared so greatly during his lifetime – all this induced me to publish a short statement attacking the wretched Blind, which, however, did not deal with the *content* of Lassalle's activities. (Hatzfeld sent the statement to the *Nordstern*.)[30] For the same reasons and in the hope of being able to remove elements which seem dangerous to me, Engels and I promised to contribute to the *Social-Demokrat* (they have published a translation of the 'Address'[31] and at their request I wrote an article on Proudhon when he died[32]) and after Schweitzer had sent us a *satisfactory editorial programme* we gave permission for our names to be made known as contributors. The fact that W. Liebknecht was an unofficial member of the editorial board served as a further guarantee for us. However, it soon became clear – the evidence came into our possession – that Lassalle had in fact *betrayed* the party. He had entered into a formal contract with Bismarck (naturally *without the least* guarantee in *his* hand). At the end of September 1864 he was to go to Hamburg, where (together with the crazy Schramm[33] and the Prussian police spy Marr[34]) he was to *'force'* Bismarck to annex Schleswig-Holstein; that is, he was to proclaim its annexation in the name of the 'workers', etc. In return Bismarck promised universal suffrage and a bit of socialist charlatanry. It is a pity that Lassalle was not able to play this farce through to the end! It would have condemned him and made him look ridiculous! It would have put a stop to all attempts of that sort once and for all!

Lassalle went astray because he was a *'Realpolitiker'* of the Miquel[35] type, but on a larger scale and with grander aims! (By the bye, I had long since sufficiently made up my mind about Miquel to be able to explain his actions by the fact that the

30. Karl Blind was a German democratic refugee in London, who attacked Lassalle after his death in a purely personalistic way. The *Nordstern* was a Lassallean paper published in Hamburg.

31. I.e. the Inaugural Address of the International.

32. *MECW* 20, pp. 26–33.

33. Rudolph Schramm, a democratic refugee in London after the 1848 revolution, returned to Germany after the 1861 amnesty and became a supporter of Bismarck.

34. Wilhelm Marr was a journalist from Hamburg and a supporter of the 'Young Germany' movement in the 1840s.

35. Johannes Miquel was a former member of the Communist League who went over to the bourgeoisie in the 1850s, became a banker and eventually German Minister of Finance.

National Association[36] provided a splendid opportunity for a petty lawyer from Hanover to gain an audience in Germany beyond his own four walls and to bring the enhanced authority of a *Realpolitiker* to bear back home in Hanover – playing the role of a 'Hanoverian' Mirabeau under *'Prussian'* protection.) Miquel and his present friends seized the opportunity presented by the 'New Era' inaugurated by the Prussian prince regent and together with the members of the National Association they attached themselves to 'Prussian leadership', cultivating their 'civic pride' under *Prussian protection*; in the same way Lassalle intended to play the Marquis Posa of the proletariat to the Philip II of the Uckermark,[37] with Bismarck acting as the pimp between him and the Prussian monarchy. Lassalle only imitated the gentlemen of the National Association. But while they invoked Prussian 'reaction' in the interests of the middle class, he shook hands with Bismarck in the interests of the proletariat. Those gentlemen were more justified than Lassalle, in so far as the bourgeois is accustomed to regard the interests lying immediately before his nose as 'reality' and as this class has in fact everywhere made compromises, even with feudalism, while the working class, in the very nature of things, must be honestly 'revolutionary'.

For the theatrically vain nature of a Lassalle (who, however, could not be bribed with such trifles as political office, a position as mayor, etc.) it was a very seductive thought: a direct act on behalf of the proletariat, carried out by Ferdinand Lassalle! In fact he was too ignorant of the actual economic conditions involved in such an act to be critically true to himself! On the other hand, as a result of the base *'practical politics'* which led the German bourgeoisie to tolerate the reaction of 1849–59 and to watch the stupefaction of the people, the German workers had become too *'dispirited'* not to hail such a quack saviour who promised to lead them to the promised land overnight!

Well, to pick up the thread broken above. Hardly had the *Social-Demokrat* been founded than it became evident that old

36. The National Association was formed by the pro-Prussian wing of the German liberal bourgeoisie in September 1859, to campaign for a 'little Germany' under Prussian hegemony.

37. A reference to Schiller's drama *Don Carlos*. The Philip II of the Uckermark was evidently William I of Prussia. The Uckermark was a quintessentially junker district in Brandenburg, the heartland of the Prussian monarchy.

Hatzfeld wanted to execute Lassalle's 'testament'.[38] She was in touch with Bismarck through Wagener (of the *Kreuz-Zeitung*).[39] She placed the General Association of German Workers, the *Social-Demokrat* etc. at his disposal. The annexation of Schleswig-Holstein was to be proclaimed in the *Social-Demokrat*, Bismarck was to be generally recognized as patron etc. The whole merry plan was *frustrated*, as we had Liebknecht in Berlin on the editorial board of the *Social-Demokrat*. Although Engels and I did not like the editorial policy of the paper, the lickspittle Lassalle cult, the occasional flirtation with Bismarck etc., it was naturally more important to remain identified with the paper in public in order to thwart the intrigues of old Hatzfeld and the total compromising of the workers' party. We therefore made *bonne mine à mauvais jeu*[40] although privately we were always writing to the *Social-Demokrat* that they should oppose Bismarck just as much as they opposed the Progressives. We even tolerated the intrigues conducted *against* the International Working Men's Association by that affected fop Bernhard Becker,[41] who takes quite seriously the importance conferred on him in Lassalle's testament.

Meanwhile, Herr Schweitzer's articles in the *Social-Demokrat* became more and more Bismarckian. I had written to him before saying that the Progressives could be *intimidated* on the 'combination question' but that *neither now nor at any time* would the '*Prussian government*' concede the complete abolition of the combination laws.[42] Such an abolition would lead to a breach in the bureaucratic apparatus, the release of the workers from state tutelage, the overthrow of the *Gesindeordnung*,[43] the abolition of the aristocracy's flogging of rural backsides etc.: it would be altogether incompatible with the *bureaucratic* Prussian state, and

38. Lassalle did leave a political testament, which among other things recommended the election of Bernhard Becker as president of the ADAV. But Marx seems to be referring here to Lassalle's 'testament' in the broader sense, i.e. his unfulfilled political aspirations.

39. Hermann Wagener was the founder and editor of the *Neue Preussische Zeitung*. See p. 130, n. 12.

40. The best of a bad job.

41. Bernhard Becker was elected president of the ADAV on Lassalle's testamentary recommendation, but was soon forced to resign on the grounds of incompetence. His place was taken in December 1864 by Johann von Schweitzer. In a letter to Schweitzer of 16 January 1865 Marx complained of an article by Becker attacking the International.

42. On 13 February 1865. See above, p. 147.

43. See p. 147, n. 26.

Bismarck would never allow it. I added that if the Chamber rejected the combination laws the government would take refuge in empty phrases (for example, to the effect that the social question demands 'more fundamental' measures etc.) in order to preserve them. All this indeed proved to be the case. And what did Herr von Schweitzer do? He wrote an article *in support of* Bismarck[44] and now saves up all his heroic courage for such *infiniments petits*[45] as Schulze, Faucher, etc.[46]

I believe Schweitzer, etc. to be *sincere*, but they are *'Realpolitiker'*. They want to accommodate themselves to the *existing* situation and not leave this privilege of *'Realpolitik'* to Herr Miquel and Co. alone. The latter seem to want to reserve for themselves the right of intermixture with the Prussian government. They know that the workers' newspapers and workers' movement only exist *par la grâce de la police*.[47] So they want to take circumstances as they are and not provoke the government etc., just like our *'republican' Realpolitiker* who are willing to settle for a Hohenzollern kaiser. But as I am not a *'Realpolitiker'* I have found it necessary, together with Engels, to announce my withdrawal from the *Social-Demokrat* in a public statement[48] (which you will probably soon see in one paper or another).

You will see, therefore, why I can do *nothing* in Prussia at this moment. The government has flatly rejected my renaturalization in Prussia.[49] I would only be allowed to conduct *agitation* there in a form amenable to Herr von Bismarck.

I prefer a hundred times over to agitate here through the International Association. The influence on the *English* proletariat is direct and of the greatest importance. We are creating a stir

44. The third part of Schweitzer's article 'The Bismarck Ministry' appeared in the *Social-Demokrat* on 17 February 1865. Here Schweitzer explicitly came out in support of Bismarck's policy of unifying Germany under Prussian hegemony by 'blood and iron'. This led to Liebknecht's immediate resignation from the editorship, and to Marx and Engels withdrawing their collaboration.

45. Infinitely small fry.

46. Julius Faucher, like Schulze-Delitzsch, was a leader of the Progressive party.

47. By the grace of the police.

48. *MECW* 20, p. 80.

49. After the amnesty granted by William I in January 1861, following his accession to the throne, Marx applied for renaturalization, but his request was refused (see *MECW* 19, p. 339ff).

here at the present moment on the general suffrage question,[50] which naturally has *quite another significance* in England than it has in Prussia.

On the whole the progress of this Association is *beyond all expectations* – here, in Paris, in Belgium, Switzerland and Italy. Only in Germany, of course, do Lassalle's successors oppose me, 1. because they have a stupid fear of losing their importance; 2. because they are aware of my avowed opposition to what the Germans call *Realpolitik*. (It is this sort of '*reality*' which places Germany so far behind all civilized countries.)

As anyone who pays a shilling for a card can become a member of the Association; as the French have chosen the form of individual membership (as have the Belgians) because the law forbids them to join us as an 'association'; as the situation in Germany is similar, I have decided to call upon my friends to form small societies, irrespective of the number of members in each place, in which every member buys an English card of membership. As the English society is *public* nothing stands in the way of this procedure in France. I would welcome it if you would also establish contact with London in this way in your immediate area.

Thank you for your prescription. Strangely enough, three days before it arrived the disgusting illness broke out again. So the prescription was very convenient.

In a few days I shall send you twenty-four more 'Addresses'. I have just been interrupted by a friend and as I would like to send off this letter I shall take up the other points in your letter next time.

Yours truly,

K.M.

MARX TO SCHWEITZER[51]

London, 13 October 1868

Dear Sir,

The fact that you have not received a reply to your letter of 15 September is due to a misunderstanding on my part. I understood from your letter that you intended to send me your 'drafts' to

50. The day that Marx wrote this letter the Reform League was founded in London, on the initiative of the International's General Council, to campaign for manhood suffrage.

51. The actual letter sent to Schweitzer has not survived, and the following text is Marx's original draft.

look at. I waited for them. Then came your Congress[52] and (being much overworked) I no longer regarded an answer as pressing. In my capacity as secretary of the International for Germany I had *repeatedly* urged the necessity for *peace* before your letter of 8 October arrived. I received the answer (together with quotations from the *Social-Demokrat*) that you yourself were provoking the *war*. I declared that my role must necessarily be limited to that of the umpire in the duel.

I think that I cannot better repay the great confidence in me which you have expressed in your letter than by informing you openly and unequivocally of my view of the situation. I do this in the confidence that your only concern, as mine, is the success of the movement.

I recognize without reservation the intelligence and energy of your activities in the workers' movement. I have disguised this view from none of my friends. Whenever I have to speak in public – in the General Council of the International Working Men's Association and the German Workers' Educational Association here – I have always treated you as a man of our party and have never uttered *the least word about points of disagreement*.

Nevertheless, such points of disagreement exist.

D'abord,[53] as far as the Lassallean Association is concerned, it was founded in a period of reaction. It is to Lassalle's eternal credit that he re-awakened the workers' movement in Germany after it had slumbered for fifteen years. But he committed great mistakes. He allowed himself to be governed too much by the immediate circumstances of the day. He transformed a minor starting-point – his opposition to a dwarf like Schulze-Delitzsch – into the central point of his agitation: state aid versus self-help. In doing so he only re-adopted the slogan which Buchez, the leader of Catholic socialism, had issued against the real workers' movement in France in 1843 and the following years. As he was much too intelligent to regard this slogan as anything but a transitory *pis aller*,[54] he could only justify it by its (supposed) immediate practicability. For this purpose he had to maintain that it could be brought about in the near future. Thus, *the* 'state'

52. This was the congress called by the ADAV to found a trade-union federation, and held at Hamburg in September 1868. Supporters of Liebknecht's Union of German Workers Societies were not allowed to take part. The 'drafts' referred to above are Schweitzer's draft rules for the trade-union federation – see below.

53. First of all.   54. Makeshift.

transformed itself into the Prussian state. As a result he was forced to make concessions to the Prussian monarchy, the forces of Prussian reaction (the feudal party) and even the clerical party. He combined the Chartist cry of universal suffrage with Buchez's state aid for workers' associations. He overlooked the fact that conditions in Germany and England are different. He overlooked what the *bas-empire*[55] had taught about universal suffrage. Furthermore, he gave his agitation from the very beginning the character of a religious sect, as does every man who claims to have in his pocket a panacea for the suffering masses. In fact, every sect is religious. Furthermore, precisely because he was a founder of a sect, he denied any natural connection with the earlier movement in Germany or abroad. He fell into the same error as Proudhon, of not seeking the real basis for his agitation in the actual elements of the class movement, but of trying to prescribe the course of the movement according to a certain doctrinaire recipe.

Most of what I am now saying after the event I already told Lassalle when he came to London in 1862 and invited me to place myself with him at the head of the new movement.

You yourself have had personal experience of the contradictions between a sectarian and a class movement. The sect seeks its *raison d'être* and point of honour not in what it has in common with the class movement but in the *particular shibboleth* which distinguishes it from the class movement. When, therefore, in Hamburg[56] you proposed the congress for the foundation of trade unions you were only able to defeat the sectarian opposition by threatening to resign from the office of president. You were furthermore forced to play a dual role, to declare that you were acting on the one hand as the head of the sect and on the other as the organ of the class movement.

The dissolution of the General Association of German Workers[57] gave you the opportunity to accomplish a great step forward and to declare, *s'il le fallait*,[58] that a new stage of development had

55. Marx's name for the French Second Empire; the original 'lower empire' was the Byzantine.

56. The Hamburg Congress of the ADAV was held in August 1868. Its resolutions marked a weakening of that organization's sectarianism, and a rapprochement with the International.

57. On 16 Septemer 1868 the ADAV headquarters in Leipzig were closed by the Saxon police. Three weeks later, however, a new ADAV headquarters was opened in Berlin, with the implicit tolerance of the Prussian authorities.

58. If it was necessary.

been reached and that the sectarian movement was now ready to merge into the class movement and to completely abandon its separation. As far as its true aims were concerned, the sect, like all earlier working-class sects, would bring them as an enriching element into the general movement. Instead you have in fact demanded of the class movement that it subordinate itself to a particular sectarian movement. Those who are not your friends have concluded from this that you are trying under all circumstances to preserve your 'own workers' movement'.

As far as the Berlin Congress is concerned, there was first of all no urgency, as there has not yet been a vote on the combination law.[59] So you should have come to a mutual understanding with the leaders *outside* the Lassallean circle and drawn up the plan and convened the Congress together with them. Instead, you left them only the alternative of joining *you* openly or of *opposing* you. The Congress itself seemed only a repetition of the Hamburg Congress.

As for the draft of the rules, I regard it as fundamentally misguided and I think I have as much experience as any contemporary in the field of trade unions. Without going into details here I would only remark that the *centralist* organization, no matter how valuable it may be for secret societies and sectarian movements, contradicts the essence of trade unions. Even if it were possible – and I declare *toute bonnement*[60] that it is not – it would not be necessary, least of all in Germany. There, where the worker is subject to bureaucratic discipline from his infancy and believes in officialdom and higher authority, it is above all a question of teaching him to *walk by himself*.

Your plan is impractical anyway. In the 'Association' you have three independent authorities of different origin: 1) The *Committee* elected by the *trades*; 2) the President (a completely superfluous figure in this context)[61] elected by *all members*; 3) the

59. The law granting the right to form trade unions and to strike was passed by the North German Reichstag on 29 May 1869.

60. Quite frankly.

61. In the rules of the International Working Men's Association a president also figures. But in reality he never had any function other than chairing the meeting of the General Council. At my suggestion the office, which I turned down in 1866, was abolished completely and replaced by a chairman, who is elected at each weekly meeting of the General Council. The *London Trades Council* likewise only has a chairman. The secretary is its only permanent official, because he performs a continuous function [Marx].

Congress elected by the *localities*. The result – conflicts everywhere. And is this supposed to promote 'rapid action'! Lassalle made a big blunder when he borrowed the *'président élu du suffrage universel'*[62] from the French Constitution of 1852. And now the same sort of thing in a trade-union movement! Such a movement is largely concerned with questions of money, and you will soon discover that in such a situation all dictatorship has to come to an end.

However, whatever the mistakes in the organization, they can perhaps be more or less removed if affairs are conducted rationally. I am ready, as secretary of the International,[63] to function as arbitrator between you and the Nuremberg majority,[64] which has joined the International directly – on a rational basis, needless to say. I have written the same thing to Leipzig. I recognize the difficulties of your position and do not forget that each of us is guided more by the requirements of the situation than by his own will.

I promise you under all circumstances the neutrality which I feel to be my duty. On the other hand I cannot promise that one day, as a *private writer* – as soon as I regard it as absolutely necessary in the interests of the workers' movement – I will not openly criticize the superstitious doctrines of Lassalle, as I have criticized those of Proudhon.

Assuring you of my best wishes,
Yours respectfully,
K.M.

62. President elected by universal suffrage.

63. I.e. as the General Council's corresponding secretary for Germany.

64. The Union of German Workers Societies' Nuremberg Congress was held in September 1868. The minority of liberal bourgeois representatives left the Union at this point, and a programme was adopted that brought the Union into line with the International. The headquarters of the Union was in Leipzig.

Letters on Ireland[1]

MARX TO ENGELS

London, 2 November 1867

Dear Fred,
... I used to regard Ireland's separation from England as impossible. I now think it inevitable, although *federation* may follow separation. The policy of the English is revealed in the *Agricultural Statistics*[2] for this year, published a few days ago. Also the form which eviction is taking. The Irish viceroy, Lord Abicorn[3] (the name is *something* like that) has 'cleared' his estate in the last few weeks by forcibly evicting thousands of people, among them well-to-do tenant farmers whose improvements and capital investments have in this way been confiscated! Foreign rule has not taken this direct form of expropriation of the natives in any other European country. The Russians confiscate merely for political reasons; in West Prussia the Prussians buy out the land.

MARX TO ENGELS

London, 30 November 1867

Dear Fred,
... If you have read the papers you will have seen that 1) the International Council sent the Memorial for the Fenians to

---

1. Marx's letters to Engels and other close friends, basically written in German, sometimes lapse into an idiosyncratic composite of German and English. The frequent English words and phrases in the original have not been marked. These letters are translated from the texts printed in *MEW* 31 & 32.
2. *Agricultural Statistics, Ireland*, Dublin, 1867.
3. The name was in fact James Hamilton, Duke of Abercorn.

Hardy,[4] 2) the debate on Fenianism (the Tuesday before last) was public and *The Times* reported it. Reporters from the Dublin *Irishman* and *Nation* were there too. I didn't arrive until very late (I have had fever for about two weeks and it only disappeared two days ago) and in fact didn't intend to speak, firstly because of my uncomfortable state of health and secondly because of the ugly situation. However, Weston,[5] the chairman, wanted to force me to speak, and so I moved the adjournment, as a result of which I was obliged to speak last Tuesday. In fact I did not have a speech prepared for Tuesday last, but only the points of a speech.[6] However, the Irish reporters did not come and we waited until nine o'clock although the public house only remained open until 10.30 p.m. At my suggestion Fox[7] (he had not put in an appearance for two weeks because of a quarrel in the Council and had furthermore submitted his resignation as a member of the Council, accompanied by crude attacks on Jung) had prepared a long speech. After the sitting opened I thus announced that because of the belated hour I would allow Fox to speak in my place. In fact – as a result of the execution which had taken place in Manchester in the meantime – our topic, 'Fenianism', had become charged with passion and heated feeling, which would have forced me (though not the abstract Fox) to deliver a thundering revolutionary tirade instead of the intended sober analysis of the situation and the movement. Thus, by staying away and causing the sitting to begin late, the Irish reporters did me a great service. I don't like being involved with people like Roberts, Stephens, etc.[8]

Fox's speech was good, firstly because it was given by *an Englishman*, secondly, in its treatment of the purely political and

4. This refers to the General Council's 'Memorial' (written by Marx) sent on 20 November 1867 to Gathorne-Hardy, the Home Secretary, petitioning for the commutation of the death sentences on the five Fenian prisoners condemned at Manchester for the murder of a policeman in the course of an attempt to rescue two Fenian leaders. In the event, Michael Larkin, William Allen and Michael O'Brien were executed on 23 November.

5. John Weston, an Owenist, was a founding member of the International and its General Council.

6. Marx's 'Notes for an undelivered speech on Ireland' are printed in *MECW* 21, pp. 189–93.

7. Peter Fox, a journalist and a follower of Comte, was active in the Reform League and a member of the General Council.

8. James Stephens, a Fenian leader, had in fact emigrated to the United States in 1866. William Roberts was a lawyer prominent in the Fenians' defence.

international aspects. But with these he only touched the surface. The resolution which he submitted was insipid and vacuous. I opposed it and had it referred back to the Standing Committee.[9]

What the English do not yet know is that since 1846 the economic content of English rule in Ireland, and therefore also its political aims, has entered a new phase, and it is for this very reason that Fenianism is characterized by a socialist tendency (in a negative sense: in being opposed to the appropriation of the soil and as a lower orders movement). What could be more ridiculous than to confuse the barbarities of Elizabeth or Cromwell, who wanted to supplant the Irish by English colonists (in the Roman sense), with the present system, which is trying to supplant the Irish with sheep, pigs and oxen! The system from 1801 to 1846[10] (evictions during the period were exceptional, occurring most often in Leinster, where the land is particularly suited to cattle-raising), with its rack-rents and middlemen, collapsed in 1846. The repeal of the Corn Laws, partly the result of the Irish famine, at any rate accelerated by it, deprived Ireland of its *monopoly* on corn supplies to England during normal times. Wool and meat became the watchword: that is, the conversion of tillage into pasture. Hence, from then on, the systematic consolidation of farms. The Encumbered Estates Act,[11] which turned a mass of earlier, enriched middlemen into land-lords, accelerated the process. Clearing of the Estate of Ireland is now the sole significance of English rule there. Of course, the *stupid* English government in London itself knows nothing of this immense change since 1846. But the Irish know. From *Meagher's Proclamation* (1848)[12] down to the *election address of Hennessy* (Tory and Urquhartite) (1866), the Irish have expressed their awareness of it in the clearest and most forcible manner.

9. For Fox's speech and resolution see *IWMA* II, p. 181. The Standing Committee was the executive committee of the General Council.

10. In 1782 the Dublin Parliament, which represented the Protestant land-owners and bourgeoisie, had achieved a measure of independence from English control, and went on to pass various protectionist measures. Following the United Irishmen's rebellion of 1798, the Act of Union, operative from 1 January 1801, abolished the Irish Parliament. From 1801 onwards there was free trade between England and Ireland.

11. This Act, passed in 1853, accelerated the consolidation of Irish agricul-ture into larger units by facilitating the forced sale of the land of indebted farmers.

12. Thomas Meagher, of the Young Ireland movement, called in 1848 for a natio-nal armed uprising.

The question now is what advice *we* should give the *English* workers? In my view they must make the *Repeal of the Union* (in short, the *arrangement of* 1783, but democratized and adapted to the times) an article of their *pronunziamento*. This is the only *legal* and hence the only possible form of Irish emancipation which can be included in the programme of an *English* party. Experience must show later whether a mere personal union between the two countries could continue. I am half inclined to believe this, if it happens in time.

What the Irish need are:

1. Self-government and independence from England.

2. Agrarian revolution. With the best will in the world the English cannot make this revolution for them, but they can give them the legal means of making it for themselves.

3. *Protective tariffs against England*. Between 1783 and 1801 all branches of Irish industry prospered. With the overthrow of the protective tariffs which the Irish Parliament had established, the Union destroyed all industrial life in Ireland. The small linen industry is in no way a substitute. The Union of 1801 affected Irish industry in just the same way as the measures passed by the English Parliament under Anne and George II for the suppression of the Irish woollen industry, etc. Once the Irish got their independence, need would immediately force them to turn protectionist, just like Canada and Australia etc. Before I present my views in the General Council (next Tuesday, this time fortunately *without* the presence of reporters)[13] I should be glad if you would give me your opinion in a few lines.

> *Salut.*
> Regards,
> K.M.

MARX TO KUGELMANN

London, 6 April 1868

Dear Kugelmann,

... The Irish question is the dominant issue here at present. Gladstone and Co. have, of course, exploited the problem only

---

13. In the event, Marx did not deliver his speech to the General Council as planned, but used his notes for a speech to the German Workers Educational Association on 16 December 1867 (*MECW* 21, pp. 194–206).

in order to have an electoral cry at the next elections, which will be based on household suffrage.[14] *For the moment* this turn of events is harmful for the workers' party, as the *intriguers* among the workers who want to get into the next Parliament, such as Odger, Potter, etc., now have a new *pretext* for joining the bourgeois Liberals.

However, this is only a punishment which England – and therefore the English working class as well – is suffering in payment for the great crime which it has committed against Ireland over many centuries. And in the long run the English working class will itself profit. For the English Established Church in Ireland – or what they used to call here the Irish Church – is the religious bulwark of English landlordism in Ireland and at the same time the outpost of the Established Church in England itself (I am speaking of the Established Church as a *landowner*). With its overthrow in Ireland the Established Church will collapse in England, and both will be followed by the collapse of landlordism, first in Ireland and then in England. But I have always been convinced from the very first that the social revolution can only *seriously* begin from the bottom up; that is, with landlordism.[15]

However, the whole business will have the very useful result that, once the Irish Church is dead, the Protestant Irish tenants in the province of Ulster will join forces with the Catholic tenants and their movement in the other three provinces of Ireland, whereas hitherto landlordism has been able to exploit this *religious* antagonism . . .

Regards,
K. MARX

14. Household suffrage was granted by the Second Reform Act of 1867. It still left all women and two thirds of all adult males unfranchised, and did not apply in Scotland or Ireland. Gladstone, who won the General Election of December 1868 as leader of the Liberal party, had compared the repressive regime in Ireland to that of William the Conqueror.

15. The German, '*von Grund aus*' (from the bottom up) and '*Grund-und-Boden-Eigentum*' (landlordism), contains a play on words based on the dual meaning of the word '*Grund*'.

MARX TO ENGELS

London, 18 November 1869

Dear Fred,

... Last Tuesday I opened the discussion about point no. 1, *the attitude of the British government to the Irish Amnesty question.*[16] Made a speech lasting about one and a quarter hours, much cheered, and then proposed the following resolution on point no. 1.

Resolved,

That in his reply to the Irish demands for the release of the imprisoned Irish patriots – a reply contained in his letter to Mr O'Shea etc. etc. – Mr Gladstone deliberately insults the Irish nation;

That he clogs political amnesty with conditions alike degrading to the victims of misgovernment and the people they belong to;

That having, in the teeth of his responsible position, publicly and enthusiastically cheered on the American slaveholders' rebellion,[17] he now steps in to preach to the Irish people the doctrine of passive obedience;

That his whole proceedings with reference to the Irish Amnesty question are the true and genuine offspring of that *'policy of conquest'*, by the fiery denunciation of which Mr Gladstone ousted his Tory rivals from office;

That the *General Council* of the *'International Working Men's Association'* express their admiration of the spirited, firm and high-souled manner in which the Irish people carry on their Amnesty movement;

That these resolutions be communicated to all branches of, and working men's bodies connected with the *International Working Men's Association* in Europe and America.

16. Marx is referring to the meeting of the General Council on 16 November; see *IWMA* III, pp. 178–94. The amnesty movement, to press the British government to release Fenian prisoners, saw a new upsurge of popular struggle in Ireland, and Marx, for reasons that he states in his letter to Kugelmann of 29 November (below, pp. 164–6), actively mobilized the General Council in support of the Irish amnesty. 'Point no. 2', which Marx had also proposed that the General Council should discuss, was 'the attitude of the English working class towards the Irish' (*IWMA* III, p. 177), but Marx refrained from introducing this question into the debate.

17. This refers to Gladstone's speech at Newcastle on 7 October 1862, in which he sent greetings to Jefferson Davis, the Confederate president.

Harris (an O'Brien man[18]) agreed to second. But the president (Lucraft) pointed to the clock (we can only stay until eleven o'clock); hence meeting adjourned until next Tuesday. However, Lucraft, Weston, Hales, etc.,[19] in fact the whole Council, provisionally declared their agreement in [an] informal way.

Another O'Brienite – Milner – declared the language of the resolution was too weak (i.e. not declamatory enough); furthermore, he demands that everything that I said by way of an explanation should be included in the resolution. (That's asking quite a lot!)

So, as the debate continues on Tuesday, now [is] the time for you to say or write to me what you perhaps want *changed* or *added* in the resolutions. If, for example, you want another clause added about the amnesties throughout Europe, e.g. Italy, formulate it straightaway as a resolution . . .

Regards,
K.M.

MARX TO KUGELMANN

London, 29 November 1869

Dear Kugelmann,

. . . You will probably have seen in the *Volksstaat* the resolutions which I proposed against Gladstone on the Irish Amnesty question.[20] I have now attacked Gladstone – and it caused quite a stir here – in just the same way I attacked Palmerston earlier.[21]

18. The O'Brienite organization to which George Harris and George Milner belonged was the National Reform League. A former Chartist, Bronterre O'Brien through his League kept up a semi-socialist propaganda centred on land reform throughout the barren years of the 1850s. The National Reform League affiliated to the International in 1867, and its members played an important role in founding the Land and Labour League (see p. 29, n. 47).

19. Benjamin Lucraft was a leader of the furniture-workers' union, and a founder member of the General Council. In June 1871 he resigned from the International following the publication of *The Civil War in France*. John Hales was a leader of the weavers' union, a member of the General Council and its secretary from 1871–2.

20. The *Volksstaat*, edited by Wilhelm Liebknecht, was the official paper of the SDAP (Eisenach party), founded in August 1869 (see pp. 23–4). The resolution against Gladstone is that reproduced by Marx in his letter to Engels of 18 November 1869 (above, p. 163).

21. Marx is referring to his articles on Palmerston published in the *People's Paper*, the *New York Daily Tribune* and as a pamphlet in 1853 (*MECW* 12, pp. 341–406).

The demagogic refugees here are very fond of assailing the continental despots from a safe distance. That sort of thing only attracts me if it is done *vultu instantis tyranni*.[22]

Nevertheless, both my activities on this Irish Amnesty question and my further suggestion in the General Council that we discuss the relation of the English working class to Ireland and pass resolutions on the problem have, of course, other aims beyond that of speaking out loudly and decisively on behalf of the oppressed Irish against their oppressors.

I have become more and more convinced – and it remains a matter of driving the point home to the English working class – that it can never do anything decisive here in England until it makes a decisive break with the ruling class in its policy on Ireland, until it not only makes common cause with the Irish but actually takes the initiative in dissolving the *Union* founded in 1801 and replacing it with a free federal relationship. And, indeed, this must be done not as a matter of sympathy with Ireland but as a demand based on the interests of the English proletariat. Otherwise the English people will be kept in tether by the ruling classes, because they will have to establish a common front with them against Ireland. Every one of its movements in England remains paralysed by the quarrel with the Irish, who form a very considerable section of the working class in England itself. The *first condition* for emancipation here – the overthrow of the English landed oligarchy – remains an impossibility, because its bastion here cannot be stormed as long as it holds its strongly entrenched outpost in Ireland. But once the Irish people takes matters into its own hands there, once it is made its own legislator and ruler, once it becomes autonomous, the overthrow of the landed aristocracy (for the most part *the same people* as the English landlords) will be infinitely easier than here, because in Ireland it is not only a simple economic question but at the same time a *national* question, because the landlords there are not, as in England, the traditional dignitaries and representatives of the nation but its mortally hated oppressors. And not only England's inner social development but also its foreign policy, particularly with regard to Russia and the United States, remain paralysed by its present relationship with Ireland.

But, as the English working class undeniably casts the decisive weight into the scales of social emancipation in general, the

22. To the tyrant's face.

important thing is to apply the lever here. In fact the English republic under Cromwell came to grief – in Ireland.[23] *Non bis in idem!*[24] The Irish have played a delightful trick on the English government by electing the 'convict felon' O'Donovan Rossa[25] to Parliament. The government papers are already threatening a renewed suspension of the Habeas Corpus Act and a renewed system of terror! The fact is that England has never ruled and *can* never rule Ireland any other way, as long as the present relationship lasts – than by the most atrocious reign of terror and the most damnable corruption . . .

Regards,

K. MARX

MARX TO ENGELS

London, 10 December 1869

Dear Fred,

. . . *Ad vocem: Irish question*. Although I had undertaken to open the debates, I didn't go to the Central Council last Tuesday. My 'family' didn't allow me to go in this *fog* and in my present state of health . . .

The way I shall present the matter next Tuesday[26] is this: I shall say that quite apart from all the 'international' and 'humane' phrases about justice-for-Ireland – which are taken for granted in the International Council – it is in *the direct and absolute interests of the English working class* to get rid of their present connection with Ireland. And this is my firm conviction, for reasons which, in part, I *cannot* tell the English workers themselves. I long believed it was possible to overthrow the Irish regime by way of

23. From 1649 to 1652 Cromwell was engaged in reconquering Ireland, the greater part of which had been liberated from English rule by the insurrection of October 1641. Cromwell expropriated Irish land and allotted it to officers and soldiers in his army, but the effect of this was to weaken the resistance to the restoration of the Stuart monarchy.

24. Let this not happen a second time.

25. Jeremiah O'Donovan Rossa was co-founder of the Fenian movement, and published the *Irish People* from 1863 to 1865. In 1865 he was condemned to life imprisonment, but amnestied in 1870.

26. In fact the General Council's discussion of the Irish question came to an end at this point. On 14 December the council did not discuss the Irish question, but postponed it until 4 January, and on that day Marx proposed the adjournment of the discussion (see *IWMA* III, p. 200).

English working-class ascendancy. This is the position I always represented in the *New York Tribune*.[27] A deeper study has now convinced me of the opposite. The English working class will never achieve anything before it has got rid of Ireland. The lever must be applied in Ireland. This is why the Irish question is so important for the social movement in general ...

Regards,
K. MÖHR[28]

MARX TO MEYER AND VOGT

London, 9 April 1870

Dear Meyer and dear Vogt,[29]

... Among what I have sent you you will also find some copies of the familiar resolutions passed by the General Council on 30 November on the *Irish Amnesty* question[30] which I drew up; also an Irish pamphlet on the treatment of the Fenian convicts.

I intended to introduce more resolutions on the necessary transformation of the present Union (which amounts to the enslavement of Ireland) in[to] a free and equal federation with Great Britain. The prosecution of this matter has been suspended for the time being, as far as public resolutions go, because of my enforced absence from the General Council. No other member of the Council knows enough about Irish affairs and possesses enough authority in the eyes of the *English* members of the General Council to be able to replace me in this matter.

Meanwhile time has not passed unused and I would ask you to pay particular attention to what follows.

After occupying myself with the Irish question for many years I have come to the conclusion that the decisive blow against the English ruling classes (and it will be decisive for the workers' movement all over the world) *cannot* be struck *in England*, but *only in Ireland*.

On 1 January 1870 the General Council issued a secret circular

27. See for example Marx's article of 1853 on 'Forced Emigration', *MECW* 11, pp. 528–34.

28. 'The Moor' was a nickname of Marx's.

29. Siegfried Meyer and August Vogt were German supporters of Marx who emigrated to the US in the late 1860s and were active in the International in New York.

30. The resolutions proposed by Marx on 16 November 1869 (above, p. 163).

which I had drawn up in French[31] – for a reaction in England only the French, not the German papers are important – on the relation of the Irish national struggle to the emancipation of the working class and hence on the attitude which the International Working Men's Association should adopt on the Irish question.

I shall give you only the main points here quite briefly. Ireland is the bulwark of the *English landed aristocracy*. The exploitation of this country is not only one of the main sources of their material wealth; it is their greatest *moral* strength. They represent in fact *England's dominion over Ireland*. Ireland is, therefore, the *grand moyen*[32] by which the English aristocracy maintains *its rule in England* itself.

On the other hand, if the English army and police withdrew tomorrow, you would have an agrarian revolution in Ireland immediately. But the overthrow of the English aristocracy in Ireland involves and would necessarily be followed by its overthrow in England. Thus one prerequisite for the proletarian revolution in England would be fulfilled. Quite apart from the more passionate and more revolutionary character of the Irish compared with the English, the destruction of the English landed aristocracy in Ireland is an infinitely easier operation than in England itself, because in Ireland the *land question* has up till now been the *exclusive form* which the social question has taken, because it is a question of existence, a *question of life and death* for the majority of the Irish people, because at the same time it is inseparable from the *national* question.

As far as the English *bourgeoisie* is concerned, it has *d'abord*[33] a common interest with the English aristocracy in transforming Ireland into mere pasture land, to supply the English market with meat and wool at the cheapest possible prices. It has the same interest in reducing the Irish population to such a small number, by eviction and forcible emigration, that *English capital* (invested in leasehold farmland) can operate in this country with 'security'. It has the same interest in clearing the estate of Ireland that it had in the clearing of the agricultural districts of England and Scotland. The £6,000–£10,000 absentee and other Irish revenues which at present flow annually to London must also be taken into account.

---

31. 'The General Council to the Federal Council of French Switzerland'; see above, pp. 117–18.
32. Great means.   33. First of all.

But the English bourgeoisie has other, much more important interests in the present structure of the Irish economy. As a result of the steadily increasing concentration of farms Ireland supplies the English labour market with its surplus [labour] and thus lowers the wages and the material and moral position of the English working class.

And most important of all! All English industrial and commercial centres now possess a working class *split* into two *hostile* camps: English proletarians and Irish proletarians. The ordinary English worker hates the Irish worker because he sees in him a competitor who lowers his standard of life. Compared with the Irish worker he feels himself a member of the *ruling nation* and for this very reason he makes himself into a tool of the aristocrats and capitalists *against Ireland* and thus strengthens their domination *over himself*. He cherishes religious, social and national prejudices against the Irish worker. His attitude is much the same as that of the 'poor whites' towards the 'niggers' in the former slave states of the American Union. The Irishman pays him back with interest in his own money. He sees in the English worker both the accomplice and the stupid tool of *English rule in Ireland*.

This antagonism is artificially sustained and intensified by the press, the pulpit, the comic papers, in short, by all the means at the disposal of the ruling classes. *This antagonism* is the *secret of the impotence of the English working class*, despite its organization. It is the secret which enables the capitalist class to maintain its power, as this class is perfectly aware.

The evil does not stop here. It continues on the other side of the ocean. The antagonism between the English and the Irish is the secret basis of the conflict between the United States and England. It makes any serious and honest cooperation between the working classes of the two countries impossible. It allows the governments of the two countries, whenever they think fit, to blunt the edge of the social conflict by their mutual bullying and in case of need by going to war with one another.

England, as the metropolis of capital, as the power which has up to now ruled the world market, is for the time being the most important country for the workers' revolution; moreover it is the *only* country where the material conditions for this revolution have developed to a certain degree of maturity. To accelerate the social revolution in England is therefore the most important object of the International Working Men's Association. The only means of accelerating it is to bring about the independence of Ireland. It is therefore the task of the 'International' to bring the conflict between England and Ireland into the foreground and everywhere to side openly with Ireland. It is the special task of the General Council in London to arouse the consciousness in the English working class that *for them* the *national emancipation of Ireland* is not a question of abstract justice or humanitarian sentiment but the first condition of their own social emancipation.

These are roughly the main points contained in the circular, which are thus also the *raison d'être* of the General Council's resolutions on the Irish Amnesty. Shortly afterwards I sent an anonymous, vehement article[34] about the English treatment of the Fenians etc., attacking Gladstone etc., to the *Internationale* (the organ of our Belgian Central Committee in Brussels). In the article I also accused the French republicans – (the *Marseillaise* had printed some nonsense on Ireland by the wretched Talandier)[35] – of being led by their national egoism to save all their *colères*[36] for the Empire.

The article had an effect. My daughter, Jenny, under the pseudonym J. Williams (she called herself Jenny Williams in a private letter to the editor), wrote a series of articles for the *Marseillaise* and published, among other things, the letter from O'Donovan Rossa. Hence immense noise. *As a result*, after many years of cynical refusal, *Gladstone* has been forced to agree to a *parliamentary inquiry* into the treatment of the Fenian prisoners. She is now regular correspondent on Irish affairs for the *Marseillaise*. (*This is, of course, a secret between us*.) The English government and press are furious that the Irish question is thus *ordre du jour*[37] and that these scoundrels are now being watched and exposed via Paris all over the Continent.

We have killed another bird with the same stone. We have forced the Irish leaders and press people in Dublin to make contact with us, which the *General Council* had failed to achieve hitherto.

You have great scope in America to work in the same way. *A*

34. 'The English Government and the Fenian Prisoners'; *MECW* 21, pp. 101–7.

35. Pierre Talandier was a former member of the General Council, later a Bakuninist. The *Marseillaise* was a left republican newspaper.

36. Anger.

37. On the agenda.

combination between the German and Irish workers (and, of course, also with those English and American workers who show an interest) is the most important task to embark on now, and it must be done in the name of the 'International'. The social significance of the Irish question must be made clear.

I shall soon send you a special letter on the situation among the English workers.

Salut et fraternité![38]

KARL MARX

38. Greetings and brotherhood.

The Franco-Prussian War

*To the Members of the International Working Men's Association
in Europe and the United States*

In the Inaugural Address of the International Working Men's Association, of November 1864, we said: 'If the emancipation of the working classes requires their fraternal concurrence, how are they to fulfil that great mission with a foreign policy in pursuit of criminal designs, playing upon national prejudices, and squandering in piratical wars the people's blood and treasure?' We defined the foreign policy aimed at by the International in these words: 'Vindicate the simple laws of morals and justice, which ought to govern the relations of private individuals, as the rules paramount of the intercourse of nations.'[2]

No wonder that Louis Bonaparte, who usurped his power by exploiting the war of classes in France, and perpetuated it by periodical wars abroad, should from the first have treated the International as a dangerous foe. On the eve of the plebiscite he ordered a raid on the members of the administrative committees of the International Working Men's Association throughout France, at Paris, Lyons, Rouen, Marseilles, Brest, etc., on the pretext that the International was a secret society dabbling in a complot for his assassination, a pretext soon after exposed in its

1. The Franco-Prussian war broke out on 19 July 1870. The same day, the General Council commissioned Marx to draft this Address, which was adopted at the following council meeting of 26 July. It was published in the *Pall Mall Gazette* on 28 July 1870, and a few days later as a leaflet. It is reproduced here from the pamphlet, *The General Council of the International Working Men's Association on the War*, Truelove, September 1870.

2. See above, p. 81.

full absurdity by his own judges.[3] What was the real crime of the French branches of the International? They told the French people publicly and emphatically that voting the plebiscite was voting despotism at home and war abroad. It has been, in fact, their work that in all the great towns, in all the industrial centres of France, the working class rose like one man to reject the plebiscite. Unfortunately the balance was turned by the heavy ignorance of the rural districts. The stock exchanges, the cabinets, the ruling classes and the press of Europe celebrated the plebiscite as a signal victory of the French emperor over the French working class; and it was the signal for the assassination, not of an individual, but of nations.

The war plot of July 1870 is but an amended edition of the coup d'état of December 1851.[4] At first view the thing seemed so absurd that France would not believe in its real good earnest. It rather believed the deputy[5] denouncing the ministerial war talk as a mere stock-jobbing trick. When, on 15 July, war was at last officially announced to the Corps Législatif,[6] the whole opposition refused to vote the preliminary subsidies, even Thiers branded it as 'detestable'; all the independent journals of Paris condemned it, and, wonderful to relate, the provincial press joined in almost unanimously.

Meanwhile, the Paris members of the International had again set to work. In the *Réveil* of 12 July they published their manifesto 'To the workmen of all nations', from which we extract the following few passages:

Once more, on the pretext of the European equilibrium, of national honour, the peace of the world is menaced by political ambitions. French, German, Spanish workmen! Let our voices unite in one cry of reprobation against war! ... War for a question of preponderance of a dynasty can, in the eyes of workmen, be nothing but a criminal

3. In the plebiscite of 8 May 1870, the French people were asked to approve Louis Napoleon's liberal reforms. The Paris Federation of the International called on the workers to boycott the plebiscite, an action which provoked the government to initiate this frame-up. In July 1870 thirty-eight members of the Paris Federation were imprisoned simply for belonging to the International, but the charges of conspiracy could not be made to stick.

4. Louis Bonaparte, elected president of the French republic in 1848, overthrew the constitution by his coup of 2 December 1851, and established the Second Empire.

5. Jules Favre.

6. The French legislature under the Second Empire.

absurdity. In answer to the warlike proclamations of those who exempt themselves from the impost of blood, and find in public misfortunes a source of fresh speculations, we protest, we who want peace, labour and liberty! . . . Brothers of Germany! Our division would only result in the complete triumph of *despotism* on both sides of the Rhine . . . Workmen of all countries! Whatever may for the present become of our common efforts, we, the members of the International Working Men's Association, who know of no frontiers, we send you as a pledge of indissoluble solidarity the good wishes and the salutations of the workmen of France.

This manifesto of our Paris section was followed by numerous similar French addresses, of which we can here only quote the declaration of Neuilly-sur-Seine, published in the *Marseillaise* of 22 July:

The war, is it just? – No! The war, is it national? – No! It is merely dynastic. In the name of humanity, of democracy, and the true interests of France, we adhere completely and energetically to the protestation of the International against the war.

These protestations expressed the true sentiments of the French working people, as was soon shown by a curious incident. The Society of 10 December,[7] first organized under the presidency of Louis Bonaparte, having been masqueraded into *blouses* and let loose on the streets of Paris, there to perform the contortions of war fever, the real workmen of the *faubourgs* came forward with public peace demonstrations so overwhelming that Piétri, the Prefect of Police, thought it prudent to at once stop all further street politics, on the plea that the real Paris people had given sufficient vent to their pent-up patriotism and exuberant war enthusiasm.

Whatever may be the incidents of Louis Bonaparte's war with Prussia, the death knell of the Second Empire has already sounded at Paris. It will end as it began, by a parody. But let us not forget that it is the governments and the ruling classes of Europe who enabled Louis Bonaparte to play during eighteen years the ferocious farce of the *restored Empire*.

On the German side, the war is a war of defence, but who put Germany to the necessity of defending herself? Who enabled

7. See *The Eighteenth Brumaire of Louis Bonaparte*, *Surveys from Exile*, pp. 197–8. The Society had in fact been dissolved as early as 1850, but the Bonapartist police continued to organize secret paramilitary forces, which Marx assimilates to the original Society of 10 December.

Louis Bonaparte to wage war upon her? *Prussia!* It was Bismarck who conspired with that very same Louis Bonaparte for the purpose of crushing popular opposition at home, and annexing Germany to the Hohenzollern dynasty. If the battle of Sadowa[8] had been lost instead of being won, French battalions would have overrun Germany as the allies of Prussia. After her victory did Prussia dream one moment of opposing a free Germany to an enslaved France? Just the contrary. While carefully preserving all the native beauties of her old system, she superadded all the tricks of the Second Empire, its real despotism and its mock democratism, its political shams and its financial jobs, its high-flown talk and its low legerdemains. The Bonapartist regime, which till then only flourished on one side of the Rhine, had now got its counterfeit on the other. From such a state of things, what else could result but *war?*

If the German working class allow the present war to lose its strictly defensive character and to degenerate into a war against the French people, victory or defeat will prove alike disastrous. All the miseries that befell Germany after her war of independence[9] will revive with accumulated intensity.

The principles of the International are, however, too widely spread and too firmly rooted amongst the German working class to apprehend such a sad consummation. The voices of the French workmen have re-echoed from Germany. A mass meeting of workmen, held at Brunswick on 16 July, expressed its full concurrence with the Paris manifesto, spurned the idea of national antagonism to France, and wound up its resolutions with these words:

We are enemies of all wars, but above all of dynastic wars . . . With deep sorrow and grief we are forced to undergo a defensive war as an unavoidable evil; but we call, at the same time, upon the whole German working class to render the recurrence of such an immense social misfortune impossible by vindicating for the peoples themselves the power to decide on peace and war, and making them masters of their own destinies.

At Chemnitz, a meeting of delegates representing 50,000 Saxon workers adopted unanimously a resolution to this effect:

8. The battle of Sadowa or Königgrätz, 3 July 1866, was Prussia's decisive victory in the Austro-Prussian war.

9. I.e. the war against Napoleon of 1813–14, which fired hopes for democracy and unification, but led to the reimposition of the old regimes.

In the name of the German democracy and especially of the workmen forming the Social-Democratic Workers' Party, we declare the present war to be exclusively dynastic . . . We are happy to grasp the fraternal hand stretched out to us by the workmen of France . . . Mindful of the watchword of the International Working Men's Association: *Proletarians of all countries, unite*, we shall never forget that the workmen of *all* countries are our *friends* and the despots of *all* countries our *enemies*.

The Berlin branch of the International has also replied to the Paris manifesto:

We join with heart and hand your protestation . . . Solemnly we promise that neither the sound of the trumpet, nor the roar of the cannon, neither victory nor defeat shall divert us from our common work for the union of the children of toil of all countries.

Be it so!

In the background of this suicidal strife looms the dark figure of Russia. It is an ominous sign that the signal for the present war should have been given at the moment when the Muscovite government had just finished its strategical lines of railway and was already massing troops in the direction of the Pruth. Whatever sympathy the Germans may justly claim in a war of defence against Bonapartist aggression, they would forfeit at once by allowing the Prussian government to call for, or accept, the help of the Cossacks. Let them remember that, after their war of independence against the first Napoleon, Germany lay for generations prostrate at the feet of the tsar.

The English working class stretch the hand of fellowship to the French and German working people. They feel deeply convinced that whatever turn the impending horrid war may take, the alliance of the working classes of all countries will ultimately kill war. The very fact that while official France and Germany are rushing into a fratricidal feud, the workmen of France and Germany send each other messages of peace and goodwill, this great fact, unparalleled in the history of the past, opens the vista of a brighter future. It proves that in contrast to old society, with its economical miseries and its political delirium, a new society is springing up, whose international rule will be *Peace*, because its national ruler will be everywhere the same – *Labour!* The pioneer of that new society is the International Working Men's Association.

LETTER TO THE BRUNSWICK COMMITTEE
OF THE SOCIAL-DEMOCRATIC WORKERS' PARTY[10]

... The military camarilla, professoriat, bourgeoisie and saloonbar politicians present this[11] as the way for Germany to prevent war with France permanently. On the contrary, it is the most certain way to convert this war into a *European institution*. It is in fact the surest way to perpetuate military despotism in the rejuvenated Germany, as a necessity for maintaining a *western Poland*, Alsace and Lorraine. It is the unfailing way to convert the approaching peace into a mere ceasefire, until France is sufficiently recovered to demand the lost territory back. It is the most unfailing way to ruin Germany and France by reciprocal self-mutilation.

The rogues and fools who have discovered these guarantees of perpetual peace, should know from Prussian history, from the results of Napoleon's Tilsit peace,[12] how such forcible measures of pacification have on a lively people the opposite of the planned effect. And look at France, even after the loss of Alsace and Lorraine, compared with Prussia after the Tilsit peace.

If French chauvinism had a certain material justification even in the context of the old state system, in that since 1815 Paris, the capital, and therefore France in general, was defenceless after a few lost battles – what new nourishment will it not derive once the frontier lies along the Vosges to the east, and at Metz to the north?

Even the most fanatical Teuton would not venture to maintain that the people of Alsace and Lorraine desire the blessings of *German* government. It is the principle of pan-Germanism and 'secure' frontiers that is being proclaimed, and what fine results this would have for Germany and Europe if applied on the eastern side.

10. The following excerpt from Marx and Engels's letter, the only extant part, was reproduced in a leaflet published by the Social-Democratic Workers' Party (SDAP). It is translated here from the text of the leaflet, as printed in *MEW* 17. A few words replaced in the leaflet by ellipses have been restored after markings by Engels in a copy of the leaflet.

11. The planned annexation by Prussia of Alsace and eastern Lorraine.

12. The Treaty of Tilsit, signed between France, Prussia and Russia in July 1807, after the defeat of the fourth anti-French coalition, confined Prussia to its territories east of the Elbe and formed western Germany into a confederation subordinate to the French Empire. This oppressive regime prepared the ground for the German national liberation movement of 1813–14.

Whoever is not completely deafened by the clamour of the moment, or does not have an *interest* in deafening the German people, must realize that the war of 1870 is just as necessarily pregnant with a *war between Germany and Russia* as the war of 1866 was with the war of 1870.

I say *necessarily, unavoidably*, except in the unlikely event of a prior outbreak of *revolution in Russia*. If this unlikely event does not occur, then a war between Germany and Russia must already be considered a *fait accompli*.

It depends completely on the behaviour of the German victors whether the present war will be useful or damaging.

If Alsace and Lorraine are taken, then France will later make war on Germany in conjunction with Russia. It is unnecessary to go into the unholy consequences.

If an honourable peace is made with France, then the war will have emancipated Europe from the Muscovite dictatorship, made Prussia merge into Germany, and allowed the western Continent a peaceful development; finally, it will have helped the outbreak of the Russian social revolution, whose elements only need such a push from outside in order to develop; it would thus also benefit the Russian people.

But I fear that the rogues and fools will drive on with their mad game unhindered, unless the German working class raises its voices *en masse*.

The present war opens a new world-historical epoch, in so far as Germany has shown that, even with the exclusion of German Austria, it is prepared to go its own way *independent of foreign influence*. If it has at first found its *unity* in *Prussian barracks*, this is a punishment that it has richly deserved. But *one* result has even so been directly achieved. Petty trivialities such as the conflict between National Liberal north Germans and Peoples' Party south Germans will no longer stand in the way.[13] Conditions will develop on a larger scale, and will be more unified. If the German working class does not play the historic role that has fallen to it, that will be its own fault. *This war has shifted the centre*

13. 'National Liberal' was the new title adopted by the majority of the bourgeois Progressive party in autumn 1866, when, following the defeat of Austria and the formation of the North German Confederation, they made their peace with Bismarck. The German Peoples' Party, formed in 1865, expressed the opposition of the south German bourgeoisie and petty bourgeoisie to Prussian hegemony, and their aspiration for a 'great Germany', including German Austria, with a federal constitution.

of gravity of the continental workers' movement from France to Germany. This has pinned on the German working class a greater responsibility . . .

To the Members of the International Working Men's Association in Europe and the United States

In our first Manifesto of 23 July we said:

> The death knell of the Second Empire has already sounded at Paris. It will end as it began, by a parody. But let us not forget that it is the governments and the ruling classes of Europe who enabled Louis Napoleon to play during eighteen years the ferocious farce of the *restored Empire*.[15]

Thus, even before war operations had actually set in, we treated the Bonapartist bubble as a thing of the past.

If we were not mistaken as to the vitality of the Second Empire, we were not wrong in our apprehension lest the German war should 'lose its strictly defensive character and degenerate into a war against the French people'.[16] The war of defence ended, in point of fact, with the surrender of Louis Bonaparte, the Sedan capitulation, and the proclamation of the republic at Paris.[17] But long before these events, the very moment that the utter rottenness of the Imperialist[18] arms became evident, the Prussian military camarilla had resolved upon conquest. There lay an ugly obstacle in their way – *King William's own proclamations at the commencement of the war*. In his speech from the throne to the North German Reichstag, he had solemnly declared to make war upon

14. The Second Empire collapsed on 4 September 1870, after the defeat of Sedan. Two days later the General Council commissioned Marx to draft this Address, which was adopted at a special meeting on 9 September. It was issued as a leaflet on 11 September, and is reproduced here from the pamphlet *The General Council of the International Working Men's Association on the War*, Truelove, September 1870.

15. Above, p. 174.

16. Above, p. 175.

17. On 2 September 1870, at Sedan, 80,000 French soldiers, led by Louis Napoleon himself, surrendered to the Prussian army. The republic was declared two days later, following a workers' rising in Paris.

18. See p. 34, n. 62.

the emperor of the French, and not upon the French people. On 11 August he had issued a manifesto to the French nation, where he said:

The emperor Napoleon having made, by land and sea, an attack on the German nation, which desired and still desires to live in peace with the French people, I have assumed the command of the German armies *to repel his aggression*, and I have been led by *military events to cross the frontiers of France*.

Not content to assert the defensive character of the war by the statement that he only assumed the command of the German armies '*to repel aggression*', he added that he was only 'led by military events' to cross the frontiers of France. A defensive war does, of course, not exclude offensive operations dictated by 'military events'.

Thus this pious king stood pledged before France and the world to a strictly defensive war. How to release him from his solemn pledge? The stage-managers had to exhibit him as giving, reluctantly, way to the irresistible behest of the German nation. They at once gave the cue to the liberal German middle class, with its professors, its capitalists, its aldermen, and its penmen. That middle class which in its struggle for civil liberty had, from 1846 to 1870, been exhibiting an unexampled spectacle of irresolution, incapacity, and cowardice, felt, of course, highly delighted to bestride the European scene as the roaring lion of German patriotism. It revindicated its civic independence by affecting to force upon the Prussian government the secret designs of that same government. It does penance for its long-continued and almost religious faith in Louis Bonaparte's infallibility, by shouting for the dismemberment of the French republic. Let us for a moment listen to the special pleadings of those stout-hearted patriots!

They dare not pretend that the people of Alsace and Lorraine pant for the German embrace; quite the contrary. To punish their French patriotism, Strasbourg, a town with an independent citadel commanding it, has for six days been wantonly and fiendishly bombarded by 'German' explosive shells, setting it on fire, and killing great numbers of its defenceless inhabitants! Yet the soil of those provinces once upon a time belonged to the whilom German Empire.[19] Hence, it seems, the soil and the human

19. I.e. the Holy Roman Empire of the German Nation. France moved into Alsace in 1639, and occupied Lorraine in 1670.

beings grown on it must be confiscated as imprescriptible German property. If the map of Europe is to be remade in the anti-quary's vein, let us by no means forget that the Elector of Branden-burg, for his Prussian dominions, was the vassal of the Polish republic.[20]

The more knowing patriots, however, require Alsace and the German-speaking part of Lorraine as a 'material guarantee' against French aggression. As this contemptible plea has bewil-dered many weak-minded people, we are bound to enter more fully upon it.

There is no doubt that the general configuration of Alsace, as compared with the opposite bank of the Rhine, and the presence of a large fortified town like Strasbourg, about halfway between Basle and Germersheim, very much favour a French invasion of south Germany, while they offer peculiar difficulties to an inva-sion of France from south Germany. There is, further, no doubt that the addition of Alsace and German-speaking Lorraine would give south Germany a much stronger frontier, inasmuch as she would then be master of the crest of the Vosges mountains in its whole length, and of the fortresses which cover its northern passes. If Metz were annexed as well, France would certainly for the moment be deprived of her two principal bases of operation against Germany, but that would not prevent her from constructing a fresh one at Nancy or Verdun. While Germany owns Coblenz, Mainz, Germersheim, Rastatt, and Ulm, all bases of operation against France, and plentifully made use of in this war, with what show of fair play can she begrudge France Strasbourg and Metz, the only two fortresses of any importance she has on that side? Moreover, Strasbourg endangers south Germany only while south Germany is a separate power from north Germany. From 1792 to 1795 south Germany was never invaded from that direc-tion, because Prussia was a party to the war against the French Revolution; but as soon as Prussia made a peace of her own in 1795, and left the south to shift for itself, the invasions of south Germany, with Strasbourg for a base, began, and continued till 1809. The fact is, a *united* Germany can always render Strasbourg and any French army in Alsace innocuous by concentrating all her troops, as was done in the present war, between Saarlouis and

20. The Electorate of Brandenburg grew into the Kingdom of Prussia. From 1618 to 1657, when the Elector first acquired the Duchy of Prussia, he was in respect of his Prussian lands a vassal of Poland.

Landau, and advancing, or accepting battle, on the line of road between Mainz and Metz. While the mass of the German troops is stationed there, any French army advancing from Strasbourg into south Germany would be outflanked, and have its communications threatened. If the present campaign has proved anything, it is the facility of invading France from Germany.

But, in good faith, is it not altogether an absurdity and an anachronism to make military considerations the principle by which the boundaries of nations are to be fixed? If this rule were to prevail, Austria would still be entitled to Venetia and the line of the Mincio, and France to the line of the Rhine, in order to protect Paris, which lies certainly more open to an attack from the north-east than Berlin does from the south-west. If limits are to be fixed by military interests, there will be no end to claims, because every military line is necessarily faulty, and may be improved by annexing some more outlying territory; and, moreover, they can never be fixed finally and fairly, because they always must be imposed by the conqueror upon the conquered, and consequently carry within them the seed of fresh wars.

Such is the lesson of all history. Thus with nations as with individuals. To deprive them of the power of offence, you must deprive them of the means of defence. You must not only garrotte but murder. If ever conqueror took 'material guarantees' for breaking the sinews of a nation, the first Napoleon did so by the Tilsit treaty,[21] and the way he executed it against Prussia and the rest of Germany. Yet, a few years later, his gigantic power split like a rotten reed upon the German people. What are the 'material guarantees' Prussia, in her wildest dreams, can, or dare impose upon France, compared to the 'material guarantees' the first Napoleon had wrenched from herself? The result will not prove the less disastrous. History will measure its retribution, not by the extent of the square miles conquered from France, but by the intensity of the crime of reviving, in the second half of the nineteenth century, *the policy of conquest*!

But, say the mouthpieces of Teutonic patriotism, you must not confound Germans with Frenchmen. What *we* want is not glory, but safety. The Germans are an essentially peaceful people. In their sober guardianship, conquest itself changes from a condition of future war into a pledge of perpetual peace. Of course, it is not Germans that invaded France in 1792, for the sublime purpose of

21. See p. 177, n. 12.

bayoneting the revolution of the eighteenth century. It is not Germans that befouled their hands by the subjugation of Italy, the oppression of Hungary, and the dismemberment of Poland. Their present military system, which divides the whole adult male population into two parts – one standing army on service, and another standing army on furlough, both equally bound in passive obedience to rulers by divine right – such a military system is, of course, a 'material guarantee' for keeping the peace, and the ultimate goal of civilizing tendencies! In Germany, as everywhere else, the sycophants of the powers that be poison the popular mind by the incense of mendacious self-praise.

Indignant as they pretend to be at the sight of French fortresses in Metz and Strasbourg, those German patriots see no harm in the vast system of Muscovite fortifications at Warsaw, Modlin and Ivangorod. While gloating at the terrors of Imperialist invasion, they blink at the infamy of autocratic tutelage.

As in 1865 promises were exchanged between Louis Bonaparte and Bismarck, so in 1870 promises have been exchanged between Gorchakov and Bismarck.[22] As Louis Bonaparte flattered himself that the war of 1866, resulting in the common exhaustion of Austria and Prussia, would make him the supreme arbiter of Germany, so Alexander flattered himself that the war of 1870, resulting in the common exhaustion of Germany and France, would make him the supreme arbiter of the western Continent. As the Second Empire thought the North German Confederation incompatible with its existence, so autocratic Russia must think herself endangered by a German empire under Prussian leadership. Such is the law of the old political system. Within its pale the gain of one state is the loss of the other. The tsar's paramount influence over Europe roots in his traditional hold on Germany. At a moment when in Russia herself volcanic social agencies threaten to shake the very base of autocracy, could the tsar afford to bear with such a loss of foreign prestige? Already the Muscovite journals repeat the language of the Bonapartist journals after the war of 1866. Do the Teuton patriots really believe that liberty and peace will be guaranteed to Germany by forcing France into the arms of Russia? If the fortune of her arms, the arrogance of success, and dynastic intrigue lead Germany to a dismemberment of France, there will then only remain two courses open to her. She

22. Prince Gorchakov was the Russian foreign minister under Tsar Alexander II.

must at all risks become the *avowed* tool of Russian aggrandize-
ment, or, after some short respite, make again ready for another
'defensive' war, not one of those new-fangled 'localized' wars,
but a *war of races* – a war with the combined Slavonian and
Roman races.

The German working class has resolutely supported the war, which
it was not in their power to prevent, as a war for German independence
and the liberation of France and Europe from that pestilential incubus,
the Second Empire. It was the German workmen who, together with
the rural labourers, furnished the sinews and muscles of heroic hosts,
leaving behind their half-starved families. Decimated by the battles
abroad, they will be once more decimated by misery at home. In their
turn they are now coming forward to ask for 'guarantees' – guarantees
that their immense sacrifices have not been bought in vain, that they
have conquered liberty, that the victory over the Imperialist armies will
not, as in 1815, be turned into the defeat of the German people – and,
as the first of these guarantees, they claim an *honourable peace for
France*, and the *recognition of the French republic*.

The Central Committee of the German Social-Democratic
Workers' Party issued, on 5 September, a manifesto, energetically
insisting upon these guarantees.

> We protest against the annexation of Alsace and Lorraine. And we are
> conscious of speaking in the name of the German working class. In the
> common interest of France and Germany, in the interest of peace and liberty,
> in the interest of western civilization against eastern barbarism, the German
> workmen will not patiently tolerate the annexation of Alsace and Lorraine . . .
> We shall faithfully stand by our fellow-workmen in all countries for the
> common international cause of the Proletariat!

Unfortunately, we cannot feel sanguine of their immediate success.
If the French workmen amidst peace failed to stop the aggressor,
are the German workmen more likely to stop the victor amidst the
clangour of arms? The German workmen's manifesto demands the
extradition of Louis Bonaparte as a common felon to the French
republic. Their rulers are, on the contrary, already trying hard to
restore him to the Tuileries as the best man to ruin France. However
that may be, history will prove that the German working class are not
made of the same malleable stuff as the German middle class. They
will do their duty.

Like them, we hail the advent of the republic in France, but at the same time we labour under misgivings which we hope will prove groundless. That republic has not subverted the throne, but only taken its place become vacant. It has been proclaimed, not as a social conquest, but as a national measure of defence. It is in the hands of a Provisional Government composed partly of notorious Orleanists,[23] partly of middle-class republicans, upon some of whom the insurrection of June 1848[24] has left its indelible stigma. The division of labour amongst the members of that government looks awkward. The Orleanists have seized the strongholds of the army and the police, while to the professed republicans have fallen the talking departments. Some of their first acts go far to show that they have inherited from the Empire, not only ruins, but also its dread of the working class. If eventual impossibilities are in wild phraseology demanded from the republic, is it not with a view to prepare the cry for a 'possible' government? Is the republic, by some of its middle-class managers, not intended to serve as a mere stopgap and bridge over [to] an Orleanist restoration?

The French working class moves, therefore, under circumstances of extreme difficulty. Any attempt at upsetting the new government in the present crisis, when the enemy is almost knocking at the doors of Paris, would be a desperate folly. The French workmen must perform their duties as citizens; but, at the same time, they must not allow themselves to be deluded by the national souvenirs of 1792, as the French peasants allowed themselves to be deluded by the national souvenirs of the First Empire.[25] They have not to recapitulate the past, but to build up the future. Let them calmly and resolutely improve the opportunities of republican liberty, for the work of their own class organization. It will gift them with fresh Herculean powers for the regeneration of

23. Supporters of the cadet branch of the French royal family, which ruled from 1830 to 1848 in the person of Louis Philippe. The Orleanists represented the 'aristocracy of finance' and the big bourgeoisie. See 'The Class Struggles in France', *Surveys from Exile*, pp. 88–9 and 173–4.

24. The workers' uprising against the Provisional Government of 1848, acclaimed by Marx as 'the first great battle . . . between the two great classes which divide modern society' . . . 'a fight for the preservation or destruction of the bourgeois order'. 'The Class Struggles in France', *Surveys from Exile*, pp. 58–9.

25. In 1792 the plebeian classes of Paris were instrumental in overthrowing the constitutional monarchy and convening the more radical Convention. The French peasantry had made the mistake of attempting to relive the past by electing Louis Bonaparte President of the Republic in 1848 and supporting his coup d'état of December 1851.

France, and our common task – the emancipation of labour. Upon their energies and wisdom hinges the fate of the republic.

The English workmen have already taken measures to overcome, by a wholesome pressure from without, the reluctance of their government to recognize the French republic.[26] The present dilatoriness of the British government is probably intended to atone for the anti-Jacobin war and its former indecent haste in sanctioning the coup d'état. The English workmen call also upon their government to oppose by all its power the dismemberment of France, which part of the English press is so shameless enough to howl for. It is the same press that for twenty years deified Louis Bonaparte as the providence of Europe, that frantically cheered on the slaveholders' rebellion.[27] Now, as then, it drudges for the slaveholder.

Let the sections of the International Working Men's Association in every country stir the working classes to action. If they forsake their duty, if they remain passive, the present tremendous war will be but the harbinger of still deadlier international feuds, and lead in every nation to a renewed triumph over the workman by the lords of the sword, of the soil, and of capital.

Vive la république.

26. Demonstrations for the recognition of the French republic were held in London and other English cities as early as 5 September.

27. I.e. the Confederate side in the United States civil war.

The Civil War in France

THE CIVIL WAR IN FRANCE:
ADDRESS OF THE GENERAL COUNCIL[1]

To All the Members of the Association in Europe and the United States

I

On 4 September 1870, when the working men of Paris proclaimed the republic, which was almost instantaneously acclaimed throughout France, without a single voice of dissent, a cabal of place-hunting barristers, with Thiers for their statesman and Trochu[2] for their general, took hold of the Hôtel de Ville.[3] At that time they were imbued with so fanatical a faith in the mission of Paris to represent France in all epochs of historical crisis, that, to legitimate their usurped titles as governors of France, they thought it quite sufficient to produce their lapsed mandates as representatives of Paris. In our second Address on the late war, five days after the rise of these men, we told you who they were.[4] Yet, in the turmoil of surprise, with the real leaders of the working class still shut up in Bonapartist prisons and the Prussians already marching upon Paris, Paris bore with their assumption of power, on the express condition that it was to be wielded for the single purpose of national defence. Paris, however, was not to be defended without arming its working class, organizing them into

1. On 18 April 1871 the General Council commissioned Marx to draft an address on the Paris Commune. Marx read *The Civil War in France* to the General Council meeting of 30 May 1871, two days after the final defeat of the Commune; it was adopted unanimously and published as a pamphlet on 13 June 1871, running through three editions in a matter of weeks. It is reproduced here from the third edition.

2. Louis Trochu was a general and Orleanist politician, Chairman of the Government of National Defence (September 1870–January 1871) and commander-in-chief of the Paris armed forces during the siege of Paris by the Prussians.

3. The Paris town hall.   4. See above, p. 185.

an effective force, and training their ranks by the war itself. But Paris armed was the revolution armed. A victory of Paris over the Prussian aggressor would have been a victory of the French workman over the French capitalist and his state parasites. In this conflict between national duty and class interest, the Government of National Defence did not hesitate one moment to turn into a Government of National Defection.

The first step they took was to send Thiers on a roving tour to all the courts of Europe, there to beg mediation by offering the barter of the republic for a king. Four months after the commencement of the siege,[5] when they thought the opportune moment had come for breaking the first word of capitulation, Trochu, in the presence of Jules Favre[6] and others of his colleagues, addressed the assembled mayors of Paris in these terms:

> The first question put to me by my colleagues on the very evening of 4 September was this: Paris, can it with any chance of success stand a siege by the Prussian army? I did not hesitate to answer in the negative. Some of my colleagues here present will warrant the truth of my words and the persistence of my opinion. I told them, in these very terms, that, under the existing state of things, the attempt of Paris to hold out a siege by the Prussian army would be a folly. Without doubt, I added, it would be an heroic folly; but that would be all . . . The events (managed by himself) have not given the lie to my prevision.

This nice little speech of Trochu was afterwards published by M. Corbon, one of the mayors present.[7]

Thus, on the very evening of the proclamation of the republic, Trochu's 'plan' was known to his colleagues to be the capitulation of Paris. If national defence had been more than a pretext for the personal government of Thiers, Favre, and Co., the upstarts of 4 September would have abdicated on the 5th – would have initiated the Paris people into Trochu's 'plan', and called upon them to surrender at once, or to take their own fate into their own hands. Instead of this, the infamous impostors resolved upon

5. Paris was besieged by the Prussians from 19 September 1870 to 28 January 1871, when the Government of National Defence signed an armistice. This provided, among other things, for the occupation of Paris, the payment of a large war indemnity, and the immediate election of a National Assembly to make peace.

6. Jules Favre was a lawyer and republican politician, and Foreign Minister in the Government of National Defence.

7. In *Le Figaro*, 19 March 1871.

curing the heroic folly of Paris by a regimen of famine and broken heads, and to dupe her in the meanwhile by ranting manifestoes, holding forth that Trochu, 'the governor of Paris, will never capitulate', and Jules Favre, the Foreign Minister, will 'not cede an inch of our territory, nor a stone of our fortresses'. In a letter to Gambetta,[8] that very same Jules Favre avows that what they were 'defending' against were not the Prussian soldiers, but the working men of Paris. During the whole continuance of the siege the Bonapartist cut-throats, whom Trochu had wisely entrusted with the command of the Paris army, exchanged, in their intimate correspondence, ribald jokes at the well-understood mockery of defence. (See, for instance, the correspondence of Adolphe Simon Guiod, supreme commander of the artillery of the army of defence of Paris and Grand Cross of the Legion of Honour, to Susane, general of division of artillery, a correspondence published by the *Journal officiel* of the Commune.)[9] The mask of imposture was at last dropped on 28 January 1871. With the true heroism of utter self-debasement, the Government of National Defence, in their capitulation, came out as the government of France by Bismarck's prisoners – a part so base that Louis Bonaparte himself had, at Sedan, shrunk from accepting it. After the events of 18 March, on their wild flight to Versailles, the *capitulards* left in the hands of Paris the documentary evidence of their treason, to destroy which, as the Commune says in its manifesto to the provinces, 'those men would not recoil from battering Paris into a heap of ruins washed by a sea of blood'.

To be eagerly bent upon such a consummation, some of the leading members of the Government of Defence had, besides, most peculiar reasons of their own.

Shortly after the conclusion of the armistice, M. Millière,[10] one of the representatives of Paris to the National Assembly, now shot

8. Léon Gambetta was a republican politician, Minister of War and of the Interior in the Government of National Defence. See p. 194, n. 27.

9. The *Journal officiel de la République française* was first published in Paris on 5 September 1870, as the official organ of the newly founded Government of Defence. From 20 March 1871 the Paris edition of this paper became the organ of the Commune, while the Versailles government continued to publish its own *Journal officiel*. On 30 March the Commune's paper was retitled *Journal officiel de la Commune de Paris*, and appeared under that title until 24 May. The letter referred to here was published on 25 April.

10. Jean-Baptiste Millière was a journalist and a left-wing Proudhonist, who sat in the Versailles Assembly but defended the Paris Commune.

by express order of Jules Favre, published a series of authentic legal documents in proof that Jules Favre, living in concubinage with the wife of a drunkard resident at Algiers, had, by a most daring concoction of forgeries, spread over many years, contrived to grasp, in the name of the children of his adultery, a large succession, which made him a rich man, and that, in a lawsuit undertaken by the legitimate heirs, he only escaped exposure by the connivance of the Bonapartist tribunals. As these dry legal documents were not to be got rid of by any amount of rhetorical horse-power, Jules Favre, for the first time in his life, held his tongue, quietly awaiting the outbreak of the civil war, in order, then, frantically to denounce the people of Paris as a band of escaped convicts in utter revolt against family, religion, order and property. This same forger had hardly got into power, after 4 September, when he sympathetically let loose upon society Pic and Taillefer, convicted, even under the Empire, of forgery, in the scandalous affair of the *'Étendard'*.[11] One of these men, Taillefer, having dared to return to Paris under the Commune, was at once reinstated in prison; and then Jules Favre exclaimed, from the tribune of the National Assembly, that Paris was setting free all her jailbirds!

Ernest Picard, the Joe Miller[12] of the Government of National Defence, who appointed himself Finance Minister of the Republic after having in vain striven to become the Home Minister of the Empire, is the brother of one Arthur Picard, an individual expelled from the Paris Bourse as a blackleg (see report of the Prefecture of Police, dated 31 July 1867), and convicted, on his own confession, of a theft of 300,000 francs, while manager of one of the branches of the Société Générale,[13] Rue Palestro, no. 5. (See report of the Prefecture of Police, 11 December 1868.) This Arthur Picard was made by Ernest Picard the editor of his paper, *L'Électeur libre*. While the common run of stock-jobbers were led astray by the official lies of this Finance Office paper, Arthur was running backwards and forwards between the Finance Office and the Bourse, there to discount the disasters of the French army. The whole financial correspondence of that worthy pair of brothers fell into the hands of the Commune.

11. *L'Étendard* was a Bonapartist newspaper, forced to close in 1868 after the exposure of its involvement in financial frauds.

12. Joe Miller was an eighteenth-century English comic actor.

13. The Société Générale du Crédit Mobilier; see above, p. 103, n. 47.

Jules Ferry, a penniless barrister before 4 September, contrived, as mayor of Paris during the siege, to job a fortune out of famine. The day on which he would have to give an account of his mal-administration would be the day of his conviction.

These men, then, could find, in the ruins of Paris only, their tickets-of-leave: they were the very men Bismarck wanted. With the help of some shuffling of cards, Thiers, hitherto the secret prompter of the government, now appeared at its head, with the ticket-of-leave men for his ministers.

Thiers, that monstrous gnome, has charmed the French bourgeoisie for almost half a century, because he is the most consummate intellectual expression of their own class-corruption. Before he became a statesman he had already proved his lying powers as a historian. The chronicle of his public life is the record of the misfortunes of France. Banded, before 1830, with the republicans, he slipped into office under Louis Philippe by betraying his protector Laffitte,[14] ingratiating himself with the king by exciting mob riots against the clergy, during which the church of Saint Germain l'Auxerrois and the Archbishop's palace were plundered, and by acting the minister-spy upon, and the jail-*accoucheur* of, the Duchess de Berry.[15] The massacre of the republicans in the rue Transnonain, and the subsequent infamous laws of September against the press and the right of association, were his work.[16] Reappearing as the chief of the Cabinet in March 1840, he astonished France with his plan of fortifying Paris. To the republicans, who denounced this plan as a sinister plot against the liberty of Paris, he replied from the tribune of the Chamber of Deputies:

What! To fancy that any works of fortification could ever endanger liberty! And first of all you calumniate any possible government in supposing that it could some day attempt to maintain itself by bom-

14. Jacques Laffitte was a big banker and Louis Philippe's first Prime Minister (1830–31).

15. The Duchess de Berry was the mother of the Legitimist pretender, the Count de Chambord. In 1831 she attempted to organize a Legitimist revolt, and after its failure went into hiding. She was captured later in the year, and Thiers, as Minister of the Interior, had her officially examined to establish the fact of her pregnancy (she had in fact secretly re-married a minor Italian count) and thus discredit her.

16. A republican rising in April 1834 was suppressed by Thiers to the accompaniment of various atrocities. The September laws were passed in 1835.

barding the capital . . . but that government would be a hundred times more impossible after its victory than before.

Indeed, no government would ever have dared to bombard Paris from the forts, but that government which had previously surrendered these forts to the Prussians.

When King Bomba[17] tried his hand at Palermo, in January 1848, Thiers, then long since out of office, again rose in the Chamber of Deputies:

> You know, gentlemen, what is happening at Palermo. You, all of you, shake with horror (in the parliamentary sense) on hearing that during forty-eight hours a large town has been bombarded – by whom? Was it by a foreign enemy exercising the rights of war? No, gentlemen, it was by its own government. And why? Because that unfortunate town demanded its rights. Well, then, for the demand of its rights it has got forty-eight hours of bombardment . . . Allow me to appeal to the opinion of Europe. It is doing a service to mankind to arise, and to make reverberate, from what is perhaps the greatest tribune in Europe, some words (indeed words) of indignation against such acts . . . When the regent Espartero, who had rendered services to his country (which M. Thiers never did), intended bombarding Barcelona, in order to suppress its insurrection, there arose from all parts of the world a general outcry of indignation.[18]

Eighteen months afterwards, M. Thiers was amongst the fiercest defenders of the bombardment of Rome by a French army.[19] In fact, the fault of King Bomba seems to have consisted in this only, that he limited his bombardment to forty-eight hours.

A few days before the revolution of February, fretting at the long exile from place and pelf to which Guizot[20] had condemned him, and sniffing in the air the scent of an approaching popular commotion, Thiers, in that pseudo-heroic style which won him the nickname of *Mirabeau-mouche*,[21] declared to the Chamber of Deputies:

17. Ferdinand II of Naples acquired his nickname from his bombardments of Palermo in January 1848 and Messina in the autumn of the same year, to suppress the Italian national movement.

18. This is quoted from *Le Moniteur universel*, 1 February 1848.

19. This was in May 1849, to overthrow the Roman republic and restore the temporal power of the Pope. See 'The Class Struggles in France', *Survey from Exile*, p. 85.

20. François Guizot was a historian and Orleanist politician, and Louis Philippe's chief minister from 1840 to 1848.

21. 'The fly-weight Mirabeau', an allusion to the hero of the first French revolution.

I am of the party of revolution, not only in France, but in Europe. I wish the government of the revolution to remain in the hands of moderate men . . . but if that government should fall into the hands of ardent minds, even into those of radicals, I shall, for all that, not desert my cause. I shall always be of the party of the revolution.[22]

The revolution of February came. Instead of displacing the Guizot cabinet by the Thiers cabinet, as the little man had dreamt, it superseded Louis Philippe by the republic. On the first day of the popular victory he carefully hid himself, forgetting that the contempt of the working men screened him from their hatred. Still, with his legendary courage, he continued to shy the public stage, until the June massacres had cleared it for his sort of action. Then he became the leading mind of the 'party of Order'[23] and its parliamentary republic, that anonymous interregnum, in which all the rival factions of the ruling class conspired together to crush the people, and conspired against each other to restore each of them its own monarchy. Then, as now, Thiers denounced the republicans as the only obstacle to the consolidation of the republic; then, as now, he spoke to the republic as the hangman spoke to Don Carlos:[24] 'I shall assassinate thee, but for thy own good.' Now, as then, he will have to exclaim on the day after his victory: *L'empire est fait* – the empire is consummated. Despite his hypocritical homilies about necessary liberties and his personal grudge against Louis Bonaparte, who had made a dupe of him, and kicked out parliamentarism – and outside of its factitious atmosphere the little man is conscious of withering into nothingness – he had a hand in all the infamies of the Second Empire, from the occupation of Rome by French troops to the war with Prussia, which he incited by his fierce invective against German unity – not as a cloak of Prussian despotism, but as an encroachment upon the vested right of France in German disunion. Fond of brandishing, with his dwarfish arms, in the face of Europe the sword of the first Napoleon, whose historical shoe-black he had

22. *Le Moniteur universel*, 3 February 1848.
23. The coalition of Legitimist and Orleanist monarchists, which represented the big bourgeoisie as a whole and was the preponderant force in the short-lived Second Republic of 1848–51. See 'The Class Struggles in France', *Surveys from Exile*, pp. 88–90.
24. The rebellious son of Philip II of Spain. From Schiller's drama *Don Carlos*.

become, his foreign policy always culminated in the utter humiliation of France, from the London Convention of 1840[25] to the Paris capitulation of 1871 and the present civil war, where he hounds on the prisoners of Sedan and Metz[26] against Paris by special permission of Bismarck. Despite his versatility of talent and swiftness of purpose, this man has his whole lifetime been wedded to the most fossil routine. It is self-evident that to him the deeper undercurrents of modern society remained forever hidden; but even the most palpable changes on its surface were abhorrent to a brain all the vitality of which had fled to the tongue. Thus he never tired of denouncing as a sacrilege any deviation from the old French protective system. When a minister of Louis Philippe, he railed at railways as a wild chimera; and when in opposition under Louis Bonaparte, he branded as a profanation every attempt to reform the rotten French army system. Never in his long political career has he been guilty of a single – even the smallest – measure of any practical use. Thiers was consistent only in his greed for wealth and his hatred of the men that produce it. Having entered his first ministry under Louis Philippe poor as Job, he left it a millionaire. His last ministry under the same king (of 1 March 1840) exposed him to public taunts of peculation in the Chamber of Deputies, to which he was content to reply by tears – a commodity he deals in as freely as Jules Favre, or any other crocodile. At Bordeaux[27] his first measure for saving France from impending financial ruin was to endow himself with three millions a year, the first and the last word of the 'economical republic', the vista of which he had opened to his Paris electors in 1869. One of his former colleagues of the Chamber of Deputies of 1830, himself a capitalist and, nevertheless, a devoted member of the Paris

25. The European great powers, with the exclusion of France, signed the London Convention of July 1840 in aid of the Turkish Sultan against the French-supported Egyptian ruler Mohammed Ali, who was resisting Turkish suzerainty. The French government was forced to abandon its support of Mohammed.

26. An entire French army had also surrendered to the Germans at Metz, in October 1870.

27. When the siege of Paris cut the capital off from the rest of France, the Government of National Defence sent Gambetta by balloon across the German lines to establish a governmental delegation at Tours. In January 1871, under pressure from the German advance, the Tours delegation withdrew to Bordeaux, and it was at Bordeaux that the hastily elected National Assembly met soon after the armistice, before moving to Versailles.

Commune, M. Beslay,[28] lately addressed Thiers thus in a public placard:

> The enslavement of labour by capital has always been the cornerstone of your policy, and from the very day you saw the Republic of Labour installed at the Hôtel de Ville, you have never ceased to cry out to France: 'These are criminals!'

A master in small-state roguery, a virtuoso in perjury and treason, a craftsman in all the petty strategems, cunning devices, and base perfidies of parliamentary party-warfare; never scrupling, when out of office, to fan a revolution, and to stifle it in blood when at the helm of the state; with class prejudices standing him in the place of ideas, and vanity in the place of a heart; his private life as infamous as his public life is odious – even now, when playing the part of a French Sulla,[29] he cannot help setting off the abomination of his deeds by the ridicule of his ostentation.

The capitulation of Paris, by surrendering to Prussia not only Paris, but all France, closed the long-continued intrigues of treason with the enemy, which the usurpers of 4 September had begun, as Trochu himself said, on that very same day. On the other hand, it initiated the civil war they were now to wage, with the assistance of Prussia, against the republic and Paris. The trap was laid in the very terms of the capitulation. At that time above one third of the territory was in the hands of the enemy, the capital was cut off from the provinces, all communications were disorganized. To elect under such circumstances a real representation of France was impossible, unless ample time were given for preparation. In view of this, the capitulation stipulated that a National Assembly must be elected within eight days; so that in many parts of France the news of the impending election arrived on its eve only. This assembly, moreover, was, by an express clause of the capitulation, to be elected for the sole purpose of deciding on peace or war, and, eventually, to conclude a treaty of peace. The population could not but feel that the terms of the armistice rendered the continuation of the war impossible, and that for

28. Charles Beslay was a Proudhonist, and a member of the Commune's finance committee. As delegate to the Bank of France, he was especially responsible for the Commune's failure to establish political control over the Bank's activities.

29. The Roman dictator in 82–79 BC, notorious for his brutality towards the people.

sanctioning the peace imposed by Bismarck, the worst men in France were the best. But not content with these precautions, Thiers, even before the secret of the armistice had been broached to Paris, set out for an electioneering tour through the provinces, there to galvanize back into life the Legitimist party,[30] which now, along with the Orleanists, had to take the place of the then impossible Bonapartists. He was not afraid of them. Impossible as a government of modern France, and, therefore, contemptible as rivals, what party were more eligible as tools of counter-revolution than the party whose action, in the words of Thiers himself (Chamber of Deputies, 5 January 1833), 'had always been confined to the three resources of foreign invasion, civil war, and anarchy'?

They verily believed in the advent of their long-expected retrospective millennium. There were the heels of foreign invasion trampling upon France; there was the downfall of an empire, and the captivity of a Bonaparte; and there they were themselves. The wheel of history had evidently rolled back to stop at the *Chambre introuvable* of 1816.[31] In the Assemblies of the Republic, 1848 to 1851, they had been represented by their educated and trained parliamentary champions; it was the rank-and-file of the party which now rushed in – all the Pourceaugnacs[32] of France.

As soon as this Assembly of 'Rurals' had met at Bordeaux, Thiers made it clear to them that the peace preliminaries must be assented to at once, without even the honours of a parliamentary debate, as the only condition on which Prussia would permit them to open the war against the republic and Paris, its stronghold. The counter-revolution had, in fact, no time to lose. The Second Empire had more than doubled the national debt, and plunged all the large towns into heavy municipal debts. The war had fearfully swelled the liabilities, and mercilessly ravaged the resources of the nation. To complete the ruin, the Prussian Shylock was there with his bond for the keep of half a million of his soldiers on French soil, his indemnity of five milliards, and interest at

30. The Legitimists were the supporters of the elder branch of the French royal family, driven from the throne for the second and last time in 1830 in the person of Charles X. They represented the large landed proprietors. On the Orleanists see above, p. 185, n. 23.

31. The 'matchless' Chamber of 1815–16 was matchless only in its rabid reaction.

32. After Molière's Monsieur de Pourceaugnac, the typical philistine landed proprietor.

five per cent on the unpaid instalments thereof.[33] Who was to pay the bill? It was only by the violent overthrow of the republic that the appropriators of wealth could hope to shift on the shoulders of its producers the cost of a war which they, the appropriators, had themselves originated. Thus, the immense ruin of France spurred on these patriotic representatives of land and capital, under the very eyes and patronage of the invader, to graft upon the foreign war a civil war – a slaveholders' rebellion.

There stood in the way of this conspiracy one great obstacle – Paris. To disarm Paris was the first condition of success. Paris was therefore summoned by Thiers to surrender its arms. Then Paris was exasperated by the frantic anti-republican demonstrations of the 'Rural' Assembly and by Thiers's own equivocations about the legal status of the republic; by the threat to decapitate and decapitalize Paris; the appointment of Orleanist ambassadors; Dufaure's laws on overdue commercial bills and house-rents,[34] inflicting ruin on the commerce and industry of Paris; Pouyer-Quertier's[35] tax of two centimes upon every copy of every imaginable publication; the sentences of death against Blanqui and Flourens;[36] the suppression of the republican journals; the transfer of the National Assembly to Versailles; the renewal of the state of siege declared by Palikao,[37] and expired on 4 September; the appointment of Vinoy,[38] the *Décembriseur*, as governor of Paris – of Valentin,[39] the Imperialist *gendarme*,

33. The preliminary peace treaty signed at Versailles on 26 February ceded to the new German Reich Alsace and eastern Lorraine, and provided that France was to pay a war indemnity of five milliard francs. The final peace treaty was signed at Frankfurt on 10 May.

34. Jules Dufaure was an advocate and Orleanist politician, and Minister of Justice in 1871. The *loi Dufaure* of 10 March 1871 failed to provide the moratorium needed for the majority of those indebted as a result of the war and the siege of Paris.

35. Augustin Pouyer-Quertier was a large manufacturer, and Minister of Finance in 1871.

36. Gustave Flourens was a follower of Blanqui and a martyr of the Commune. Blanqui, who was imprisoned after the attempted insurrection of 31 October 1870, and Flourens, who organized the further attempt of 22 January 1871, were sentenced to death for their part in these actions.

37. Charles Cousin-Montauban, Count de Palikao, was a Bonapartist general, Minister of War and head of government in August–September 1870.

38. Joseph Vinoy was a general who had helped to organize Louis Bonaparte's coup d'état of December 1851.

39. Louis Valentin was another Bonapartist general.

as its prefect of police – and of d'Aurelle de Paladines,[40] the Jesuit general, as the commander-in-chief of its National Guard.

And now we have to address a question to M. Thiers and the men of national defence, his under-strappers. It is known that, through the agency of M. Pouyer-Quertier, his finance minister, Thiers had contracted a loan of two milliards. Now, is it true, or not –

1. That the business was so managed that a consideration of several hundred millions was secured for the private benefit of Thiers, Jules Favre, Ernest Picard, Pouyer-Quertier, and Jules Simon?[41] and –

2. That no money was to be paid down until after the 'pacification' of Paris?[42]

At all events, there must have been something very pressing in the matter, for Thiers and Jules Favre, in the name of the majority of the Bordeaux Assembly, unblushingly solicited the immediate occupation of Paris by Prussian troops. Such, however, was not the game of Bismarck, as he sneeringly, and in public, told the admiring Frankfurt[43] philistines on his return to Germany.

II

Armed Paris was the only serious obstacle in the way of the counter-revolutionary conspiracy. Paris was, therefore, to be disarmed. On this point the Bordeaux Assembly was sincerity itself. If the roaring rant of its Rurals had not been audible enough, the surrender of Paris by Thiers to the tender mercies of the triumvirate of Vinoy the *Décembriseur*, Valentin the Bonapartist *gendarme*, and d'Aurelle de Paladines the Jesuit general, would have cut off even the last subterfuge of doubt. But while insultingly exhibiting the true purpose of the disarmament of Paris, the conspirators asked her to lay down her arms on a

40. Louis d'Aurelle de Paladines was a supporter of the clericalist Legitimist party.

41. Jules Simon was a Republican politician, and Minister of Public Instruction in the Government of National Defence and Thiers's government of 1871.

42. These accusations against Thiers and his friends were made in the Communard press; Thiers himself admitted later that the prospective financiers were pressing for the rapid suppression of the Commune. The loan bill was passed by the National Assembly on 20 June 1871.

43. A reference to the German Federal Diet at Frankfurt, transformed by the new constitution of the German Reich into the Federal Council.

pretext which was the most glaring, the most barefaced of lies. The artillery of the Paris National Guard, said Thiers, belonged to the state, and to the state it must be returned. The fact was this: From the very day of the capitulation, by which Bismarck's prisoners had signed the surrender of France, but reserved to themselves a numerous bodyguard for the express purpose of cowing Paris, Paris stood on the watch. The National Guard reorganized themselves and entrusted their supreme control to a Central Committee elected by their whole body, save some fragments of the old Bonapartist formations.[44] On the eve of the entrance of the Prussians into Paris, the Central Committee took measures for the removal to Montmartre, Belleville, and La Villette of the cannon and mitrailleuses treacherously abandoned by the *capitulards* in and about the very quarters the Prussians were to occupy. That artillery had been furnished by the subscriptions of the National Guard. As their private property, it was officially recognized in the capitulation of 28 January, and on that very title exempted from the general surrender, into the hands of the conqueror, of arms belonging to the government. And Thiers was so utterly destitute of even the flimsiest pretext for initiating the war against Paris, that he had to resort to the flagrant lie of the artillery of the National Guard being state property!

The seizure of her artillery was evidently but to serve as the preliminary to the general disarmament of Paris, and, therefore, of the revolution of 4 September. But that revolution had become the legal status of France. The republic, its work, was recognized by the conqueror in the terms of the capitulation. After the capitulation, it was acknowledged by all the foreign powers, and in its name the National Assembly had been summoned. The Paris working men's revolution of 4 September was the only legal title of the National Assembly seated at Bordeaux, and of its executive. Without it, the National Assembly would at once have to give way to the Corps Législatif, elected in 1869, by universal suffrage under French, not under Prussian, rule, and forcibly dispersed by the arm of the revolution. Thiers and his ticket-

44. The Central Committee of the National Guard was elected by 215 out of 270 battalions, almost entirely working class or petty-bourgeois in composition, which formed themselves on 3 March 1870 into the Republican Federation of the National Guard. The Commune's soldiers were hence known as *fédérés* (Federals).

of-leave men would have had to capitulate for safe conducts signed by Louis Bonaparte, to save them from a voyage to Cayenne.[45] The National Assembly, with its power of attorney to settle the terms of peace with Prussia, was but an incident of that revolution, the true embodiment of which was still armed Paris, which had initiated it, undergone for it a five months' siege, with its horrors of famine, and made her prolonged resistance, despite Trochu's plan, the basis of an obstinate war of defence in the provinces. And Paris was now either to lay down her arms at the insulting behest of the rebellious slaveholders of Bordeaux, and acknowledge that her revolution of 4 September meant nothing but a simple transfer of power from Louis Bonaparte to his royal rivals; or she had to stand forward as the self-sacrificing champion of France, whose salvation from ruin, and whose regeneration were impossible, without the revolutionary overthrow of the political and social conditions that had engendered the Second Empire, and, under its fostering care, matured into utter rottenness. Paris, emaciated by a five months' famine, did not hesitate one moment. She heroically resolved to run all the hazards of a resistance against the French conspirators, even with Prussian cannon frowning upon her from her own forts. Still, in its abhorrence of the civil war into which Paris was to be goaded, the Central Committee continued to persist in a merely defensive attitude, despite the provocations of the Assembly, the usurpations of the executive, and the menacing concentration of troops in and around Paris.

Thiers opened the civil war by sending Vinoy, at the head of a multitude of *sergents-de-ville*[46] and some regiments of the line, upon a nocturnal expedition against Montmartre, there to seize, by surprise, the artillery of the National Guard. It is well known how this attempt broke down before the resistance of the National Guard and the fraternization of the line with the people.[47] Aurelle de Paladines had printed beforehand his bulletin of victory, and Thiers held ready the placards announcing his measures of coup d'état. Now these had to be replaced by Thiers's appeals, imparting his magnanimous resolve to leave

45. The penal settlement in French Guiana.
46. Police constables.
47. The women of Montmartre prevailed on the rank-and-file soldiers not to fire on the people, and thus assured the bloodless victory of the revolution of 18 March.

the National Guard in the possession of their arms, with which, he said, he felt sure they would rally round the government against the rebels. Out of 300,000 National Guards only 300 responded to this summons to rally round little Thiers against themselves. The glorious working men's revolution of 18 March took undisputed sway of Paris. The Central Committee was its provisional government. Europe seemed, for a moment, to doubt whether its recent sensational performances of state and war had any reality in them, or whether they were the dreams of a long bygone past.

From 18 March to the entrance of the Versailles troops into Paris, the proletarian revolution remained so free from the acts of violence in which the revolutions, and still more the counter-revolutions, of the 'better classes' abound, that no facts were left to its opponents to cry out about but the execution of Generals Lecomte and Clément Thomas, and the affair of the Place Vendôme.

One of the Bonapartist officers engaged in the nocturnal attempt against Montmartre, General Lecomte, had four times ordered the 81st line regiment to fire at an unarmed gathering in the Place Pigalle, and on their refusal fiercely insulted them. Instead of shooting women and children, his own men shot him. The inveterate habits acquired by the soldiery under the training of the enemies of the working class are, of course, not likely to change the very moment these soldiers changed sides. The same men executed Clément Thomas.

'General' Clément Thomas, a malcontent ex-quartermaster-sergeant, had, in the latter times of Louis Philippe's reign, enlisted at the office of the republican newspaper *Le National*, there to serve in the double capacity of responsible man-of-straw (*gérant responsable*) and of duelling bully to that very combative journal. After the revolution of February, the men of *Le National* having got into power, they metamorphosed this old quartermaster-sergeant into a general on the eve of the butchery of June, of which he, like Jules Favre, was one of the sinister plotters, and became one of the most dastardly executioners. Then he and his generalship disappeared for a long time, to again rise to the surface on 1 November 1870. The day before, the Government of Defence, caught at the Hôtel de Ville, had solemnly pledged their parole to Blanqui, Flourens and other representatives of the working class, to abdicate their usurped power into the hands of a

Commune to be freely elected by Paris. Instead of keeping their word, they let loose on Paris the Bretons of Trochu, who now replaced the Corsicans of Bonaparte.[48] General Tamisier alone, refusing to sully his name by such a breach of faith, resigned the commandership-in-chief of the National Guard, and in his place Clément Thomas for once became again a general. During the whole of his tenure of command, he made war, not upon the Prussians, but upon the Paris National Guard. He prevented their general armament, pitted the bourgeois battalions against the working men's battalions, weeded out the officers hostile to Trochu's 'plan', and disbanded, under the stigma of cowardice, the very same proletarian battalions whose heroism has now astonished their most inveterate enemies. Clément Thomas felt quite proud of having reconquered his June pre-eminence as the personal enemy of the working class of Paris. Only a few days before 18 March, he laid before the War Minister, Le Flô, a plan of his own for 'finishing off *la fine fleur* (the cream) of the Paris *canaille*'. After Vinoy's rout, he must needs appear upon the scene of action in the quality of an amateur spy. The Central Committee and the Paris working men were as much responsible for the killing of Clément Thomas and Lecomte as the Princess of Wales was for the fate of the people crushed to death on the day of her entrance into London.

The massacre of unarmed citizens in the Place Vendôme is a myth which M. Thiers and the Rurals persistently ignored in the Assembly, entrusting its propagation exclusively to the servants' hall of European journalism. 'The men of order', the reactionists of Paris, trembled at the victory of 18 March. To them it was the signal of popular retribution at last arriving. The ghosts of the victims assassinated at their hands from the days of June 1848 down to 22 January 1871,[49] arose before their faces. Their panic was their only punishment. Even the *sergents-de-ville*, instead of being disarmed and locked up, as ought to have been done, had the gates of Paris flung wide open for their safe retreat to Versailles.

---

48. On 31 October 1870, after the defeat of the French army and the rumours of capitulationist plans, Blanqui and his followers attempted to force the resignation of the Government of National Defence. The attempt was defeated by the middle-class sections of the National Guard, and by the Breton Mobile Guard, whom Trochu used to police Paris. Louis Napoleon had relied on similarly backward Corsicans.

49. The second attempted insurrection by the Blanquists during the siege of Paris was the signal for the violent suppression of the popular movement.

The men of order were left not only unharmed, but allowed to rally and quietly to seize more than one stronghold in the very centre of Paris. This indulgence of the Central Committee – this magnanimity of the armed working men – so strangely at variance with the habits of the 'party of Order', the latter misinterpreted as mere symptoms of conscious weakness. Hence their silly plan to try, under the cloak of an unarmed demonstration, what Vinoy had failed to perform with his cannon and mitrailleuses. On 22 March a riotous mob of swells started from the quarters of luxury, all the *petits crevés*[50] in their ranks, and at their head the notorious familiars of the Empire – the Heeckeren, Coëtlogon, Henri de Pène, etc. Under the cowardly pretence of a pacific demonstration, this rabble, secretly armed with the weapons of the bravo, fell into marching order, ill-treated and disarmed the detached patrols and sentries of the National Guards they met with on their progress, and, on debouching from the rue de la Paix, with the cry of 'Down with the Central Committee! Down with the assassins! The National Assembly for ever!' attempted to break through the line drawn up there, and thus to carry by surprise the headquarters of the National Guard in the Place Vendôme. In reply to their pistol-shots, the regular *sommations* (the French equivalent of the English Riot Act) were made, and, proving ineffective, fire was commanded by the general of the National Guard.[51] One volley dispersed into wild flight the silly coxcombs, who expected that the mere exhibition of their 'respectability' would have the same effect upon the revolution of Paris as Joshua's trumpets upon the wall of Jericho. The runaways left behind them two National Guards killed, nine severely wounded (among them a member of the Central Committee[52]), and the whole scene of their exploit strewn with revolvers, daggers, and sword-canes, in evidence of the 'unarmed' character of their 'pacific' demonstration. When, on 13 June 1849, the National Guard made a really pacific demonstration in protest against the felonious assault of French troops upon Rome,[53] Changarnier, then general of the party of Order, was acclaimed by the National Assembly, and especially by M. Thiers, as the saviour of society, for having launched his

50. Fops.
51. Jules Bergeret, a member of the Paris Commune.
52. Maljournal, also a member of the International.
53. See 'The Class Struggles in France', *Surveys from Exile*, pp. 94–100.

troops from all sides upon these unarmed men, to shoot and sabre them down, and to trample them under their horses' feet. Paris, then, was placed under a state of siege. Dufaure hurried through the Assembly new laws of repression. New arrests, new proscriptions – a new reign of terror set in. But the lower orders manage these things otherwise. The Central Committee of 1871 simply ignored the heroes of the 'pacific demonstration'; so much so that only two days later they were enabled to muster under Admiral Saisset for that *armed* demonstration, crowned by the famous stampede to Versailles. In their reluctance to continue the civil war opened by Thiers's burglarious attempt on Montmartre, the Central Committee made itself, this time, guilty of a decisive mistake in not at once marching upon Versailles, then completely helpless, and thus putting an end to the conspiracies of Thiers and his Rurals. Instead of this, the party of Order was again allowed to try its strength at the ballot box, on 26 March, the day of the election of the Commune. Then, in the *mairies* of Paris, they exchanged bland words of conciliation with their too generous conquerors, muttering in their hearts solemn vows to exterminate them in due time.

Now look at the reverse of the medal. Thiers opened his second campaign against Paris in the beginning of April. The first batch of Parisian prisoners brought into Versailles was subjected to revolting atrocities, while Ernest Picard, with his hands in his trouser pockets, strolled about jeering them, and while Mesdames Thiers and Favre, in the midst of their ladies of honour (?), applauded, from the balcony, the outrages of the Versailles mob. The captured soldiers of the line were massacred in cold blood; our brave friend General Duval,[54] the iron-founder, was shot without any form of trial. Galliffet, the kept man of his wife, so notorious for her shameless exhibitions at the orgies of the Second Empire, boasted in a proclamation of having commanded the murder of a small troop of National Guards, with their captain and lieutenant, surprised and disarmed by his Chasseurs. Vinoy, the runaway, was appointed by Thiers Grand Cross of the Legion of Honour, for his general order to shoot down every soldier of the line taken in the ranks of the Federals. Desmarest, the gendarme, was decorated for the treacherous butcher-like chopping in pieces of the high-souled and chivalrous Flourens,

54. Émile Duval, a general of the National Guard, was an iron-founder, a member of the International and of the Paris Commune.

who had saved the heads of the Government of Defence on 31 October 1870. 'The encouraging particulars' of his assassination were triumphantly expatiated upon by Thiers in the National Assembly. With the elated vanity of a parliamentary Tom Thumb, permitted to play the part of a Tamerlane, he denied the rebels against his littleness every right of civilized warfare, up to the right of neutrality for ambulances. Nothing more horrid than that monkey, allowed for a time to give full fling to his tigerish instincts, as foreseen by Voltaire.[55] (See note I [pp. 233–4].)

After the decree of the Commune of 7 April, ordering reprisals and declaring it to be its duty 'to protect Paris against the cannibal exploits of the Versailles banditti, and to demand an eye for an eye, a tooth for a tooth',[56] Thiers did not stop the barbarous treatment of prisoners, moreover insulting them in his bulletins as follows: 'Never have more degraded countenances of a degraded democracy met the afflicted gazes of honest men' – honest like Thiers himself and his ministerial ticket-of-leave men. Still the shooting of prisoners was suspended for a time. Hardly, however, had Thiers and his Decembrist generals become aware that the Communal decree of reprisals was but an empty threat, that even their gendarme spies caught in Paris under the disguise of National Guards, that even *sergents-de-ville*, taken with incendiary shells upon them, were spared – when the wholesale shooting of prisoners was resumed and carried on uninterruptedly to the end. Houses to which National Guards had fled were surrounded by gendarmes, inundated with petroleum (which here occurs for the first time in this war), and then set fire to, the charred corpses being afterwards brought out by the ambulance of the press at the Ternes. Four National Guards having surrendered to a troop of mounted Chasseurs at Belle Épine, on 25 April, were afterwards shot down, one after another, by the captain, a worthy man of Galliffet's. One of his four victims, left for dead, Scheffer, crawled back to the Parisian outposts, and deposed to this fact before a commission of the Commune. When Tolain interpellated the War Minister upon the report of this commission, the Rurals drowned his voice and forbade Le Flô to answer. It would be an insult to their 'glorious' army to speak of its deeds. The flippant

55. In *Candide*, ch. 22.
56. The decree of reprisals was in fact adopted on 5 April. It provided for the killing of selected hostages in return for Communards executed by the Versaillais.

tone in which Thiers's bulletins announced the bayoneting of the Federals surprised asleep at Moulin Saquet, and the wholesale fusillades at Clamart shocked the nerves even of the not over-sensitive London *Times*. But it would be ludicrous today to attempt recounting the merely preliminary atrocities committed by the bombarders of Paris and the fomenters of a slaveholders' rebellion protected by foreign invasion. Amidst all these horrors, Thiers, forgetful of his parliamentary laments on the terrible responsibility weighing down his dwarfish shoulders, boasts in his bulletins that *l'Assemblée siège paisiblement* (the Assembly continues meeting in peace), and proves by his constant carousals, now with Decembrist generals, now with German princes, that his digestion is not troubled in the least, not even by the ghosts of Lecomte and Clément Thomas.

III

On the dawn of 18 March, Paris arose to the thunderburst of *'Vive la Commune!'* What is the Commune, that sphinx so tantalizing to the bourgeois mind? 'The proletarians of Paris,' said the Central Committee in its manifesto of 18 March,

amidst the failures and treasons of the ruling classes, have understood that the hour has struck for them to save the situation by taking into their own hands the direction of public affairs . . . They have understood that it is their imperious duty and their absolute right to render themselves masters of their own destinies, by seizing upon the governmental power.

But the working class cannot simply lay hold of the readymade state machinery, and wield it for its own purposes.

The centralized state power, with its ubiquitous organs of standing army, police, bureaucracy, clergy, and judicature – organs wrought after the plan of a systematic and hierarchic division of labour –originatesfromthedaysofabsolutemonarchy,servingnascentmiddle-lass society as a mighty weapon in its struggles against feudalism. Still, its development remained clogged by all manner of medieval rubbish, seignorial rights, local privileges, municipal and guild monopolies and provincial constitutions. The gigantic broom of the French revolution of the eighteenth century swept away all these relics of bygone times, thus clearing simultaneously the social soil of its last hindrances to the superstructure of the modern state edifice raised under the First Empire, itself the offspring of the coalition wars of old semi-feudal Europe against modern France. During the subsequent regimes the government, placed under parliamentary control – that is, under the direct control of the propertied classes – became not only a hotbed of huge national debts and crushing taxes; with its irresistible allurements of place, pelf, and patronage, it became not only the bone of contention between the rival factions and adventurers of the ruling classes; but its political character changed simultaneously with the economic changes of society. At the same pace at which the progress of modern industry developed, widened, intensified the class antagonism between capital and labour, the state power assumed more and more the character of the national power of capital over labour, of a public force organized for social enslavement, of an engine of class despotism. After every revolution marking a progressive phase in the class struggle, the purely repressive character of the state power stands out in bolder and bolder relief. The revolution of 1830, resulting in the transfer of government from the landlords to the capitalists, transferred it from the more remote to the more direct antagonists of the working men. The bourgeois republicans, who, in the name of the revolution of February [1848], took the state power, used it for the June massacres, in order to convince the working class that 'social' republic meant the republic ensuring their social subjection, and in order to convince the royalist bulk of the bourgeois and landlord class that they might safely leave the cares and emoluments of government to the bourgeois 'republicans'. However, after their one heroic exploit of June, the bourgeois republicans had, from the front, to fall back to the rear of the 'party of Order' – a combination formed by all the rival fractions and factions of the appropriating class in their now openly declared antagonism to the producing classes. The proper form of their joint-stock government was the *parliamentary republic*, with Louis Bonaparte for its President. Theirs was a regime of avowed class terrorism and deliberate insult toward the 'vile multitude'. If the parliamentary republic, as M. Thiers said, 'divided them' (the different fractions of the ruling class) 'least', it opened an abyss between that class and the whole body of society outside their spare ranks. The restraints by which their own divisions had under former regimes still checked the state power, were removed by their union; and in view of the threatening upheaval of the proletariat, they now used that state power mercilessly and ostentatiously as the national war-engine of capital against labour. In their uninterrupted crusade against the producing masses they were, however, bound not only to invest the executive with continually increased powers of repression, but at the same time to divest their own parliamentary stronghold – the National Assembly – one by one, of all its own means of defence against the executive. The executive, in the person of Louis Bonaparte, turned them out. The natural offspring of the 'party-of-Order' republic was the Second Empire.

The Empire, with the coup d'état for its certificate of birth, universal suffrage for its sanction, and the sword for its sceptre, professed to rest upon the peasantry, the large mass of producers not directly involved in the struggle of capital and labour. It professed to save the working class by breaking down parliamentarism, and, with it, the undisguised subserviency of government to the propertied classes. It professed to save the propertied classes by upholding their economic supremacy over the working class; and, finally, it professed to unite all classes by reviving for all the chimera of national glory. In reality, it was the only form of government possible at a time when the bourgeoisie had already lost, and the working class had not yet acquired, the faculty of ruling the nation. It was acclaimed throughout the world as the saviour of society. Under its sway, bourgeois society, freed from political cares, attained a development unexpected even by itself. Its industry and commerce expanded to colossal dimensions; financial swindling celebrated cosmopolitan orgies; the misery of the masses was set off by a shameless display of gorgeous, meretricious and debased luxury. The state power, apparently soaring high above society, was at the same time itself the greatest scandal of that society and the very hotbed of all its corruptions. Its own rottenness, and the rottenness of the society it had saved, were laid bare by the bayonet of Prussia, herself eagerly bent upon transferring the supreme seat of that regime from Paris to Berlin. Imperialism is, at the same time, the most prostitute and the ultimate form of the state power which nascent middle-class society had commenced to elaborate as a means of its own emancipation from feudalism, and which full-grown bourgeois society had finally transformed into a means for the enslavement of labour by capital.

The direct antithesis to the Empire was the Commune. The cry of 'social republic', with which the revolution of February was ushered in by the Paris proletariat, did but express a vague aspiration after a republic that was not only to supersede the monarchical form of class rule, but class rule itself. The Commune was the positive form of that republic.

Paris, the central seat of the old governmental power, and, at the same time, the social stronghold of the French working class, had risen in arms against the attempt of Thiers and the Rurals to restore and perpetuate that old governmental power bequeathed to them by the Empire. Paris could resist only because, in consequence of the siege, it had got rid of the army, and replaced it by a National Guard, the bulk of which consisted of working men. This fact was now to be transformed into an institution. The first decree of the Commune, therefore, was the suppression of the standing army, and the substitution for it of the armed people.

The Commune was formed of the municipal councillors, chosen by universal suffrage in the various wards of the town, responsible and revocable at short terms. The majority of its members were naturally working men, or acknowledged representatives of the working class. The Commune was to be a working, not a parliamentary body, executive and legislative at the same time. Instead of continuing to be the agent of the central government, the police was at once stripped of its political attributes, and turned into the responsible and at all times revocable agent of the Commune. So were the officials of all other branches of the administration. From the members of the Commune downwards, the public service had to be done at *workmen's wages*. The vested interests and the representation allowances of the high dignitaries of state disappeared along with the high dignitaries themselves. Public functions ceased to be the private property of the tools of the central government. Not only municipal administration, but the whole initiative hitherto exercised by the state was laid into the hands of the Commune.

Having once got rid of the standing army and the police, the physical force elements of the old government, the Commune was anxious to break the spiritual force of repression, the 'parson-power', by the disestablishment and disendowment of all churches as proprietary bodies. The priests were sent back to the recesses of private life, there to feed upon the alms of the faithful in imitation of their predecessors, the apostles. The whole of the educational institutions were opened to the people gratuitously, and at the same time cleared of all interference of church and state. Thus, not only was education made accessible to all, but science itself freed from the fetters which class prejudice and governmental force had imposed upon it.

The judicial functionaries were to be divested of that sham independence which had but served to mask their abject subserviency to all succeeding governments to which, in turn, they had taken, and broken, the oaths of allegiance. Like the rest of public servants, magistrates and judges were to be elective, responsible, and revocable.

The Paris Commune was, of course, to serve as a model to all the great industrial centres of France. The communal regime once established in Paris and the secondary centres, the old centralized government would in the provinces, too, have to give way to the self-government of the producers. In a rough sketch of national organization which the Commune had no time to develop, it states clearly that the commune was to be the political form of even the smallest country hamlet, and that in the rural districts the standing army was to be replaced by a national militia, with an extremely short term of service. The rural communes of every district were to administer their common affairs by an assembly of delegates in the central town, and these district assemblies were again to send deputies to the national delegation in Paris, each delegate to be at any time revocable and bound by the *mandat impératif* (formal instructions) of his constituents. The few but important functions which still would remain for a central government were not to be suppressed, as has been intentionally misstated, but were to be discharged by Communal, and therefore strictly responsible agents. The unity of the nation was not to be broken, but, on the contrary, to be organized by the Communal constitution and to become a reality by the destruction of the state power which claimed to be the embodiment of that unity independent of, and superior to, the nation itself, from which it was but a parasitic excrescence. While the merely repressive organs of the old governmental power were to be amputated, its legitimate functions were to be wrested from an authority usurping pre-eminence over society itself, and restored to the responsible agents of society. Instead of deciding once in three or six years which member of the ruling class was to misrepresent the people in parliament, universal suffrage was to serve the people, constituted in communes, as individual suffrage serves every other employer in the search for the workmen and managers in his business. And it is well known that companies, like individuals, in matters of real business generally know how to put the right man in the right place, and, if they for once make a mistake, to redress it promptly. On the other hand, nothing could be more foreign to the spirit of the Commune than to supersede universal suffrage by hierarchic investiture.

It is generally the fate of completely new historical creations to be mistaken for the counterpart of older and even defunct forms of social life, to which they may bear a certain likeness. Thus, this new Commune, which breaks the modern state power, has been mistaken for a reproduction of the medieval communes, which first preceded, and afterwards became the substratum of, that very state power. The Communal constitution has been mistaken for an attempt to break up into a federation of small states, as dreamt of by Montesquieu and the Girondins,[57] that unity of great nations which, if originally brought about by political force, has now become a powerful coefficient of social production. The antagonism of the Commune against the state power has been mistaken for an exaggerated form of the ancient struggle against over-centralization. Peculiar historical circumstances may have prevented the classical development, as in France, of the bourgeois form of government, and may have allowed, as in England, to complete the great central state organs by corrupt vestries, jobbing councillors, and ferocious poor-law guardians in the towns, and virtually hereditary magistrates in the counties. The Communal constitution would have restored to the social body all the forces hitherto absorbed by the state parasite feeding upon, and clogging the free movement of, society. By this one act it would have initiated the regeneration of France. The provincial French middle class saw in the Commune an attempt to restore the sway their order had held over the country under Louis Philippe, and which, under Louis Napoleon, was supplanted by the pretended rule of the country over the towns. In reality, the Communal constitution brought the rural producers under the intellectual lead of the central towns of their districts, and these secured to them, in the working men, the natural trustees of their interests. The very existence of the Commune involved, as a matter of course, local municipal liberty, but no longer as a check upon the, now superseded, state power. It could only enter into the head of a Bismarck, who, when not engaged on his intrigues of blood and iron, always likes to resume his old trade, so befitting his mental

57. The party of the big bourgeoisie during the first French revolution.

calibre, of contributor to *Kladderadatsch* (the Berlin *Punch*), it could only enter into such a head, to ascribe to the Paris Commune aspirations after that caricature of the old French municipal organization of 1791, the Prussian municipal constitution which degrades the town governments to mere secondary wheels in the police machinery of the Prussian state.

The Commune made that catchword of bourgeois revolutions, cheap government, a reality, by destroying the two greatest sources of expenditure – the standing army and state functionarism. Its very existence presupposed the non-existence of monarchy, which, in Europe at least, is the normal incumbrance and indispensable cloak of class rule. It supplied the republic with the basis of really democratic institutions. But neither cheap government nor the 'true republic' was its ultimate aim; they were its mere concomitants.

The multiplicity of interpretations to which the Commune has been subjected, and the multiplicity of interests which construed it in their favour, show that it was a thoroughly expansive political form, while all previous forms of government had been emphatically repressive. Its true secret was this. It was essentially a working-class government, the produce of the struggle of the producing against the appropriating class, the political form at last discovered under which to work out the economical emancipation of labour.

Except on this last condition, the Communal constitution would have been an impossibility and a delusion. The political rule of the producer cannot coexist with the perpetuation of his social slavery. The Commune was therefore to serve as a lever for uprooting the economical foundations upon which rests the existence of classes, and therefore of class rule. With labour emancipated, every man becomes a working man, and productive labour ceases to be a class attribute.

It is a strange fact. In spite of all the tall talk and all the immense literature, for the last sixty years, about emancipation of labour, no sooner do the working men anywhere take the subject into their own hands with a will, than up rises at once all the apologetic phraseology of the mouthpieces of present society with its two poles of capital and wage slavery (the landlord now is but the sleeping partner of the capitalist), as if capitalist society was still in its purest state of virgin innocence, with its antagonisms still undeveloped, with its delusions still unexploded, with its prostitute realities not yet laid bare. The Commune, they exclaim, intends to abolish property, the basis of all civilization! Yes, gentlemen, the Commune intended to abolish that class property which makes the labour of the many the wealth of the few. It aimed at the expropriation of the expropriators. It wanted to make individual property a truth by transforming the means of production, land and capital, now chiefly the means of enslaving and exploiting labour, into mere instruments of free and associated labour. But this is communism, 'impossible' communism! Why, those members of the ruling classes who are intelligent enough to perceive the impossibility of continuing the present system – and they are many – have become the obtrusive and full-mouthed apostles of cooperative production. If cooperative production is not to remain a sham and a snare; if it is to supersede the capitalist system; if united cooperative societies are to regulate national production upon a common plan, thus taking it under their own control, and putting an end to the constant anarchy and periodical convulsions which are the fatality of capitalist production – what else, gentlemen, would it be but communism, 'possible' communism?

The working class did not expect miracles from the Commune. They have no ready-made utopias to introduce *par décret du peuple*.[58] They know that in order to work out their own emancipation, and along with it that higher form to which present society is irresistibly tending by its own economical agencies, they will have to pass through long struggles, through a series of historic processes, transforming circumstances and men. They have no ideals to realize, but to set free the elements of the new society with which old collapsing bourgeois society itself is pregnant. In the full consciousness of their historic mission, and with the heroic resolve to act up to it, the working class can afford to smile at the coarse invective of the gentlemen's gentlemen with the pen and inkhorn, and at the didactic patronage of well-wishing bourgeois doctrinaires, pouring forth their ignorant platitudes and sectarian crotchets in the oracular tone of scientific infallibility.

When the Paris Commune took the management of the revolution in its own hands; when plain working men for the first time dared to infringe upon the governmental privilege of their 'natural superiors', and, under circumstances of unexampled difficulty, performed their work modestly, conscientiously, and efficiently –

58. By decree of the people.

performed it at salaries the highest of which barely amounted to one fifth of what, according to high scientific authority,[59] is the minimum required for a secretary to a certain metropolitan school board – the old world writhed in convulsions of rage at the sight of the red flag, the symbol of the republic of labour, floating over the Hôtel de Ville.

And yet, this was the first revolution in which the working class was openly acknowledged as the only class capable of social initiative, even by the great bulk of the Paris middle class – shopkeepers, tradesmen, merchants – the wealthy capitalists alone excepted. The Commune had saved them by a sagacious settlement of that ever-recurring cause of dispute among the middle classes themselves – the debtor and creditor accounts.[60] The same portion of the middle class, after they had assisted in putting down the working men's insurrection of June 1848, had been at once unceremoniously sacrificed to their creditors by the then Constituent Assembly.[61] But this was not their only motive for now rallying round the working class. They felt that there was but one alternative – the Commune, or the Empire – under whatever name it might reappear. The Empire had ruined them economically by the havoc it made of public wealth, by the wholesale financial swindling it fostered, by the props it lent to the artificially accelerated centralization of capital, and the concomitant expropriation of their own ranks. It had suppressed them politically, it had shocked them morally by its orgies, it had insulted their Voltaireanism by handing over the education of their children to the *frères ignorantins*,[62] it had revolted their national feeling as Frenchmen by precipitating them headlong into a war which left only one equivalent for the ruins it made – the disappearance of the Empire. In fact, after the exodus from Paris of the high Bonapartist and capitalist *bohème*, the true middle-class party of Order came out in the shape of the 'Union Républicaine',[63] enrolling themselves

59. Professor Huxley [note by Marx to the German edition of 1871].

60. On 16 April 1871 the Commune decreed a three-year moratorium on all debts incurred as a result of the war, and the cancellation of interest payments.

61. This refers to the rejection of the *concordats à l'amiable* on 22 August 1848; see 'The Class Struggles in France', *Surveys from Exile*, pp. 66–7.

62. The Brothers Ignoramus were an actual Catholic religious order. Marx uses the term here, however, to allude more generally to the clerical and obscurantist character of education under the Second Empire.

63. This was in fact the Alliance Républicaine des Départements, a petty-bourgeois group of provincial representatives in Paris loyal to the Commune.

under the colours of the Commune and defending it against the wilful misconstruction of Thiers. Whether the gratitude of this great body of the middle class will stand the present severe trial, time must show.

The Commune was perfectly right in telling the peasants that 'its victory was their only hope'.[64] Of all the lies hatched at Versailles and re-echoed by the glorious European penny-a-liner, one of the most tremendous was that the Rurals represented the French peasantry. Think only of the love of the French peasant for the men to whom, after 1815, he had to pay the milliard of indemnity![65] In the eyes of the French peasant, the very existence of a great landed proprietor is in itself an encroachment on his conquests of 1789. The bourgeois, in 1848, had burdened his plot of land with the additional tax of forty-five cents in the franc;[66] but then he did so in the name of the revolution; while now he had fomented a civil war against the revolution, to shift on to the peasant's shoulders the chief load of the five milliards of indemnity to be paid to the Prussian. The Commune, on the other hand, in one of its first proclamations, declared that the true originators of the war would be made to pay its cost. The Commune would have delivered the peasant of the blood tax,[67] would have given him a cheap government, transformed his present blood-suckers, the notary, advocate, executor, and other judicial vampires, into salaried communal agents, elected by, and responsible to, himself. It would have freed him of the tyranny of the *garde champêtre*,[68] the gendarme, and the prefect; would have put enlightenment by the schoolmaster in the place of stultification by the priest. And the French peasant is, above all, a man of reckoning. He would find it extremely reasonable that the pay of the priest, instead of being extorted by the tax-gatherer, should only depend upon the spontaneous action of the parishioners' religious instincts. Such were the great immediate boons which the rule of the Commune – and that rule alone – held out to the French peasantry. It is, therefore, quite superfluous here to expatiate upon the more com-

64. An apparent reference to the Commune's appeal 'To the rural workers', issued at the end of April.

65. In 1825 Louis XVIII's government granted landowners who had been expropriated during the first French revolution compensation of the order of a thousand million francs.

66. See 'The Class Struggles in France', *Surveys from Exile*, p. 51.

67. I.e. conscription.

68. Village policeman.

plicated but vital problems which the Commune alone was able, and at the same time compelled, to solve in favour of the peasant, viz., the hypothecary debt, lying like an incubus upon his parcel of soil, the *prolétariat foncier* (the rural proletariat), daily growing upon it, and his expropriation from it enforced, at a more and more rapid rate, by the very development of modern agriculture and the competition of capitalist farming.

The French peasant had elected Louis Bonaparte President of the Republic; but the party of Order created the Empire. What the French peasant really wants he commenced to show in 1849 and 1850, by opposing his *maire* to the government's prefect, his schoolmaster to the government's priest, and himself to the government's gendarme. All the laws made by the party of Order in January and February 1850[69] were avowed measures of repression against the peasant. The peasant was a Bonapartist, because the great Revolution, with all its benefits to him, was, in his eyes, personified in Napoleon. This delusion, rapidly breaking down under the Second Empire (and in its very nature hostile to the Rurals), this prejudice of the past, how could it have withstood the appeal of the Commune to the living interests and urgent wants of the peasantry?

The Rurals – this was, in fact, their chief apprehension – knew that three months' free communication of Communal Paris with the provinces would bring about a general rising of the peasants, and hence their anxiety to establish a police blockade around Paris, so as to stop the spread of the rinderpest.

If the Commune was thus the true representative of all the healthy elements of French society, and therefore the truly national government, it was, at the same time, as a working men's government, as the bold champion of the emancipation of labour, emphatically international. Within sight of the Prussian army, that had annexed to Germany two French provinces, the Commune annexed to France the working people all over the world.

The Second Empire had been the jubilee of cosmopolitan blackleg-ism, the rakes of all countries rushing in at its call for a share in its orgies and in the plunder of the French people. Even at this moment the right hand of Thiers is Ganesco, the foul Wallachian, and his left hand is Markovsky, the Russian spy. The

---

69. See 'The Class Struggles in France', *Surveys from Exile*, pp. 118–19.

Commune admitted all foreigners to the honour of dying for an immortal cause. Between the foreign war lost by their treason, and the civil war fomented by their conspiracy with the foreign invader, the bourgeoisie had found the time to display their patriotism by organizing police-hunts upon the Germans in France. The Commune made a German working man[70] its Minister of Labour. Thiers, the bourgeoisie, the Second Empire, had continually deluded Poland by loud professions of sympathy, while in reality betraying her to, and doing the dirty work of, Russia. The Commune honoured the heroic sons of Poland[71] by placing them at the head of the defenders of Paris. And, to broadly mark the new era of history it was conscious of initiating, under the eyes of the conquering Prussians, on the one side, and of the Bonapartist army, led by Bonapartist generals, on the other, the Commune pulled down that colossal symbol of martial glory, the Vendôme column.[72]

The great social measure of the Commune was its own working existence. Its special measures could but betoken the tendency of a government of the people by the people. Such were the abolition of the nightwork of journeymen bakers; the prohibition, under penalty, of the employers' practice to reduce wages by levying upon their work-people fines under manifold pretexts – a process in which the employer combines in his own person the parts of legislator, judge, and executor, and filches the money to boot. Another measure of this class was the surrender to associations of workmen, under reserve of compensation, of all closed workshops and factories, no matter whether the respective capitalists had absconded or preferred to strike work.

The financial measures of the Commune, remarkable for their sagacity and moderation, could only be such as were compatible with the state of a besieged town. Considering the colossal robberies committed upon the city of Paris by the great financial com-

70. Leo Frankel, in fact a German-speaking Hungarian, was an active member of the International, and the only member of the Commune who was in any sense a Marxist.

71. These were Jaroslaw Dombrowski and Walery Wroblewski, both revolutionary democrats in exile after the Polish insurrection of 1863. Dombrowski was appointed commander-in-chief of the Commune's forces during its last days, and died in its defence.

72. The Vendôme column was erected in 1806–10, out of melted-down cannons, to commemorate Napoleon's victories of 1805. It was pulled down on 16 May 1871, but restored after the Versailles victory.

panies and contractors, under the protection of Haussmann,[73] the Commune would have had an incomparably better title to confiscate their property than Louis Napoleon had against the Orleans family. The Hohenzollern[74] and the English oligarchs, who both have derived a good deal of their estates from church plunder, were, of course, greatly shocked at the Commune clearing but 8,000 francs out of secularization.

While the Versailles government, as soon as it had recovered some spirit and strength, used the most violent means against the Commune; while it put down the free expression of opinion all over France, even to the forbidding of meetings of delegates from the large towns; while it subjected Versailles and the rest of France to an espionage far surpassing that of the Second Empire; while it burned by its gendarme inquisitors all papers printed at Paris, and sifted all correspondence from and to Paris; while in the National Assembly the most timid attempts to put in a word for Paris were howled down in a manner unknown even to the *Chambre introuvable* of 1816; with the savage warfare of Versailles outside, and its attempts at corruption and conspiracy inside Paris – would the Commune not have shamefully betrayed its trust by affecting to keep up all the decencies and appearances of liberalism as in a time of profound peace? Had the government of the Commune been akin to that of M. Thiers, there would have been no more occasion to suppress party-of-Order papers at Paris than there was to suppress Communal papers at Versailles.

It was irritating indeed to the Rurals that at the very same time they declared the return to the church to be the only means of salvation for France, the infidel Commune unearthed the peculiar mysteries of the Picpus nunnery, and of the Church of Saint Laurent.[75] It was a satire upon M. Thiers that, while he showered grand crosses upon the Bonapartist generals in acknowledgement of their mastery in losing battles, signing capitulations, and turning cigarettes at Wilhelmshöhe,[76] the Commune dismissed and

73. Georges Haussmann, a Bonapartist politician and prefect of the Seine department, supervised the extensive planned rebuilding of Paris that was carried out under the Second Empire, which, among other things, created straight broad avenues for artillery fire, as a precaution against popular insurrection.   74. The Prussian royal family.

75. The Commune discovered at these places evidence of torture, incarceration and murder committed within religious orders.

76. The castle where the captured French generals, and Louis Napoleon himself, were interned.

arrested its generals whenever they were suspected of neglecting their duties. The expulsion from, and arrest by, the Commune of one of its members[77] who had slipped in under a false name, and had undergone at Lyons six days' imprisonment for simple bankruptcy, was it not a deliberate insult hurled at the forger, Jules Favre, then still the Foreign Minister of France, still selling France to Bismarck, and still dictating his orders to that paragon government of Belgium? But indeed the Commune did not pretend to infallibility, the invariable attribute of all governments of the old stamp. It published its doings and sayings, it initiated the public into all its shortcomings.

In every revolution there intrude, at the side of its true agents, men of a different stamp; some of them survivors of and devotees to past revolutions, without insight into the present movement, but preserving popular influence by their known honesty and courage, or by the sheer force of tradition; others mere bawlers, who, by dint of repeating year after year the same set of stereotyped declamations against the government of the day, have sneaked into the reputation of revolutionists of the first water. After 18 March, some such men did also turn up, and in some cases contrived to play pre-eminent parts. As far as their power went, they hampered the real action of the working class, exactly as men of that sort have hampered the full development of every previous revolution. They are an unavoidable evil: with time they are shaken off; but time was not allowed to the Commune.

Wonderful, indeed, was the change the Commune had wrought in Paris! No longer any trace of the meretricious Paris of the Second Empire. No longer was Paris the rendezvous of British landlords, Irish absentees, American ex-slaveholders and shoddy men, Russian ex-serfowners, and Wallachian boyards. No more corpses at the morgue, no nocturnal burglaries, scarcely any robberies; in fact, for the first time since the days of February 1848 the streets of Paris were safe, and that without any police of any kind. 'We', said a member of the Commune, 'hear no longer of assassination, theft and personal assault; it seems indeed as if the police had dragged along with it to Versailles all its conservative friends.'

The *cocottes*[78] had refound the scent of their protectors – the absconding men of family, religion, and, above all, of property.

77. Stanislas Blanchet, in fact a police agent.
78. High-class prostitutes.

In their stead, the real women of Paris showed again at the surface – heroic, noble, and devoted, like the women of antiquity. Working, thinking, fighting, bleeding Paris – almost forgetful, in its incubation of a new society, of the cannibals at its gates – radiant in the enthusiasm of its historic initiative!

Opposed to this new world at Paris, behold the old world at Versailles – that assembly of the ghouls of all defunct regimes, Legitimists and Orleanists, eager to feed upon the carcass of the nation – with a tail of antediluvian republicans, sanctioning, by their presence in the Assembly, the slaveholders' rebellion, relying for the maintenance of their parliamentary republic upon the vanity of the senile mountebank at its head, and caricaturing 1789 by holding their ghastly meetings in the Jeu de Paume.[79] There it was, this Assembly, the representative of everything dead in France, propped up to the semblance of life by nothing but the swords of the generals of Louis Bonaparte. Paris all truth, Versailles all lie; and that lie vented through the mouth of Thiers.

Thiers tells a deputation of the mayors of the Seine-et-Oise, 'You may rely upon my word, which I have *never* broken!'

He tells the Assembly itself that it was 'the most freely elected and most liberal Assembly France ever possessed'; he tells his motley soldiery that it was 'the admiration of the world, and the finest army France ever possessed'; he tells the provinces that the bombardment of Paris by him was a myth: 'If some cannon-shots have been fired, it is not the deed of the army of Versailles, but of some insurgents trying to make believe that they are fighting, while they dare not show their faces.'

He again tells the provinces that 'the artillery of Versailles does not bombard Paris, but only cannonades it'.

He tells the Archbishop of Paris that the pretended executions and reprisals (!) attributed to the Versailles troops were all moonshine. He tells Paris that he was only anxious 'to free it from the hideous tyrants who oppress it', and that, in fact, the Paris of the Commune was 'but a handful of criminals'.

The Paris of M. Thiers was not the real Paris of the 'vile multitude', but a phantom Paris, the Paris of the *francs-fileurs*,[80] the Paris of the boulevards, male and female – the rich, the

79. The tennis court where the French Third Estate met on 20 June 1789 and vowed to exact a constitution.

80. A pun on '*franc-tireur*' (sniper or guerrilla soldier). Literally, those who 'freely filed off'.

capitalist, the gilded, the idle Paris, now thronging with its lack-eys, its blacklegs, its literary *bohème* and its *cocottes* at Versailles, Saint-Denis, Rueil, and Saint-Germain; considering the civil war but an agreeable diversion, eyeing the battle going on through telescopes, counting the rounds of cannon, and swearing by their own honour, and that of their prostitutes, that the performance was far better got up than it used to be at the Porte Saint Martin. The men who fell were really dead; the cries of the wounded were cries in good earnest; and, besides, the whole thing was so intensely historical.

This is the Paris of M. Thiers, as the emigration of Coblenz was the France of M. de Calonne.[81]

IV

The first attempt of the slaveholders' conspiracy to put down Paris by getting the Prussians to occupy it, was frustrated by Bismarck's refusal. The second attempt, that of 18 March, ended in the rout of the army and the flight to Versailles of the govern-ment, which ordered the whole administration to break up and follow in its track. By the semblance of peace negotiations with Paris, Thiers found the time to prepare for war against it. But where to find an army? The remnants of the line regiments were weak in number and unsafe in character. His urgent appeal to the provinces to succour Versailles, by their National Guards and volunteers, met with a flat refusal. Brittany alone furnished a handful of Chouans[82] fighting under a white flag, every one of them wearing on his breast the heart of Jesus in white cloth, and shouting '*Vive le roi!*' (Long live the king!). Thiers was, therefore, compelled to collect, in hot haste, a motley crew, composed of sailors, marines, Pontifical Zouaves,[83] Valentin's gendarmes, and Piétri's *sergents-de-ville* and *mouchards*.[84] This army, however, would have been ridiculously ineffective without the instal-ments of Imperialist war-prisoners, which Bismarck granted in

81. Coblenz was the main centre of the monarchist emigration during the first French revolution. Charles de Calonne, a former minister of Louis XVI, headed a government in exile there.

82. The name of the Breton royalist insurgents during the first French revolution.

83. A regiment of the Papal guard formed from the French aristocracy; the Pontifi-cal Zouaves were sent to France in 1870 to fight the Prussians.

84. Police informers.

numbers just sufficient to keep the civil war a-going, and keep the Versailles government in abject dependence on Prussia. During the war itself, the Versailles police had to look after the Versailles army, while the gendarmes had to drag it on by exposing themselves at all posts of danger. The forts which fell were not taken, but bought. The heroism of the Federals convinced Thiers that the resistance of Paris was not to be broken by his own strategic genius and the bayonets at his disposal.

Meanwhile, his relations with the provinces became more and more difficult. Not one single address of approval came in to gladden Thiers and his Rurals. Quite the contrary. Deputations and addresses demanding, in a tone anything but respectful, conciliation with Paris on the basis of the unequivocal recognition of the republic, the acknowledgement of communal liberties, and the dissolution of the National Assembly, whose mandate was extinct, poured in from all sides, and in such numbers that Dufaure, Thiers's Minister of Justice, in his circular of 23 April to the public prosecutors, commanded them to treat 'the cry of conciliation' as a crime! In regard, however, of the hopeless prospect held out by his campaign, Thiers resolved to shift his tactics by ordering, all over the country, municipal elections to take place on 30 April, on the basis of the new municipal law dictated by himself to the National Assembly. What with the intrigues of his prefects, what with police intimidation, he felt quite sanguine of imparting, by the verdict of the provinces, to the National Assembly that moral power it had never possessed, and of getting at last from the provinces the physical force required for the conquest of Paris.

His banditti-warfare against Paris, exalted in his own bulletins, and the attempts of his ministers at the establishment, throughout France, of a reign of terror, Thiers was from the beginning anxious to accompany with a little by-play of conciliation, which had to serve more than one purpose. It was to dupe the provinces, to inveigle the middle-class element in Paris, and, above all, to afford the professed republicans in the National Assembly the opportunity of hiding their treason against Paris behind their faith in Thiers. On 21 March, when still without an army, he had declared to the Assembly: 'Come what may, I will not send an army to Paris.'

On 27 March he rose again: 'I have found the republic an accomplished fact, and I am firmly resolved to maintain it.'

In reality, he put down the revolution at Lyons and Marseilles[85] in the name of the republic, while the roars of his Rurals drowned the very mention of its name at Versailles. After this exploit, he toned down the 'accomplished fact' into an hypothetical fact. The Orleans princes, whom he had cautiously warned off Bordeaux, were now, in flagrant breach of the law, permitted to intrigue at Dreux. The concessions held out by Thiers in his interminable interviews with the delegates from Paris and the provinces, although constantly varied in tone and colour, according to time and circumstances, did in fact never come to more than the prospective restriction of revenge to the 'handful of criminals implicated in the murder of Lecomte and Clément Thomas', on the well-understood premise that Paris and France were unreservedly to accept M. Thiers himself as the best of possible republics, as he, in 1830, had done with Louis Philippe. Even these concessions he not only took care to render doubtful by the official comments put upon them in the Assembly through his ministers. He had his Dufaure to act. Dufaure, this old Orleanist lawyer, had always been the justiciary of the state of siege, as now in 1871, under Thiers, so in 1839 under Louis Philippe, and in 1849 under Louis Bonaparte's presidency. While out of office he made a fortune by pleading for the Paris capitalists, and made political capital by pleading against the laws he had himself originated. He now hurried through the National Assembly not only a set of repressive laws which were, after the fall of Paris, to extirpate the last remnants of republican liberty in France;[86] he foreshadowed the fate of Paris by abridging the, for him, too slow procedure of courts-martial, and by a new-fangled, Draconic code of deportation. The revolution of 1848, abolishing the penalty of death for political crimes, had replaced it by deportation. Louis Bonaparte did not dare, at least not in theory, to re-establish the regime of the guillotine. The Rural Assembly, not yet bold enough even to hint that the Parisians were not rebels, but assassins, had therefore to confine its prospective vengeance against Paris to Dufaure's new code of deportation. Under all these circumstances Thiers himself could not have gone on with his comedy of conciliation, had it not, as he intended it to do, drawn forth shrieks of rage from the

85. At Lyons and Marseilles Communard risings took place in the wake of Paris, but were defeated after only a few days.

86. Particularly a law curbing the press.

Rurals, whose ruminating mind did neither understand the play, nor its necessities of hypocrisy, tergiversation, and procrastination.

In sight of the impending municipal elections of 30 April, Thiers enacted one of his great conciliation scenes on 27 April. Amidst a flood of sentimental rhetoric, he exclaimed from the tribune of the Assembly:

> There exists no conspiracy against the republic but that of Paris, which compels us to shed French blood. I repeat it again and again. Let those impious arms fall from the hands which hold them, and chastisement will be arrested at once by an act of peace excluding only the small number of criminals.

To the violent interruption of the Rurals he replied:

> Gentlemen, tell me, I implore you, am I wrong? Do you really regret that I could have stated the truth that the criminals are only a handful? Is it not fortunate in the midst of our misfortunes that those who have been capable to shed the blood of Clément Thomas and General Lecomte are but rare exceptions?

France, however, turned a deaf ear to what Thiers flattered himself to be a parliamentary siren's song. Out of 700,000 municipal councillors returned by the 35,000 communes still left to France, the united Legitimists, Orleanists and Bonapartists did not carry 8,000. The supplementary elections which followed were still more decidedly hostile. Thus, instead of getting from the provinces the badly needed physical force, the National Assembly lost even its last claim to moral force, that of being the expression of the universal suffrage of the country. To complete the discomfiture, the newly chosen municipal councils of all the cities of France openly threatened the usurping Assembly at Versailles with a counter assembly at Bordeaux.

Then the long-expected moment of decisive action had at last come for Bismarck. He peremptorily summoned Thiers to send to Frankfurt plenipotentiaries for the definitive settlement of peace. In humble obedience to the call of his master, Thiers hastened to dispatch his trusty Jules Favre, backed by Pouyer-Quertier. Pouyer-Quertier, an 'eminent' Rouen cotton-spinner, a fervent and even servile partisan of the Second Empire, had never found any fault with it save its commercial treaty with England,[87]

---

87. The 'Cobden treaty' of January 1860, which substantially reduced French protective tariffs on imported industrial goods.

prejudicial to his own shop-interest. Hardly installed at Bordeaux as Thiers's Minister of Finance, he denounced that 'unholy' treaty, hinted at its near abrogation, and had even the effrontery to try, although in vain (having counted without Bismarck), the immediate enforcement of the old protective duties against Alsace, where, he said, no previous international treaties stood in the way. This man, who considered counter-revolution as a means to put down wages at Rouen, and the surrender of French provinces as a means to bring up the price of his wares in France, was he not *the one* predestined to be picked out by Thiers as the helpmate of Jules Favre in his last and crowning treason?

On the arrival at Frankfurt of this exquisite pair of plenipotentiaries, bully Bismarck at once met them with the imperious alternative: Either the restoration of the Empire, or the unconditional acceptance of my own peace terms! These terms included a shortening of the intervals in which the war indemnity was to be paid and the continued occupation of the Paris forts by Prussian troops until Bismarck should feel satisfied with the state of things in France; Prussia thus being recognized as the supreme arbiter in internal French politics! In return for this he offered to let loose, for the extermination of Paris, the captive Bonapartist army, and to lend them the direct assistance of Emperor William's troops. He pledged his good faith by making payment of the first instalment of the indemnity dependent on the 'pacification' of Paris. Such a bait was, of course, eagerly swallowed by Thiers and his plenipotentiaries. They signed the treaty of peace on 10 May, and had it endorsed by the Versailles Assembly on the 18th.

In the interval between the conclusion of peace and the arrival of the Bonapartist prisoners, Thiers felt the more bound to resume his comedy of conciliation, as his republican tools stood in sore need of a pretext for blinking their eyes at the preparations for the carnage of Paris. As late as 8 May he replied to a deputation of middle-class conciliators: 'Whenever the insurgents will make up their minds for capitulation, the gates of Paris shall be flung wide open during a week for all except the murderers of Generals Clément Thomas and Lecomte.'

A few days afterwards, when violently interpellated on these promises by the Rurals, he refused to enter into any explanations; not, however, without giving them this significant hint:

I tell you there are impatient men amongst you, men who are in too great a hurry. They must have another eight days; at the end of these eight days there will be no more danger, and the task will be proportionate to their courage and to their capacities.

As soon as MacMahon[88] was able to assure him that he could shortly enter Paris, Thiers declared to the Assembly that he would enter Paris with the *laws* in his hands, and demand a full expiation from the wretches who had sacrificed the lives of soldiers and destroyed public monuments.

As the moment of decision drew near he said – to the Assembly, 'I shall be pitiless!' – to Paris, that it was doomed; and to his Bonapartist banditti, that they had state licence to wreak vengeance upon Paris to their hearts' content. At last, when treachery had opened the gates of Paris to General Douay, on 21 May, Thiers, on the 22nd, revealed to the Rurals the 'goal' of his conciliation comedy, which they had so obstinately persisted in not understanding. 'I told you a few days ago that we were approaching *our goal*; today I come to tell you *the goal* is reached. The victory of order, justice and civilization is at last won!'

So it was. The civilization and justice of bourgeois order comes out in its lurid light whenever the slaves and drudges of that order rise against their masters. Then this civilization and justice stand forth as undisguised savagery and lawless revenge. Each new crisis in the class struggle between the appropriator and the producer brings out this fact more glaringly. Even the atrocities of the bourgeois in June 1848 vanish before the ineffable infamy of 1871. The self-sacrificing heroism with which the population of Paris – men, women and children – fought for eight days after the entrance of the Versaillais, reflects as much the grandeur of their cause, as the infernal deeds of the soldiery reflect the innate spirit of that civilization of which they are the mercenary vindicators. A glorious civilization, indeed, the great problem of which is how to get rid of the heaps of corpses it made after the battle was over!

To find a parallel for the conduct of Thiers and his bloodhounds we must go back to the times of Sulla and the two trium-

88. Marie Édmé MacMahon was a Bonapartist marshal, and commander-in-chief of the Versailles army that put down the Commune. He was subsequently President of the Third Republic (1873–9).

virates of Rome.[89] The same wholesale slaughter in cold blood; the same disregard, in massacre, of age and sex; the same system of torturing prisoners; the same proscriptions, but this time of a whole class; the same savage hunt after concealed leaders, lest one might escape; the same denunciations of political and private enemies; the same indifference for the butchery of entire strangers to the feud. There is but this difference, that the Romans had no mitrailleuses for the despatch, in the lump, of the proscribed, and that they had not 'the law in their hands', nor on their lips the cry of 'civilization'.

And after those horrors, look upon the other, still more hideous, face of that bourgeois civilization as described by its own press! The Paris correspondent of a London Tory paper writes:

With stray shots still ringing in the distance, and untended wounded wretches dying amid the tombstones of Père Lachaise – with 6,000 terror-stricken insurgents wandering in an agony of despair in the labyrinth of the catacombs, and wretches hurried through the streets to be shot down in scores by the mitrailleuse – it is revolting to see the *cafés* filled with the votaries of absinthe, billiards, and dominoes; female profligacy perambulating the boulevards, and the sound of revelry disturbing the night from the *cabinets particuliers*[90] of fashionable restaurants.

M. Edouard Hervé writes in the *Journal de Paris*, a Versaillist journal suppressed by the Commune:

The way in which the population of Paris (!) manifested its satisfaction yesterday was rather more than frivolous, and we fear it will grow worse as time progresses. Paris has now a *fête* day appearance, which is sadly out of place; and, unless we are to be called the *Parisiens de la décadence*, this sort of thing must come to an end.

And then he quotes the passage from Tacitus:

Yet, on the morrow of that horrible struggle, even before it was completely over, Rome – degraded and corrupt – began once more to wallow in the voluptuous slough which was destroying its body and polluting its soul – *alibi proelia et vulnera, alibi balnea popinaeque* [here fights and wounds, there baths and restaurants].

M. Hervé only forgets to say that the 'population of Paris' he speaks of is but the population of the Paris of M. Thiers – the

89. The first (60–53 BC) and second (46–43 BC) triumvirates were, like Sulla's dictatorship, notorious for their brutality against the Roman population.

90. Private rooms.

francs-fileurs returning in throngs from Versailles, Saint-Denis, Rueil and Saint-Germain – *the* Paris of the 'Decline'.

In all its bloody triumphs over the self-sacrificing champions of a new and better society, that nefarious civilization, based upon the enslavement of labour, drowns the moans of its victims in a hue-and-cry of calumny, reverberated by a world-wide echo. The serene working men's Paris of the Commune is suddenly changed into a pandemonium by the bloodhounds of 'order'. And what does this tremendous change prove to the bourgeois mind of all countries? Why, that the Commune has conspired against civilization! The Paris people die enthusiastically for the Commune in numbers unequalled in any battle known to history. What does that prove? Why, that the Commune was not the people's own government but the usurpation of a handful of criminals! The women of Paris joyfully give up their lives at the barricades and on the place of execution. What does this prove? Why, that the demon of the Commune has changed them into Megaeras and Hecates! The moderation of the Commune during two months of undisputed sway is equalled only by the heroism of its defence. What does that prove? Why, that for months the Commune carefully hid, under a mask of moderation and humanity, the bloodthirstiness of its fiendish instincts, to be let loose in the hour of its agony!

The working men's Paris, in the act of its heroic self-holocaust, involved in its flames buildings and monuments. While tearing to pieces the living body of the proletariat, its rulers must no longer expect to return triumphantly into the intact architecture of their abodes. The government of Versailles cries, 'Incendiarism!' and whispers this cue to all its agents, down to the remotest hamlet, to hunt up its enemies everywhere as suspect of professional incendiarism. The bourgeoisie of the whole world, which looks complacently upon the wholesale massacre after the battle, is convulsed by horror at the desecration of brick and mortar!

When governments give state licences to their navies to 'kill, *burn* and destroy', is that a licence for incendiarism? When the British troops wantonly set fire to the Capitol at Washington and to the summer palace of the Chinese emperor,[91] was that in-

91. British troops fired on the Capitol and the White House in August 1814, during the war of 1812–14. The Summer Palace outside Peking was burned down by English and French troops during the expedition of 1860 to force China to ratify the oppressive treaty of Tsientsin.

cendiarism? When the Prussians, not for military reasons, but out of the mere spite of revenge, burned down, by the help of petroleum, towns like Châteaudun and innumerable villages, was that incendiarism? When Thiers, during six weeks, bombarded Paris, under the pretext that he wanted to set fire to those houses only in which there were people, was that incendiarism? In war, fire is an arm as legitimate as any. Buildings held by the enemy are shelled to set them on fire. If their defenders have to retire, they themselves light the flames to prevent the attack from making use of the buildings. To be burnt down has always been the inevitable fate of all buildings situated in the front of battle of all the regular armies of the world. But in the war of the enslaved against their enslavers, the only justifiable war in history, this is by no means to hold good! The Commune used fire strictly as a means of defence. They used it to stop up to the Versailles troops those long, straight avenues which Haussmann had expressly opened to artillery-fire; they used it to cover their retreat, in the same way as the Versaillais, in their advance, used their shells which destroyed at least as many buildings as the fire of the Commune. It is a matter of dispute, even now, which buildings were set fire to by the defence, and which by the attack. And the defence resorted to fire only then, when the Versaillais troops had already commenced their wholesale murdering of prisoners. Besides, the Commune had, long before, given full public notice that, if driven to extremities, they would bury themselves under the ruins of Paris, and make Paris a second Moscow, as the Government of Defence, but only as a cloak for its treason, had promised to do. For this purpose Trochu had found them the petroleum. The Commune knew that its opponents cared nothing for the lives of the Paris people, but cared much for their own Paris buildings. And Thiers, on the other hand, had given them notice that he would be implacable in his vengeance. No sooner had he got his army ready on one side, and the Prussians shutting up the trap on the other, than he proclaimed: 'I shall be pitiless! The expiation will be complete, and justice will be stern!' If the acts of the Paris working men were vandalism, it was the vandalism of defence in despair, not the vandalism of triumph, like that which the Christians perpetrated upon the really priceless art treasures of heathen antiquity; and even that vandalism has been justified by the historian as an unavoidable and comparatively trifling concomitant to the titanic struggle between a new society arising and an old one breaking down. It was still less the vandalism of Haussmann, razing historic Paris to make place for the Paris of the sightseer!

But the execution by the Commune of the sixty-four hostages, with the Archbishop of Paris at their head! The bourgeoisie and its army, in June 1848, re-established a custom which had long disappeared from the practice of war – the shooting of their defenceless prisoners. This brutal custom has since been more or less strictly adhered to by the suppressors of all popular commotions in Europe and India; thus proving that it constitutes a real 'progress of civilization'! On the other hand, the Prussians, in France, had re-established the practice of taking hostages – innocent men, who, with their lives, were to answer to them for the acts of others. When Thiers, as we have seen, from the very beginning of the conflict, enforced the humane practice of shooting down the Communal prisoners, the Commune, to protect their lives, was obliged to resort to the Prussian practice of securing hostages. The lives of the hostages had been forfeited over and over again by the continued shooting of prisoners on the part of the Versaillais. How could they be spared any longer after the carnage with which MacMahon's praetorians celebrated their entrance into Paris? Was even the last check upon the unscrupulous ferocity of bourgeois governments – the taking of hostages – to be made a mere sham of? The real murderer of Archbishop Darboy is Thiers. The Commune again and again had offered to exchange the archbishop, and ever so many priests in the bargain, against the single Blanqui, then in the hands of Thiers. Thiers obstinately refused. He knew that with Blanqui he would give to the Commune a head; while the archbishop would serve his purpose best in the shape of a corpse. Thiers acted upon the precedent of Cavaignac. How, in June 1848, did not Cavaignac and his men of order raise shouts of horror by stigmatizing the insurgents as the assassins of Archbishop Affre! They knew perfectly well that the archbishop had been shot by the soldiers of order. M. Jacquemet, the archbishop's vicar-general, present on the spot, had immediately afterwards handed them in his evidence to that effect.

All this chorus of calumny, which the party of Order never fail, in their orgies of blood, to raise against their victims, only proves that the bourgeois of our days considers himself the legitimate successor to the baron of old, who thought every weapon in his own hand fair against the plebeian, while in the hands of the plebeian a weapon of any kind constituted in itself a crime.

The conspiracy of the ruling class to break down the revolution by a civil war carried on under the patronage of the foreign invader – a conspiracy which we have traced from the very 4th of September down to the entrance of MacMahon's praetorians through the gate of Saint-Cloud – culminated in the carnage of Paris. Bismarck gloats over the ruins of Paris, in which he saw perhaps the first instalment of that general destruction of great cities he had prayed for when still a simple Rural in the Prussian *chambre introuvable* of 1849.[92] He gloats over the cadavers of the Paris proletariat. For him this is not only the extermination of revolution, but the extinction of France, now decapitated in reality, and by the French government itself. With the shallowness characteristic of all successful statesmen, he sees but the surface of this tremendous historic event. Whenever before has history exhibited the spectacle of a conqueror crowning his victory by turning into, not only the gendarme, but the hired bravo of the conquered government? There existed no war between Prussia and the Commune of Paris. On the contrary, the Commune had accepted the peace preliminaries, and Prussia had announced her neutrality. Prussia was, therefore, no belligerent. She acted the part of a bravo, a cowardly bravo, because incurring no danger; a hired bravo, because stipulating beforehand the payment of her blood-money of 500 millions on the fall of Paris. And thus, at last, came out the true character of the war, ordained by Providence as a chastisement of godless and debauched France by pious and moral Germany! And this unparalleled breach of the law of nations, even as understood by the old-world lawyers, instead of arousing the 'civilized' governments of Europe to declare the felonious Prussian government, the mere tool of the St Petersburg cabinet, an outlaw amongst nations, only incites them to consider whether the few victims who escape the double cordon around Paris are not to be given up to the hangman at Versailles!

That after the most tremendous war of modern times, the conquering and the conquered hosts should fraternize for the common massacre of the proletariat – this unparalleled event does indicate, not, as Bismarck thinks, the final repression of a new society upheaving, but the crumbling into dust of bourgeois society. The highest heroic effort of which old society is still capable is

92. Like the original *Chambre introuvable* of 1815–16 (see p. 196, n. 31), the Prussian Chamber elected in January 1849 was also noted for its arch-reactionary character.

national war; and this is now proved to be a mere governmental humbug, intended to defer the struggle of classes, and to be thrown aside as soon as that class struggle bursts out into civil war. Class rule is no longer able to disguise itself in a national uniform; the national governments are *one* as against the proletariat!

After Whit Sunday 1871, there can be neither peace nor truce possible between the working men of France and the appropriators of their produce. The iron hand of a mercenary soldiery may keep for a time both classes tied down in common oppression. But the battle must break out again and again in ever-growing dimensions, and there can be no doubt as to who will be the victor in the end – the appropriating few, or the immense working majority. And the French working class is only the advanced guard of the modern proletariat.

While the European governments thus testify, before Paris, to the international character of class rule, they cry down the International Working Men's Association – the international counter-organization of labour against the cosmopolitan conspiracy of capital – as the head fountain of all these disasters. Thiers denounced it as the despot of labour, pretending to be its liberator. Picard ordered that all communications between the French Internationalists and those abroad should be cut off; Count Jaubert,[93] Thiers's mummified accomplice of 1835, declares it the great problem of all civilized governments to weed it out. The Rurals roar against it, and the whole European press joins the chorus. An honourable French writer,[94] completely foreign to our Association, speaks as follows:

> The members of the Central Committee of the National Guard, as well as the greater part of the members of the Commune, are the most active, intelligent, and energetic minds of the International Working Men's Association . . . men who are thoroughly honest, sincere, intelligent, devoted, pure, and fanatical in the *good* sense of the word.

The police-tinged bourgeois mind naturally figures to itself the International Working Men's Association as acting in the manner of a secret conspiracy, its central body ordering, from time to time, explosions in different countries. Our association is, in fact,

93. Hippolyte François, Count Jaubert, served in Thiers's cabinet of 1840 and was a deputy to the National Assembly of 1871.

94. Apparently Jean Robinet, a physician and historian, and a follower of Comte, who attempted to mediate between Versailles and the Commune.

nothing but the international bond between the most advanced working men in the various countries of the civilized world. Wherever, in whatever shape, and under whatever conditions the class struggle obtains any consistency, it is but natural that members of our association should stand in the foreground. The soil out of which it grows is modern society itself. It cannot be stamped out by any amount of carnage. To stamp it out, the governments would have to stamp out the despotism of capital over labour – the condition of their own parasitical existence.

Working men's Paris, with its Commune, will be for ever celebrated as the glorious harbinger of a new society. Its martyrs are enshrined in the great heart of the working class. Its exterminators history has already nailed to that eternal pillory from which all the prayers of their priests will not avail to redeem them.

Notes

I

The column of prisoners halted in the avenue Uhrich, and was drawn up, four or five deep, on the footway facing to the road. General Marquis de Galliffet and his staff dismounted and commenced an inspection from the left of the line. Walking down slowly and eyeing the ranks, the general stopped here and there, tapping a man on the shoulder or beckoning him out of the rear ranks. In most cases, without further parley, the individual thus selected was marched out into the centre of the road, where a small supplementary column was, thus, soon formed . . . It was evident that there was considerable room for error. A mounted officer pointed out to General Galliffet a man and woman for some particular offence. The woman, rushing out of the ranks, threw herself on her knees, and, with outstretched arms, protested her innocence in passionate terms. The general waited for a pause, and then with most impassible face and unmoved demeanour, said, 'Madame, I have visited every theatre in Paris, your acting will have no effect on me' ('*ce n'est pas la peine de jouer la comédie*') . . . It was not a good thing on that day to be noticeably taller, dirtier, cleaner, older, or uglier than one's neighbours. One individual in particular struck me as probably owing his speedy release from the ills of this world to his having a broken nose . . . Over a hundred being thus chosen, a firing party told off, and the column resumed its march, leaving them behind. A few minutes afterwards a dropping fire in our rear commenced, and continued for over a quarter of an hour. It was the execution of these summarily convicted wretches – Paris Correspondent, *Daily News*, 8 June.

This Galliffet, 'the kept man of his wife, so notorious for her shameless exhibitions at the orgies of the Second Empire', went, during the war, by the name of the French 'Ensign Pistol'.

The *Temps* which is a careful journal, and not given to sensation, tells a dreadful story of people imperfectly shot and buried before life was extinct. A great number were buried in the square round Saint Jacques-la-Bouchière; some of them very superficially. In the daytime the roar of the busy streets prevented any notice being taken; but in the stillness of the night the inhabitants of the houses in the neighbourhood were roused by distant moans, and in the morning a clenched hand was seen protruding through the soil. In consequence of this, exhumations were ordered to take place . . . That many wounded have been buried alive I have not the slightest doubt. One case I can vouch for. When Brunel was shot with his mistress on the 24th ult. in the courtyard of a house in the Place Vendôme, the bodies lay there until the afternoon of the 27th. When the burial party came to remove the corpses, they found the woman living still and took her to an ambulance. Though she had received four bullets she is now out of danger – Paris Correspondent, *Evening Standard*, 8 June.

II

The following letter appeared in *The Times* of 13 June:

To the Editor of *The Times*

Sir, On 6 June 1871, M. Jules Favre issued a circular to all the European powers, calling upon them to hunt down the International Working Men's Association. A few remarks will suffice to characterize that document.

In the very preamble of our Statutes it is stated that the International was founded '28 September 1864, at a public meeting held at St Martin's Hall, Long Acre, London'. For purposes of his own Jules Favre puts back the date of its origin behind 1862.

In order to explain our principles, he professes to quote 'their (the International's) sheet of 25 March 1869'. And then what does he quote? The sheet of a society which is not the International. This sort of manoeuvre he already recurred to when, still a comparatively young lawyer, he had to defend the *National* newspaper, prosecuted for libel by Cabet.[95] Then he pretended to read extracts from Cabet's pamphlets while reading interpolations of his own – a trick exposed while the court was sitting, and which, but for the indulgence of Cabet, would have

95. Étienne Cabet was a utopian communist and the author of *Voyage en Icarie* (1839).

been punished by Jules Favre's expulsion from the Paris bar. Of all the documents quoted by him as documents of the International, not one belongs to the International. He says, for instance, ' "The Alliance declares itself Atheist," says the General Council, constituted in London in July 1869'.

The General Council never issued such a document. On the contrary, it issued a document which quashed the original statutes of the 'Alliance' – L'Alliance de la Démocratie Socialiste at Geneva – quoted by Jules Favre.[96]

Throughout his circular, which pretends in part also to be directed against the Empire, Jules Favre repeats against the International but the police inventions of the public prosecutors of the Empire, which broke down miserably even before the law courts of that Empire.

It is known that in its two Addresses (of July and September last) on the late war,[97] the General Council of the International denounced the Prussian plans of conquest against France. Later on, Mr Reitlinger, Jules Favre's private secretary, applied, though of course in vain, to some members of the General Council for getting up by the Council a demonstration against Bismarck, in favour of the Government of National Defence; they were particularly requested not to mention the republic. The preparations for a demonstration with regard to the expected arrival of Jules Favre in London were made – certainly with the best of intentions – in spite of the General Council, which, in its address of 9 September, had distinctly forewarned the Paris workmen against Jules Favre and his colleagues.

What would Jules Favre say if, in its turn, the International were to send a circular on Jules Favre to all the cabinets of Europe, drawing their particular attention to the documents published at Paris by the late M. Millière?[98]

I am, Sir, your obedient servant,

JOHN HALES.[99]
Secretary to the General Council
of the International Working Men's Association

London, 12 June 1871

In an article on 'The International Society and its aims', that pious informer, the London *Spectator* (24 June), amongst other similar tricks, quotes, even more fully than Jules Favre has done, the above document of the 'Alliance' as the work of the Inter-

96. This document was 'The International Working Men's Association and the International Alliance of Socialist Democracy'; see below, pp. 278–80.

97. Above, pp. 172–6 and 179–86.

98. Above, pp. 189–90.

99. This letter was in fact drafted by Marx and Engels.

national, and that eleven days after the refutation had been published in *The Times*. We do not wonder at this. Frederick the Great used to say that of all Jesuits the worst are the Protestant ones.

FIRST DRAFT OF *THE CIVIL WAR IN FRANCE*[1]   [*Extract*]

The Commune

1. Measures for the Working Class

Nightwork of Journeymen Bakers Suppressed (*20 April*). *The private jurisdiction*, usurped by the seigneurs of mills, etc. (manufacturers) (employers, great and small) being at the same time judges, executors, gainers and parties in the disputes, that right of *a penal code of their own*, enabling them to rob the labourers' wages by fines and deductions as punishment etc., abolished in public and private workshops; penalties impended upon the employers in case they infringe upon this law; *fines and deductions* extorted since 18 March to be paid back to the workmen (*27 April*). Sale of pawned articles at pawnshops suspended (*29 March*).

A great lot of workshops and manufactories have been closed in Paris, their owners having run away. This is the old method of the industrial capitalists, who consider themselves entitled 'by the spontaneous action of the laws of political economy' not only to make a profit out of labour, as the condition of labour, but to stop it altogether and throw the workmen on the pavement – to produce an artificial crisis whenever a victorious revolution threatens the 'order' of their 'system'. The Commune, very wisely, has appointed a Communal commission which, in cooperation with delegates chosen by the different trades, will inquire into the ways of handing over the deserted workshops and manufactories to cooperative workmen's societies with some indemnity for the capitalist

1. This text is a section of Marx's original draft of *The Civil War in France*, roughly corresponding to section III of the published version. It is reproduced here from the *Archiv Marksa i Engelsa* edited by Adoratsky, vol. III (VIII), Moscow, 1934. Adoratsky's text sticks very close to Marx's manuscript, which is in extremely unpolished and often ungrammatical English, with a lot of French words interspersed, and the present version has been somewhat edited in the interest of greater clarity. See p. 33, n. 58.

deserters (*16 April*); (this commission has also to make statistics of the abandoned workshops).

The Commune has given order to the *mairies*[2] to make no distinction between the wives called illegitimate, the mothers and widows of National Guards, as to the indemnity of seventy-five centimes.[3]

The public prostitutes till now kept for the 'men of order' at Paris, but for their 'safety' kept in personal servitude under the arbitrary rule of the police – the Commune has liberated the prostitutes from this degrading slavery, but swept away the soil upon which, and the men by whom, prostitution flourishes. The higher prostitutes – the *cocottes* – were of course, under the rule of order, not the slaves, but the masters of the police and the governors.

There was, of course, no time to reorganize public instruction (education); but by removing the religious and clerical element from it, the Commune has taken the initiative in the mental emancipation of the people. It has appointed a commission for the organization of education (primary – elementary – and professional) (*28 April*). It has ordered that all tools of instruction, like books, maps, paper, etc. be given gratuitously by the schoolmasters who receive them in their turn from the respective *mairies* to which they belong. No schoolmaster is allowed on any pretext to ask payment from his pupils for these instruments of instruction (*28 April*).

Pawnshops.   All pawn tickets issued by the Mont-de-Piété[4] prior to 25 April 1871, pledging articles of clothing, furniture, linen, books, bedding and instruments of labour valued at not more than 20 francs, may be redeemed free of charge as from 12 May (*7 May*).

2. Measures for the Working Class, but Mostly for the Middle Classes

House-Rent for the Last Three Quarters up to April Wholly

2. The town halls of the *arrondissements* into which Paris is divided.

3. The significance of 'seventy-five centimes' is unclear. This seems to be a reference to the Commune's decree of 10 April, which granted a pension of 600 francs p.a. to the widows of National Guards killed in defence of the Commune, whether they were married or not – a very important point among the nineteenth-century Parisian working class. Widows were also entitled to 365 francs p.a. for each child under eighteen.

4. The Mont-de-Piété was a municipal pawnshop with several branches.

Remitted. Whoever had paid any of these three quarters shall have right of setting that sum against future payments. The same law to prevail in the case of furnished apartments. No notice to quit coming from landlords to be valid for three months to come (*29 March*).

Échéances. Payment of bills of exchange due (*expiration of bills*): all prosecutions for bills of exchange fallen due suspended (*12 April*).

All commercial papers of that sort to be repaid in (repayments spread over) two years, to begin 15 July next, the debt being not chargeable with interest. The total amount of the sums due divided in eight *equal instalments payable quarterly* (first quarter to be dated from *15 July*). Only on these partial payments when fallen due judicial prosecutions permitted (*16 April*). The Dufaure laws[5] on leases and bills of exchange entailed the bankruptcy of the majority of the respectable shopkeepers of Paris.

The notaries, bailiffs, auctioneers, bum-bailiffs and other judicial officers making till now a fortune of their functions, transformed into agents of the Commune receiving from it fixed salaries like other workmen.

As the professors of the École de Médecine have run away, the Commune appointed a commission for the foundation of *free universities*, no longer state parasites; given to the students that had passed their examination, means to practise independent of doctoral titles (titles to be conferred by the faculty).

Since the judges of the *Civil Tribunal of the Seine*, like the other magistrates always ready to function under any class government, had run away, the Commune appointed an advocate to do the most urgent business until the reorganization of tribunals on the basis of general suffrage (*26 April*).

3. General Measures

Conscription Abolished. In the present war every able man (National Guard) must serve. This measure excellent to get rid of all traitors and cowards hiding in Paris (*29 March*).

Games of Hazard Suppressed (*2 April*). Church separated from state; the religious budget suppressed; all clerical estates declared

5. See p. 197, n. 34.

national properties (*3 April*). The Commune, having made inquiries consequent upon private information, found that besides the old guillotine the '*government of order*' had commanded the construction of a new guillotine (more expeditious and portable) and paid in advance. The Commune ordered both the old and the new guillotines to be burned publicly on 6 April. The Versailles journals, re-echoed by the press of order all over the world, narrated that the Paris people, as a demonstration against the bloodthirstiness of the Communards, had burnt these guillotines! (*6 April*). All political prisoners were set free at once after the revolution of 18 March. But the Commune knew that under the regime of L. Bonaparte and his worthy successor the Government of Defence, many people were simply incarcerated on no charge whatever as political suspects. Consequently it charged one of its members – Protot[6] – to make inquiries. By him 150 people were set free who, being arrested six months before, had not yet undergone any judicial examination; many of them, already arrested under Bonaparte, had been for a year in prison without any charge or judicial examination (*9 April*). This fact, so characteristic of the Government of Defence, enraged them. They asserted that the Commune had liberated all felons. But who liberated convicted felons? The forger Jules Favre. Hardly got into power, he hastened to liberate Pic and Taillefer, condemned for theft and forgery in the affaire of the *Étendard*.[7] One of these men, Taillefer, daring to return to Paris, has been reinstated in his convenient abode. But this is not all. The Versailles government has delivered, in the Maisons Centrales[8] all over France, convicted thieves on the condition of entering M. Thiers's army.

Decree on the Demolition of the Column of the Place Vendôme. As 'a monument of barbarism, symbol of brute force and false glory, an affirmation of militarism, a negation of international right' (*12 April*).[9]

Election of Frankel[10] (German member of the International) to the Commune declared valid: 'considering that the flag of the Commune is that of the Universal Republic and that foreigners

6. Eugène Protot was a lawyer, doctor and journalist, a right-wing Blanquist and a member of the justice commission of the Paris Commune.

7. See p. 190, n. 11. 8. Prisons.

9. See p. 217, n. 72. 10. See p. 217, n. 70.

can have a seat in it' (*4 April*); Frankel afterwards chosen a member of the executive of the Commune (*21 April*).

The *Journal officiel* has inaugurated the publicity of the sittings of the Commune (*15 April*).

Decree of Pascal Grousset[11] for the protection of foreigners against requisitions. Never a government in Paris so courteous to foreigners (*27 April*).

The Commune has abolished political and professional oaths (*27 April*).

Destruction of the monument known as 'Chapelle expiatoire de Louis XVI'[12], rue d'Anjoy St Thérèse (the work of the *Chambre introuvable* of 1816) (*7 May*).

4. Measures of Public Safety

Disarmament of the 'loyal' National Guards (*30 March*); Commune declares incompatibility between seats in its ranks and at Versailles (*29 March*).

Decree of Reprisals. Never executed.[13] Only the fellows arrested, *Archbishop of Paris and Curé of the Madeleine*; whole staff of the college of Jesuits; incumbents of all the principal churches; *part of these fellows arrested* as hostages, part as conspirators with Versailles, part because they tried to save church property from the clutches of the Commune (*6 April*). 'The monarchists wage war like savages; they shoot prisoners, they murder the wounded, they fire on ambulances, troops raise the butt-end of their rifles in the air and then fire traitorously' (*Proclamation of Commune*).

In regard to these decrees of reprisals to be remarked:
In the first instance men of all layers of the Paris society – after the exodus of the capitalists, the idlers and the parasites – have interposed at Versailles to stop the civil war – *except the Paris*

11. Pascal Grousset, a Blanquist, was chairman of the Commune's foreign relations commission.
12. Chapel of atonement for Louis XVI (i.e. for his execution by the French revolutionary Convention).
13. After Marx wrote this draft, during the last days of the Commune's resistance, 64 hostages were executed by order of the Committee of Public Safety (see above, pp. 32 and 230).

clergy. The Archbishop and the Curé of the Madeleine have only written to Thiers because averse to '*the effusion of their own blood*,' in their quality as hostages.

Secondly: after the publication by the Commune of the decree of reprisal, the taking of hostages etc., the atrocious treatment of the Versailles prisoners by Piétri's lambs[14] and Valentin's gendarmes did not cease, but the assassination of the captive Paris soldiers and National Guard was stopped, to set in with renewed fury as soon as the Versailles government had convinced itself that the Commune was too humane to execute its decree of 6 April. Then the assassination set in again wholesale. The Commune did not execute one hostage, not one prisoner, not even some gendarme officers who under the disguise of National Guard had entered Paris as spies and were simply arrested.

Surprise of the Redoubt of Clamart (2 May). Railway station in the hands of the Parisians, massacre, bayonetting, the 22nd battalion of Chasseurs (*Galliffet?*) shoots line soldiers offhand without any formality (*2 May*). *Redoubt of Moulin Saquet*, situated between Fort Issy and Montrouge, surprised in the night by treachery on the part of the commandant *Gallien* who had sold the password to the *Versaillaise* troops. Federals surprised in their beds asleep, great part of them massacred (*4 May?*).

25 April. Four National Guards (this established by commissaries sent to Bicêtre where the only survivor of the four men, at Belle Epine, near Villejuif. His name *Scheffer*). These men being surrounded by horse Chasseurs, on their order, unable to resist, surrendered, disarmed, nothing done to them by the soldiers. But then arrives the captain of the Chasseurs, and shoots them down one after the other with his revolver. Left there on the soil. Scheffer, fearfully wounded, survived.

Thirteen soldiers of the line made prisoners at the railway station of Clamart were shot offhand, and all prisoners wearing the line uniforms who arrive in Versailles will be executed whenever doubts about their identity are cleared up. (*Liberté* at Versailles.) Alexander Dumas *fils*, now at Versailles, tells that a young man exercising the functions, if not bearing the title, of a general, was shot, by order of a Bonapartist general, after having [been]

14. An ironic reference to the *sergents de ville* trained by Piétri as prefect of police in Paris (1866–70).

marched in custody a few hundred yards along a road. Parisian troops and National Guards surrounded in houses by gendarmes, who inundate the house with petroleum and then fire it. Some cadavers of National Guards burnt to ashes have been transported by the ambulance of the press of the Ternes (*Mot d'ordre, 20 April*). 'They have no right to ambulances'.

Thiers. Blanqui. Archbishop. General Chanzy.[15] (Thiers said his Bonapartists should have liked to be shot.)

Visitation in Houses, etc. Casimir Bouis[16] named chairman of a commission of inquiry into the doings of the dictators of 4 September (*14 April*). Private houses invaded and papers seized, but no furniture has been carried away and sold by auction. (Papers of the fellows of 4 September, Thiers, etc. and Bonapartist policemen in the house of Lafont, inspector-general of prisons) (*11 April*). The houses (properties) of Thiers and Co. invaded as traitors, but *only the papers* confiscated.

Arrests among Themselves. This shocks the bourgeois who wants political idols and 'great men' immensely.

'It is *provoking* (*Daily News, 6 May*. Paris Correspondence), however, and *discouraging*, that whatever be the authority possessed by the Commune, it is continually changing hands, and we know not today with whom the power may rest tomorrow . . . In all these eternal changes one sees more than ever the want of a presiding hand. The Commune is a concourse of equivalent atoms, each one jealous of another and *none endowed with supreme control over the others*'.

Suppression of newspapers!

5. Financial Measures

See Daily News, 6 May.
Principal outlay for war!
    Only 8928 francs from seizures – all taken from ecclesiastics, etc.

Vengeur, 6 May.

15. Antoine Chanzy, a general and a deputy in the 1871 National Assembly, was taken hostage by the Commune, but released when the Versailles troops temporarily withdrew.
16. Casimir Bouis was a Blanquist member of the Commune.

The Commune: The Rise of the Commune and the Central Committee

The Commune had been proclaimed at Lyons, then Marseilles, Toulouse, etc., after Sedan. Gambetta tried his best to break it down.[17]

The different movements at Paris in the beginning of October aimed at the establishment of the Commune, as a measure of defence against the foreign invasion, as the realization of the rise of 4 September. Its establishment by the movement of 31 October[18] failed only because Blanqui, Flourens and the other then leaders of the movement believed in the men of their word who had given their word of honour to abdicate and make room for a Commune freely elected by all the *arrondissements* of Paris. It failed because they saved the lives of those men so eager for the assassination of their saviours. Having allowed Trochu and Ferry to escape, they were surprised by Trochu's Bretons. It ought to be remembered that on 31 October the self-imposed 'Government of Defence' existed only on sufferance. It had not yet gone even through the farce of a plebiscite.[19] Under the circumstances, there was of course nothing easier than to misrepresent the character of the movement, to decry it as a treasonable conspiracy with the Prussians, to improve [?] the dismissal of the only man amongst them who would not break his word,[20] to strengthen Trochu's Bretons who were for the Government of Defence what the Corsican bravos had been for L. Bonaparte by the appointment of Clément Thomas as commander-in-chief of the National Guard; there was nothing easier for these old panic-mongers [than] – appealing to the cowardly fears of the middle class [towards] working[-class] battalions who had taken the initiative, throwing distrust and dissension amongst the working[-class] battalions themselves, by an appeal to patriotism – to create one of those days of blind reaction and disastrous misunderstandings by which they have

17. The Communard risings of October–November 1870 in the south of France were crushed by the Government of Defence after a few days.

18. See pp. 201–2.

19. After the crisis of 31 October, the Government of Defence attempted to retrieve the initiative by holding a plebiscite on 3 November; it succeeded in gaining a majority by demagogy and police pressure.

20. General François Tamisier; see above, p. 202.

always contrived to maintain their usurped power. As they had slipped into power on 4 September by a surprise, they were now enabled to give it a mock sanction by a plebiscite of the true Bonapartist pattern during days of reactionary terror.

The victorious establishment in Paris of the Commune at the beginning of November 1870 (then already initiated in the great cities of the country and sure to be imitated all over France) would not only have taken the defence out of the hands of traitors, and imprinted its enthusiasm on it as the present heroic war of Paris shows, it would have altogether changed the character of the war. It would have become the war of republican France, hoisting the flag of the social revolution of the nineteenth century, against Prussia, the banner-bearer of conquest and counter-revolution. Instead of sending the hackneyed old intriguer[21] a-begging at all courts of Europe, it would have electrified the producing masses in the old and the new world. By juggling away the Commune on 31 October, Jules Favre and Co. secured the capitulation of France to Prussia and initiated the present civil war.

But this much is shown: the revolution of 4 September was not only the reinstalment of the republic, because the place of the usurper had become vacant by his capitulation at Sedan, it not only conquered that republic from the foreign invader by the prolonged resistance of Paris although fighting under the leadership of its enemies – that revolution was working its way into the heart of the working classes. The republic had ceased to be a name for a thing of the past. It was impregnated with a new world. Its real tendency, veiled from the eye of the world through the deceptions, the lies and the vulgarizing of a pack of intriguing lawyers and word fencers, came again and again to the surface in the spasmodic movements of the Paris working classes (and the south of France) whose watchword was always the same, the *Commune*!

The Commune – the positive form of the revolution against the Empire and the conditions of its existence – first essayed in the cities of southern France, again and again proclaimed in spasmodic movements during the siege of Paris and juggled away by the sleight of hand of the Government of Defence and the Bretons of Trochu, the 'plan of capitulation' hero – was at last victoriously installed on 26 March, but it had not suddenly sprung into life on that day. It was the unchangeable goal of the workmen's

21. Thiers; see above, p. 188.

revolution. The capitulation of Paris, the open conspiracy against the republic at Bordeaux, the coup d'état initiated by the nocturnal attack on Montmartre, rallied around it all the living elements of Paris, no longer allowing the Defence men to limit it to the insulated efforts of the most conscious and revolutionary portions of the Paris working class.

The Government of Defence was only undergone as a makeshift of the first surprise, a necessity of the war. The true answer of the Paris people to the Second Empire, the empire of lies – was the Commune.

Thus also the rising of all living Paris – with the exception of the pillars of Bonapartism and its official opposition, the great capitalists, the financial jobbers, the sharpers, the loungers, and the old state parasites – against the Government of Defence does not date from 18 March, although it conquered on that day its first victory against the conspiration, it dates from 31 January,[22] from the very day of the capitulation. The National Guard – that is all the armed manhood of Paris – organized itself and really ruled Paris from that day, independently of the usurpatory government of the *capitulards* installed by the grace of Bismarck. It refused to deliver its arms and artillery, which were its property, and only left them in the capitulation because of its property. It was not the magnanimity of Jules Favre that saved these arms from Bismarck, but the readiness of armed Paris to fight for its arms against Jules Favre and Bismarck. In view of the foreign invader and the peace negotiations, Paris would not complicate the situation. It was afraid of civil war. It observed a mere attitude of defence and content with the *de facto* self-rule of Paris. But it organized itself quietly and steadfastly for resistance. Even in the terms of the capitulation itself the *capitulards* had unmistakably shown their tendency to make the surrender to Prussia at the same time the means of their domination over Paris. The only concession by Prussia they insisted upon, a concession which Bismarck would have imposed upon them as a condition, if they had not begged it as a concession – was 40,000 soldiers for subduing Paris. In the face of its 300,000 National Guards – more than sufficient for securing Paris from an attempt by the foreign enemy, and for the defence of its internal order – the demand of these 40,000 men – a thing which was besides avowed – could have no other purpose.

22. The armistice was in fact signed on 28 January; see above, p. 188, n. 5.

On its existing military organization it grafted a political federation according to a very simple plan. It was the alliance of all the National Guard, put in connection the one with the other *by the delegates* of each company, appointing in their turn the delegates of the battalions, who in their turn appointed general delegates, generals of legions, who were to represent an *arrondissement* and to cooperate with the delegates of the nineteen other *arrondissements*. Those twenty delegates, chosen by the majority of the battalions of the National Guard, composed the Central Committee, which on 18 March initiated the greatest revolution of this century and still holds its post in the present glorious struggle of Paris. Never were elections more sifted, never delegates fuller representing the masses from which they had sprung. To the objection of the outsiders that they were unknown – in point of fact, that they only were known to the working classes, but no old stagers, no men illustrious by the infamies of their past, by their chase after pelf and place – they proudly answered, 'So were the twelve apostles', and they answered by their deeds.

The Character of the Commune

The centralized state machinery which, with its ubiquitous and complicated military, bureaucratic, clerical and judiciary organs, entoils (enmeshes) the living civil society like a boa constrictor, was first forged in the days of absolute monarchy as a weapon of nascent modern society in its struggle of emancipation from feudalism. The seignorial privileges of the medieval lords and cities and clergy were transformed into the attributes of a unitary state power, displacing the feudal dignitaries by salaried state functionaries, transferring the arms from medieval retainers of the landlords and the corporations of townish citizens to a standing army; substituting for the checkered (parti-coloured) anarchy of conflicting medieval powers the regulated plan of a state power, with a systematic and hierarchic division of labour. The first French revolution with its task to found national unity (to create a nation) had to break down all local, territorial, townish and provincial independence. It was, therefore, forced to develop what absolute monarchy had commenced, the centralization and organization of state power, and to expand the circumference and the attributes of the state power, the number of its tools, its independence, and its supernaturalist sway over real society which in fact took the place of the medieval supernaturalist heaven, with its saints. Every minor solitary interest engendered by the relations of social groups was separated from society itself, fixed and made independent of it and opposed to it in the form of state interest, administered by state priests with exactly determined hierarchical functions.

This parasitical [excrescence upon] civil society, pretending to be its ideal counterpart, grew to its full development under the sway of the first Bonaparte. The Restoration and the monarchy of July [1830] added nothing to it but a greater division of labour, growing at the same measure in which the division of labour within civil society created new groups of interests, and therefore new material for state action. In their struggle against the revolution of 1848, the parliamentary republic of France and the governments of all continental Europe were forced to strengthen, with their measures of repression against the popular movement, the means of action and the centralization of that governmental power. All revolutions thus only perfected the state machinery instead of throwing off this deadening incubus. The fractions and parties of the ruling classes which alternately struggled for supremacy, considered the occupancy (control) (seizure) and the direction of this immense machinery of government as the main booty of the victor. It centred in the creation of immense standing armies, a host of state vermin, and huge national debts. During the time of the absolute monarchy it was a means of the struggle of modern society against feudalism, crowned by the French revolution, and under the first Bonaparte it served not only to subjugate the revolution and annihilate all popular liberties, it was an instrument of the French revolution to strike abroad, to create for France on the Continent, instead of feudal monarchies, more or less states after the image of France. Under the Restoration and the monarchy of July it became not only a means of the forcible class domination of the middle class, and a means of adding to the direct economic exploitation a second exploitation of the people by assuring to their families all the rich places of the state household. During the time of the revolutionary struggle of 1848 at last it served as a means of annihilating that revolution and all aspirations at the emancipation of the popular masses. But the state parasite received only its last development during the Second Empire. The governmental power with its standing army, its all-directing bureaucracy, its stultifying clergy and its servile tribunal hierarchy had grown so independent of society itself that a grotesquely mediocre adventurer with a hungry band of desperadoes behind him sufficed to wield it. It did no longer want the pretext of an armed coalition of old Europe against the modern world founded by the revolution of 1789. It appeared no longer as a means of class domination, subordinate to its parliamentary ministry or legislature. Humbling under its sway even the interests of the ruling classes, whose parliamentary show work it supplanted by self-elected Corps Législatifs and self-paid Senates,[23] sanctioned in its absolute sway by universal suffrage, the acknowledged necessity for keeping up 'order', that is the rule of the landowner and the capitalist over the producer, cloaking under the tatters of a masquerade of the past, the orgies of the corruption of the present and the victory of the most parasite fraction, the financial swindler, the *debauchery* of all the reactionary influences of the past let loose – a pandemonium of infamies – the state power had received its last and supreme expression in the Second Empire. Apparently the final victory of this governmental power over society, it was in fact the orgy of all the corrupt elements of that society. To the eye of the uninitiated it appeared only as the victory of the executive over the legislative, of the final defeat of the form of class rule pretending to be the autocracy of society by its form pretending to be a superior power to society. But in fact it was only the last degraded and the only possible form of that class ruling, as humiliating to those classes themselves as to the working classes which they kept fettered by it.

4 September was only the revindication of the republic against the grotesque adventurer that had assassinated it. The true antithesis to the *Empire itself* – that is to the state power, the centralized executive, of which the Second Empire was only the exhausting formula – was *the Commune*. This state power forms in fact the creation of the middle class, first a means to break down feudal-

23. The legislature of the Second Empire comprised the Corps Législatif (Legislative Body) and the Senate. The Corps Législatif was elected by universal male suffrage, but besides the absence of freedom of the press, association and assembly, and frequent police terrorism against the opposition, the Bonapartist regime constantly manipulated the elections. The Senate was partly elected, and partly consisted of government functionaries sitting *ex officio*.

ism, then a means to crush the emancipatory aspirations of the producers, of the working class. All reactions and all revolutions had only served to transfer that organized power – that organized force of the slavery of labour – from one hand to the other, from one fraction of the ruling classes to the other. It had served the ruling classes as a means of subjugation and of pelf. It had sucked new forces from every new change. It had served as the instrument of breaking down every popular rise and served it to crush the working classes after they had fought and been ordered to secure its transfer from one part of its oppressors to the others. This was, therefore, a revolution not against this or that Legitimate, Constitutional, Republican or Imperialist form of state power. It was a revolution against the *state* itself, this supernaturalist abortion of society, a resumption by the people for the people of its own social life. It was not a revolution to transfer it from one fraction of the ruling classes to the other, but a revolution to break down this horrid machinery of class domination itself. It was not one of those dwarfish struggles between the executive and the parliamentary forms of class domination, but a revolt against both these forms, integrating each other, and of which the parliamentary form was only the deceitful by-work of the executive. The Second Empire was the final form of this state usurpation. The Commune was its definite negation, and, therefore, the initiation of the social revolution of the nineteenth century. Whatever therefore its fate at Paris, it will make its way round the world. It was at once acclaimed by the working class of Europe and the United States as the magic word of delivery. The glories and the antediluvian deeds of the Prussian conqueror seemed only hallucinations of a bygone past.

It was only the working class that could formulate by the word 'Commune' – and initiate by the fighting Commune of Paris – this new aspiration. Even the last expression of that state power in the Second Empire, although humbling for the pride of the ruling classes and casting to the winds their parliamentary pretensions of self-government, had been only the last possible form of their class rule. While politically dispossessing them, it was the orgy under which all the economic and social infamies of their regime got full sway. The middling bourgeoisie and the petty middle class were by their economical conditions of life excluded from initiating a new revolution and induced to follow in the track of the ruling classes or be the followers of the working class. The peasants were the passive economical basis of the Second Empire, of that last triumph of a *state* separate of and independent from society. Only the proletarians, fired by a new social task to accomplish by them for all society, to do away with all classes and class rule, were the men to break the instrument of that class rule – the state, the centralized and organized governmental power usurping to be the master instead of the servant of society. In the active struggle against them by the ruling classes, supported by the passive adherence of the peasantry, the Second Empire, the last crowning at the same time as the most signal prostitution of the state – which had taken the place of the medieval church – had been engendered. It had sprung into life against them. By them it was broken, not as a peculiar form of governmental (centralized) power, but as its most powerful, elaborated into seeming independence from society, expression, and, therefore, also its most prostitute reality, covered by infamy from top to bottom, having centred in absolute corruption at home and absolute powerlessness abroad.

But this one form of class rule had only broken down to make the executive, the governmental state machinery, the great and single object of attack to the revolution.

Parliamentarism in France had come to an end. Its last term and fullest sway was the parliamentary republic from May 1848 to the coup d'état. The Empire that killed it was its own creation. Under the Empire with its Corps Législatif and its Senate – in this form it has been reproduced in the military monarchies of Prussia and Austria – it had been a mere farce, a mere by-word for despotism in its crudest form. Parliamentarism then was dead in France, and the workmen's revolution certainly was not to awaken it from this death.

The *Commune* – the reabsorption of the state power by society as its own living forces instead of as forces controlling and subduing it, by the popular masses themselves, forming their own force instead of the organized force of their suppression – the political form of their social emancipation, instead of the artificial force (appropriated by their oppressors) (their own force opposed to and organized against them) of society wielded for their oppression by their enemies. The form was simple, like all great things. The reaction of former revolutions – the time wanted for all historical developments, and in the past always lost in all revolutions, in the very days of popular triumph, whenever it had rendered its victorious arms, to be turned against itself – first by displacing the army by the National Guard. 'For the first time since 4 September the republic is liberated from the *government of its enemies* . . . to the city a national militia that defends the citizens against the power (the government) *instead of a permanent army that defends the government* against the citizens'. (Proclamation of Central Committee of 22 March.) (The people had only to organize this militia on a national scale, to have done away with the standing armies; the first economical condition *sine qua non* for all social improvements, discarding at once this source of taxes and state debt, and this constant danger to government usurpation of class rule – of the regular class rule or an adventurer pretending to save all classes); at the same time the safest guarantee against foreign aggression and making in fact the costly military apparatus impossible in all other states; the emancipation of the peasant from the blood-tax and [from being] the most fertile source of all state taxation and state debts. Here already the point in which the Commune is a *luck for the peasant*, the first word of his emancipation. With the 'independent police' abolished, and its ruffians supplanted by servants of the Commune. The general suffrage, till now abused either for the parliamentary sanction of the Holy State Power, or a play in the hands of the ruling classes, only employed by the people to sanction (choose the instruments of) parliamentary class rule once in many years, adapted to its real purposes, to choose by the communes their own functionaries of administration and initiation. The delusion as if administration and political governing were mysteries, transcendent functions only to be trusted to the hands of a trained caste – state parasites, richly paid sycophants and sinecurists, in the higher posts, absorbing the intelligence of the masses and turning them against themselves in the lower places of the hierarchy. Doing away with the state hierarchy altogether and replacing the haughty masters of the people by always removable servants, a mock responsibility by a real responsibility, as they act continuously under public supervision. Paid like skilled workmen, £12 a month, the highest salary not exceeding £240 a year, a salary somewhat more than a fifth, according to a great scientific authority, Professor Huxley, [of that needed] to satisfy a clerk for the Metropolitan School Board. The whole sham of state mysteries and state pretensions was done away with by a Commune, mostly consisting of simple working men, organizing the defence of Paris, carrying war against the praetorians of Bonaparte, securing the supplies for that immense town, filling all the posts hitherto divided between government, police, and prefecture, doing their work publicly, simply, under the most difficult and complicated circumstances, and doing it, as Milton did his *Paradise Lost*, for a few pounds, acting in bright daylight, with no pretensions to infallibility, not hiding itself behind circumlocution offices, not ashamed to confess blunders by correcting them. Making in one order the public functions – military, administrative, political – *real workmen's functions*, instead of the hidden attributes of a trained caste; (keeping order in the turbulence of civil war and revolution) (initiating measures of general regeneration). Whatever the merits of the single measures of the Commune, its greatest measure was its own organization, extemporized with the foreign enemy at one door, and the class enemy at the other, proving by its life its vitality, confirming its thesis by its action. Its appearance was a victory over the victors of France. Captive Paris resumed by one bold spring the leadership of Europe, not depending on brute force, but by taking the lead of the social movement, by giving body to the aspirations of the working class of all countries.

With all the great towns organized into communes after the model of Paris, no government could have repressed the movement by the surprise of sudden reaction. Even by this preparatory step the time of incubation, the guarantee of the movement [would have been won]. All France organized into self-working and self-governing communes, the standing army replaced by the popular militias, the army of state parasites removed, the clerical hierarchy displaced by the schoolmaster, the state judges transformed into Communal organs, the suffrage for the national representation not a matter of sleight of hand for an all-powerful government but the deliberate expression of organized communes, the state functions reduced to a few functions for general national purposes.

Such is the *Commune – the political form of the social emancipation*, of the liberation of labour from the usurpations (slave-holding) of the monopolists of the means of labour, created by the labourers themselves or forming the gift of nature. As the state machinery and parliamentarism are not the real life of the ruling classes, but only the organized general organs of their dominion, the political guarantees and forms and expressions of the old order of things, so the Commune is not the social movement of the working class and therefore of a general regeneration of mankind, but the organized means of action. The Commune does not do away with the class struggles, through which the working classes strive to the abolition of all classes and, therefore, of all [class rule] (because it does not represent a peculiar interest. It represents the liberation of 'labour', that is the fundamental and natural condition of individual and social life which only by usurpation, fraud, and artificial contrivances can be shifted from the few upon the many), but it affords the rational medium in which that class struggle can run through its different phases in the most rational and humane way. It could start violent reactions and as violent revolutions. It begins the *emancipation of labour* – its great goal – by doing away with the unproductive and mischievous work of the state parasites, by cutting away the springs which sacrifice an immense portion of the national produce to the feeding of the state monster on the one side, by doing, on the other, the real work of administration, local and national, for workingmen's wages. It begins therefore with an immense saving, with economical reform as well as political transformation.

The Communal organization once firmly established on a national scale, the catastrophes it might still have to undergo would be sporadic slaveholders' insurrections, which, while for a moment interrupting the work of peaceful progress, would only accelerate the movement, by putting the sword into the hand of the social revolution.

The working class know that they have to pass through different phases of class struggle. They know that the superseding of the economical conditions of the slavery of labour by the conditions of free and associated labour can only be the progressive work of time (that economical transformation), that they require not only a change of distribution, but a new organization of production, or rather the delivery (setting free) of the social forms of production in present organized labour (engendered by present industry), of the trammels of slavery, of their present class character, and their harmonious national and international coordination. They know that this work of regeneration will be again and again relented and impeded by the resistance of vested interests and class egotisms. They know that the present 'spontaneous action of the natural laws of capital and landed property' – can only be superseded by 'the spontaneous action of

the laws of the social economy of free and associated labour'
by a long process of development of new conditions, as was the
'spontaneous action of the economic laws of slavery' and the
'spontaneous action of the economic laws of serfdom'. But they
know at the same time that great strides may be [made] at once
through the Communal form of political organization and that
the time has come to begin that movement for themselves and
mankind.

Peasantry

(*War indemnity.*) Even before the instalment of the Commune, the
Central Committee had declared through its *Journal officiel*: '*The
greater part of the war indemnity should be paid by the authors
of war*'. This is the great 'conspiracy against civilization' the men
of order are most afraid of. This is the most practical question.
With the Commune victorious, the authors of the war will have
to pay its indemnity; with Versailles victorious, the producing
masses who have already paid in blood, ruin, and contribution,
will have again to pay, and the financial dignitaries will even
contrive to make a profit out of the transaction. The liquidation
of the war costs is to be decided by the civil war. The Commune
represents on this vital point not only the interests of the working
class, the petty middle class, in fact, all the middle class with the
exception of the *bourgeoisie* (the wealthy capitalists) (the rich
landowners, and their state parasites). It represents above all the
interest of the *French peasantry*. On them the greater part of the
war taxes will be shifted, if Thiers and his 'Rurals' are victorious.
And people are silly enough to repeat the cry of the 'Rurals' that
they – the great landed proprietors – 'represent the peasant', who
is of course, in the naivety of his soul, exceedingly anxious to
pay for these good 'landowners' the milliards of the war indemnity, who made him already pay the milliard of indemnity: the
revolution indemnity.[24]

The same men deliberately compromised the republic of February
[1848] by the additional 45 centimes tax on the peasant,[25] but
this they did in the name of the revolution, in the name of the
'Provisional Government' created by it. It is now in their own

24. See p. 215, n. 65. On the 'Rurals' see above, pp. 195–6.
25. See 'The Class Struggles in France', *Surveys from Exile*, p. 51.

name that they wage a civil war against the Communal republic to shift the war indemnity from their own shoulders upon those of the peasant! He will of course be delighted by it!

The Commune will abolish conscription, the party of Order will fasten this blood-tax on the peasant. The party of Order will fasten upon him the tax-collector for the payment of a parasitical and costly state machinery, the Commune will give him a cheap government. The party of Order will continue to grind him down by the townish usurer, the Commune will free him of the incubus of the mortgages resting upon his plot of land. The Commune will replace the parasitical judiciary body eating the heart of his income – the notary, the bailiff, etc. – by Communal agents doing their work at workmen's salaries, instead of enriching themselves out of the peasant's work. It will break down this whole judiciary cobweb which entangles the French peasant and gives abodes to the judiciary bench and mayors of the bourgeois spiders that suck its blood! The party of Order will keep him under the rule of the gendarme, the Commune will restore him to independent social and political life! The Commune will enlighten him by the rule of the schoolmaster, the party of Order force upon him the stultification by the rule of the priest! But the French peasant is above all a man of reckoning! He will find it exceedingly reasonable that the payment of the clergy will no longer be exacted from him by the tax-collector, but will be left to the 'spontaneous action' of his religious instinct!

The French peasant had elected Louis Bonaparte President of the Republic, but the party of Order (during the anonymous regime of the republic under the Constituent and the Legislative Assemblies) was the creator of the Empire! What the French peasant really wants, he commenced to show in 1849 and 1852 by opposing his mayor to the government's prefect, his schoolmaster to the government's parson, himself to the government's gendarme! The nucleus of the reactionary laws of the party of Order in 1849 – and peculiarly in January and February 1850 – were specifically directed against the French peasantry! If the French peasant had made Louis Bonaparte President of the Republic because in his tradition all the benefits he had derived from the first revolution were fantastically transferred on the first Napoleon, the armed risings of peasants in some departments of France and the gendarme hunting upon them after the coup d'état proved that that delusion was rapidly breaking down! The Empire was founded on the delusions artificially nourished into power and traditional prejudices, the Commune would be founded on his living interests and his real wants.

The hatred of the French peasant is centring on the 'Rurals', the men of the *châteaux*, the men of the milliard of indemnity, and the townish capitalists masqueraded into landed proprietors, whose encroachment upon him marched never more rapidly than under the Second Empire, partly fostered by artificial state means, partly naturally growing out of the very development of modern agriculture. The 'Rurals' know that three months' rule of the republican Commune in France would be the signal for the rising of the peasantry and the agricultural proletariat against them. Hence their ferocious hatred of the Commune! What they fear even more than the emancipation of the townish proletariat is the emancipation of the peasants. The peasants would soon acclaim the townish proletariat as their own leaders and seniors. There exists of course in France as in most continental countries a deep antagonism between the townish and rural producers, between the industrial proletariat and the peasantry. The aspirations of the proletariat, the material basis of its movement, is labour organized on a grand scale, although now despotically organized, and the means of production centralized, although now centralized in the hands of the monopolist, not only as a means of production, but as a means of the exploitation and enslavement of the producer. What the proletariat has to do is to transform the present capitalist character of that organized labour and those centralized means of labour, to transform them from the means of class rule and class exploitation into forms of free associated labour and social means of production. On the other hand, the labour of the peasant is insulated and the means of production are parcelled, dispersed. On these economical differences rests super-constructed a whole world of different social and political views. But this peasant proprietorship has long since outgrown its normal phase, that is the phase in which it was a reality, a mode of production and a form of property which responded to the economical wants of society and placed the rural producers themselves in normal conditions of life. It has entered its period of decay. On the one side a large *prolétariat foncier* (rural proletariat) has grown out of it whose interests are identical with those of the townish wage

labourers. The mode of production itself has become super-
annuated by the modern progress of agronomy. Lastly – the
peasant proprietorship itself has become nominal, leaving to the
peasant the delusion of proprietorship and expropriating him from
the fruits of his own labour. The competition of the great farm
producers, the blood-tax, the state tax, the usury of the townish
mortgagee and the multitudinous pilfering of the judiciary system
thrown around him, have degraded him to the position of a Hindu
ryot,[26] while expropriation – even expropriation from his nominal
proprietorship – and his degradation into a rural proletarian is an
every day fact. What separates the peasant from the proletarian is,
therefore, no longer his real interest, but his delusive prejudice. If
the Commune, as we have shown, is the only power that can give
him immediate great loans even in its present economical conditions, it is the only form of government that can secure to him the
transformation of his present economical conditions, rescue him
from expropriation by the landlord on the one hand, save him from
grinding, drudging and misery on the pretext of proprietorship on
the other, that can convert his nominal proprietorship of the land
into real proprietorship of the fruits of his labour, that can combine
for him the profits of modern agronomy, dictated by social wants
and every day now encroaching upon him as a hostile agency,
without annihilating his position as a really independent producer.
Being immediately benefited by the Communal republic, he would
soon confide in it.

Union (Ligue) Républicaine

The party of disorder, whose regime topped [?] under the corruption of the Second Empire, has left Paris (exodus from Paris),
followed by its appurtenances, its retainers, its menials, its state
parasites, its *mouchards*,[27] its *'cocottes'*, and the whole band of
low *bohème* (the common criminals) that form the complement of
that *bohème of quality*. But the true vital elements of the middle
classes, delivered by the workmen's revolution from their sham
representatives, have for the first time in the history of French revolutions separated from them and come out in their true colours.
This is the 'League of Republican Liberty'[28] acting the inter-

26. An impoverished Indian peasant proprietor under a land tenure system introduced by the British. See Marx's article 'Indian Affairs', *Surveys from Exile*, pp. 316–19.
27. Police spies.   28. See above, p. 214.

mediary between Paris and the provinces, disavowing Versailles and marching under the banners of the Commune.

The Communal Revolution as the Representative of all Classes of Society not Living upon Foreign Labour

We have seen that the Paris proletarian fights for the French peasant, and Versailles fights against him; that the greatest anxiety of the 'Rurals' is that Paris be heard by the peasants and no longer separated from them through the blockade; that at the bottom of its war upon Paris is the attempt to keep the peasant as its bond-man and treat him as before as its material *'taillable à merci et miséricorde'*.[29]

For the first time in history the petty and middling middle class has openly rallied round the workmen's revolution, and proclaimed it as the only means of their own salvation and that of France! It forms with them the bulk of the National Guard, it sits with them in the Commune, it mediates for them in the Union Républicaine!

The principal measures taken by the Commune are taken for the salvation of the middle class – the debtor class of Paris against the creditor class! That middle class had rallied in the June insurrection (1848) against the proletariat under the banners of the capitalist class, their generals and their state parasites. It was punished at once on 19 September 1848 by the rejection of the *'concordats à l'amiable'*.[30] The victory over the June insurrection showed itself at once also as the victory of the creditor, the wealthy capitalist over the debtor, the middle class. It insisted mercilessly on its pound of flesh. On 13 June 1849 the National Guard of that middle class was disarmed and sabred down by the army of the bourgeoisie![31] During the Empire, [as a result of] the dilapidation of the state resources upon which the wealthy capitalist fed, this middle class was delivered to the plunder of the stock-jobbers, the railway kings, the swindling associations of the Crédit Mobilier,[32] etc., and expropriated by capitalist association (joint-stock company). If lowered in its political position, attacked in its economical interests, it was morally revolted by the orgies of that

29. Taxable at its pleasure and at its mercy.
30. See 'The Class Struggles in France', *Surveys from Exile*, pp. 66–7.
31. Ibid., pp. 97–100.   32. See p. 103, n. 47.

regime. The infamies of the war gave the last shock and roused its feelings as Frenchmen. The disasters bestowed upon France by that war, its crisis of national breakdown and its financial ruin, this middle class feels that not the corrupt class of the would-be slave-holders of France, but only the manly aspirations and the herculean power of the working class, can come to the rescue!

They feel that only the working class can emancipate them from priest rule, convert science from an instrument of class rule into a popular force, convert the men of science themselves from the panderers to class prejudice, place-hunting parasites, and allies of capital into free agents of thought! Science can only play its genuine part in the republic of labour.

Republic Only Possible as Avowedly Social Republic

This civil war has destroyed the last delusions about the 'republic', as the Empire the delusion of unorganized 'universal suffrage' in the hands of the state gendarme and the parson. All vital elements of France acknowledge that a republic is only possible in France and Europe as a 'social republic', that is a republic which disowns the capital and landowner class of the state machinery to supersede it by the Commune, that frankly avows 'social emancipation' as the great goal of the republic and guarantees thus that social transformation by the Communal organization. The other republic can be nothing but the *anonymous* terrorism of all monarchical fractions, of the combined Legitimists, Orleanists, and Bonapartists, to land in an empire of some kind as its final goal, the *anonymous* terror of class rule which, having done its dirty work, will always burst into an empire!

The professional republicans of the Rural Assembly are men who really believe, despite the experiments of 1848–51, despite the civil war against Paris – the *republican form* of class despotism a possible, lasting form, while the 'party of Order' demands it only as a form of conspiracy for fighting the republic and reintroducing its only adequate form, monarchy or rather Imperialism,[33] as the form of class despotism. In 1848 these voluntary dupes were

33. See p. 34, n. 62.

pushed in the foreground till, by the insurrection of June, they had paved the way for the *anonymous* rule of all fractions of the would-be slave-holders in France. In 1871, at Versailles, they are from the beginning pushed into the background, there to figure as the 'republican' decoration of Thiers's rule and sanction by their presence the war of the Bonapartist generals upon Paris! In unconscious self-irony these wretches hold their party meeting in the Salle de Paume (tennis court) to show how they have degenerated from their predecessors in 1789! By their Schölchers,[34] etc. they tried to coax Paris into tendering its arms to Thiers and to force it into disarmament by the National Guard of 'order' under Saisset! We do not speak of the so-called socialist Paris deputies like Louis Blanc.[35] They undergo meekly the insults of a Dufaure and the Rurals, dote upon Thiers's 'legal' rights, and whining in the presence of the banditti cover themselves with infamy!

Workmen and Comte

If the workmen have outgrown the time of socialist sectarianism, it ought not [to] be forgotten that they have never been in the leading strings of Comtism. This sect has never afforded the International but a *branch* of about half a dozen men, whose programme was rejected by the General Council.[36] Comte is known to the Parisian workmen as the prophet in politics of Imperialism (of personal *dictatorship*), of capitalist rule in political economy, of hierarchy in all spheres of human action, even in the sphere of science, and as the author of a new catechism with a new pope and new saints in place of the old ones.

If his followers in England play a more popular part than those in France it is not by preaching their sectarian doctrines, but by their personal valour, and by the acceptance by their sect of the

34. Victor Schölcher was a left-wing republican deputy to the National Assembly of 1871. As the commander of an artillery legion of the National Guard in Paris, he attempted, on 17 March, to bring about the capitulation of Paris to the Versailles government.

35. This veteran social reformist of the 1840s, prominent in the Provisional Government of 1848, was elected to the 1871 National Assembly, and sat in Versailles during the rise and fall of the Commune.

36. Early in 1870 the Comtist 'Society of Positivist Proletarians' was allowed to affiliate to the International, although the General Council criticized its programme. See below, p. 288.

forms of working men's class struggle created without them, as for instance the trade unions and strikes in England which, by the bye, are denounced as heresy by their Paris co-religionists.

The Commune (*Social Measures*)

That the workmen of Paris have taken the initiative of the present revolution and in heroic self-sacrifice bear the brunt of this battle, is nothing new. It is the striking fact of all French revolutions! It is only a repetition of the past! That the revolution is made in *the name of* and confessedly *for* the popular masses, that is the producing masses, is a feature this revolution has in common with all its predecessors. The new feature is that the people, after the first rise, have not disarmed themselves and surrendered their power into the hands of the republican mountebanks of the ruling classes, that, by the constitution of the *Commune*, they have taken the actual management of their revolution into their own hands and found at the same time, in the case of success, the means to hold it in the hands of the people itself, displacing the state machinery, the governmental machinery of the ruling classes by a governmental machinery of their own. This is their ineffable crime! Workmen infringing upon the governmental privilege of the upper 10,000 and proclaiming their will to break the economical basis of that class despotism which for its own sake wielded the organized state force of society! This it is that has thrown the respectable classes in Europe as in the United States into a paroxysm of convulsions and accounts for their shrieks of abomination (it is blasphemy), their fierce appeals to assassination of the people and the Billingsgate of abuse and calumny from their parliamentary tribunes and their journalistic servants' hall!

The greatest measure of the Commune is its own existence, working, acting under circumstances of unheard-of difficulty! The red flag, hoisted by the Paris Commune, crowns in reality only the government of workmen for Paris! They have clearly, consciously proclaimed the emancipation of labour, and the transformation of society, as their goal! But the actual 'social' character of their republic consists only in this, that workmen govern the Paris Commune! As to their measures, they must, by the nature of things, be principally confined to the military defence of Paris and its supply!

Some patronizing friends of the working class, while hardly dissembling their disgust even at the few measures they consider as 'socialist', although there is nothing socialist in them except their tendency – express their satisfaction and try to coax genteel sympathies for the Paris Commune by the great discovery that, after all, workmen are rational men and whenever in power always resolutely turn their back upon socialist enterprises! They do in fact neither try to establish in Paris a *phalanstère* nor an *Icarie*.[37] Wise men of their generation! These benevolent patronizers, profoundly ignorant of the real aspirations and the real movement of the working classes, forget one thing. All the socialist founders of sects belong to a period in which the working classes themselves were neither sufficiently trained and organized by the march of capitalist society itself to enter as historical agents upon the world's stage, nor were the material conditions of their emancipation sufficiently matured in the old world itself. Their misery existed, but the conditions of their own movement did not yet exist. The utopian founders of sects, while in their criticism of present society clearly describing the goal of the social movement, the supersession of the wages system with all its economical conditions of class rule, found neither in society itself the material conditions of its transformation, nor in the working class the organized power and the conscience of the movement. They tried to compensate for the historical conditions of the movement by fantastic pictures and plans of a new society in whose propaganda they saw the true means of salvation. From the moment the working men's class movement became real, the fantastic utopias evanesced, not because the working class had given up the end aimed at by these utopians, but because they had found the real means to realize them, and in their place came a real insight into the historic conditions of the movement and a more and more gathering force of the militant organization of the working class. But the last two ends of the movement proclaimed by the utopians are the last ends proclaimed by the Paris revolution and by the International. Only the means are different, and the real conditions of the movement are no longer clouded in utopian fables. These patronizing friends of the proletariat, in glossing over the loudly proclaimed socialist tendencies of this revolution, are therefore but the dupes of their own ignorance. It is not the fault of the Paris proletariat, if for them the utopian creations of the prophets

37. Utopian communities envisaged by Charles Fourier and Étienne Cabet respectively.

of the working men's movement are still the 'social revolution', that is to say, if the social revolution is for them still 'utopian'.

*

Journal officiel of the Central Committee, 20 March:
'The proletarians of the capital, amidst the failures and the treasons of the governing (ruling) classes, have understood that the hour has arrived for them *to save the situation by taking into their own hands the direction (management) of public affairs* (the state business)'. They denounce 'the political incapacity and the moral decrepitude of the bourgeoisie' as the source of 'the misfortunes of France'.

'The workmen, who produce everything and enjoy nothing, who suffer from misery in the midst of their accumulated products, the fruit of their work and their sweat . . . *shall they never be allowed to work for their emancipation*? . . . The proletariat, in face of the permanent menace against its rights, of the absolute negation of all its legitimate aspirations, of the ruin of the country and all its hopes, has understood that it was its imperious duty and its absolute right to take into its hands its own destinies and to assure their triumph in seizing the state power'.

It is here plainly stated that the government of the working class is, in the first instance, necessary to save France from the ruins and the corruption impended upon it by the ruling classes, that the dislodgement of these classes from power (of these classes who have lost the capacity of ruling France) is *a necessity of national safety*.

But it is no less clearly stated that the government by the working class can only save France and do the national business by working for its *own emancipation*, the conditions of that emancipation being at the same time the conditions of the regeneration of France.

It is proclaimed as a war of labour upon the monopolists of the means of labour, upon capital.

The *chauvinism* of the bourgeoisie is only a vanity, giving a national cloak to all their own pretensions. It is a means, by permanent armies, to perpetuate international struggles, to subjugate in each country the producers by pitching them against their brothers in each other country, a means to prevent the international cooperation of the working classes, the first condition of their emancipation. The true character of that chauvinism (long since become a mere phrase) has come out during the war of defence after Sedan, everywhere paralysed by the chauvinist bourgeoisie in the capitulation of France, in the civil war carried on under that high priest of chauvinism, Thiers, on Bismarck's sufferance! It came out in the petty police intrigue of the Anti-German League, in foreigner-hunting in Paris after the capitulation. It was hoped that the Paris people (and the French people) could be stultified into the passion of national hatred and by factitious outrages to the foreigner forget its real aspiration and its home betrayers!

How has this factitious movement disappeared (vanished) before the breath of revolutionary Paris! Loudly proclaiming its international tendencies – because the cause of the producer is everywhere the same and its enemy everywhere the same, whatever its nationality (in whatever national garb) – it proclaimed as a principle the admission of foreigners into the Commune, it even chose a foreign workman (a member of the International) onto its executive,[38] it decreed [the destruction of] the symbol of French chauvinism – the Vendôme column!

And while the bourgeois *chauvins* have dismembered France, and act under the dictatorship of the foreign invasion, the Paris workmen have beaten the foreign enemy by striking at their own class rulers, have abolished fractions, in conquering the post as the vanguard of the workmen of all nations!

The genuine patriotism of the bourgeoisie – so natural for the real proprietors of the different 'national' estates – has faded into a mere sham consequent upon the cosmopolitan character imprinted upon their financial, commercial, and industrial enterprise. Under similar circumstances it would explode in all countries as it did in France.

Decentralization by the Rurals and the Commune

It has been said that Paris, and with it the other French towns, were oppressed by the rule of the peasants, and that its present struggle is for its emancipation from the rule of the peasantry! Never was a more foolish lie uttered!

Paris, as the central seat and the stronghold of the centralized government machinery, subjected the peasantry to the rule of the

38. Leo Frankel.

gendarme, the tax-collector, the prefect, the priest, and the rural magnates, that is to the despotism of its enemies, and deprived it of all life (took the life out of it). It repressed all organs of independent life in the rural districts. On the other hand, the government, the rural magnate, the gendarme and the priest, into whose hands the whole influence of the provinces was thus thrown by the centralized state machinery centring at Paris, brought this influence to bear for the government and the classes whose government it was, not against the Paris of the government, the parasite, the capitalist, the idle, the cosmopolitan stew, but against the Paris of the workman and the thinker. In this way, by the government centralization with Paris as its base, the peasants were suppressed by the Paris of the government and the capitalist, and the Paris of the workmen was suppressed by the provincial power handed over into the hands of the enemies of the peasants.

The Versailles *Moniteur* (29 March) declares that 'Paris cannot be a *free city*, because it is *the capital*'. This is the true thing. Paris, the capital of the ruling classes and its government, cannot be a 'free city', and the provinces cannot be 'free', because such a Paris is the capital. The provinces can only be free with the Commune at Paris. The party of Order is still less infuriated against Paris because it has proclaimed its own emancipation from them and their government, than because, by doing so, it has sounded the alarm signal for the emancipation of the peasant and the provinces from their sway.

Journal officiel de la Commune, 1 April: 'The revolution of 18 March had not for its only object the securing to Paris of communal representation elected, but subject to the *despotic tutelage of a national power strongly centralized. It is to conquer and secure independence for all the communes* of France, and also of all superior groups, departments, and provinces, united amongst themselves for their common interest by a really national pact; it is to guarantee and perpetuate the republic . . . Paris has *renounced her apparent omnipotence* which is identical with her forfeiture, she has not renounced that moral power, that intellectual influence, which so often has made her victorious in France and Europe in her propaganda.'

'This time again Paris works and suffers for all France, of which it prepares by its combats and its sacrifices the intellectual, moral, administrative and economical regeneration, the glory and the prosperity' (*Programme*[39] of the *Commune de Paris* sent out by balloon).

Mr Thiers, in his tour through the provinces, managed the elections, and above all, his own manifold elections. But there was one difficulty. The Bonapartist provincials had for the moment become impossible. (Besides, he did not want them, nor did they want him.) Many of the Orleanist old stagers had merged into the Bonapartist lot. It was therefore necessary to appeal to the rusticated Legitimist landowners who had kept quite aloof from politics and were just the men to be duped. They have given its apparent character to the Versailles assembly, its character of the '*Chambre introuvable*' of Louis XVIII, its 'Rural' character. In their vanity they believed, of course, that their time had at last come with the downfall of the second Bonapartist empire and under the shelter of foreign invasion, as it had come in 1814 and 1815. Still they are mere dupes. So far as they act, they can only act as elements of the 'party of Order' and its 'anonymous' terrorism, as in 1848–51. Their own party effusions lend only the comical character to that association. They are, therefore, forced to suffer as President the jail-*accoucheur* of the Duchess de Berry and as their ministers the pseudo-republicans of the Government of Defence. They will be pushed aside as soon as they have done their service. But – a trick of history – by this curious combination of circumstances they are forced to attack Paris for revolting against the '*republique une et indivisible*'[40] (Louis Blanc expresses it so, Thiers calls it unity of France), while their very first exploit was to revolt against unity by declaring for the 'decapitation and decapitalization' of Paris, by wanting the Assembly to sit in a provincial town. What they really want is to go back to what preceded the centralized state machinery, become more to less independent of its prefects and its ministers, and put into its place the provincial and local domainal influence of the *châteaux*. They want a reactionary *decentralization* of France. What Paris wants is to supplant that centralization which has done its service against feudality, but has become the mere unity of an artificial body, resting on gendarmes, red and black armies, repressing the life of real society, resting as an incubus upon it, giving Paris an 'apparent omnipotence' by enclosing it and leaving the provinces outside – to supplant this unitarian France which

39. This is quoted from the manifesto 'To the French People'.
40. One and indivisible republic.

exists besides the French society – by the political union of French society itself through the Communal organization.

The true partisans of breaking up the unity of France are therefore the Rurals, opposed to the united state machinery so far as it interferes with their own local importance (seignorial rights), so far as it is the antagonist of feudalism.

What Paris wants is to break up that factitious unitarian system, so far as it is the antagonist of the real living union of France and a mere means of class rule.

Comtist View

Men completely ignorant of the existing economical system are of course still less able to comprehend the workmen's negation of that system. They can of course not comprehend that the social transformation the working class aim at is the necessary, historical, unavoidable birth of the present system itself. They talk in deprecatory tones of the threatened abolition of 'property', because in their eyes their present class form of property – a transitory historical form – *is* property itself, and the abolition of that form would therefore be the abolition of property. As they now defend the 'eternity' of capital rule and the wages system, if they had lived in feudal times or in times of slavery they would have defended the feudal system and the slave system, as founded on the nature of things, as a spontaneous outgrowth [?] springing from nature, fiercely declaimed against their 'abuses', but at the same time from the height of their ignorance answering to the prophecies of their abolition by the dogma of their eternity righted by 'moral checks' ('constraints').

They are as right in their appreciation of the aims of the Paris working classes, as is Mr Bismarck in declaring that what the Commune wants is the Prussian municipal order.

Poor men! They do not even know that every *social form* of property has 'morals' of its own, and that the form of social property which makes property the attribute of labour, far from creating individual 'moral constraints', will emancipate the 'morals' of the individual from its class constraints.

*

How the breath of the popular revolution has changed Paris! The revolution of February was called the revolution of moral contempt. It was proclaimed by the cries of the people, '*À bas les grands voleurs! À bas les assassins!*' [41] Such was the sentiment of the people. But as to the bourgeoisie, they wanted broader sway for corruption! They got it under Louis Bonaparte's (Napoleon the little) reign. Paris, the gigantic town, the town of historic initiative, was transformed in[to] the *maison dorée* [42] of all the idlers and swindlers of the world, into a cosmopolitan stew! After the exodus of the 'better class of people', the Paris of the working class reappeared, heroic, self-sacrificing, enthusiastic in the sentiment of its herculean task! No cadavers in the morgue, no insecurity of the streets. Paris was never more quiet within. Instead of the *cocottes*, the heroic women of Paris! Manly, stern, fighting, working, thinking Paris! Magnanimous Paris! In view of the cannibalism of their enemies, making their prisoners only dangerless! . . . What Paris will no longer stand is yet the existence of the *cocottes* and *cocodès*. [43] What it is resolved to drive away or transform is this useless, sceptical and egotistical race which has taken possession of the gigantic town, to use it as its own. No celebrity of the Empire shall have the right to say, 'Paris is very pleasant in the best quarters, but there are too many paupers in the others.' (*Vérité*, 23 April): 'Private crime wonderfully diminished at Paris. The absence of thieves and *cocottes*, of assassinations and street attacks: all the conservatives have fled to Versailles!' 'There has not been signalized one single nocturnal attack even in the most distant and less frequented quarters since the citizens do their police business themselves'.

41. Down with the big thieves! Down with the murderers!
42. Brothel.   43. Fops.

Documents of the First International: 1871–2

RESOLUTION OF THE LONDON CONFERENCE ON
WORKING-CLASS POLITICAL ACTION[1]

Karl Marx and Frederick Engels

Considering the following passage of the preamble to the Rules:
'The economical emancipation of the working classes is the great
end to which every political movement ought to be subordinate *as
a means*';[2]

That the Inaugural Address of the International Working Men's
Association (1864) states: 'The lords of land and the lords of capital
will always use their political privileges for the defence and perpetuation of their economical monopolies. So far from promoting, they
will continue to lay every possible impediment in the way of the
emancipation of labour . . . To conquer political power has therefore
become the great duty of the working classes';[3]

That the Congress of Lausanne (1867) has passed this resolution:
'The social emancipation of the workmen is inseparable from their
political emancipation';[4]

That the declaration of the General Council relative to the
pretended plot of the French Internationalists on the eve of the
plebiscite (1870) says: 'Certainly by the tenor of our Statutes,[5]

1. This text is Resolution IX adopted by the London Conference of the International in September 1871, headed 'Political Action of the Working Class'. A draft
resolution on this question, originally introduced by the Blanquist Edouard Vaillant
on behalf of Marx's bloc, was passed in principle, and the final drafting left to the
General Council, a job that was in fact performed by Marx and Engels. The finished
resolution was published in the pamphlet *Resolutions of the Conference of Delegates
of the International Working Men's Association*, London, 1871.

2. Above, p. 82. (Emphasis added by Marx in the present text.)

3. Above, p. 80.

4. '*Procès-verbaux du congrès de l'Association Internationale des Travailleurs
réuni à Lausanne du 2 au 8 septembre 1867*', printed in J. Freymond (ed.), *La
Première Internationale*, vol. I, Geneva, 1962, p. 121.

5. By 'Statutes' Marx refers to the Rules of the International.

all our branches in England, on the Continent, and in America have the special mission not only to serve as centres for the militant organization of the working class, but also to support, in their respective countries, every political movement tending towards the accomplishment of our ultimate end – the economical emancipation of the working class';[6]

That false translations of the original Statutes have given rise to various interpretations which were mischievous to the development and action of the International Working Men's Association;[7]

In presence of an unbridled reaction which violently crushes every effort at emancipation on the part of the working men, and pretends to maintain by brute force the distinction of classes and the political domination of the propertied classes resulting from it;

Considering, that against this collective power of the propertied classes the working class cannot act, as a class, except by constituting itself into a political party, distinct from, and opposed to, all old parties formed by the propertied classes;

That this constitution of the working class into a political party is indispensable in order to ensure the triumph of the social revolution and its ultimate end – the abolition of classes;

That the combination of forces which the working class has already effected by its economical struggles ought at the same time to serve as a lever for its struggles against the political power of landlords and capitalists –

The Conference recalls to the members of the *International*:

That in the militant state of the working class, its economical movement and its political action are indissolubly united.

SPEECH ON THE SEVENTH ANNIVERSARY OF THE
INTERNATIONAL[8]

Concerning the International, [Marx] said that the great success which had hitherto crowned its efforts was due to circumstances

6. *IWMA* III, pp. 231–2.

7. See 'The General Council to the Federal Council of French Switzerland', above, pp. 118–19.

8. This text is an excerpt from a report published in the New York *World* on 15 October 1871, headed 'The Reds in Session. Authentic Account of the Seventh Anniversary of the International in London'. The anniversary cele-

over which the members themselves had no control. The foundation of the International itself was the result of these circumstances, and by no means due to the efforts of the men engaged in it. It was not the work of any set of clever politicians; all the politicians in the world could not have created the situation and circumstances requisite for the success of the International. The International had not put forth any particular creed. Its task was to organize the forces of labour and link the various working men's movements and combine them. The circumstances which had given such a great development to the association were the conditions under which the work-people were more and more oppressed throughout the world, and this was the secret of success. The events of the last few weeks had unmistakably shown that the working class must fight for its emancipation. The persecutions of the governments against the International were like the persecutions of ancient Rome against the primitive Christians. They, too, had been few in numbers at first, but the patricians of Rome had instinctively felt that if the Christians succeeded the Roman empire would be lost. The persecutions of Rome had not saved the empire, and the persecutions of the present day against the International would not save the existing state of things.

What was new in the International was that it was established by the working men themselves and for themselves. Before the foundation of the International all the different organizations had been societies founded by some radicals among the ruling classes for the working classes, but the International was established by the working men for themselves. The Chartist movement in this country had been started with the consent and assistance of middle-class radicals, though if it had been successful it could only have been for the advantage of the working class. England was the only country where the working class was sufficiently developed and organized to turn universal suffrage to its proper account. He then alluded to the revolution of February as a movement that had been favoured by a portion of the bourgeoisie against the ruling party. The revolution of February had only given promises to the working classes and had replaced one set of men of the

bration took the form of a dinner on 26 September, which the *World*'s correspondent, probably R. Landor who interviewed Marx three months before (see below, p. 393), apparently attended. The dinner was held two days after the close of the London Conference of the International, and the participants included many of the Conference delegates.

ruling class by another. The insurrection of June had been a revolt against the whole ruling class, including the most radical portion. The working men who had lifted the new men into power in 1848 had instinctively felt that they had only exchanged one set of oppressors for another and that they were betrayed.

The last movement was the Commune, the greatest that had yet been made, and there could not be two opinions about it – the Commune was the conquest of the political power of the working classes. There was much misunderstanding about the Commune. The Commune could not found a new form of class government. In destroying the existing conditions of oppression by transferring all the means of labour to the productive labourer, and thereby compelling every able-bodied individual to work for a living, the only base for class rule and oppression would be removed. But before such a change could be effected a proletarian dictature would become necessary, and the first condition of that was a proletarian army. The working classes would have to conquer the right to emancipate themselves on the battlefield. The task of the International was to organize and combine the forces of labour for the coming struggle.

THE ALLEGED SPLITS IN THE INTERNATIONAL[9]

Private Circular from the General Council of the International Working Men's Association

Karl Marx and Frederick Engels

Up to now the General Council has maintained a total reserve over struggles within the International, and has never made any public answer to the public attacks made against it over the past two years by members of the Association.

And still, had it only been a question of a few trouble-makers persisting in purposely sowing confusion between the International and a society which has from the first been hostile to it, that

9. Marx and Engels wrote this text in French between January and March 1872, as part of their preparations for the Hague Congress of September 1872. It was adopted by the General Council on 5 March, printed in Geneva in May, and distributed privately to the International's federations and sections. It is translated here from the pamphlet, *Les Prétendues Scissions dans l'Internationale. Circulaire privée du Conseil Général de l'Association Internationale des Travailleurs*, Geneva, 1872.

silence might have been preserved. But in view of the support given to reactionary forces all over Europe by the scandals that society has provoked – just at a moment when the International is passing through the most serious crisis it has faced since it was founded – it becomes necessary for the General Council to give a full account of these intrigues.

I

After the fall of the Paris Commune, the first act of the General Council was to publish its Address on *The Civil War in France*, in which it expressed its solidarity with everything done by the Commune, at a point when the bourgeoisie, the press and every government in Europe were all pouring out a stream of calumnies upon the defeated Communards. There were even some among the working class who failed to recognize their own cause, and joined in the abuse. The Council received one proof of this, among others, when two of its members, citizens Odger and Lucraft, resigned to dissociate themselves from the Address.[10] But in general it may be said that the united attitude of the working class towards the events in Paris dates from its publication in all the countries of the civilized world.

Furthermore, the International discovered a most powerful means of propaganda in the bourgeois press, and above all the leading English papers, because they felt obliged to attack the Address and the replies of the General Council maintained a full-scale debate in being.[11]

The arrival of numbers of Communard refugees in London made it necessary for the General Council to form itself into a relief committee, a function quite outside its normal activities which it carried on for over eight months. It goes without saying that the defeated and exiled Communards had nothing to hope for from the bourgeoisie; as for the working class, their calls for help came at a difficult time. Switzerland and Belgium had already received

10. After the Second Reform Bill of 1867 Odger worked for labour parliamentary representation through the Liberal party, and under pressure from his middle-class political allies he resigned from the General Council in June 1871, after the publication of *The Civil War in France*. Benjamin Lucraft, leader of the furniture-makers' union, was, like Odger, a founding member of the International and the General Council.

11. A selection of Marx and Engels's letters on behalf of the General Council is published in *MECW* 22, p. 285ff.

their contingents of refugees, whom they had either to support, or help on their way to London, and money collected in Germany, Austria and Spain was sent to Switzerland. In England, the battle for the nine-hour working day – whose final decisive engagement took place in Newcastle[12] – had absorbed both the individual contributions of the workers, and the organized funds of the trade unions; the latter, in any case, could statutorily only be used in the industrial struggle as such. However, by dint of continuous activity and correspondence, the Council managed to collect enough in small sums to distribute a little money each week. American working people responded most generously to its appeal. But, as so often, how wonderful it would have been if the Council had had anything like the millions attributed to it by the terrified imagination of the bourgeoisie!

After May 1871, a certain number of Communard refugees were called upon to replace the French members whom the war had removed from the Council. Among those thus brought in were former members of the International, and a minority of well-known revolutionaries whose election represented our homage to the Paris Commune.[13]

In the midst of such preoccupations, the Council had also to do the preparatory work for the Conference of delegates it had just convened.

The violent measures taken against the International by the Bonapartist government[14] had made it impossible to hold a Congress in Paris, as determined by the Basle Congress. The General Council, in virtue of the right conferred upon it in article 4 of the Rules,[15] sent out a circular on 12 July 1870, to convene the Congress in Mainz.[16] At the same time, in letters addressed to the various federations, it proposed that the seat of the General Council be transferred from England to another country, and

12. This refers to the Newcastle builders and engineers' strike of May–October 1871, led by the *ad hoc* Nine Hours League.

13. These 'well-known revolutionaries' who had formerly been outside of the International were Blanquists, who after the Commune accepted the Marxist position of the need for a working-class political party, and worked with Marx against Bakunin's intrigues.

14. See p. 173, n. 3.

15. References to the General Rules and Administrative Regulations of the International are given here according to the 1871 English edition, printed in *IWMA* IV, pp. 451–69.

16. 'The Fifth Annual Congress of the IWMA', *IWMA* III, pp. 372–3.

asked that the delegates be given a mandate to do this.[17] However the federations were unanimous in asking that it remain in London. The outbreak of the Franco-Prussian war, a few days later, made it impossible to hold any Congress at all, and the federations consulted gave us the power to fix a date for the next Congress as circumstances should allow.

As soon as the political situation seemed to make it possible, the General Council summoned a private Conference; the precedents for our doing this were the 1865 Conference, and the private administrative sessions of each Congress. It was impossible to hold a public Congress, for that would merely have served to get the continental delegates denounced at the height of the positive orgy of reaction then taking place in Europe: with Jules Favre demanding the extradition of refugees as common-law criminals from all other governments, even the English,[18] with Dufaure proposing in the Rural Assembly a law banning the International[19] – later plagiarized by Malou[20] for use against the Belgians; with a refugee from the Commune being taken into preventive custody in Switzerland while the Federal government was making up its mind whether or not to grant extradition; with a combined operation against Internationalists forming the ostensible basis for an alliance between Beust and Bismarck,[21] and Victor Emmanuel hurrying to adopt the clause directed against the International;[22] with the Spanish government doing everything demanded by the executioners of Versailles and forcing the Madrid Federal Coun-

17. The General Council in fact proposed Brussels as its future seat (see *IWMA* III, pp. 266–70). Marx's probable reason for this proposal, which there was little chance of the federations supporting, was to forestall objections to the strengthening of the General Council's authority.

18. Jules Favre, the French foreign minister, circularized the European governments on 6 June 1871, calling on them to hunt down the International.

19. Jules Dufaure was Minister of Justice in Thiers's government. The *loi Dufaure*, passed on 14 March 1872, made membership of the International in France an offence punishable by imprisonment. On the 'Rural Assembly' see above, pp. 195–6.

20. Jules Malou was the Belgian Prime Minister.

21. Friedrich, Count Beust, was the Austro-Hungarian chancellor. In August and September 1871, after preparatory exchanges between Beust and Bismarck, emperors Francis Joseph of Austria and William I of Germany held two meetings, in Bad Gastein and in Salzburg, specifically to coordinate measures against the International.

22. The Italian government banned the Naples section of the International in August 1871.

cil to seek refuge in Portugal.[23] In short, it was a situation in which the International's first task was to get its own organization back into order, so as to take up the challenge of the various governments.

All sections in regular communication with the General Council were invited to the Conference in good time; but even though it was not a public Congress, it still had serious difficulties to contend with. Obviously France, in its present state, could not elect delegates. The only section then functioning in Italy was the one in Naples, and just as it was appointing its delegate, it was dissolved by the army. In Austria and Hungary, all the most active members were in prison.[24] In Germany, some of the best-known members were wanted for the crime of high treason, while others were in prison, and all the party's funds were needed for the support of their families.[25] The Americans, though they sent the Conference a detailed memorandum on the situation of the International in their country, spent the money that could have paid for sending a delegation on supporting refugees. Clearly, all the federations recognized the need for holding a private Conference rather than a public congress.

The Conference, having sat in London from 17 to 23 September 1871, entrusted the General Council with the task of publishing its resolutions, of codifying the Administrative Regulations and putting them out, together with the revised and corrected General Rules, in three languages, of putting into effect the resolution to substitute adhesive stamps for membership cards, of reorganizing the International in England, and lastly, of finding the money needed for all these objects.[26]

The moment the Conference's activities were made public, the reactionary press – from Paris to Moscow, from London to New

23. The Spanish government moved to the offensive against the International in spring and summer 1871.

24. The leaders of the Austrian Social-Democratic party were arrested in July 1870, after a wave of strikes, and charged with high treason.

25. The Brunswick committee of the German Social-Democratic Workers' Party (SDAP) was arrested in September 1870 and its members held for over a year in prison, while Bebel and Liebknecht were arrested in December 1870, charged with high treason, and sentenced in March 1872 to two years' imprisonment.

26. See 'Resolutions of the London Conference', *IWMA* IV, pp. 440–50. The English reorganization involved the formation of an English Federal Council separate from the General Council.

York – attacked the resolution on working-class political action;[27] it enshrined, they said, designs so dangerous ('coldly calculated audacity', accused *The Times*) that it was vital that the International be outlawed at once. On the other hand, the resolution unmasking the fraudulent sectarian section[27a] provided a pretext for the ever-watchful international police to make loud demands in favour of the freedom of their protégés, the workers, as against the appalling despotism of the General Council and the Conference. So 'heavily oppressed' did the workers feel, indeed, that the General Council received new members, and notifications that new branches had been formed, from Europe, America, Australia and even the East Indies!

II

The attacks of the bourgeois press and the laments of the international police even found a certain sympathetic echo within our Association. Plots, directed apparently against the General Council, but in reality against the Association itself, began taking shape, and at the bottom of them all there was inevitably to be found the International Alliance of Socialist Democracy, that brain-child of the Russian Michael Bakunin. On his return from Siberia he preached pan-Slavism and racial war in Herzen's *Kolokol*, as the fruit of his long experience. Later, during his time in Switzerland, he was appointed to the governing committee of the 'League of Peace and Freedom' founded in opposition to the International. Since the affairs of this bourgeois society went from bad to worse, its president, Mr G. Vogt, acting on Bakunin's advice, proposed an alliance when the International's Congress met in Brussels in September 1868. But the Congress unanimously declared that *either* the League was pursuing the same aim as the International, in which case there was no point in its existing, *or* its aim was different, in which case no merger was possible. At the League's own congress in Berne a few days later, Bakunin underwent a conversion. He put forward an outworn programme, whose scientific value can be judged from this one phrase: '*the economic and social equalization of classes*'. With only a tiny minority supporting him, he broke with the League and joined the International, bent on replacing the International's General Rules with his own makeshift programme, which the League had rejected, and the General Council with himself as a virtual

27. See above, pp. 269–70.   27a. See above, p. 48.

dictator. With this object, he formed a new instrument, the 'International Alliance of Socialist Democracy', intending it to become an International within the International.

Bakunin found the people he needed to establish that society from among the friendships he had formed during his stay in Italy, and in a group of Russian exiles who acted as his emissaries and 'recruiting officers' among members of the International in Switzerland, France and Spain. However it was only the repeated refusals of the Belgian and Paris Federal Councils to recognize his 'Alliance' that made him decide to present the rules of his new society to the General Council for approval, rules which were simply a reproduction of his 'unappreciated' Berne programme. The Council replied with the following circular, dated 22 December 1868:

The International Working Men's Association and the International Alliance of Socialist Democracy[28]

About a month ago, a number of citizens established themselves in Geneva as the 'Inaugural Central Committee' of a new International society, known as 'The International Alliance of Socialist Democracy', which took as its '*special mission* the study of political and philosophical questions actually on the basis of this great principle of *equality*, etc . . .'

The printed programme and rules of this inaugural committee were only communicated to the General Council of the International Working Men's Association on 15 December 1868. According to these documents, the aforesaid Alliance is 'wholly founded within the International' – though at the same time it is wholly founded outside this Association. Alongside the General Council of the International, elected by the successive Congresses of Geneva, Lausanne and Brussels, there would seem, to judge by these documents, to be another General Council in Geneva, appointed by itself. Alongside the local groups of the International, there would seem to be local groups of the 'Alliance' which, through their own national bureaux functioning quite apart from the national bureaux of the International, 'will ask the Central Bureau of the Alliance to admit them into the International' – in other words, the Central Committee of the '*Alliance*' is taking upon itself the right to admit people into the *International*. Finally, the General Congress of the International Working Men's Association also has its counterpart in the 'General Congress of the Alliance', for, as the rules of the inaugural committee tell us, at the annual working men's Congress, the delegation of the International Alliance of Socialist Demo-

28. This circular was written by Marx in French, on the mandate of the General Council, and distributed by private letter.

cracy, as a branch of the International Working Men's Association, 'will hold its public sessions in another place'.

Considering:

That the presence of a second international body functioning both inside and outside the International Working Men's Association would infallibly succeed in reducing it to chaos;

That any other group of individuals living anywhere would have a right to imitate the Geneva inaugural group, and under various pretexts, whether expressed or not, to graft other International Associations with their own special missions onto the International Working Men's Association;

That in this way the International Working Men's Association could easily become the plaything of intriguers from all countries and all parties;

That in any case the Rules of the International Working Men's Association only include in its framework local and national branches (see articles 1 and 7 of the Rules);

That no section of the International Working Men's Association is allowed to adopt rules and administrative regulations contrary to the General Rules and Administrative Regulations of the International Working Men's Association (see article V/1 of the Administrative Regulations);

That the Rules and Administrative Regulations of the International Working Men's Association can only be revised by a General Congress at which two thirds of the delegates present are in favour (see article 12 of the General Rules);

That the question has already been settled by the resolutions unanimously adopted at the Brussels General Congress against the League of Peace;[29]

That in those resolutions Congress declared that the League of Peace served no purpose, given that its recent declarations made it clear that its aims and principles were identical with those of the International Working Men's Association;

That several members of the inaugural group of the Alliance, as delegates to the Brussels Congress, themselves voted for those resolutions;

The General Council of the International Working Men's Association, at its meeting of 22 December 1868, has unanimously resolved:

1. All the articles of the rules of the International Alliance of Socialist Democracy concerning its relationship with the International Working Men's Association are declared null and void;

29. See 'Resolutions of the First and Third Congresses of the International Working Men's Association', *IWMA* III, pp. 297–8.

2. The International Alliance of Socialist Democracy is not admitted as a branch of the International Working Men's Association.

G. ODGER, Chairman of the meeting
R. SHAW, General Secretary

London, 22 December, 1868

A few months later, the Alliance once again approached the General Council, asking whether or not its *principles* were acceptable to it. If the answer were 'Yes', then the Alliance declared itself ready to dissolve itself into sections of the International. In reply to this, it received the following circular of 9 March 1869:

The General Council to the Central Committee of the International Alliance of Socialist Democracy[30]

According to article 1 of our Rules, the Association admits all working men's societies 'aiming at the same end, viz. *the protection, advancement and complete emancipation of the working class*'.

Since the sections of the working class in various countries have reached different stages of development, it follows that their theoretical opinions, which reflect the real movement, will be equally divergent.

However, the community of action established by the International Working Men's Association, the exchange of ideas fostered by the publicity provided by the organs of the various national sections, and finally the face-to-face discussions at the general Congresses, cannot fail gradually to give rise to a common theoretical programme.

Thus it is no part of the functions of the General Council to make a critical study of the Alliance's programme. It is not for us to analyse whether or not it is a genuine expression of the proletarian movement. All we need to know is that it contains nothing counter to the *general tendency* of our Association, in other words, the *complete emancipation of the working class*. There is one sentence in your programme which fails this test. We read in article 2: 'It [the Alliance] desires above all the political, economic and social equalization of classes.'

The *equalization of classes*, if taken literally, amounts to the *harmony between capital and labour*, which is precisely what bourgeois socialists so unfortunately preach.[31] It is not the *equalization* of classes, a logical impossibility and therefore incapable of achievement, but on the con-

---

30. This circular was written by Marx and distributed by private letter. Since there are minor differences between the English original printed in *IWMA* III, pp. 310–11, and the French version reproduced by Marx in *Les Prétendues Scissions . . .* , we have followed the French text as published in the *Scissions* (the only contemporary published variant) rather than the English manuscript.

31. For Marx's critique of 'bourgeois socialism', see the 'Manifesto of the Communist Party', section III/2, *R1848*, pp. 93–4.

trary the *abolition* of classes which is the true secret of the proletarian movement, and the prime object of the International Working Men's Association. However, in view of the context in which the phrase 'equalization of classes' stands, it may perhaps have resulted merely from a slip of the pen. The General Council has no doubt that you would be willing to remove from your programme a phrase which could give rise to such dangerous misunderstanding. Apart from cases in which our Association's general tendency is positively contradicted, it is part of our principles to leave each section free to formulate its own theoretical programme.

Thus there is no obstacle to *converting* the sections of the Alliance into sections of the International Working Men's Association.

If it is definitely decided to *dissolve* the Alliance, and have its sections individually join the International, then by our Regulations it would become necessary to inform the Council of each new section's location and numerical strength.

Meeting of the General Council, 9 March 1869

The Alliance, having accepted these conditions, was admitted into the International by the General Council, which, owing to some of the signatures to the Bakunin programme, erroneously presumed it to be recognized by the French-Swiss[32] Federal Committee in Geneva – whereas in fact the opposite was the case. It had now achieved its immediate object of being represented at the Basle Congress. Despite the dishonest means used by his supporters (the only time such means were ever used in a Congress of the International), Bakunin was disappointed in his attempt to get the Congress to transfer the seat of the General Council to Geneva, and sanction officially the old Saint-Simonian rubbish of the immediate abolition of the right of inheritance, which Bakunin considered the practical starting-point of socialism. This marked the opening of the open and unremitting war waged by the Alliance not just against the General Council, but also against all sections of the International which refused to adopt the programme of their sectarian coterie, and above all the doctrine of total abstention from political activity.

Before the Basle Congress, when Nechayev came to Geneva, Bakunin had made contact with him and founded a secret society among students in Russia. Always concealing his own identity under the name of various 'revolutionary committees', he assumed autocratic powers, and adopted all the trickeries and

32. 'French-Swiss' has been used to translate *'Romand'*, the French name for the French-speaking districts and people of Switzerland.

mystifications from the time of Cagliostro.[33] This society's major means of propaganda consisted in compromising innocent people with the Russian police by sending them communications from Geneva in yellow envelopes, marked on the outside, in Russian, with the stamp of the Secret Revolutionary Committee. Public reports of the Nechayev trial show what infamous things were done in the name of the International.[34]

During that time, the Alliance began a public polemic against the General Council, first in *Progrès* (Le Locle), then in *Égalité* (Geneva), the official newspaper of the French-Swiss Federation, into which some members of the Alliance had followed Bakunin. The General Council paid no heed to the attacks in *Progrès*, Bakunin's own personal paper, but it could not ignore those in *Égalité* since these gave the appearance of having the Federation's approval. So it published the circular of 1 January 1870,[35] in which it said:

We read in *Égalité*, 11 December 1869: 'It is *certain* that the General Council is neglecting matters of great importance. We would remind it of its obligations under Regulation II/2: "The General Council is *bound* to execute the Congress resolutions, etc . . ." We could ask the General Council enough questions for its answers to make a somewhat lengthy document. These will come later . . . Meanwhile, etc. etc . . .' The General Council knows of no article, either in the Rules or the Regulations, which would oblige it to enter into correspondence or debate with *Égalité*, or provide any 'answers to questions' from newspapers. Only the Federal Committee in Geneva represents the branches of French Switzerland to the General Council. Whenever the Federal Committee addresses requests or objections to us by the one and only legitimate channel, i.e. through its secretary, the General Council will always be ready to reply. But the Federal Committee has no right either to hand over its functions to the editors of *Égalité* and *Progrès*, or to

33. Guiseppe Balsano, known as Allessandro Cagliostro, was an eighteenth-century Italian adventurer.

34. An extract from the trial will soon be published. There the reader will find a sample of the kind of maxims – at once ridiculous and evil – which through Bakunin's friends have been attributed to the International [Marx].

Nechayev's activities included the extortion of money under threat of assassination from a publisher with whom Bakunin had contracted to translate Marx's *Capital* into Russian. Evidence of this particular incident tipped the scales in securing Bakunin's expulsion from the International at the Hague Congress [Ed.].

35. 'The General Council to the Federal Council of French Switzerland'. See above, p. 113ff.

permit those journals to usurp its functions. Generally speaking, administrative correspondence between the General Council and the national and local committees cannot be made public without doing considerable damage to the general interests of the Association. Therefore, if other organs of the International were to imitate *Progrès* and *Égalité*, the General Council would be forced either to remain silent and thus earn the discredit of the public, or to violate its obligations by making a public reply. *Égalité* has combined with *Progrès* in urging *Le Travail* (a Paris newspaper) also to attack the General Council. This is virtually a *ligue du bien public*.

However, even before it learnt of this circular, the French-Swiss Federal Committee had already removed all Alliance supporters from editorial positions on *Égalité*.

The circular of 1 January 1870, like those of 22 December 1868 and 9 March 1869, was approved by all sections of the International.

It goes without saying that none of the conditions agreed by the Alliance was ever fulfilled. Its so-called sections remained a mystery to the General Council. Bakunin tried to keep under his personal authority the scattered groups in Spain and Italy, and the Naples section which he had prised away from the International. In the other towns of Italy, he was in correspondence with small groups made up not of working men, but of lawyers, journalists and other bourgeois doctrinaires. In Barcelona his influence was kept alive by a few friends. In certain towns in the south of France, the Alliance tried to establish separatist sections under the leadership of Albert Richard and Gaspard Blanc of Lyons, of whom we shall have more to say later on. In brief, the International within the International continued to stir up trouble.

The Alliance's master stroke, its attempt to seize the leadership of French Switzerland, was to take place at the Congress of La Chaux-de-Fonds, which opened on 4 April 1870.

Though, according to their own estimates, the supporters of the Alliance amounted to no more than one fifth of the members of the Federation, they managed, thanks to a repetition of the manoeuvres which had been so successful at Basle, to win an apparent majority of one or two votes – a majority which, on the admission of their own organ (see *Solidarité* for 7 May 1870), represented no more than *fifteen* sections, though there were thirty in Geneva alone! With this vote, the Congress split into two parts, which continued their sessions separately. The supporters of the

Alliance, considering themselves the legal representatives of the whole Federation, transferred the seat of the Federal Committee to La Chaux-de-Fonds, and established their official organ, *Solidarité*, edited by citizen Guillaume, in Neuchâtel. The special job of this young writer was to abuse the 'factory workers' of Geneva as disgraceful 'bourgeois', to attack *Égalité*, the Federation's own paper, and to urge total abstention from all political activity. The most trenchant articles on this latter subject were written by Bastelica[36] in Marseilles, and by those two great pillars of the Alliance in Lyons, Albert Richard and Gaspard Blanc.

On their return, the Geneva delegates convoked their sections to a general assembly which, despite the opposition of Bakunin and his friends, gave its approval to what they had done at the Chaux-de-Fonds Congress. Shortly afterwards, Bakunin and his most active disciples were expelled from the original French-Swiss Federation.

Barely had the Congress closed when the new La Chaux-de-Fonds Committee appealed to the General Council to intervene, in a letter signed by F. Robert, secretary, and Henri Chevalley, president – who, two months later was denounced as a *thief* by the Committee's organ, *Solidarité*, on 7 July. Having closely studied the apologias of both parties, the General Council decided on 28 June 1870 to maintain the Geneva Federal Committee in its former functions, and ask the new Federal Committee of La Chaux-de-Fonds to adopt a local title. For this decision, which ran wholly counter to their wishes, the Chaux-de-Fonds Committee denounced the General Council's *authoritarianism* – quite forgetting that it was they who had asked it to intervene in the first place. The problems created in the Swiss Federation by their continuing to usurp the title of the French-Swiss Federal Committee forced the General Council to suspend all official relations with them.

Louis Bonaparte had just surrendered his army at Sedan. Protests arose from the International's supporters everywhere against the continuance of the war. The General Council in its Address of 9 September,[37] denouncing Prussia's plans for conquest, showed

36. André Bastelica was a printer and a follower of Bakunin. He was active in the Communard risings in Marseilles, October–November 1870, then in the Paris Commune.

37. 'The Second Address of the General Council on the Franco-Prussian War', above, pp. 179–86.

how damaging its victory would be to the proletarian cause, and warned the workers of Germany that they would be the first to suffer. Meetings were called in England to create a counter-weight to the pro-Prussian leanings of the court. In Germany Internationalist workers organized demonstrations demanding the recognition of the republic, and 'a peace that would be honourable to France . . .'

The ebullient and bellicose Guillaume (in Neuchâtel) had the brilliant idea of producing an *anonymous* manifesto, published as a supplement to the official paper *Solidarité*, demanding the formation of a Swiss free corps to go and fight the Prussians – though when it came to the point, his abstentionist convictions would presumably have prevented his actually doing this.

Then came the Lyons uprising. Bakunin hastened to the spot, and with the support of Albert Richard, Gaspard Blanc and Bastelica, he established himself on 28 September in the town hall – though he made no attempt to guard the building in any way, since that would have been a political act. He was ignomini-ously driven out by a few National Guards just as, after a painful labour, he had at last given birth to his decree on the '*Abolition of the state*'.

In October 1870, the General Council, in the absence of its French members, coopted as a member citizen Paul Robin, a refugee from Brest, one of the best-known of the Alliance's supporters, and also the author of the attacks published against the General Council in *Égalité* – whose correspondent from the Chaux-de-Fonds Committee he still remained. On 14 March 1871, he suggested that a private conference of the International be summoned to settle the Swiss dispute. The Council, realizing that major events would soon be taking place in Paris, refused outright. Robin returned several times to the question, and even suggested that the Council itself pronounce a final settlement of the dispute. On 25 July, the General Council decided that this matter must be one of the questions laid before the Conference due to be convened in September 1871.

On 10 August, the Alliance, far from anxious to have its doings looked into closely by any conference, declared itself dissolved as from the sixth of that month. But on 15 September it reap-peared, and asked to be admitted to the Council in the guise of the 'Atheist Socialist Section'. According to Administrative Regulation II/5, adopted by the Basle Congress, the Council could not admit it without prior consultation with the Geneva Federal Committee, now worn out after two years of struggle with the various sectarian sections. Besides, the Council had already informed the Young Men's Christian Association that the International could not recognize any theological sections.

On 6 August, the date of the Alliance's 'dissolution', the Federal Committee of La Chaux-de-Fonds, while renewing its request to enter into official relations with the Council, informed it that it would continue to ignore the resolution of 28 June and present itself as the French-Swiss Federal Committee, as against Geneva – on the grounds 'that it is for the General Congress to judge the matter'. On 4 September, that same Committee sent a protest against the competence of the Conference – though it had been the first to demand that it be convened. The Conference might well have asked in return what competence the Paris Federal Committee possessed for judging the Swiss dispute, as the Chaux-de-Fonds Committee had also asked it to do before the siege.[38] However, it merely confirmed the General Council's decision of 28 June 1870. (See *Égalité*, 21 October 1871.)

III

The presence in Switzerland of some of the outlawed French who had found refuge there brought a fresh spark of life to the Alliance.

The Geneva members of the International did everything in their power for these people. They provided them with help and agitated strongly to prevent the Swiss authorities from conceding their extradition, as demanded by the Versailles government. Several people ran serious risks by going to France to help refugees to reach the frontier. One can therefore imagine the surprise with which the workers of Geneva saw certain such ringleaders as B. Malon[39] at once getting into contact with members

38. The first siege of Paris lasted from October 1870 to January 1871.

39. One wonders whether the friends of Malon who, in a mimeographed announcement three months later, described him as the 'founder of the International', and his book as the 'only independent work on the Commune', knew of the attitude taken by the deputy from Les Batignolles on the eve of the February elections. At that time, Malon, who did not anticipate the Commune, and was planning only for the success of his own election to the Assembly, was conspiring to get himself put on the list of the four committees as a member of the International. With this in mind, he had the effrontery to deny the existence of the Paris Federal Council, and submitted to the com-

of the Alliance, and, with the aid of N. Zhukovsky,[40] the former secretary of the Alliance, trying to establish a new 'Socialist Revolutionary Propaganda and Action Section' in Geneva, quite outside the French-Swiss Federation. In the first article of its rules, this organization 'declares its adherence to the General Rules of the International Working Men's Association, *while reserving to itself all the freedom of action* and initiative allowed it as a logical consequence of the principle of autonomy and federation recognized by the Rules and Congresses of the Association'. In other words, it held itself entirely free to carry on the work of the Alliance.

In a letter from Malon, dated 20 October 1871, this new section asked the General Council for the third time to admit it into the International. In conformity with Regulation II/5, adopted by the Basle Congress, the Council consulted the Geneva Federal Committee, which protested in no uncertain terms against the Council's granting recognition to this fresh 'centre of intrigue and dissension'. And, in fact, the Council *was* 'authoritarian' enough to refuse to impose the wishes of Malon and Zhukovsky upon an entire federation.

Solidarité no longer existed, so the new members of the Alliance founded *La Révolution sociale* under the chief editorship of Madame André Léo, who had just stated to the Peace Congress at Lausanne that 'Raoul Rigault and Ferré were the two sinister figures in the Commune who did not cease to demand bloodshed, albeit in vain up to the execution of the hostages'.[41]

---

mittees the names of a section founded by himself in Les Batignolles as though it came from the entire Association. Later, on 19 March, he insulted in a public document the leaders of the great revolution carried out the day before. Today this unbounded anarchist is printing or allowing to be printed what he said to the four committees a year ago: *'L'Internationale c'est moi!'* [I am the International!] Malon has thus managed to parody both Louis XIV, and Perron the chocolate-maker – though even Perron never claimed that his was the *only* edible chocolate [Marx].

Benoît Malon was a dyer, a left-wing Proudhonist and a member of the Paris Commune [Ed.].

40. Nikolai Zhukovsky was a Russian *émigré* and a close collaborator of Bakunin.

41. Marx's source here is the pamphlet, *La Guerre sociale*, Neuchâtel 1871. André Léo was the pseudonym of Léodile Champseix, the wife of Benoît Malon, who played an active part in the Commune. Raoul Rigault and Théophile Ferré were Blanquists, and respectively procurator and deputy-procurator of the Paris Commune. Both were shot by the Versailles forces.

From its first issue, this paper tried to equal or even out-do *Figaro, Gaullois, Paris-Journal* and other abusive papers, whose slanders against the General Council it was happy to repeat. It seemed an opportune moment to kindle, even within the International, the fire of nationalist hatreds. According to it, the General Council was a German committee with a Bismarckian brain behind it.[42]

Having clearly established that certain members of the General Council could not claim to be 'Gauls first and foremost', *La Révolution sociale* could do no more than adopt the second slogan of the European police, and attack the Council's 'authoritarianism'.

What then was the evidence on which these puerile attacks rested? The General Council had let the Alliance die a natural death, and in consort with the Geneva Federal Committee, had prevented its resurrection. In addition, it had asked that the Chaux-de-Fonds Committee take a title which would enable it to live in peace with the great majority of Swiss Internationalists.

Apart from these 'authoritarian' acts, what other use had the General Council made, from October 1869 to October 1871, of the wide-ranging powers granted it by the Basle Congress?

1. On 8 February 1870, the 'Society of Positivist Proletarians' in Paris asked the General Council for admission. The Council replied that the positivist principles enshrined in those rules of the society that dealt with capital were in flagrant contradiction with the preamble to the General Rules; that they must therefore strike them out, and join the International not as 'positivists' but as 'proletarians', though they would still be perfectly free to reconcile their theories with the general principles of the Association. The section, recognizing the justice of this ruling, joined the International.

2. In Lyons, there had been a split between the 1865 section and a section of recent origin in which, in addition to perfectly honest workers, the Alliance was represented by Albert Richard and Gaspard Blanc. As so often happens in such cases, the judgement of an arbitration court set up in Switzerland was not recognized. On 15 February 1870, the recently formed section did not merely

42. In point of fact that national make-up of the Council is as follows: 20 English, 15 French, 7 German (5 of them founders of the International), 2 Swiss, 2 Hungarian, 1 Polish, 1 Belgian, 1 Irish, 1 Danish and 1 Italian [Marx].

demand that the General Council should pronounce on the dispute in virtue of Regulation II/7, but actually sent it a 'judgement' to give – expelling and slandering the members of the 1865 section – to be signed and sent back *by return of post*! The Council deplored such an unheard-of proceeding, and demanded that some justification be given. To that demand, the 1865 section replied that the evidence for charges against Albert Richard had been laid before the arbitration court, but Bakunin had taken possession of it, and refused to return it, thus making it impossible to send it to the General Council. The Council's decision in this matter, dated 8 March, aroused no objection from either side.

3. The French branch in London, having accepted members of a doubtful character (to say the least), had gradually developed into the fief of M. Félix Pyat. He used it to organize highly compromising demonstrations in favour of the assassination of Louis Bonaparte, etc., and, under cover of the International, to get his ridiculous manifestoes sent all over France. The General Council merely stated in the Association's organs that M. Pyat was no longer a member of the International, and that it therefore bore no responsibility for anything he might say or do.[43] The French branch then declared that it recognized neither the General Council nor the Congresses; it stuck notices up all over London stating that apart from itself, the rest of the International was an anti-revolutionary society. The arrest of the French members on the eve of the plebiscite, on grounds of conspiracy (in fact contrived by the police, but given a certain semblance of probability by Pyat's manifestoes), forced the General Council to publish in *Marseillaise* and *Réveil* its resolution of 10 May 1870,[44] declaring that the so-called French branch had not belonged to the International for over two years, and that its actions were actually the work of the police. The need for this step was proved by the declaration in those same newspapers by the Paris Federal Committee, and those of the Parisian Internationalists during their trial – both of which were based on the Council's resolution.[45] The French branch had disappeared when the war began, but like

43. Félix Pyat was a petty-bourgeois democrat and a member of the Paris Commune. For the General Council's statement, see *IWMA* II, p. 224.

44. See *IWMA* III, pp. 235–6.

45. The resolution alluded to here is that of 7 July 1868, repudiating the actions of Félix Pyat. See *IWMA* II, p. 224.

the Alliance in Switzerland, it was to reappear in London, with new allies and under other names.

In the final days of the Conference, some of the exiled Communards formed a 'French section of 1871', some thirty-five strong. The first 'authoritarian' act of the General Council was a public denunciation of the secretary of that section, Gustave Durand, as a French police spy. The evidence in our possession proves that the police intended to help Durand, first of all at the Conference, and later by getting him onto the General Council. The rules of the new section bound its members to 'accept no delegation to the General Council other than from their own section', so citizens Theisz[46] and Bastelica resigned from the Council.

On 17 October, the section delegated two of its members to the Council, with formal instructions, one of whom was none other than M. Chautard, a former member of the artillery committee,[47] whom the Council refused to accept after an examination of the rules of the 1871 section.[48] It will be sufficient here to recall the major points in the debate to which these rules gave rise. They refer to article 2:

'To be accepted as a member of the section, one must justify one's means of existence, present guarantees of morality, etc.' In its resolution of 17 October 1871, the Council proposed that the phrase 'justify one's means of existence' be struck out. 'In cases of doubt,' said the Council, 'a section can certainly investigate a man's means of existence as a "guarantee of morality"; but in other cases, as with refugees, workers on strike etc., the absence of means of existence may well in itself be a guarantee of morality. To demand that candidates justify their means of existence as a general condition for joining the International would be a bourgeois innovation, contrary to both the spirit and the letter of the General Rules'. The section replied that the General Rules made the sections responsible for the morality of their members, and consequently allowed their right to secure such guarantees *as they thought fit*. To this the General Council replied on 7 November:[49]

46. Albert Theisz was a metal-cutter, a Proudhonist and a member of the Paris Commune.

47. I.e. the artillery committee of the Paris National Guard.

48. Shortly afterwards, this man whom they had tried to force upon the General Council was expelled from his section as being an agent of the Thiers police. He was accused by the very people who had earlier thought him the best man to represent them on the Council [Marx].

49. See *IWMA* V, pp. 339–45.

According to this view, an International section founded by teetotallers could insert in its special rules some such article as: 'To be a member of the section, one must swear to abstain from all alcoholic drink.' In short, the most ridiculous and extraordinary conditions of admission into the International could be laid down by the sections in their special rules, especially if this is done on the pretext of securing the morality of their members . . .

The French section of 1871 have added that 'the means of existence' of strikers are to be found in 'the strike fund'. To this one must reply, first that there is often no such 'fund'.

Further, official English inquiries have proved that the majority of English working men . . . are obliged, whether by strikes or lack of work, by inadequate wages or unfair terms of payment or a number of other possible causes, to have constant recourse to pawn-shops and money-lenders, 'means of existence' of which one cannot demand justification without making quite unacceptable inquiries into the private lives of citizens.

Now there can be one of two possibilities: either the section does not inquire into 'means of existence' as 'guarantees of morality', in which case the General Council's proposition is quite apt . . . Or the section, in article 2 of its rules, has intentionally made the justification of one's 'means of existence' a condition for admission in addition to 'guarantees of morality' . . . in which case the Council declares that this is a bourgeois innovation contrary in letter and spirit to the General Rules.

Article 11 of the section's rules reads: 'One or several delegates shall be sent to the General Council.' The Council asked that this article be struck out, 'because the General Rules of the International do not allow any sections the right to send delegates to the General Council'. It added:

The General Rules only recognize two means of electing members to the General Council: either they are elected by the Congress, or they are coopted by the General Council . . . It is quite true that the various sections existing in London were invited to send delegates to the General Council, but in order not to infringe the General Rules, they always did it as follows: The General Council first determined the number of delegates to be sent by each section, reserving to itself the right to accept or reject them in accordance with the Council's estimate of each one's ability to fulfil the general functions demanded of him. These delegates became members of the General Council not in virtue of being delegated by their sections, but in virtue of the Council's statutory right to coopt new members. Having until the decision of the last Conference functioned both as General Council of the International Association and as the Central Council for England, the London Council considered it valuable, in addition to the members it adopted directly, to accept members first delegated by their respective sections. It would be oddly mistaken to compare the method by which the General Council is elected to that used for the Paris Federal Council, which was not even a national Council appointed by a national Congress (as, for instance, the Federal Councils of Brussels or Madrid). The Paris Federal Council was entirely made up of delegates from the Paris sections . . . The way the General Council is elected is determined by the General Rules . . . and its members can accept no overriding mandate other than that of the Rules and Administrative Regulations . . . If one reads it in the light of the preceding paragraph, article 11 can only mean a complete change in the make-up of the General Council whereby, contrary to article 5 of the General Rules, it would consist only of delegates from the London sections, with the influence of local groups replacing that of the entire International Working Men's Association.

In conclusion, the General Council, whose prime duty is to carry out the resolutions of the Congresses (see Administrative Regulation II/2, adopted by the Geneva Congress), said that it considered as quite irrelevant to the question . . . the ideas put forward by the French section of 1871 concerning radical changes to be made in the articles of the General Rules bearing on its constitution.[50]

The Council further declared that it would admit two delegates from the section on the same conditions as those it accepted from the other London sections.

The '1871 section', far from finding this response satisfactory, put out a 'Declaration' on 14 December, signed by all its members – including the new secretary who was shortly afterwards expelled by the refugee society for unbefitting conduct. According to that declaration, the General Council, by refusing to usurp the functions of a legislative body, was guilty 'of a completely naturalistic distortion of the social idea' [*sic*].

Here then are a few examples of the kind of good faith which characterizes the formulation of this document.

The London Conference had approved the conduct of the German workers during the war. Obviously that resolution, proposed by a Swiss delegate, seconded by a Belgian, and accepted unanimously, referred only to those German members of the International who were – or still are – in prison for their anti-

---

50. This paragraph appears to continue quoting from the General Council's resolutions of 7 November, but the passages in question do not appear in Marx's manuscript as printed in *IWMA* V.

chauvinist activities during the war. In order further to avoid any possibility of its being interpreted pejoratively, the General Council's secretary for France had made very clear the exact meaning of the resolution in a letter published in *Qui Vive!*, *La Constitution*, *Le Radical*, *L'Émancipation*, *L'Europe*, and else-where. A week later, however, on 20 November 1871, fifteen members of the '1871 French section' sent to *Qui Vive!* a 'protest' filled with attacks on the German workers, and denouncing the resolution of the Conference as irrefutable proof that the General Council was possessed by 'the pan-Germanic idea'. The whole of the feudalist, liberal and police-controlled press of Germany was not slow to seize upon this incident to show the German work-ers how vain were their dreams of international unity. Finally, the protest of 20 November was endorsed by the entire 1871 section in its Declaration of 14 December.

To indicate 'the general tendency to authoritarianism into which the General Council was slipping', it referred to 'the publication by that same General Council of an *official* edition of the General Rules *revised by itself*'. A glance at the new edition of the Rules is enough to establish that every paragraph has a reference in the appendix to the sources proving its authenticity! As for the phrase '*official* edition', the first Congress of the International had decided that the '*official* and *obligatory* text of the Rules and Regulations is to be published by the General Council'. (See *Congrès ouvrier de l'Association Internationale des Travailleurs, tenu à Genève du 3 au 8 septembre 1866*,[51] p. 27, note.)

Needless to say, the 1871 section was in continuous contact with the dissidents of Geneva and Neuchâtel. One of its members – Chalain – who had used far more energy in attacking the General Council than he had ever used in defending the Commune, was suddenly rehabilitated by Malon, who had shortly beforehand made highly serious accusations against him in a letter to a member of the Council. In any case, the '1871 French section' had barely put out its declaration when civil war broke out within its ranks. First Theisz, Avrial and Camélinat[52] resigned. It then went on to break up into several small groups, one of which was led by a certain gentleman, Pierre Vesinier, who had been expelled from

51. Printed in Freymond, op. cit., vol. I.

52. Augustin Avrial was a mechanic, a left-wing Proudhonist and a member of the Paris Commune. Zephyrin Camélinat was a bronze-worker, a Proudhonist and a member of the Paris Commune.

the General Council for his slanders against Varlin and others, and then expelled from the International by the Belgian Commission appointed by the Brussels Congress in 1868.[53] Another of these groups was founded by B. Landeck, who was freed from his 'scrupulously regarded' commitment 'to take no further part in *political affairs* or the International in France' by the unexpected absconding of Prefect of Police Piétri on 4 September! (See *Troisième procès de l'Association Internationale des Travailleurs de Paris*, 1870, p. 4.) On the other hand, the mass of French refugees in London established a section which was completely in harmony with the General Council.

IV

The partisans of the Alliance, in the guise of the Neuchâtel Federal Committee,[54] trying yet another attempt to break up the International, this time on a far larger scale, summoned a Congress of their sections to be held at Sonvillier on 12 November 1871. Back in July, two letters from Master Guillaume to his friend Robin[55] had threatened the General Council with a campaign of this kind if it persisted in refusing to recognize them as against 'the Geneva brigands'.

The Sonvillier Congress consisted of sixteen delegates, representing nine sections in all, among them the new 'Socialist Revolutionary Propaganda and Action Section' in Geneva.

The Sixteen began with an anarchist decree, declaring the French-Swiss Federation dissolved – to which the Federation responded by immediately expelling the Alliance supporters from all its sections, and letting them go off to enjoy their own 'autonomy'. Apart from that, the Council had to admit that they had one flash of good sense in deciding to accept the title of 'Jura Federation' which the London Conference had bestowed on them.

This Congress of Sixteen then proceeded to the 'reorganization' of the International, putting out against the Conference and the General Council a 'Circular to all Federations of the International Working Men's Association'.[56]

53. Vesinier had nevertheless been a member of the Commune.

54. I.e. the Chaux-de-Fonds Committee.

55. Paul Robin, like Guillaume, was a schoolteacher and a leading member of Bakunin's Alliance.

56. Printed in Freymond, op. cit., vol. II, pp. 261–5.

The authors of this circular began by accusing the General Council of having summoned a Conference in 1871 instead of a Congress. From the explanations given above, it is clear that such attacks in fact involved the whole International since it had, as a body, accepted the summoning of a Conference – at which, furthermore, the Alliance had had no objection to being represented by citizens Robin and Bastelica.

The General Council has had delegates at each Congress; at Basle, for instance, there were six. The Sixteen now claimed that 'the majority of the Conference was rigged in advance by the admission of six delegates from the General Council with the right to vote'. The fact was that, of the delegates sent to the Conference by the General Council, the French refugees were none other than the representatives of the Paris Commune, while its English and Swiss members could not normally take any part in the sessions, as is clear from the minutes to be submitted to the next Congress. One Council delegate had a mandate from a national federation. According to a letter sent to the Conference, the mandate of another one was withdrawn because his death had been announced in the newspapers. There remained only one other, with the result that the Belgians alone outnumbered the General Council by six to one.[57]

The international police, watching from the sidelines in the person of Gustave Durand, complained bitterly that the General Rules had been violated by holding a 'secret' Conference. They did not even know our Administrative Regulations well enough to know that the administrative sessions of the Congresses *have* to be held in private.

Their complaints none the less found a sympathetic echo among the Sonvillier Sixteen, who declared: 'And to crown everything, one decision of this Conference allows the General Council itself to fix the date and place for the next Congress, or the *Conference to be held in its stead*; thus we are threatened with the suppression of general Congresses, those great public sessions of the International.'

The Sixteen refused to recognize that this decision was merely a way of informing all governments that, whatever repressive

57. Marx's statistics here are rather tendentious. Although several General Council members did hold mandates from sections or federations, thirteen of the twenty-two delegates at the London Conference were in fact on the General Council.

measures they might take, the International was unshakeably resolved to continue its general meetings by hook or by crook.

At the general assembly of the Geneva sections on 2 December 1871, which gave citizens Malon and Lefrançais a bad reception,[58] the latter submitted a proposition that would help to confirm the decrees passed by the Sonvillier Sixteen, and reinforce their complaint against the General Council and their rejection of the legitimacy of the Conference. The Conference had decided that 'the resolutions not intended for publicity will be communicated to the *Federal Councils or Committees of the various countries* by the corresponding secretaries of the *General Council*.'[59] This resolution, in complete conformity with the General Rules and Regulations, was falsified by Malon and his friends as follows: '*A part* of the resolutions of the Conference *will only be* communicated *to the* Federal Councils *and* to the corresponding secretaries'. Once again they accused the General Council of having 'failed in the *principle of sincerity*' by refusing to make use of 'publicity' which would inform the police of the resolutions whose sole object was the reorganization of the International in those countries where it was banned by law.

Citizens Malon and Lefrançais further objected, 'The Conference has infringed on freedom of thought and expression . . . by giving the General Council the right to denounce and disavow any press organ of the sections and federations that discusses either the principles on which the Association is based, or the respective interests of sections and federations, or finally the general interests of the whole Association (see *Égalité*, 21 October).' What do we find in *Égalité*? A resolution in which the Conference 'gives a warning that henceforth the General Council will be bound to publicly denounce and disavow organs of the International which, following the precedents of *Progrès* and *Solidarité*, should discuss in their columns, before the middle-class public, questions exclusively reserved for the local or Federal Committees and the General Council, or for the private and administrative sittings of the Federal or General Congresses'.[60]

To get the full flavour of Malon's lament, one must remember that this resolution has put an end once and for all to the efforts

58. Gustave Lefrançais was a teacher, a left-wing Proudhonist and a member of the Paris Commune.

59. *IWMA* IV, p. 449.

60. Resolution XVII/2 of the London Conference, ibid.

of certain journalists whose aim is to replace the official committees of the International, and play the same part there as the journalistic bohemia plays in the bourgeois world. Following an attempt of that kind, the Geneva Federal Committee were faced with members of the Alliance editing the official journal of the French-Swiss Federation, *Égalité*, in a manner that was totally hostile to them.

In any case, the General Council hardly needed the London Conference in order to publicly denounce and disavow such journalistic malpractice, for the Basle Congress had declared: 'Wherever attacks against the International are published, the nearest branch or committee is held to send at once a copy of such publication to the General Council' (Administrative Regulation V/7). 'It is obvious,' said the French-Swiss Federal Committee in its statement of 20 December 1871 (see *Égalité*, 24 December),

that this article did not imply that the General Council should simply file in its archives the newspapers which attack the Association, but should reply, and if need be, undo the harmful effect of slanders and malicious attacks. It is equally obvious that this article relates to all newspapers in general, and that if we are not prepared to put up freely with attacks from the bourgeois papers, then *a fortiori* we must use the instrument of our central delegation, the General Council, to disavow papers whose attacks upon us are made in the name of our own Association.

We may note, incidentally, that *The Times*, that Leviathan of the capitalist press, the Lyons *Progrès*, a newspaper of the liberal bourgeoisie, and the *Journal de Genève*, an ultra-reactionary paper, made the same attacks on the Conference, indeed in almost the same words, as citizens Malon and Lefrançais.

Having attacked first the calling of the Conference, then its membership and so-called secret character, the circular from Sonvillier went on to attack the resolutions themselves.

Declaring, first, that the Basle Congress had abdicated its authority 'by giving the General Council the right to refuse, to admit, or to suspend sections of the International', it goes on to impute this crime to the Conference: 'This Conference has ... taken resolutions ... which are directed towards turning the International, a free federation of autonomous sections, into a hierarchical and authoritarian organization of disciplined sections, entirely under the control of a General Council which may at its own whim refuse to admit them or suspend their activity!' Returning later to the Basle Congress, it describes it as having 'denatured the powers of the General Council'.

All the contradictions in the Sonvillier circular boil down to this: The 1871 Conference is accountable for the voting at the Basle Congress of 1869, and the General Council is guilty of having obeyed the Regulations which require it to carry out Congress resolutions.

In point of fact, the true motive for all these attacks on the Conference is something far less obvious than might seem at first. To start with, the Conference had, by its resolutions, totally undermined the intrigues by the Alliance group in Switzerland. Then, the supporters of the Alliance, in Italy, in Spain, in part of Switzerland and in Belgium, had established and maintained with incredible persistence a calculated confusion between Bakunin's outworn programme and the programme of the International Working Men's Association.

The Conference brought into the open this intentional misunderstanding in its two resolutions on working-class political action and on sections with sectarian interests. The first, giving its due to the political abstention preached in Bakunin's programme, was wholly justified by all that had gone before, and supported by the General Rules, the resolution of the Lausanne Congress and other similar precedents.[61]

Let us now consider the question of the sectarian sections:

The first phase in the struggle of the proletariat against the bourgeoisie is marked by sectarianism. This is because the proletariat has not yet reached the stage of being sufficiently developed to act as a class. Individual thinkers provide a critique of social antagonisms, and put forward fantastic solutions which the mass of workers can only accept, pass on, and put into practice. By their very nature, the sects established by these initiators are abstentionist, strangers to all genuine action, to politics, to strikes, to coalitions, in brief, to any unified movement. The mass of the proletariat always remains unmoved by, if not hostile to, their propaganda. The workers of Paris and Lyons did not want the Saint-Simonians, Fourierists or Icarians, any more than the Chartists and trade-unionists of England wanted the Owenists.

61. A footnote at this point in the text quotes in full Resolution IX of the London Conference, on the political action of the working class. This resolution is printed above, pp. 269–70.

All these sects, though at first they provide an impetus to the movement, become an obstacle to it once it has moved further forward; they then become reactionary, as witness the sects in France and England, and more recently the Lassalleans in Germany who, having for years hampered the organization of the proletariat, have finally become nothing less than tools of the police. In fact, we have here the proletarian movement still in its infancy, comparable perhaps to the time when astrology and alchemy were the infancy of science. For the founding of the International to become a possibility, the proletariat had to develop further.[62]

In comparison with the fantastic and mutually antagonistic organizations of the sects, the International is the real and militant organization of the proletarian class in every country, linked together in common struggle against the capitalists, the landowners, and their class power organized by the state. Thus the Rules of the International only speak of *workers'* societies, all seeking the same object, and all accepting the same programme – a programme limited to outlining the major features of the proletarian movement, and leaving the details of theory to be worked out as inspired by the demands of the practical struggle, and as growing out of the exchange of ideas among the sections, with an equal hearing given to all socialist views in their journals and congresses.

Just as in any other new stage of history, the old errors come to the surface for a time, only to disappear soon again; so the International has seen sectarian sections arise within it, though never in any very marked form.

By considering the resurrection of the sects as a great advance, the Alliance has shown conclusively that its time is past. For, though it did at first represent certain elements of progress, the Alliance's programme, like a kind of 'Mahommed without the Koran', amounts to no more than a collection of dead ideas, wrapped up in high-sounding phrases whose only function could be to frighten the more foolish of the bourgeois, or provide ammunition against the Internationalists for Bonapartist or other prosecutors.[63]

62. cf. 'Manifesto of the Communist Party', section III/3, *The Revolutions of 1848*, pp. 94–7.

63. Comments published recently by the police about the International, not excepting Jules Favre's circular to the European powers, nor deputy Sacaze's report on Dufaure's draft law, are stuffed with quotations from the pompous manifestoes of the Alliance. The phraseology they use, radical only in its verbiage, provides reactionaries with just what they are looking for [Marx].

The Conference, at which every shade of socialism was represented, unanimously acclaimed the resolution against sectarian sections; everyone was convinced that that resolution, by bringing the International back onto its own ground, marked a new phase in its forward movement. The supporters of the Alliance, realizing that this resolution was their death-blow, could only see it in terms of a victory of the General Council over the International whereby, as their circular put it, it managed to win sole recognition for the 'special programme' of some members, 'their personal doctrine', 'the orthodox doctrine', 'the official theory alone having any right to be heard in the Association'. However, this was not the fault of those few members, but the necessary result, 'the corrupting effect' of their belonging to the General Council, for 'it is absolutely impossible for any man who has power (!) over his peers to remain a moral man. The General Council has become a circle of intrigue.'

According to the opinion of the Sonvillier Sixteen, the General Rules committed a very serious error in allowing the General Council to coopt new members. With that power, they said, 'the Council could afterwards coopt a whole group of people who would totally alter the tendency of the majority'. It would seem that to them, the mere fact of belonging to the General Council is enough to destroy not only a man's morality, but even his common sense. How else can it be supposed that a majority would transform itself voluntarily into a minority by coopting new members?

However, the Sixteen themselves do not appear wholly convinced on this point; for later on they complain that the General Council has been 'made up of *the same men, continually re-elected*, for five years running' – yet they go on to say that 'most of them are not our regularly elected delegates, since they were not chosen by any Congress'.

The truth of the matter is that the membership of the General Council has kept changing, though certain of the founding members have remained, as in the Federal Councils of Belgium, Switzerland, etc.

The General Council has to fulfil three essential conditions in order to carry out its mandate. First, there must be a large enough membership to do the amount of work involved; second, it must be made up of 'working men from the different countries represented in the International Association';[64] and finally, the

64. 'General Rules', *IWMA* IV, p. 453.

working-class element must predominate. Since, for workers, the demands of their jobs mean that there is inevitably a continual change in the membership of the General Council, how could it fulfil these conditions without having the right to coopt new members? However, more precise definition of that right seems needed, and this was raised at the recent Conference.

The re-election of the General Council as it stood, by successive Congresses – at which England was barely represented – would seem to prove that it was doing its duty within the limits of its possibilities. The Sixteen, however, saw this only as a proof of 'the blind faith of the Congresses', a faith which at Basle was pushed 'to the point of a voluntary abdication of power in favour of the General Council'.

According to them, the 'normal role' of the Council should be 'simply that of an office for correspondence and statistics'. This definition was derived from an incorrect translation of the Rules.

Unlike the rules of any bourgeois society, the General Rules of the International barely touch on its administrative organization. They leave that to be worked out through experience and formulated by future Congresses. None the less, since it is only unity and common action, among the sections in the various countries that can confer a distinctively international character, the Rules are more concerned with the General Council than with any other element in the organization.

Rule 6 states: 'The General Council shall form an international agency between the different national and local groups,' and goes on to give examples of the way in which it is to act. Actually among those examples is the instruction that the Council should see that, 'when immediate practical steps should be needed – as, for instance in the case of international quarrels – the action of the associated societies be simultaneous and uniform'. This article continues: 'Whenever it seems opportune, the General Council shall take the initiative of proposals to be laid before the different national or local societies'.[65] Furthermore, the Rules define the part the Council is to play in summoning and preparing for Congresses, and give it certain specific work to be done and laid before them. The Rules see so little opposition between the spontaneous action of groups and the unified action of the Association that they state:

Since the success of the working men's movement in each country

65. Ibid.

cannot be secured but by the power of union and combination, while, on the other hand, the usefulness of the International General Council must greatly depend [on the circumstance whether it has to deal with a few national centres of working men's associations, or with a great number of small and disconnected local societies]; the members of the International Association shall use their utmost efforts to combine the disconnected working men's societies of their respective countries into national bodies, represented by central national organs.[66]

Administrative Regulation II/2, adopted by the Geneva Congress, states: 'The General Council is *bound to execute* the Congress resolutions.'[67] This regulation rendered official the position occupied by the General Council from the first of being the Association's *executive arm*. It would be difficult to carry out orders without moral 'authority' in the absence of any other 'freely given authority'. The Geneva Congress also at that time ordered the General Council to publish 'the official and obligatory text of the Rules'.[68]

The same Congress also resolved: 'Every branch is at liberty to make rules and bye-laws for its local administration, adapted to local circumstances and the laws of its country. But these rules and bye-laws must not contain anything contrary to the General Rules and Regulations.'[69]

We may note first of all that there is not the slightest allusion to special declarations of principle, nor to special missions to be undertaken by any group on its own initiative outside the common objective being pursued by all the groups in the International. It is simply a matter of each section's right to adapt the General Rules and Regulations 'to local circumstances and the laws of its country'.

In the second place, who is to pronounce on the conformity of such special rules with the General Rules? Obviously if there does not exist any 'authority' empowered to do so, then the resolution is null and void. Not merely could hostile and police sections be formed, but the Association might also be infiltrated by bourgeois philanthropists and sectarians who have abandoned their own class; these would not only alter the whole character of the Association, but if there were enough of them, they could outnumber the workers at Congresses.

66. Ibid., p. 454.　　67. Ibid., p. 457, Marx's emphasis.
68. See p. 82, n. 15.
69. 'General Rules', *IWMA* IV, p. 460.

From the first, the national or local federations have assumed the right in their respective areas to admit or refuse admittance to new sections, depending on whether or not the rules of those sections were in conformity with the General Rules. That this same function should be carried out by the General Council is envisaged in article 7 of the General Rules, which allows *local independent societies*, i.e. societies established outside the federal network of their country, the right to form their own direct links with it. The Alliance did not deign to make use of that right, and did not therefore fulfil the conditions for sending delegates to the Basle Congress.

Article 7 of the Rules also considers the legal obstacles which stand in the way of the formation of national federations in some countries, where the General Council is therefore called on to act as a substitute for a federal council.

Since the fall of the Commune, such legal obstacles have become more numerous in a number of countries, and made the action of the General Council more necessary still if dubious elements are to be kept out of the Association. Thus, recently, committees in France have asked the General Council to intervene to rid them of police spies; while in another major country,[70] the Internationalists have asked it to refuse recognition to any section not founded through a direct mandate either from itself or from them. Their request was motivated by the need to get rid of the kind of *agents provocateurs* whose overwhelming zeal took the form of setting up, one after another, new sections of unparalleled radicalism. From a different direction, certain so-called anti-authoritarian sections had no hesitation in appealing to the Council the moment any internal dispute arose, even demanding that it do all in its power to discipline the opposing side – as happened during the dispute in Lyons. More recently, since the Conference, the Turin 'Workers' Federation' resolved to declare itself a section of the International. There was then a split, with the minority group becoming a 'Society for the Emancipation of the Proletariat'. It joined the International and its first act was to pass a resolution in favour of the Jura Federation. Its paper, *Il Proletario*, was full of angry comments on all forms of authoritarianism. On sending in the subscriptions from the society, its secretary informed the General Council that the older Federation would probably also be sending in subscriptions. He continued:

70. This refers to Austria.

'As you will have read in *Il Proletario*, the Society for the Emancipation of the Proletariat . . . has determined . . . to reject all solidarity with the bourgeoisie who make up the Workers' Federation and pretend to be workers', and he asks the General Council to 'communicate this resolution to all the sections, and to refuse their ten-centime subscriptions should they be sent in'.[71]

Like all the International's groups, the General Council has the duty of issuing propaganda. This it does in its manifestoes, and through its agents who have established the foundations of the International in North America, Germany, and a number of towns in France.

Another of the General Council's functions is to assist during strikes, providing help on behalf of the entire International. (See the reports of the General Council to the various Congresses.) The following instance, among others, indicates how valuable its action has been during strikes. The English Iron-Founders' Resistance Society is in itself an international trade union, with branches in other countries, particularly the United States. However, in a strike by the American foundrymen, the latter found it necessary to get the General Council to intervene to stop English foundrymen being imported to take their places.

The development of the International has forced the General Council, as also the various Federal Councils, into the role of arbitrator.

The Brussels Congress resolved: 'The Federal Councils or Committees shall transmit to the General Council every three months a report on the administration and financial state of their respective branches' (Administrative Regulation IV/3).

Finally, the Basle Congress, which aroused such blind rage among the Sixteen, did no more than formalize the administrative relationship which had grown up as the Association developed. If it did extend the powers of the General Council excessively, whose fault was it if not that of Bakunin, Schwitzguebel, Robert,[72]

71. Such were at that time the *apparent* views of the Society for the Emancipation of the Proletariat, represented by its corresponding secretary, a friend of Bakunin's. In fact, the tendencies of this branch were very different. The society, having expelled this representative for the double disloyalty of mis-appropriating funds and being on terms of close friendship with the chief of police in Turin, provided further explanations which dispelled all mis-understanding between it and the General Council [Marx].

72. Adhemar Schwitzguebel was a Swiss engraver; Fritz Robert, a Swiss teacher.

Guillaume, and the other Alliance delegates, who were loud in demanding that very thing? Would they by chance accuse themselves of 'blind faith' in the General Council in London?

Here are two of the Administrative Regulations adopted by the Basle Congress:

II/4: 'Every new branch or society intending to join the International is bound immediately to announce its adhesion to the General Council;' and II/5: 'The General Council has the right to admit or to refuse the affiliation of any new branch or group, subject to appeal to the next Congress.' As for local independent societies coming into existence outside the federal networks, these articles merely confirm the practice observed from the very beginning of the International – a practice whose continuation is really a matter of life and death for the Association. But it would be going too far to generalize the practice by applying it without distinction to any section or society in the process of formation. What these articles really give the General Council is the right to interfere in the internal affairs of the federations, but they have never in fact been applied by the General Council in that way. Indeed it defies the Sixteen to find a single instance of its having interfered in the affairs of new sections wishing to become affiliated to existing federations or groups.

The resolutions just quoted relate to sections in the process of formation; the following refer to sections already granted recognition:

II/6: 'The General Council has also the right of suspending till the meeting of the next Congress any branch of the International.

II/7: 'In case of conflict between the societies or branches of a national group, or between groups of different nationalities, the General Council shall have the right to decide the conflict, subject to appeal at the next Congress, which will decide definitively.'

These two articles are necessary for extreme situations, but up to now the General Council has never in fact made use of them. The account given above shows that it has not suspended a single section, and that in any matter of dispute, it has done no more than act as an arbitrator at the request of both parties.

We come finally to one function which the needs of the struggle oblige the General Council to assume. However it may distress the supporters of the Alliance, the General Council, simply because of the persistence of the attacks made against it by all the enemies of the proletarian movement, stands in the forefront of those who must defend the International Working Men's Association.

V

Having shown the International in its true colours, the Sixteen go on to tell us what it *should* be like.

First, the General Council should officially be no more than an office for correspondence and providing statistics. Its administrative functions being abandoned, its correspondence would obviously be reduced simply to reproducing information already published in the Association's various journals. The correspondence office would therefore barely exist. As for providing statistics, that is a job that cannot be done without a powerful organization, and even more, as expressly stated in the original Rules, without a common objective. Now since these things smack strongly of 'authoritarianism', while there should perhaps *be* an office, it should not be a statistical office. In brief, the General Council should go. The same logic would also disband Federal Councils, local committees and all other centres of 'authority'. All that would remain would be autonomous sections.

And what would then be the mission of those 'autonomous sections', freely federated, and joyfully unshackled by any authority, 'even authority chosen and constituted by workers'?

At this point, one had to fill in the gaps in the Circular from the report of the Jura Federal Committee submitted to the Congress of the Sixteen. 'To make the working class the true representative of the new interests of mankind', their organization must be 'guided by the *idea* to which all else is subordinate. To *formulate* that idea out of the needs of our age, and the inner tendencies of human beings through a prolonged study of the phenomena of social life, and then to *bring that idea home* to our working men's organizations, such must be our object . . . etc.' Finally, there must be established 'within our working population a truly revolutionary socialist *school*'.

So, all of a sudden, our autonomous working men's sections have become so many *schools*, with these gentlemen from the Alliance as their teachers. They *formulate the idea* through 'prolonged study'. They then 'bring it home to our working men's associations'. To them, the working class is so much raw material, a chaos which needs the breath of their Holy Spirit to give it form.

All of this is simply a paraphrase of the Alliance's own old programme,[73] opening with the words: 'The socialist minority in the League of Peace and Freedom having left that League' proposes to found 'a new Alliance of Socialist Democracy . . . taking as its *special mission* the study of political and philosophical questions . . .' That is where their 'idea' first came from! 'Such an undertaking . . . will give the sincere socialist democrats of Europe and America the *means* of communicating with one another, and strengthening *their ideas*.'[74]

Thus, by their own admission, the minority group within a bourgeois society only wormed their way into the International shortly before the Basle Congress in order to use it *as a means* of presenting themselves to the mass of workers as the hieratic practitioners of a secret science, a science summed up in four sentences, culminating in the 'economic and social equality of the classes'.

Apart from this theoretical 'mission', there was also a practical side to the new organization being proposed for the International. 'The society of the future', says the Circular of the Sixteen, 'must be nothing but the universalization of the organization adopted by the International. We must therefore hasten to make that organization as close as possible to our ideal.'

'How can a free and egalitarian society emerge from an authoritarian organization? It is impossible. The International, the embryo of the future human society, must begin now to be the faithful reflection of our principles of liberty and federation.'

In other words, just as the monasteries of the Middle Ages were a reflection of the life of heaven, so the International must be a reflection of the new Jerusalem, whose 'embryo' is borne within

73. The original programme of the Alliance, which dates from October 1868, is reproduced in the German version as an appendix to Marx and Engels's pamphlet *Ein Komplott gegen die Internationale Arbeiterassoziation, MEW* 18, pp. 467–8, and in the French version, with Marx's marginal comments in *IWMA* III, pp. 273–8.

74. The Alliance supporters, who never stop reproving the General Council for having convened a private Conference at a time when summoning a public Congress would have been the height either of treason or idiocy, these absolute partisans of being open and above board, have – in complete disregard of our Rules – organized a truly secret society actually within the International, directed against the International, and aimed at getting the sections unwittingly under the priestly control of Bakunin. The General Council intends to demand an inquiry at the next Congress into this secret organization and those running it in certain countries, Spain for instance [Marx].

the womb of the Alliance. Had the Communards realized that the Commune was 'the embryo of the future human society', they would have thrown away all discipline and all weapons – things which must disappear as soon as there are no more wars – and they would not have been defeated!

But to make it quite clear that, despite their 'prolonged study', the Sixteen were not hatching this charming plan for disorganizing and disarming the International at a time when it was fighting for its life, Bakunin has just published the original text in his memorandum on the organization of the International.[75] (See *Almanach du Peuple pour 1872*, Geneva.)

VI

Now read the report presented by the Jura Committee to the Congress of the Sixteen. 'To read this', says their official journal, *La Révolution sociale* (16 November), 'will give the *true measure* of what may be expected in the way of dedication and practical intelligence from the members of the Jura Federation'. It begins by attributing to 'those terrible events', the Franco-Prussian war and the civil war in France, 'a somewhat *demoralizing* influence . . . on the situation of sections of the International'.

Though in fact the Franco-Prussian war may have tended to *disorganize* the sections by taking away a large number of workers into both armies, it is equally true to say that the fall of the Empire and Bismarck's open declaration of a war of conquest, gave rise in Germany and England to an impassioned struggle between the bourgeoisie who sided with the Prussians, and the proletariat who affirmed their internationalism more strongly than ever. In this way the International was to gain ground in both countries. In America, its doing so created a split in the vast body of German proletarian immigrants; the internationalist group broke away completely from the chauvinist one.

From yet another point of view, the advent of the Commune in Paris gave an unprecedented impulse to the external development of the International, and to the vigorous support for its principles by the sections in every country – except however the Jura Federation, whose report continues thus: since 'the beginning of the battle of the giants . . . we have been forced to reflect . . . that

75. English excerpts in G. D. Maximoff (ed.), *The Political Philosophy of Bakunin*, Collier-Macmillan, 1964.

some people are merely concealing their weakness ... To many people this situation (in their ranks) is a sign of decrepitude', but, 'on the contrary, it is ... an ideal situation *for a total transformation* of the International' – according to their image. A closer look at this advantageous situation will make their modest wish clearer.

Leaving aside the Alliance, which had been dissolved and its place taken by the Malon section, the Committee had to report on the situation in twenty sections. Among them, seven repudiated it totally; here is what the report has to say:

The cabinet-makers' section, and the engravers' and engine-turners' section of Bienne, have never replied to *any* of the communications we have sent them.

The trades' sections of Neuchâtel, consisting of carpenters, cabinet-makers, engravers and engine-turners, have made *no* reply to the communications of the Federal Committee.

We have not been able to hear *any* news from the Val-de-Ruz section.

The Le Locle section of engravers and engine-turners have given *no* reply to the communications of the Federal Committee.

This is presumably what is meant by the *free* relationship between autonomous sections and their Federal Committee.

Another section, that of 'the engravers and engine-turners of the district of Courtelary, after three years of stubborn persistence ... are now ... forming a resistance society' *outside the International*, a fact which did not deter them from sending two delegates to represent them at the Congress of the Sixteen.

We then come to four sections that are well and truly dead:

The central Bienne section has for the moment collapsed; one of its keenest members however wrote recently that all hope of seeing the International born again in Bienne was not lost.

The Saint-Blaise section has fallen.

The Catébat section, after a splendid career, was forced to yield in face of the intrigues of the lords (!) of the district to dissolve this *valiant* section.

Finally, the Corgémont section too fell victim to intrigues by the bosses.

We then come to the central section of the Courtelary district which 'took the wise step of *suspending* activities' – though it still sent two delegates to the Congress of the Sixteen.

There are then four sections whose existence is doubtful to say the least.

The Grange section has been reduced to a tiny kernel of socialist workers . . . Their local action is hampered by their small numbers.

The central section of Neuchâtel has had a great deal to suffer from circumstances, and had it not been for the dedication and activity of certain of its members, it would certainly have collapsed.

The central section of Le Locle, having hung between life and death for several months, finally broke up. Quite recently it has been reconstituted . . .

– clearly for the one object of sending two delegates to the Congress of the Sixteen!

The socialist propaganda section of La Chaux-de-Fonds is in a critical situation . . . Its position, far from improving, is in fact tending to grow worse.

Two sections then follow, the study circles of Saint-Imier and Sonvillier, which are only mentioned by the way, with nothing said as to their condition.

There remains one model section which, judging from its being called the '*central* section' would seem to be no more than the remainder of all the sections that no longer exist.

'The central section of Moutier has certainly suffered least . . . Its committee has been in continuous contact with the Federal Committee . . . (although) *sections are not yet consolidated . . .*' The explanation for this is that 'the action of the Moutier section is especially facilitated by the *excellent attitude* of a working-class population . . . with plebeian ways of living; we should like to see the working class of this district become still more independent of political elements.'

It is quite clear that this report does 'give the *precise measure* of what can be expected from the dedication and *practical intelligence* of the members of the Jura Federation'. They might have completed it by adding that the workers of La Chaux-de-Fonds, the original seat of their committee, have always refused to have any dealing with them! In fact, quite recently, at the general assembly of 18 January 1872, they replied to the Circular of the Sixteen with a unanimous vote confirming the resolution of the London Conference as well as that of the French-Swiss Congress of May 1871: 'to exclude permanently from the International Bakunin, Guillaume and their disciples'.

Does there remain anything more to be said as to the value of this so-called Sonvillier Congress, which, by its own admission caused 'an outbreak of war – open war – within the International'?

Undoubtedly these people, whose influence is out of all proportion to their numbers, have had considerable success. All the liberal and police press has openly supported them; they were echoed in their personal attacks on the General Council and their generalized attacks on the International by self-styled reformers from many countries; in England, by bourgeois republicans, whose intrigues had been unmasked by the General Council; in Italy, by dogmatic free-thinkers who have just founded a 'Universal Society of Rationalists' under the banner of Stefanoni,[76] to have its statutory headquarters in Rome, an 'authoritarian' and 'hierarchical' organization with its atheist monks and nuns, with statutes allowing for a marble bust to be placed in its congress hall of any bourgeois prepared to donate ten thousand francs or more; and finally in Germany, by Bismarckian socialists who not only run a police-backed paper, *Neuer Social-Demokrat*, but also sport the white shirts of the Prusso-German empire.[77]

In a touching appeal, the Sonvillier conclave asks that all International sections stress the urgency of holding an immediate Congress in order, as citizens Malon and Lefrançais put it, 'to fight off the successive encroachments of the London Council'; though what they really mean is to replace the International with the Alliance. This appeal received so encouraging a response that they were immediately reduced to falsifying one of the votes of the last Belgian Congress. They say in their official organ (*La Révolution sociale*, 4 January 1872): 'Finally, more important still, the Belgian sections met in Congress in Brussels on 24 and 25 December, and unanimously voted a resolution identical to that voted by the Sonvillier Congress, on the urgency of summoning a General Congress.' It is worth noting that this Belgian Congress did nothing of the kind: it charged the Belgian Congress, which is not due to meet until June, to work out a set of projected new General Rules to submit to the *next Congress* of the International.

In accordance with the wish of the vast majority of the Inter-

76. Luigi Stefanoni was a bourgeois democrat who had taken part in Garibaldi's campaign.

77. The *Neuer Social-Demokrat* was the organ of Schweitzer's die-hard Lassallean faction after the ADAV split in 1869 and the section led by Bracke united with Liebknecht and Bebel's Union of German Workers' Societies to form the SDAP ('Eisenach party'). The *blouses blanches* (white shirts) were working-class *provocateurs* organized by the Bonapartist police under the Second Empire.

national, the General Council is only convening the annual Congress for September 1872.

VII

A few weeks after the Conference, Messrs Albert Richard and Gaspard Blanc, the most influential and enthusiastic members of the Alliance, arrived in London with the task of recruiting from among the French refugees auxiliaries prepared to work for the restoration of the Empire, which seemed to them the only way of getting rid of Thiers without being reduced to penury. The General Council issued warnings to all whose interests might be at stake, including the Brussels Federal Council, of their Bonapartist manoeuvres.

In January 1872, they abandoned all pretence, and published a pamphlet: *'The Empire and the new France. An appeal to the French conscience from the people and youth'*.[78]

With the usual modesty of Alliance charlatans, they are loud in their own praise:

We who formed the great army of the French proletariat . . . we, the most influential leaders of the International in France[79] . . . having had the good fortune to be spared death by shooting, we remain here to set up against . . . ambitious parliamentarians, well-fed republicans, and self-styled democrats of every kind . . . the flag under which we fight and, despite all slanders, threats and attacks, we cry from the depths of our

78. Albert Richard and Gaspard Blanc, *L'Empire et la France nouvelle*, Brussels, 1872.

79. Under the headline 'To the Pillory!', *Égalité* said on 15 February:

'The time has not yet come when the whole story of the Communal movement's defeat in the south of France can be told; but what we can say now, we who have for the most part been witness to the deplorable defeat of the Lyons rising of 30 April, is that this rising failed partly because of the cowardice, the treason and the dishonesty of G. Blanc, who infiltrated everything, carrying out the orders of A. Richard who remained in the background. By their well-planned manoeuvres, these wretched men succeeded in compromising a number of those who took part in the preliminary work of the insurrectionary committees. Furthermore, these traitors succeeded in discrediting the International in Lyons – so much so that when the revolution took place in Paris, the workers in Lyons regarded the International with the utmost mistrust. Hence the total lack of organization; hence, further, the defeat of the rising, a defeat which inevitably brought with it the fall of the Commune, thus left isolated and defenceless. It was only this bloody lesson that made it possible for us to win the workers of Lyons over and get them to rally to the flag of the International. Albert Richard was the spoilt child, the prophet indeed, of Bakunin and his friends' [Marx].

hearts to an astonished Europe the call soon to resound in the hearts of all Frenchmen: 'Long live the Emperor!'.

For Napoleon III, dishonoured and scorned, there must be a magnificent rehabilitation.

So Messrs Albert Richard and Gaspard Blanc, paid out of the secret funds of Invasion III,[80] are, it appears, specially entrusted with that rehabilitation.

Furthermore, they admit: 'We have become Imperialists through the normal progression of our ideas.' There is a confession to warm the hearts of their co-religionists in the Alliance. As in the good old days of *Solidarité*, Richard and Blanc retail their old tags about 'political abstentionism' which, as is clear from their 'normal progression', only becomes a reality where there is absolute despotism, for then the workers abstain from all political activity in the same way as the prisoner abstains from going for walks in the sun.

'The age of the revolutionaries,' they say, 'is over . . . communism is limited to Germany and England, Germany especially. It is there, certainly, that it has been receiving serious formulation for a long time before gradually spreading through the whole of the International; and this disquieting progress of *German influence* in the Association has contributed more than a little to hampering its development, or rather, to giving it a new direction in the sections of central and southern France which have never yet taken their slogans from a German.'

One might almost be listening to the great hierophant himself,[81] attributing to himself, as a Russian, a special mission to represent the *Latin races*, dating back to the foundation of the Alliance; or 'the genuine missionaries' of *La Révolution sociale* (2 November 1871) denouncing 'the backward movement which German and Bismarckian thinkers are trying to impose on the International'.

How fortunate that the genuine tradition has not been lost, and that Messrs Richard and Blanc were not shot! So their special 'work' consists in 'giving a new direction' to the International in central and southern France, trying to found Bonapartist sections which would *ipso facto* be essentially 'autonomous'.

As for forming the proletariat into a political party, as recommended by the London Conference, '*After the restoration of the Empire*, we', i.e. Richard and Blanc, 'will soon have done, not just

80. A nickname for Napoleon III.
81. I.e. Bakunin.

with socialist theories, but with the beginnings of their realization as seen in the revolutionary organization of the masses'.

In short, by exploiting the great 'principle of the autonomy of each section' which 'constitutes the real strength of the International . . . especially in *Latin countries*' (*La Révolution sociale*, 4 January), these gentlemen are counting on creating anarchy in the International.

Anarchy – that is the great warhorse of their master, Bakunin, whose doctrines only use certain catch-phrases from socialist theory. To all socialists anarchy means this: the aim of the proletarian movement – that is to say the abolition of social classes – once achieved, the power of the state, which now serves only to keep the vast majority of producers under the yoke of a small minority of exploiters, will vanish, and the functions of government become purely administrative. But to the Alliance it means something different. It designates anarchy in the ranks of the proletariat as *the* infallible means of destroying the powerful concentration of social and political forces in the hands of the exploiters. It is therefore demanding that the International replace its organization with anarchy – just at a time when the old world is in any case trying to destroy it. The international police could ask no better means to prolong the Thiers republic forever, while covering it with the mantle of empire.[82]

REPORT TO THE HAGUE CONGRESS[83]

Citizens,

Since our last Congress at Basle, two great wars have changed the face of Europe: the Franco-German war and the civil war in

---

82. In his report on the Dufaure law, deputy Sacaze makes his prime object of attack the International's 'organization'. That organization is his *bête noire*. Having noted 'the tremendous advance of this alarming Association', he goes on: 'That Association rejects . . . the shady practices of the sects which came before it. Its organization takes place and undergoes changes in the public view. Thanks to the power of that organization . . . it has gradually extended its sphere of action and influence. It is breaking new ground everywhere.' He then gives a summary description of that organization, and concludes: 'Such, in its carefully planned unity . . . is the plan of this vast organization. Its strength lies in its very conception. It also lies in the mass of its followers, joined in simultaneous action, and ultimately in the unconquerable impulse urging them on' [Marx].

83. This report was adopted by the General Council at a meeting in August 1872 (the precise date is unclear). The Hague Congress of September 1872 was

France. Both of these wars were preceded, accompanied, and followed by a third war – the war against the International Working Men's Association.

The Paris members of the International had told the French people, publicly and emphatically, that voting the plebiscite[84] was voting despotism at home and war abroad. Under the pretext of having participated in a plot for the assassination of Louis Bonaparte, they were arrested on the eve of the plebiscite, 23 April 1870. Simultaneous arrests of Internationalists took place at Lyons, Rouen, Marseilles, Brest, and other towns. In its declaration of 3 May 1870, the General Council stated:[85]

This last plot will worthily range with its two predecessors of grotesque memory. The noisy and violent measures against our French sections are exclusively intended to serve one single purpose – the manipulation of the plebiscite.

In point of fact, after the downfall of the December empire its governmental successors published documentary evidence to the effect that this last plot had been fabricated by the Bonapartist police itself,[86] and that on the eve of the plebiscite, Ollivier,[87] in a private circular, directly told his subordinates, 'The leaders of the International must be arrested or else the voting of the plebiscite can not be satisfactorily proceeded with.'

The plebiscitary farce once over, the members of the Paris Federal Council were indeed condemned, on 8 July, by Louis Bonaparte's own judges, but for the simple crime of belonging to the International and not for any participation in the sham plot. Thus the Bonapartist government considered it necessary to initiate the most ruinous war that was ever brought down upon

the only one of the International's Congresses that Marx personally attended, and he read the report in German translation to the open session of the Congress on 5 September. It was published in the *International Herald*, 5, 12 and 19 October.

84. See p. 173, n. 3.

85. *IWMA* III, p. 232. The two predecessors were the trials of the Paris Federal Committee of March and May 1868; see 'Report to the Brussels Congress', above, p. 96.

86. Marx is referring to the *Papiers et correspondance de la famille impériale*, published by the Government of Defence in 1870.

87. Émile Ollivier was Louis Napoleon's Prime Minister from January to August 1870.

France, by a preliminary campaign against the French sections of the International Working Men's Association. Let us not forget that the working class in France rose like one man to reject the plebiscite. Let us no more forget that 'the stock exchanges, the cabinets, the ruling classes and the press of Europe celebrated the plebiscite as a signal victory of the French emperor over the French working class'.[88] (See First Address of the General Council on the Franco-Prussian War, 23 July 1870.)

A few weeks after the plebiscite, when the Imperialist press commenced to fan the war-like passions amongst the French people, the Paris Internationalists, nothing daunted by the government persecutions, issued their appeal of 12 July, 'To the workmen of all nations', denounced the intended war as a 'criminal absurdity', telling their 'brothers of Germany' that their 'division would only result in the complete triumph of despotism on both sides of the Rhine', and declaring, 'We, the members of the International Association, know of no frontiers'.[89] Their appeal met with an enthusiastic echo from Germany, so that the General Council was entitled to state:

> The very fact that while official France and Germany are rushing into a fratricidal feud, the workmen of France and Germany send each other messages of peace and goodwill, this great fact, unparalleled in the history of the past, opens the vista of a brighter future. It proves that in contrast to old society, with its economical miseries and its political delirium, a new society is springing up, whose international rule will be *Peace*, because its national ruler will be everywhere the same – *Labour!* The pioneer of that new society is the International Working Men's Association. – Address of 23 July 1870. [90]

Up to the proclamation of the republic, the members of the Paris Federal Council remained in prison, while the other members of the Association were daily denounced to the mob as traitors acting in the pay of Prussia.

With the capitulation of Sedan, when the Second Empire ended as it began, by a parody, the Franco-German war entered upon its second phase. It became a war against the French people. After her repeated solemn declarations to take up arms for the sole purpose of repelling foreign aggression, Prussia now dropped the

88. Above, p. 173.

89. This appeal was published in *Le Réveil*, a left republican Paris newspaper, on 12 July 1870.

90. Above, p. 176.

mask and proclaimed a war of conquest. From that moment she found herself compelled not only to fight the republic in France, but simultaneously the International in Germany. We can here but hint at a few incidents of that conflict.

Immediately after the declaration of war, the greater part of the territory of the North German Confederation, Hanover, Oldenburg, Bremen, Hamburg, Brunswick, Schleswig-Holstein, Mecklenburg, Pomerania, and the province of Prussia, were placed in a state of siege, and handed over to the tender mercies of General Vogel von Falkenstein. This state of siege, proclaimed as a safeguard against the threatening foreign invasion, was at once turned into a state of war against the German Internationalists.

The day after the proclamation of the republic at Paris, the Brunswick Central Committee of the German Social-Democratic Workers' Party, which forms a section of the International within the limits imposed by the law of the country, issued a manifesto[91] (5 September) calling upon the working class to oppose by all means in their power the dismemberment of France, to claim a peace honourable for that country, and to agitate for the recognition of the French republic. The manifesto denounced the proposed annexation of Alsace and Lorraine as a crime tending to transform all Germany into a Prussian barracks, and to establish war as a permanent European institution. On 9 September, Vogel von Falkenstein had the members of the Brunswick Committee arrested and marched off in chains, a distance of 600 miles, to Lötzen, a Prussian fortress on the Russian frontier, where their ignominious treatment was to serve as a foil to the ostentatious feasting of the Imperial guest at Wilhelmshöhe.[92] As arrests, the hunting of workmen from one German state to another, suppression of proletarian papers, military brutality, and police-chicane in all forms, did not prevent the International vanguard of the German working class from acting up to the Brunswick manifesto, Vogel von Falkenstein, by an ukase of 21 September, interdicted all meetings of the Social-Democratic Workers' Party. That interdict was cancelled by another ukase of 5 October, wherein he naively commands the police spies

... to denounce to him personally all individuals who, by public

91. The manifesto referred to here was based on Marx and Engels's letter to the Brunswick Committee of the SDAP (above, pp. 177–9).

92. Louis Napoleon, captured at Sedan, was imprisoned at this castle near Kassel from 5 September 1870 to 19 March 1871.

demonstrations, shall encourage France in her resistance against the conditions of peace imposed by Germany, so as to enable him to render such individuals innocuous during the continuance of the war.

Leaving the cares of the war abroad to Moltke,[93] the king of Prussia contrived to give a new turn to the war at home. By his personal order of 17 October, Vogel von Falkenstein was to lend his Lötzen captives to the Brunswick district tribunal, which, on its part, was either to find grounds for their legal durance, or else return them to the safe keeping of the dread general.

Vogel von Falkenstein's proceedings were, of course, imitated throughout Germany, while Bismarck, in a diplomatic circular, mocked Europe by standing forth as the indignant champion of the right of free utterance of opinion, free press, and free meetings, on the part of the peace party in France. At the very same time that he demanded a freely elected National Assembly for France, in Germany he had Bebel and Liebknecht imprisoned for having, in opposition to him, represented the International in the German parliament, and in order to get them out of the way during the impending general elections.[94]

His master, William the Conqueror, supported him by a decree from Versailles prolonging the state of siege, that is to say, the suspension of all civil law, for the whole period of the elections. In fact, the king did not allow the state of siege to be raised in Germany until two months after the conclusion of peace with France. The stubbornness with which he was insisting upon the state of war at home, and his repeated personal meddling with his own German captives, prove the awe in which he, amidst the din of victorious arms and the frantic cheers of the whole middle class, held the rising party of the proletariat. It was the involuntary homage paid by physical force to moral power.

If the war against the International had been localized, first in France, from the days of the plebiscite to the downfall of the Empire, then in Germany, during the whole period of the resistance of the republic against Prussia, it became general since the rise, and after the fall, of the Paris Commune.

On 6 June 1871, Jules Favre issued his circular to the foreign powers demanding the extradition of the refugees of the Com-

93. Helmuth Moltke was the Prussian commander-in-chief.

94. These elections were for the first Reichstag of the new German Empire, formed by the establishment of Prussian hegemony over the south German states and the annexation of Alsace and Lorraine.

mune as common criminals, and a general crusade against the International as the enemy of family, religion, order, and property, so adequately represented in his own person. Austria and Hungary caught the cue at once. On 13 June, a raid was made on the reputed leaders of the Pest [Budapest] Working Men's Union, their papers were seized, their persons sequestered, and proceedings were instituted against them for high treason. Several delegates of the Vienna [section of the] International, happening to be on a visit to Pest, were carried off to Vienna, there to undergo a similar treatment. Beust asked and received from his parliament a supplementary vote of £30,000, 'on behalf of expenses for political information that had become more than ever indispensable through the dangerous spread of the International all over Europe'.

Since that time a true reign of terror against the working class has set in in Austria and Hungary. In its last agonies the Austrian government seems still anxiously to cling to its old privilege of playing the Don Quixote of European reaction.

A few weeks after Jules Favre's circular, Dufaure proposed to his Rurals a law which is now in force, and punishes as a crime the mere fact of belonging to the International Working Men's Association, or of sharing its principles.[95] As a witness before the Rural committee of inquiry on Dufaure's bill, Thiers boasted that it was the offspring of his own ingenious brains and that he had been the first to discover the infallible panacea of treating the Internationalists as the Spanish Inquisition had treated the heretics. But even on this point he can lay no claim to originality. Long before his appointment as saviour of society, the true law which the Internationalists deserve at the hands of the ruling classes had been laid down by the Vienna courts.

On 26 July 1870, the most prominent men of the Austrian proletarian party were found guilty of high treason, and sentenced to years of penal servitude, with one fast day in every month. The law laid down was this:

The prisoners, as they themselves confess, have accepted and acted according to the programme of the German Working Men's Congress of Eisenach (1869). This programme embodies the programme of the International. The International is established for the emancipation of the working class from the rule of the propertied class, and from political dependence. That emancipation is incompatible with the existing institu-

95. On the *loi Dufaure*, see p. 275, n. 19. On the 'Rural Assembly', see above, pp. 195–6.

tions of the Austrian state. Hence, whoever accepts and propagates the principles of the International programme, commits preparatory acts for the overthrow of the Austrian government, and is consequently guilty of high treason.

On 27 November 1871, judgement was passed upon the members of the Brunswick Committee. They were sentenced to various periods of imprisonment. The court expressly referred, as to a precedent, to the law laid down at Vienna.

At Pest, the prisoners belonging to the Working Men's Union, after having undergone for nearly a year a treatment as infamous as that inflicted upon the Fenians by the British government, were brought up for judgement on 22 April 1872. The public prosecutor, here also, called upon the court to apply to them the law laid down at Vienna. They were, however, acquitted.

At Leipzig, on 27 March 1872, Bebel and Liebknecht were sentenced to two years' imprisonment in a fortress for attempted high treason upon the strength of the law as laid down at Vienna. The only distinctive feature of this case is that the law laid down by a Vienna judge was sanctioned by a Saxon jury.

At Copenhagen, the three members of the [Danish] Central Committee of the International, Brix, Pio, and Geleff, were thrown into prison on 5 May [1872] because they had declared their firm resolve to hold an open-air meeting in the teeth of a police order forbidding it. Once in prison they were told that the accusation against them was extended, that the socialist ideas in themselves were incompatible with the existence of the Danish state, and that consequently the mere act of propagating them constituted a crime against the Danish constitution. Again the law as laid down in Vienna! The accused are still in prison awaiting their trial.

The Belgian government, distinguished by its sympathetic reply to Jules Favre's demand of extradition, made haste to propose, through Malou, a hypocritical counterfeit of Dufaure's law.

His Holiness Pope Pius IX gave vent to his feelings in an allocation to a deputation of Swiss Catholics.[96] 'Your government,' said he,

which is republican, thinks itself bound to make a heavy sacrifice for what is called liberty. It affords an asylum to a goodly number of individuals of the worst character. It tolerates that sect of the Inter-

96. The source of this report is unclear, and it may possibly be apocryphal.

national which desires to treat all Europe as it has treated Paris. These gentlemen of the International, who are no gentlemen, are to be feared because they work for the account of the everlasting enemy of God and mankind. What is to be gained by protecting them! One must pray for them.

Hang them first and pray for them afterwards!

Supported by Bismarck, Beust, and Stieber,[97] the Prussian spy-in-chief, the emperors of Austria and Germany met at Salzburg in the beginning of September 1871, for the ostensible purpose of founding a Holy Alliance against the International Working Men's Association. 'Such a European alliance,' declared the *North German Gazette*,[98] Bismarck's private *Moniteur*, 'is the only possible salvation of state, church, property, civilization, in one word, of everything that constitutes European states.'

Bismarck's real object, of course, was to prepare alliances for an impending war with Russia, and the International was held up to Austria as a piece of red cloth is held up to a bull.

Lanza suppressed the International in Italy by simple decree.[99] Sagasta declared it an outlaw in Spain,[1] probably with a view to curry favour with the English stock exchange. The Russian government which, since the emancipation of the serfs, has been driven to the dangerous expedient of making timid concessions to popular claims today, and withdrawing them tomorrow, found in the general hue and cry against the International a pretext for a recrudescence of reaction at home. Abroad, with the intention of prying into the secrets of our Association, it succeeded in inducing a Swiss judge to search, in presence of a Russian spy, the house of Utin,[2] a Russian Internationalist, and the editor of the Geneva *Égalité*, the organ of our French-Swiss Federation. The republican

97. Wilhelm Stieber, as director of the Prussian political police, was an old enemy of Marx, who had exposed his earlier machinations in his book on *The Cologne Communist Trial* (*MECW* 11).

98. *Norddeutsche Allgemeine Zeitung*, a semi-official paper. *Le Moniteur universel* had been the official organ of the Bonapartist regime in France.

99. Giovanni Lanza, the Italian Prime Minister, banned the International on 14 August 1871 and had the Naples section forcibly closed on 20 August.

1. After the harassment that led the Madrid Federal Committee of the International to take refuge in Portugal in summer 1871, Praxedes Sagasta, the Spanish Minister of the Interior, gave instructions for the dissolution of the International's Spanish sections in January 1872.

2. Nikolai Utin was a Russian exile and a supporter of Marx in the International.

government of Switzerland has only been prevented by the agitation of the Swiss Internationalists from handing up to Thiers refugees of the Commune.

Finally, the government of Mr Gladstone, unable to act in Great Britain, at least set forth its good intentions by the police terrorism exercised in Ireland against our sections then in course of formation,[3] and by ordering its representatives abroad to collect information with respect to the International Working Men's Association.

But all the measures of repression which the combined government intellect of Europe was capable of devising, vanish into nothing before the war of calumny undertaken by the lying power of the civilized world. Apocryphal histories and mysteries of the International, shameless forgeries of public documents and private letters, sensational telegrams, followed each other in rapid succession; all the sluices of slander at the disposal of the venal respectable press were opened at once to set free a deluge of infamy in which to drown the execrated foe. This war of calumny finds no parallel in history for the truly international area over which it has spread, and for the complete accord in which it has been carried on by all shades of ruling-class opinion. When the great conflagration took place at Chicago, the telegraph round the world announced it as the infernal deed of the International; and it is really wonderful that to its demoniacal agency has not been attributed the hurricane ravaging the West Indies.

In its former annual reports, the General Council used to give a review of the progress of the Association since the meeting of the preceding Congress. You will appreciate, citizens, the motives which induce us to abstain from that course upon this occasion. Moreover, the reports of the delegates from the various countries, who know best how far their discretion may extend, will in a measure make up for this deficiency. We confine ourselves to the statement that since the Congress at Basle, and chiefly since the London Conference of September 1871, the International has been extended to the Irish in England and to Ireland itself, to Holland, Denmark, and Portugal, that it has been firmly organized in the United States, and that it has established ramifications in Buenos Aires, Australia, and New Zealand.

---

3. The General Council exposed this in a declaration entitled 'Police Terrorism in Ireland' (9 April 1872); *IWMA* V, pp. 149–50.

The difference between a working class without an International, and a working class with an International, becomes most evident if we look back to the period of 1848. Years were required for the working class itself to recognize the insurrection of June 1848 as the work of its own vanguard. The Paris Commune was at once acclaimed by the universal proletariat.

You, the delegates of the working class, meet to strengthen the militant organization of a society aiming at the emancipation of labour and the extinction of national feuds. Almost at the same moment, there meet at Berlin the crowned dignitaries of the old world in order to forge new chains and to hatch new wars.[4]

Long life to the International Working Men's Association!

SPEECH ON THE HAGUE CONGRESS[5]

In the eighteenth century, it was the custom of kings and potentates to gather in The Hague to discuss the interests of their dynasties.

Despite attempts to arouse our anxieties, we were determined to hold our workers' assembly in this selfsame place. We wanted to appear in the midst of the most reactionary population in order to reinforce the existence and expansion of our great Association and to fortify its hope in the future.

When our decision became known, people talked of the emissaries we had sent out to prepare the ground. Yes, we do not deny that we have such emissaries everywhere; but they are for the most part unknown to us. Our emissaries in The Hague were those workers whose jobs are as hard as those of our emissaries

4. In September 1872 the emperors of Germany, Austria-Hungary and Russia met in Berlin with a view to re-establishing their traditional Holy Alliance. They specifically discussed common action against the revolutionary movement.

5. After the Hague Congress of the International (2–7 September 1872) Marx and many other delegates visited Amsterdam at the invitation of the local section of the International. On 8 September Marx delivered the following speech in German and French at a public meeting. The most accurate report of Marx's speech, in French in *La Liberté*, was inaccessible to us, and it is therefore translated here from the German text printed in *MEW* 18, pp. 159–61. This is itself a translation from the French, checked against the less accurate German report given in the *Volksstaat*; the latter was bowdlerized in the places indicated.

in Amsterdam, and the latter are also workers who do a sixteen-hour working day. It is these men who are our emissaries; there are no others; and in all the countries where we show our face we find them prepared to give us a whole-hearted reception, for they very soon realize that we are fighting to improve their lot.

The Congress in The Hague produced three important results:

It proclaimed the need for the working class to fight the old, crumbling society in the political as in the social sphere; and we congratulate ourselves on the fact that this resolution of the London Conference will henceforth be included in our Rules.[6]

A group had formed in our midst which commended the abstention of the workers from political activity.

We saw it as our duty to point out how dangerous and fateful such principles seemed for the task in hand.

The workers will have to seize political power one day in order to construct the new organization of labour; they will have to overthrow the old politics which bolster up the old institutions, unless they want to share the fate of the early Christians, who lost their chance of heaven on earth because they rejected and neglected such action.

We do not claim, however, that the road leading to this goal is the same everywhere.

We know that heed must be paid to the institutions, customs and traditions of the various countries, and we do not deny that there are countries, such as America and England, and if I was familiar with its institutions, I might include Holland, where the workers may attain their goal by peaceful means. That being the case, we must recognize that in most continental countries the lever of the revolution will have to be force; a resort to force will be necessary one day in order to set up the rule of labour.[7]

The Hague Congress conferred new and even more extensive powers on the General Council.[8] Indeed, at a time when kings are gathering in Berlin for a meeting at which the powerful representatives of feudalism and of the past will plan new and more

6. Marx refers to Resolution IX of the London Conference, directed against the Bakuninists. See above, pp. 269–70.

7. In the *Volksstaat*, this sentence was replaced by, 'But this is not the case in all countries.'

8. The Basle Congress of 1869 had given the General Council power to suspend sections of the International that contravened its Rules, subject to ratification by the next Congress. The Hague Congress extended this power to whole federations.

determined repressive measures against us, at the very moment when persecution is being organized, the Hague Congress saw the appropriateness and necessity of extending the powers of the General Council and centralizing all actions for the coming struggle, because these actions would be helpless in isolation. Furthermore, who need worry about the delegation of power to the General Council except our enemies? Does the General Council have a bureaucracy or an armed police force to compel obedience? Is its authority not purely of a moral nature, and does it not submit its decisions to the judgement of the federations, which are entrusted with their implementation? If kings were forced to uphold their power under such conditions, without an army, without police and without courts, having only moral influence and moral authority, then they would present only a frail obstacle to the forward march of the revolution.

Finally, the Hague Congress moved the seat of the General Council to New York. Many people, even friends, showed surprise at this decision. Have they forgotten, then, that America is becoming the workers' part of the world *par excellence*, that each year half a million people – workers – emigrate to this other continent, and that the International must strike powerful roots into this soil, where the workers are the dominant force? Moreover, the Congress decision empowers the General Council to coopt members whose cooperation it regards as necessary and useful for the good of the common cause. Let us trust to their good judgement and expect that they will succeed in selecting people who are up to the task and who will know how to hold up the banner of our Association with a firm hand in Europe.

Citizens, let us remember the basic principle of the International: solidarity. We will only be able to attain the goal we have set ourselves if this life-giving principle acquires a secure foundation among the workers of all countries. The revolution requires solidarity, as the great example of the Paris Commune teaches us, for this most powerful uprising of the Parisian proletariat failed[9] because no great revolutionary movements equal in stature arose in any of the other centres such as Berlin, Madrid, etc.

As far as I am concerned, I shall continue my work and strive constantly to establish this solidarity, which will bear such rich

9. In the *Volksstaat*, the remainder of this sentence was replaced by, 'only because solidarity on the part of the workers of other countries was lacking'.

fruit in the future, amongst the entire working class. No, I shall not be withdrawing from the International, and all the rest of my life, like my efforts in the past, will be dedicated to the triumph of the social ideas which will one day – rest assured of this! – bring about the rule of the proletariat over the entire world.

Political Indifferentism[1]

'The working class must not constitute itself a political party; it must not, under any pretext, engage in political action, for to combat the state is to recognize the state: and this is contrary to eternal principles. Workers must not go on strike; for to struggle to increase one's wages or to prevent their decrease is like recognizing *wages*: and this is contrary to the eternal principles of the emancipation of the working class!

'If in the political struggle against the bourgeois state the workers succeed only in extracting concessions, then they are guilty of compromise; and this is contrary to eternal principles. All peaceful movements, such as those in which English and American workers have the bad habit of engaging, are therefore to be despised. Workers must not struggle to establish a legal limit to the working day, because this is to compromise with the masters, who can then only exploit them for ten or twelve hours, instead of fourteen or sixteen. They must not even exert themselves in order legally to prohibit the employment in factories of children under the age of ten, because by such means they do not bring to an end the exploitation of children over ten: they thus commit a new compromise, which stains the purity of the eternal principles.

'Workers should even less desire that, as happens in the United States of America, the state whose budget is swollen by what is taken from the working class should be obliged to give primary education to the workers' children; for primary education is not complete education. It is better that working men and working women should not be able to read or write or do sums than that they should receive education from a teacher in a school run by

1. This article was written in January 1873, and published in the Lodi *Almanacco Repubblicano per l'anno 1874*. Its companion piece in the *Almanacco* was Engels's *On Authority* (see *MECW* 23, pp. 422–5).

the state. It is far better that ignorance and a working day of sixteen hours should debase the working classes than that eternal principles should be violated.

'If the political struggle of the working class assumes violent forms and if the workers replace the dictatorship of the bourgeois class with their own revolutionary dictatorship, then they are guilty of the terrible crime of *lèse-principe*; for, in order to satisfy their miserable profane daily needs and to crush the resistance of the bourgeois class, they, instead of laying down their arms and abolishing the state, give to the state a revolutionary and transitory form. Workers must not even form single unions for every trade, for by so doing they perpetuate the social division of labour as they find it in bourgeois society; this division, which fragments the working class, is the true basis of their present enslavement.

'In a word, the workers should cross their arms and stop wasting time in political and economic movements. These movements can never produce anything more than short-term results. As truly religious men they should scorn daily needs and cry out with voices full of faith: "May our class be crucified, may our race perish, but let the eternal principles remain immaculate!" As pious Christians they must believe the words of their pastor, despise the good things of this world and think only of going to Paradise. In place of Paradise read the *social liquidation* which is going to take place one day in some or other corner of the globe, no one knows how, or through whom, and the mystification is identical in all respects.

'In expectation, therefore, of this famous social liquidation, the working class must behave itself in a respectable manner, like a flock of well-fed sheep; it must leave the government in peace, fear the police, respect the law and offer itself up uncomplaining as cannon-fodder.

'In the practical life of every day, workers must be the most obedient servants of the state; but in their hearts they must protest energetically against its very existence, and give proof of their profound theoretical contempt for it by acquiring and reading literary treatises on its abolition; they must further scrupulously refrain from putting up any resistance to the capitalist regime apart from declamations on the society of the future, when this hated regime will have ceased to exist!'

It cannot be denied that if the apostles of political indifferentism were to express themselves with such clarity, the working class would make short shrift of them and would resent being insulted by these doctrinaire bourgeois and displaced gentlemen, who are so stupid or so naive as to attempt to deny to the working class any real means of struggle. For all arms with which to fight must be drawn from society as it is and the fatal conditions of this struggle have the misfortune of not being easily adapted to the idealistic fantasies which these doctors in *social science* have exalted as divinities, under the names of *Freedom, Autonomy, Anarchy*. However the working-class movement is today so powerful that these philanthropic sectarians dare not repeat for the economic struggle those *great truths* which they used incessantly to proclaim on the subject of the political struggle. They are simply too cowardly to apply them any longer to strikes, combinations, single-craft unions, laws on the labour of women and children, on the limitation of the working day etc., etc.

Now let us see whether they are still able to be brought back to the good old traditions, to modesty, good faith and eternal principles.

The first socialists (Fourier, Owen, Saint-Simon, etc.), since social conditions were not sufficiently developed to allow the working class to constitute itself as a militant class, were necessarily obliged to limit themselves to dreams about the *model society* of the future and were led thus to condemn all the attempts such as strikes, combinations or political movements set in train by the workers to improve their lot. But while we cannot repudiate these patriarchs of socialism, just as chemists cannot repudiate their forebears the alchemists, we must at least avoid falling back into their mistakes, which, if we were to commit them, would be inexcusable.

Later, however, in 1839, when the political and economic struggle of the working class in England had taken on a fairly marked character, Bray, one of Owen's disciples and one of the many who long before Proudhon hit upon the idea of *mutualism*, published a book entitled *Labour's Wrongs and Labour's Remedy*.

In his chapter on the inefficacy of *all the remedies aimed for by the present struggle*, he makes a savage critique of all the activities, political or economic, of the English working class, condemns the political movement, strikes, the limitation of the working day, the restriction of the work of women and children in factories, since all this – or so he claims – instead of taking us out of the present state of society, keeps us there and does nothing but render the antagonisms more intense.

This brings us to the oracle of these doctors of social science, M. Proudhon. While the master had the courage to declare himself energetically opposed to all economic activities (combinations, strikes, etc.) which contradicted his redemptive theories of *mutualism*, at the same time through his writings and personal participation, he encouraged the working-class movement, and his disciples do not dare to declare themselves openly against it. As early as 1847, when the master's great work, *The System of Economic Contradictions*, had just appeared, I refuted his sophisms against the working-class movement.[2] None the less in 1864, after the *loi Ollivier*, which granted the French workers, in a very restrictive fashion, a certain right of combination, Proudhon returned to the charge in a book, *The Political Capacities of the Working Classes*, published a few days after his death.

The master's strictures were so much to the taste of the bourgeoisie that *The Times*, on the occasion of the great tailors' strike in London in 1866, did Proudhon the honour of translating him and of condemning the strikers with the master's very words. Here are some selections.

The miners of Rive-de-Gier went on strike; the soldiers were called in to bring them back to reason. Proudhon cries, 'The authority which had the miners of Rive-de-Gier shot acted disgracefully. But it was acting like Brutus of old caught between his paternal love and his consular duty: it was necessary to sacrifice his sons to save the Republic. Brutus did not hesitate, and posterity dare not condemn him.'[3] In all the memory of the proletariat there is no record of a bourgeois who has hesitated to sacrifice his workers to save his interests. What Brutuses the bourgeois must then be!

'Well, no: there is no right of combination, just as there is no right to defraud or steal or to commit incest or adultery.'[4] There is however all too clearly a right to stupidity.

2. P. J. Proudhon, *Système des contradictions economiques, ou philosophie de la misère* (1846). This was the work that Marx replied to with his book *The Poverty of Philosophy* (1847).

3. *De la Capacité politique des class ouvrières*, Paris, 1865, p. 413. To give Proudhon his due, he was not so much justifying the actions of the French authorities as exposing the 'contradictions' he saw as an inevitable evil of the present social order.

4. Ibid., p. 421.

What then are the eternal principles, in whose name the master fulminates his mystic anathema?

First eternal principle: 'Wage rates determine the price of commodities.'

Even those who have no knowledge of political economy and who are unaware that the great bourgeois economist Ricardo in his *Principles of Political Economy*, published in 1817, has refuted this long-standing error once and for all, are however aware of the remarkable fact that British industry can sell its products at a price far lower than that of any other nation, although wages are relatively higher in England than in any other European country.

Second eternal principle: 'The law which authorizes combinations is highly anti-juridical, anti-economic and contrary to any society and order.'[5] In a word 'contrary to the economic *right* of free competition'.

If the master had been a little less chauvinistic, he might have asked himself how it happened that forty years ago a law, thus contrary to the *economic rights of free competition*, was promulgated in England; and that as industry develops, and alongside it *free competition*, this law – so contrary to *any society and order* – imposes itself as a necessity even to bourgeois states themselves. He might perhaps have discovered that this right (with capital R) exists only in the *Economic Manuals* written by the Brothers Ignoramus of bourgeois political economy, in which manuals are contained such pearls as this: 'Property is the fruit of labour' ('of the labour', they neglect to add, 'of others').

Third eternal principle: 'Therefore, under the pretext of raising the working class from its condition of so-called social inferiority, it will be necessary to start by denouncing a whole class of citizens, the class of bosses, entrepreneurs, masters and bourgeois; it will be necessary to rouse workers' democracy to despise and to hate these unworthy members of the middle class; it will be necessary to prefer mercantile and industrial war to legal repression, and class antagonism to the state police.'[6]

The master, in order to prevent the working class from escaping from its so-called *social inferiority*, condemns the combinations that constitute the working class as a class antagonistic to the respectable *category of masters, entrepreneurs and bourgeois*, who for their part certainly prefer, as does Proudhon, *the state police to class antagonism*. To avoid any offence to this respectable class,

5. Ibid., p. 424.   6. Ibid., p. 426.

the good M. Proudhon recommends to the workers (up to the coming of the *mutualist regime*, and despite its serious disadvantages) freedom or competition, our 'only guarantee'.[7]

The master preached indifference in matters of economics – *so as to protect bourgeois freedom or competition*, our only guarantee. His disciples preach indifference in matters of politics – so as to protect bourgeois freedom, their only guarantee. If the early Christians, who also preached political indifferentism, needed an emperor's arm to transform themselves from oppressed into oppressors, so the modern apostles of political indifferentism do not believe that their own eternal principles impose on them abstinence from worldly pleasures and the temporal privileges of bourgeois society. However we must recognize that they display a stoicism worthy of the early Christian martyrs in supporting those fourteen or sixteen working hours such as overburden the workers in the factories.

7. Ibid., p. 422.

Conspectus of Bakunin's *Statism and Anarchy*[1]
[*Extract*]

We have already stated our deep opposition to the theory of Lassalle and Marx, which recommends to the workers, if not as final ideal then at least as the next major aim – *the foundation of a people's state*, which, as they have expressed it, will be none other than the proletariat *organized as ruling class*. The question arises, if the proletariat becomes the ruling class, over whom will it rule? It means that there will still remain another proletariat, which will be subject to this new domination, this new state.

It means that so long as the other classes, especially the capitalist class, still exists, so long as the proletariat struggles with it (for when it attains government power its enemies and the old organization of society have not yet vanished), it must employ *forcible* means, hence governmental means. It is itself still a class and the economic conditions from which the class struggle and the existence of classes derive have still not disappeared and must forcibly be either removed out of the way or transformed, this transformation process being forcibly hastened.

E.g. the *krestyanskaya chern*, the common peasant folk, the peasant mob, which as is well known does not enjoy the goodwill of the Marxists, and which, being as it is at the lowest level of culture, will apparently be governed by the urban factory proletariat.

I.e. where the peasant exists in the mass as private proprietor, where he even forms a more or less considerable majority, as in all states of the west European continent, where he has not disappeared and been replaced by the agricultural wage-labourer, as

1. During the latter part of 1874 Marx copied into a notebook, in the Russian, extensive extracts from Bakunin's recent book *Statism and Anarchy*, interspersing them, in the section reproduced below, with his own comments. This extract of Marx's 'Conspectus' is translated from the German text printed in *MEW* 18, pp. 630–36. English extracts of Bakunin's book are printed in G. P. Maximoff (ed.), *The Political Philosophy of Bakunin*.

in England, the following cases apply: either he hinders each workers' revolution, makes a wreck of it, as he has formerly done in France, or the proletariat (for the peasant proprietor does not belong to the proletariat, and even where his condition is proletarian, he believes himself not to) must as government take measures through which the peasant finds his condition immediately improved, so as to win him for the revolution; measures which will at least provide the possibility of easing the transition from private ownership of land to collective ownership, so that the peasant arrives at this of his own accord, from economic reasons. It must not hit the peasant over the head, as it would e.g. by proclaiming the abolition of the right of inheritance or the abolition of his property. The latter is only possible where the capitalist tenant farmer has forced out the peasants, and where the true cultivator is just as good a proletarian, a wage-labourer, as is the town worker, and so has *immediately*, not just indirectly, the very same interests as him. Still less should small-holding property be strengthened, by the enlargement of the peasant allotment simply through peasant annexation of the larger estates, as in Bakunin's revolutionary campaign.

Or, if one considers this question from the national angle, we would for the same reason assume that, as far as the Germans are concerned, the Slavs will stand in the same slavish dependence towards the victorious German proletariat as the latter does at present towards its own bourgeoisie.

Schoolboy stupidity! A radical social revolution depends on certain definite historical conditions of economic development as its precondition. It is also only possible where with capitalist production the industrial proletariat occupies at least an important position among the mass of the people. And if it is to have any chance of victory, it must be able to do immediately as much for the peasants as the French bourgeoisie, *mutatis mutandis*, did in its revolution for the French peasants of that time. A fine idea, that the rule of labour involves the subjugation of land labour! But here Mr Bakunin's innermost thoughts emerge. He understands absolutely nothing about the social revolution, only its political phrases. Its economic conditions do not exist for him. As all hitherto existing economic forms, developed or undeveloped, involve the enslavement of the worker (whether in the form of wage-labourer, peasant, etc.), he believes that a *radical revolution* is possible in all such forms alike. Still more! He wants the European social revolution, premised on the economic basis of capitalist production, to take place at the level of the Russian or Slavic agricultural and pastoral peoples, not to surpass this level [. . .] The *will*, and not the economic conditions, is the foundation of his social revolution.

If there is a state [*gosudarstvo*], then there is unavoidably domination [*gospodstvo*], and consequently slavery. Domination without slavery, open or veiled, is unthinkable – this is why we are enemies of the state.

What does it mean, the proletariat organized as ruling class?

It means that the proletariat, instead of struggling sectionally against the economically privileged class, has attained a sufficient strength and organization to employ general means of coercion in this struggle. It can however only use such economic means as abolish its own character as salariat,[2] hence as class. With its complete victory its own rule thus also ends, as its class character has disappeared.

Will the entire proletariat perhaps stand at the head of the government?

In a trade union,[3] for example, does the whole union form its executive committee? Will all division of labour in the factory, and the various functions that correspond to this, cease? And in Bakunin's constitution, will all 'from bottom to top' be 'at the top'? Then there will certainly be no one 'at the bottom'. Will all members of the commune simultaneously manage the interests of its territory? Then there will be no distinction between commune and territory.

The Germans number around forty million. Will for example all forty million be members of the government?

Certainly![4] Since the whole thing begins with the self-government of the commune.

The whole people will govern, and there will be no governed.

If a man rules himself, he does not do so on this principle, for he is after all himself and no other.

2. In English in the original.   3. In English in the original.
4. In English in the original.

Then there will be no government and no state, but if there is a state, there will be both governors and slaves.

I.e. only if class rule has disappeared, and there is no state in the present political sense.

This dilemma is simply solved in the Marxists' theory. By people's government they understand (i.e. Bakunin) the government of the people by means of a small number of leaders, chosen (elected) by the people.

Asine![5] This is democratic twaddle, political drivel. Election is a political form present in the smallest Russian commune and artel. The character of the election does not depend on this name, but on the economic foundation, the economic situation of the voters, and as soon as the functions have ceased to be political ones, there exists 1) no government function, 2) the distribution of the general functions has become a business matter, that gives no one domination, 3) election has nothing of its present political character.

The universal suffrage of the whole people . . .

Such a thing as the whole people in today's sense is a chimera –

. . . in the election of people's representatives and rulers of the state – that is the last word of the Marxists, as also of the democratic school – [is] a lie, behind which is concealed the despotism of the *governing minority*, and only the more dangerously in so far as it appears as expression of the so-called people's will.

With collective ownership the so-called people's will vanishes, to make way for the real will of the cooperative.

So the result is: guidance of the great majority of the people by a privileged minority. But this minority, say the Marxists . . .

Where?

. . . will consist of workers. Certainly, with your permission, of former workers, who however, as soon as they have become representatives or governors of the people, *cease to be workers* . . .

As little as a factory owner today ceases to be a capitalist if he becomes a municipal councillor . . .

and look down on the whole common workers' world from the height

5. Asinine.

of the state. They will no longer represent the people, but themselves and their pretensions to people's government. Anyone who can doubt this knows nothing of the nature of men.

If Mr Bakunin only knew something about the position of a manager in a workers' cooperative factory, all his dreams of domination would go to the devil. He should have asked himself what form the administrative function can take on the basis of this workers' state, if he wants to call it that.

But those elected will be fervently convinced and therefore educated socialists. The phrase '*educated socialism*' . . .

. . . never was used.

. . . '*scientific socialism*' . . .

. . . was only used in opposition to utopian socialism, which wants to attach the people to new delusions, instead of limiting its science to the knowledge of the social movement made by the people itself; see my text against Proudhon.

. . . which is unceasingly found in the works and speeches of the Lasalleans and Marxists, itself indicates that the so-called people's state will be nothing else than the very despotic guidance of the mass of the people by a new and numerically very small aristocracy of the genuine or supposedly educated. The people are not scientific, which means that they will be entirely freed from the cares of government, they will be entirely shut up in the stable of the governed. A fine liberation!

The Marxists sense this (!) contradiction and, knowing that the government of the educated (*quelle rêverie*)[6] will be the most oppressive, most detestable, most despised in the world, a real dictatorship despite all democratic forms, console themselves with the thought that this dictatorship will only be transitional and short.

Non, mon cher![7] – That the *class rule* of the workers over the strata of the old world whom they have been fighting can only exist as long as the economic basis of class existence is not destroyed.

They say that their only concern and aim is *to educate and uplift* the *people* (saloon-bar politicians!) both economically and politically, to such a level that all government will be quite useless and the state will lose all political character, i.e. character of domination, and will change by itself into a free organization of economic interests and

6. What a daydream.   7. No, my dear.

communes. An obvious contradiction. If their state will really be popular, why not destroy it, and if its destruction is necessary for the real liberation of the people, why do they venture to call it popular?

Aside from the harping of Liebknecht's *Volksstaat*,[8] which is nonsense, counter to the Communist Manifesto etc., it only means that, as the proletariat still acts, during the period of struggle for the overthrow of the old society, on the basis of that old society, and hence also still moves within political forms which more or less belong to it, it has not yet, during this period of struggle, attained its final constitution, and employs means for its liberation which after this liberation fall aside. Mr Bakunin concludes from this that it is better to do nothing at all . . . just wait for the *day of general liquidation* – the last judgement.

8. On the *Volksstaat*, see p. 164, n. 20. Marx and Engels privately criticized Liebknecht for his failure to break decisively with the petty-bourgeois democrats.

Critique of the Gotha Programme[1]

Marx to Bracke[2]

London, 5 May 1875

Dear Bracke,

Please be so kind as to give the following critical marginal notes on the unity programme[3] to Geib, Auer,[4] Bebel and Liebknecht for their perusal after you have read them yourself. I have too much on my plate and have already been forced to overshoot the work limit prescribed by my doctor. It was therefore not a 'pleasure' by any means to write this long screed. It was necessary, however, so that friends in the party, for whom it is meant, will not misunderstand the steps I shall later have to take.

Namely, after the unity congress Engels and I are going to publish a short statement dissociating ourselves from the said programme of principles and stating that we have had nothing to do with it.

This is essential, because people abroad hold the completely erroneous view – carefully nurtured by enemies of the party – that we are secretly steering the movement of the so-called Eisenach party from here. In a very recent Russian publication,[5]

1. Marx wrote his marginal notes on the draft of the Gotha programme at the beginning of May 1875. When the 'Critique of the Gotha Programme' was first published, in 1891, Engels omitted certain passages as a concession to the German Social-Democratic Party. The Critique is translated here from Marx's manuscript, as printed in *MEW* 19.

2. Wilhelm Bracke had led the faction of the Lassallean ADAV which broke away in 1869, and joined with Liebknecht's group to form the SDAP ('Eisenach party').

3. The draft unity programme for the Gotha Congress, at which the SDAP and the ADAV were united to form the German Social-Democratic Workers' Party (SAPD, later SPD), was written by Wilhelm Liebknecht for the SDAP and Wilhelm Hasselmann for the ADAV, and published in both groups' papers on 7 March 1875. The Gotha Congress was held in late May.

4. August Geib and Ignaz Auer were prominent SDAP figures.

5. Bakunin's book *Statism and Anarchy*; see Marx's 'Conspectus', above, pp. 333–8.

Bakunin still makes me responsible, for example, not only for all the programmes, etc. of that party, but even for every step that Liebknecht has taken since the first day of his cooperation with the People's Party.[6]

Apart from that, it is my duty not to approve, even by diplomatic silence, a programme which in my opinion is thoroughly reprehensible and demoralizing for the party.

Every step of a real movement is more important than a dozen programmes. If it was not possible, therefore, to go *further* than the Eisenach programme – and, in the present conditions, it is not – then they should simply have concluded an agreement for action against the common enemy. Drawing up a programme of principle, however (instead of postponing this until such time as it has been prepared for by a considerable period of common activity), means erecting a milestone for all the world to see, by which the progress of the party will be measured.

Conditions forced the Lassallean leaders to come. If they had been told from the start that no haggling over principles would be tolerated, then they would have *had to be* satisfied with a programme of action or with an organizational plan for common action. Instead, they are being allowed to appear wielding mandates, and these mandates are being recognized as binding. This constitutes a surrender to the favour or disfavour of the people who are themselves most in need of help. To crown the matter, they turn around and hold a congress *before* the *compromise congress*, while our own party holds its congress *post festum*. Obviously the idea was to make all criticism ineffective, and to prevent our party from having second thoughts. It is clear that the mere fact of unification will satisfy the workers, but it is a mistake to believe that this momentary success has not been bought dearly.

Furthermore, the programme is no good, even when one disregards the hallowing of Lassalle's articles of faith.

In the near future, I shall be sending you the final instalment of the French edition of *Capital*. The rest of the printing was held up for a long while by the French government's ban. It should all be settled by this week or the beginning of next. Did you get the earlier six instalments? Please also send me Bernhard Becker's address, for I have to send him the final instalment as well.

6. See above, p. 22.

The *Volksstaat* bookshop has its own peculiar manners. Up to this moment, for example, they have not sent me a single copy of their edition of the *Cologne Communist Trial*.

With best wishes,
Yours,
KARL MARX

Marginal Notes on the Programme of the German Workers' Party

I

1. Labour is the source of all wealth and culture, *and since* useful labour can only be performed in and through society, all members of society have an equal right to the undiminished proceeds of labour.

First part of the paragraph: 'Labour is the source of all wealth and culture'.

Labour is *not the source* of all wealth. Nature is just as much the source of use-values (and surely these are what make up material wealth!) as labour. Labour is itself only the manifestation of a force of nature, human labour power. This phrase can be found in any children's primer; it is correct in so far as it is *assumed* that labour is performed with the objects and instruments necessary to it. A socialist programme, however, cannot allow such bourgeois formulations to silence the *conditions* which give them the only meaning they possess. Man's labour only becomes a source of use-values, and hence also of wealth, if his relation to nature, the primary source of all instruments and objects of labour, is one of ownership from the start, and if he treats it as belonging to him. There is every good reason for the bourgeoisie to ascribe *supernatural creative power* to labour, for when a man has no property other than his labour power it is precisely labour's dependence on nature that forces him, in all social and cultural conditions, to be the slave of other men who have taken the objective conditions of labour into their own possession. He needs their permission to work, and hence their permission to live.

Let us now leave this sentence as it stands, or rather hobbles. What sort of conclusion would one have expected? Obviously the following: 'Since labour is the source of all wealth, it follows that no one in society can appropriate wealth except as the product of labour. Thus, if a person does not work himself, he must live off the labour of others, and his culture, too, must be acquired at the cost of other people's labour.'

Instead of this the words *'and since'* are used to tack on a second proposition so that a conclusion can be drawn from this one rather than the first.

Second part of the paragraph: 'Useful labour can only be performed in and through society'.

According to the first proposition, labour was the source of all wealth and culture, so that a society could not exist without labour. Now we are told the opposite: 'useful' labour cannot exist without society.

One could just as well have said that it is only in society that useless labour, or even labour harmful to the community, can become a line of business, and that only in society is it possible to live from idleness, etc., etc. – in short, one could have copied down the whole of Rousseau.

And what is 'useful' labour? Surely simply labour which brings the desired useful result. A savage – and man was a savage after he ceased to be an ape – who kills an animal with a stone, gathers fruit, etc., is performing 'useful' labour.

Thirdly: the conclusion: 'And since useful labour can only be performed in and through society, all members of society have an equal right to the undiminished proceeds of labour.'

A beautiful conclusion! If useful labour can only be performed in and through society then the proceeds of labour belong to society – even if the individual worker only receives as much of them as is not required for the maintenance of the 'condition' of labour, society.

In fact, this sentence is not new: it has been used in all periods by the *champions of the existing state of society*. First come the claims of the government and all that goes with it, since it is the social organ for the maintenance of social order; then come the claims of the various kinds of private property, since the various kinds of private property form the foundations of society, etc. Hollow phrases such as these can clearly be twisted and turned at will.

The first and second parts of the paragraph would have some intelligible connection only if worded as follows: 'Labour becomes the source of all wealth and culture only when it is social labour,' or, which comes to the same thing, only 'in and through society'.

This proposition is indisputably correct, for although isolated labour (given its material conditions) can also create use-values, it cannot create either wealth or culture.

But this other proposition is equally indisputable: 'The social development of labour, and thus its development as a source of wealth and culture, proceeds in equal proportion to the development of poverty and destitution among the workers and of wealth and culture among the non-workers.'

Up to the present day all history has been governed by this law. What was needed here, therefore, was not generalizations about 'labour' and 'society' but concrete proof that in present capitalist society the material etc. conditions have finally been created which enable and compel the worker to break this historical curse.

In fact, however, the sole purpose of this paragraph, a mess both in style and content, is to inscribe the Lassallean catchword of 'the undiminished proceeds of labour' as a slogan at the top of the party banner. I shall return to the 'proceeds of labour', 'equal right', etc. below, where the same things reappear in a somewhat different form.

2. In present society the capitalist class has a monopoly of the instruments of labour; the resultant dependence of the working class is the cause of misery and servitude in all its forms.

This sentence has been lifted from the Rules of the International but is incorrect in this 'improved' version.

In present society the instruments of labour are the monopoly of the landowners (the monopoly of landed property is even the basis of the monopoly of capital) *and* of the capitalists. Neither class of monopolists is mentioned by name in the relevant passage of the Rules of the International. This text speaks of the *'monopolizer of the means of labour, that is, the sources of life'*; the addition of the 'sources of life' is adequate indication that land and soil are included under the instruments of labour.

The amendment was made because Lassalle, for reasons now generally known, *only* attacked the capitalist class and not the landowners. In England, the capitalist generally does not even own the land and soil on which his factory stands.

3. For the emancipation of labour the instruments of labour must be elevated to the common property of society and the whole of labour must be regulated on a cooperative basis, with a just distribution of the proceeds of labour.

'The instruments of labour must be elevated to common property'!
This is probably meant to mean 'converted into common property'.
But this just incidentally.

What are the 'proceeds of labour'? Are they the product of labour
or its value? And in the latter case, is it the total value of the product
or only that part of its value which labour has created over and above
the value of the means of production consumed?

'Proceeds of labour' is a loose notion, used by Lassalle in place of
definite economic concepts.

What is 'just' distribution?

Does not the bourgeoisie claim that the present system of distribution is 'just'? And given the present mode of production is it not,
in fact, the only 'just' system of distribution? Are economic relations regulated by legal concepts of right or is the opposite not the
case, that legal relations spring from economic ones? Do not the
socialist sectarians themselves have the most varied notions of 'just'
distribution?

To discover what we are meant to understand by the phrase 'just
distribution' as used here we must take the opening paragraph and
this one together. The latter presupposes a society in which 'the
instruments of labour are common property and the whole of labour
is regulated on a cooperative basis' and from the opening paragraph
we learn that 'all members of society have an equal right to the undiminished proceeds of labour'.

'All members of society'? Including people who do not work?
Then what remains of the 'undiminished proceeds of labour'? Only
the working members of society? Then what remains of the 'equal
right' of all members of society?

'All members of society' and 'equal right', however, are obviously
mere phrases. The heart of the matter is that in this communist society
every worker is supposed to receive the 'undiminished' Lassallean
'proceeds of labour'.

If we start by taking 'proceeds of labour' to mean the product of
labour, then the cooperative proceeds of labour are the *total social
product*.

From this the following must now be deducted:

Firstly: cover to replace the means of production used up.

Secondly: an additional portion for the expansion of production.

Thirdly: a reserve or insurance fund in case of accidents, disrup-
tion caused by natural calamities, etc.

These deductions from the 'undiminished proceeds of labour' are an economic necessity and their magnitude will be determined by the means and forces available. They can partly be calculated by reference to probability, but on no account by reference to justice.

There remains the other part of the total product, designed to serve as means of consumption.

But before this is distributed to individuals the following further deductions must be made:

Firstly: the general costs of all administration not directly appertaining to production.

This part will, from the outset, be very significantly limited in comparison with the present society. It will diminish commensurately with the development of the new society.

Secondly: the amount set aside for needs communally satisfied, such as schools, health services, etc.

This part will, from the outset, be significantly greater than in the present society. It will grow commensurately with the development of the new society.

Thirdly: a fund for people unable to work, etc., in short, for what today comes under so-called official poor relief.

Only now do we come to that 'distribution' which, under the influence of the Lassalleans, is the only thing considered by this narrow-minded programme, namely that part of the means of consumption which is distributed among the individual producers within the cooperative.

The 'undiminished proceeds of labour' have meanwhile already been quietly 'diminished', although as a member of society the producer still receives, directly or indirectly, what is withheld from him as a private individual.

Just as the phrase 'undiminished proceeds of labour' has vanished, the phrase 'proceeds of labour' now disappears altogether.

Within the cooperative society based on common ownership of the means of production the producers do not exchange their products; similarly, the labour spent on the products no longer appears *as the value* of these products, possessed by them as a material characteristic, for now, in contrast to capitalist society, individual pieces of labour are no longer merely indirectly, but directly, a component part of the total labour. The phrase 'proceeds of labour', which even today is too ambiguous to be of any value, thus loses any meaning whatsoever.

We are dealing here with a communist society, not as it has *developed* on its own foundations, but on the contrary, just as it *emerges* from capitalist society. In every respect, economically, morally, intellectually, it is thus still stamped with the birth-marks of the old society from whose womb it has emerged. Accordingly, the individual producer gets back from society – after the deductions – exactly what he has given it. What he has given it is his individual quantum of labour. For instance, the social working day consists of the sum of the individual hours of work. The individual labour time of the individual producer thus constitutes his contribution to the social working day, his share of it. Society gives him a certificate stating that he has done such and such an amount of work (after the labour done for the communal fund has been deducted), and with this certificate he can withdraw from the social supply of means of consumption as much as costs an equivalent amount of labour. The same amount of labour he has given to society in one form, he receives back in another.

Clearly, the same principle is at work here as that which regulates the exchange of commodities as far as this is an exchange of equal values. Content and form have changed because under the new conditions no one can contribute anything except his labour and conversely nothing can pass into the ownership of individuals except individual means of consumption. The latter's distribution among individual producers, however, is governed by the same principle as the exchange of commodity equivalents: a given amount of labour in one form is exchanged for the same amount in another.

Hence *equal right* is here still – in principle – a *bourgeois right*, although principle and practice are no longer at loggerheads, while the exchange of equivalents in commodity exchange only exists *on the average* and not in the individual case.

In spite of such progress this *equal right* still constantly suffers a bourgeois limitation. The right of the producers is *proportional* to the labour they do; the equality consists in the fact that measurement is *by the same standard*, labour. One person, however, may be physically and intellectually superior to another and thus be able to do more labour in the same space of time or work for a longer period. To serve as a measure labour must therefore be determined by duration or intensity, otherwise it ceases to be a standard. This *equal* right is an unequal right for unequal labour. It does not acknowledge any class distinctions, because everyone is just a worker like everyone else, but it gives tacit recognition to a worker's individual endowment and hence productive capacity as natural privileges. *This right is thus in its content one of inequality, just like any other right.* A right can by its nature only consist in the application of an equal standard, but unequal individuals (and they would not be different individuals if they were not unequal) can only be measured by the same standard if they are looked at from the same aspect, if they are grasped from one *particular* side, e.g., if in the present case they are regarded *only as workers* and nothing else is seen in them, everything else is ignored. Further: one worker is married, another is not; one has more children than another, etc., etc. Thus, with the same work performance and hence the same share of the social consumption fund, one will in fact be receiving more than another, one will be richer than another, etc. If all these defects were to be avoided rights would have to be unequal rather than equal.

Such defects, however, are inevitable in the first phase of communist society, given the specific form in which it has emerged after prolonged birth-pangs from capitalist society. Right can never rise above the economic structure of a society and its contingent cultural development.

In a more advanced phase of communist society, when the enslaving subjugation of individuals to the division of labour, and thereby the antithesis between intellectual and physical labour, have disappeared; when labour is no longer just a means of keeping alive but has itself become a vital need; when the all-round development of individuals has also increased their productive powers and all the springs of cooperative wealth flow more abundantly – only then can society wholly cross the narrow horizon of bourgeois right and inscribe on its banner: From each according to his abilities, to each according to his needs!

If I have dealt at some length with the 'undiminished proceeds of labour' on the one hand, and 'equal right' and 'just distribution' on the other, it is in order to show the criminal nature of what is being attempted: on the one hand, our party is to be forced to re-accept as dogmas ideas which may have made some sense at a particular time but which are now only a load of obsolete verbal rubbish; on the other hand, the realistic outlook instilled in our party at the cost of immense effort, but now firmly rooted in it, is to be perverted by means of ideological, legal and other humbug so common among the democrats and the French socialists.

Quite apart from the points made so far, it was a mistake anyway to lay the main stress on so-called *distribution* and to make it into the central point.

The distribution of the means of consumption at any given time is merely a consequence of the distribution of the conditions of production themselves; the distribution of the latter, however, is a feature of the mode of production itself. The capitalist mode of production, for example, rests on the fact that the material conditions of production are in the hands of non-workers in the form of property in capital and land, while the masses are only in possession of their personal condition of production, labour power. If the elements of production are distributed in this way, the present distribution of the means of consumption follows automatically. If the material conditions of production were the cooperative property of the workers themselves a different distribution of the means of consumption from that of today would follow of its own accord. Vulgar socialists (and from them, in turn, a section of the democrats) have followed the bourgeois economists in their consideration and treatment of distribution as something independent of the mode of production and hence in the presentation of socialism as primarily revolving around the question of distribution. Why go back a step when the real state of affairs has been laid bare?

4. The emancipation of labour must be the work of the working class, in relation to which all other classes are *a single reactionary mass*.

The first strophe is an 'improved' version of the preamble to the Rules of the International. There it is said: 'The emancipation of the working classes must be conquered by the working classes themselves';[7] here, in contrast, 'the working class' has to emancipate – what? – labour. Understand who may.

In compensation, however, the antistrophe is a Lassallean quote of the purest ilk: 'in relation to which (the working class) all other classes are *a single reactionary mass*'.

In the Communist Manifesto it is said, 'Of all the classes that stand face to face with the bourgeoisie today, the proletariat alone is a *really revolutionary class*. The other classes decay and

7. Above, p. 82.

finally disappear in the face of modern industry; the proletariat is its special and essential product.'[8]

The bourgeoisie is here conceived of as a revolutionary class – as the bringer of large-scale industry – in relation to the feudal lords and the lower middle class, who want to retain all the social positions created by obsolete modes of production. These do not, therefore, form a single reactionary mass *together with the bourgeoisie*.

On the other hand the proletariat is revolutionary in relation to the bourgeoisie because it has itself sprung up on the ground of large-scale industry; it is struggling to divest production of its capitalist character, which the bourgeoisie seeks to perpetuate. The Manifesto adds, however, that the lower middle class is becoming revolutionary 'in view of (its) impending transfer into the proletariat'.

From this point of view, therefore, it is once again nonsense to say that in relation to the working class it 'forms a single reactionary mass', 'together with the bourgeoisie' and with the feudal lords to boot.

At the last elections, did we proclaim to the artisans, small manufacturers, etc. and *peasants*: In relation to us you, together with the bourgeoisie and the feudal lords, form a single reactionary mass?

Lassalle knew the Communist Manifesto by heart, just as his faithful followers know his own gospels. The reason for such gross falsification can thus only be that he wanted to extenuate his alliance with the absolutist and feudal opponents of the bourgeoisie.

In the above paragraph, moreover, this oracular utterance is dragged in by the scruff of its neck, without any connection to the bowdlerized quote from the Rules of the International. It is therefore simply an impertinence to include it here and one that will by no means displease Herr Bismarck – a cheap swipe typical of Berlin's would-be Marat.[9]

5. The working class must initially work for its emancipation *within the framework of the present-day national state*, conscious that the necessary result of its efforts, common to the workers of all civilized countries, will be the international brotherhood of peoples.

8. *The Revolutions of 1848*, p. 77. Marx's emphasis in the present text.

9. Presumably Wilhelm Hasselmann, editor of the Lassallean *Neuer Social-Demokrat*.

In contrast to the Communist Manifesto and all earlier forms of socialism, Lassalle approached the workers' movement from the narrowest national point of view. His approach is followed here – and this after the work of the International!

It is perfectly self-evident that in order to be at all capable of struggle the working class must organize itself *as a class* at home and that the domestic sphere must be the immediate arena for its struggle. To this extent its class struggle is national, not in content, but as the Communist Manifesto says, 'in form'. But the 'framework of the present-day national state', e.g., the German Reich, is itself in turn economically 'within the framework of the world market' and politically 'within the framework of the system of states'. Any businessman will tell you that German trade is at the same time foreign trade, and the greatness of Herr Bismarck lies exactly in the *international* orientation of his policy.

And to what is the internationalism of the German workers' party reduced? To the consciousness that the result of their efforts 'will be *the international brotherhood of peoples*' – a phrase borrowed from the bourgeois League of Peace and Freedom[10] and which is intended to pass as an equivalent for the international brotherhood of the working classes in the joint struggle against the ruling classes and their governments. Not a word, therefore, of the *international role* of the German working class! And this is how it is meant to challenge its own bourgeoisie, which is already fraternally linked with the bourgeoisie in all other countries, and Herr Bismarck's international policy of conspiracy!

In fact, the programme's commitment to internationalism is *infinitely smaller* even than that of the free trade party. The latter also claims that the result of its efforts will be the 'international brotherhood of peoples'. It is also *doing* something, however, to internationalize trade and is certainly not content with the mere consciousness that all peoples are carrying on trade at home.

The international activity of the working classes is not in any way dependent on the existence of the International Working Men's Association. This was only the first attempt to create a central organ for such activity; an attempt which will be of lasting success because of the impetus it gave but which could not be continued in its *initial historical form* following the fall of the Paris Commune.

Bismarck's *Norddeutsche* was perfectly right when it declared,

10. See above, pp. 44–5.

to the satisfaction of its master, that the German workers' party had renounced internationalism in its new programme.[11]

II

Starting from these basic principles, the German workers' party will strive, by all legal means, for a *free state and* a socialist society; the abolition of the wage system *together with* the *iron law of wages*, and of exploitation in every form; the removal of all social and political inequality.

I will come back to the 'free' state below.

So, in future, the German workers' party will have to believe in Lassalle's 'iron law of wages'! To prevent it from being lost, the programme goes through the nonsense of speaking of the 'abolition of the wage system' (which should read 'the system of wage labour') *'together with* the iron law of wages'. If I abolish wage labour I naturally abolish all its laws as well, whether they are made of iron or sponge. Lassalle's attack on wage labour, however, revolves almost exclusively around this so-called law. As proof, therefore, that the Lassallean sect has come out on top, the 'wage system' must be abolished *'together with* the iron law of wages', and never without it.

It is common knowledge that Lassalle contributed nothing to the 'iron law of wages' except the word 'iron', which he pilfered from Goethe's 'great, eternal, iron laws'. The word 'iron' is a label by which the true believers can recognize each other. But if I take the law with Lassalle's stamp on it and thus in the way he meant it, then I must also take it with his supporting arguments. And what do I get? As Lange showed only a short time after Lassalle's death, the Malthusian theory of population (preached by Lange himself).[12] But if this theory is right, then I *cannot* abolish the law, even by abolishing wage labour a hundred times over, for this law then governs not only the system of wage labour but *all* social systems. This, precisely, has been the basis of economists' proofs, for fifty years or more, that socialism cannot abolish poverty, which has its basis in nature, but can only

11. The *Norddeutsche Allgemeine Zeitung*, in its leader of 20 March.

12. F. A. Lange was a neo-Kantian philosopher. Marx refers to his book *The Workers Question in its Significance for Present and Future*, Duisburg, 1865. Engels criticized Lange's book in a letter to him of 29 March 1865; *MECW* 42, pp. 135–9.

generalize it, distributing it simultaneously over the whole surface of society.

But all that is beside the main point. *Quite apart* from the *false* Lassallean formulation of the law, the really outrageous step back consists in the following:

Since Lassalle's death the scientific insight has made headway in our party that wages are not what they *appear* to be, namely the value or price of labour, but only a disguised form of the *value or price of labour power*.[13] Thereby the whole of the former bourgeois conception of wages was thrown overboard once and for all, as well as all criticisms of it, and it became clear that the wage labourer is only allowed to work for his own livelihood, i.e., *to live*, if he works a certain amount of time without pay for the capitalist (and thus also for the latter's fellow consumers of surplus value); that the whole capitalist system of production turns on the prolongation of this free labour through the extension of the working day and through the development of productivity, the increasing intensification of labour power, etc.; and that the system of wage labour is consequently a system of slavery, increasing in severity commensurately with the development of the social productive forces of labour, irrespective of whether the worker is then better or worse paid. And now, after this insight has gained more and more ground in our party, there comes this return to the dogmas of Lassalle, even though people must be aware that Lassalle *knew nothing* of the true nature of wages and that he followed the bourgeois economists in mistaking the appearance of the matter for its essence.

It is as if, among slaves who have finally got behind the secret of slavery and broken out in rebellion, one slave, still the prisoner of obsolete ideas, were to write in the programme of the rebellion: Slavery must be abolished because the provisioning of slaves in the slave system cannot exceed a certain low maximum!

The mere fact that the representatives of our party were capable of making such a monstrous attack on an insight which has gained wide acceptance among the mass of the party is surely sufficient proof of the criminal levity and complete lack of conscience with which they set to work on the formulation of the compromise programme.

Instead of the unspecific closing phrase of the paragraph, 'the

13. Marx is referring to his own scientific results, as presented in Volume 1 of *Capital*, first published in 1867.

removal of all social and political inequality', it should have been said that with the abolition of class distinctions all forms of social and political inequality will disappear of their own accord.

III

The German workers' party, *in order to pave the way for the solution of the social questsion*, demands the creation of producers' cooperatives *with state aid under the democratic control of the working people*. These producers' cooperatives are *to be called into being* for industry and agriculture to such an extent *that the socialist organization of the whole of labour will arise out of them*.

After Lassalle's 'iron law of wages', the prophet's remedy! The way is 'paved' for it in a suitably dignified manner! The existing class struggle is discarded in favour of the hack phrase of a newspaper scribbler – *'the social question'*, for the solution of which one 'paves the way'. Instead of being the result of the revolutionary process of social transformation in society, the 'socialist organization of the whole of labour' 'arises' from 'state aid' to producers' cooperatives which the *state*, not the workers, is to 'call into being'. The notion that state loans can be used for the construction of a new society as easily as they can for the construction of a new railway is worthy of Lassalle's imagination!

A last remnant of shame induces them to put 'state aid' – 'under the democratic control of the working people'.

Firstly, the 'working people' in Germany are mainly peasants, and not proletarians.

Secondly, 'democratic' translates as 'by the rule of the people'. But what does 'control by the rule of the people of the working people' mean? Particularly in the case of a working people which in presenting the state with demands such as these is expressing its full awareness of the fact that it neither rules nor is mature enough to rule!

It would be superfluous to begin to criticize here a recipe which Buchez concocted under Louis Philippe *in opposition* to the French socialists and which was accepted by the reactionary workers of the *Atelier*.[14] The most offensive fact is not that this wonder cure has been included in the programme but that there

14. *L'Atelier* was a monthly journal published in the 1840s, influenced by Buchez's Christian socialism; it was edited by workers' representatives elected every three months.

has been a general retreat from the standpoint of a class movement to that of a sectarian one.

The workers' desire to create the conditions for cooperative production on a social and, by beginning at home, at first on a national scale, means nothing beyond that they are working to revolutionize the present conditions of production; it has nothing in common with the creation of cooperative societies with state aid! As far as the present cooperative societies are concerned, they are *only* valuable if they are independent creations of the workers, and not the protégés either of governments or of the bourgeoisie.

IV

I come now to the democratic section.

A. *The free basis of the state*.

According to section II, the first thing that the German workers' party strives for is 'a free state'.

A free state – what does that mean?

It is by no means the goal of workers who have discarded the narrow mentality of humble subjects to make the state 'free'. In the German Reich the 'state' has almost as much 'freedom' as in Russia. Freedom consists in converting the state from an organ superimposed on society into one thoroughly subordinate to it; and even today state forms are more or less free depending on the degree to which they restrict the 'freedom of the state'.

The German workers' party – at least if it adopts this programme – thus shows that its socialist values do not even go skin-deep, for instead of treating existing society (and the same holds good for any future one) as the *basis* of the existing *state* (or future state in the case of future society), it treats the state as an independent entity with its own 'intellectual, ethical and liberal foundations'.

And what of the wild misuse made in the programme of the words 'present state' and 'present society', or the even more riotous misconception of the state to which it addresses its demands?

The 'present society' is capitalist society, which exists in all civilized countries, freed in varying degrees from the admixture of medievalism, modified in varying degrees by the particular historical development of each country, and developed to a varying degree. In contrast to this, the 'present state' changes with each country's border. It differs between the Prusso-German empire and Switzerland, between England and the United States. '*The* present state' is thus a fiction.

Nevertheless, the various states of the various civilized countries, despite their motley diversity of form, do have this in common: they all stand on the ground of modern bourgeois society although the degree of capitalist development varies. They thus also share certain essential characteristics. In this sense one can speak of 'present states' in contrast to the future when their present root, bourgeois society, will have died off.

The question then arises: What transformation will the state undergo in a communist society? In other words, what social functions will remain that are analogous to the present functions of the state? This question can only be answered scientifically and even a thousandfold combination of the word 'state' and the word 'people' will not bring us a flea-hop nearer the problem.

Between capitalist and communist society lies a period of revolutionary transformation from one to the other. There is a corresponding period of transition in the political sphere and in this period the state can only take the form of a *revolutionary dictatorship of the proletariat*.

The programme, however, does not deal either with this or with the future public affairs of communist society.

There is nothing in its political demands beyond the old and generally familiar democratic litany: universal suffrage, direct legislation, popular justice, a people's army, etc. They merely echo the bourgeois People's Party or the League of Peace and Freedom. All these demands, unless exaggerated into fantastic dreams, have already been *realized*. It is just that the state to which they belong does not lie within the borders of the German Reich but in Switzerland, the United States, etc. This kind of 'state of the future' is a *'present state'*, although it exists outside the 'framework' of the German Empire.

One thing has been forgotten, however. The German workers' party expressly declares that it acts within the 'present national state'. This means their own state, the Prusso-German empire. (Most of its demands would be meaningless if this were not so, for one can only demand what one has not already got.) Under these circumstances the main point should not have been forgotten, which is that all these pretty little gewgaws depend on the recognition of the so-called sovereignty of the people and are hence only appropriate in a *democratic republic*.

Although they lack the courage – and wisely so, for the circumstances demand caution – to call for a democratic republic after the manner of the French workers' programmes under Louis Philippe and Louis Napoleon, it was wrong to resort to the subterfuge which is neither 'honest'[15] nor decent of making demands which are only feasible in a democratic republic, and to address these demands to a state which is no more than a military despotism and a police state, bureaucratically carpentered, embellished with parliamentary forms and disguised by an admixture of feudalism although already under the influence of the bourgeoisie, and then to assure this same state into the bargain that they imagine they can impose these demands on it 'by legal means'.

Even vulgar democrats, who see the millennium in the democratic republic and who have no inkling that it is precisely in this final state form of bourgeois society that the class struggle must be fought to a conclusion, even they tower mountains above this kind of democratism which keeps within the bounds of what is allowed by the police and disallowed by logic.

The fact that the 'state' here stands for the government machine or for the state in so far as it forms through the division of labour a special organism separate from society is shown by the following words: 'The German workers' party demands *as the economic basis of* the state: a single progressive income tax, etc.' Taxes provide the economic basis of the government machinery and of nothing else. In the state of the future, already existing in Switzerland, this demand has been pretty well realized. Income tax presupposes varied sources of income for varied social classes, and hence capitalist society. It is thus not surprising that the Liverpool Financial Reformers, a bourgeois group led by Gladstone's brother, are putting forward the same demands as this programme.

B. The German workers' party demands as the intellectual and ethical basis of the state:

1. Universal and *equal elementary education* by the state. Universal compulsory school attendance. Free tuition.

'Equal elementary education'? What are we meant to under-

15. 'Honest' was a nickname for the Eisenachers (SDAP).

stand by these words? Is it believed that in our present society (and this is all we have to deal with here) education can be *equal* for all classes? Or is it demanded that the upper classes ought also to be reduced to the modicum of education – the elementary school – which is all that is compatible with the economic conditions of both wage-labourers and peasants?

'Universal compulsory school attendance. Free tuition.' The first of these exists even in Germany, and the second, in the case of elementary schools, in Switzerland and the United States. If in some states of the latter higher institutions of learning are also 'free', this in fact only means that the upper classes can defray the costs of their education out of the general taxpayer's pocket. Incidentally, the same is true of the 'free administration of justice' demanded under A/5. Criminal justice can be had free anywhere; civil justice is almost exclusively concerned with property conflicts and is hence almost exclusively the concern of the propertied classes. Should their cases be paid for out of public funds?

The paragraph on schools at least ought to have demanded technical schools (theoretical and practical) in combination with elementary schooling.

The idea of '*elementary education by the state*' is completely objectionable. Specifying the means available to elementary schools, the qualification of teaching staff, the subjects to be taught, etc. by a general law, as is done in the United States, and having state inspectors to supervise the observance of these regulations, is something quite different from appointing the state as educator of the people! Rather, government and church should alike be excluded from all influence on the schools. Indeed, in the Prusso-German Empire of all places (and the lame excuse that one is speaking of a future state is no way out; we have already seen what that means), it is inversely the state that could do with a rude education by the people.

Despite its democratic clang, the whole programme is thoroughly infested with the Lassallean sect's servile belief in the state, or, what is no better, by a democratic faith in miracles, or rather, it is a compromise between these two sorts of faith in miracles, both equally far removed from socialism.

'*Freedom of science*', says one paragraph of the Prussian Constitution. Then why here?

'*Freedom of conscience*'! If one should want, in this era of the

Kulturkampf,[16] to remind the liberals of their old catchwords, then surely it should only have been done in this form: Everyone should be free to relieve himself religiously as well as physically without the police sticking their noses in. But at this point the workers' party ought to have expressed its awareness that bourgeois 'freedom of conscience' only means the toleration of every possible kind of *religious freedom of conscience*, while its own goal is rather the liberation of the conscience from all religious spookery. But it chooses not to go further than the 'bourgeois' level.

I have now come to the end, for the appendix which now follows is not a *characteristic* part of the programme. I can thus be very brief here.

2. Normal working day.

In no other country has a workers' party restricted itself to such a vague demand. The length of the working day considered normal in the given circumstances has always been specified.

3. The restriction of female labour and the prohibition of child labour.

The standardization of the working day must anyway result in the restriction of female labour as far as this refers to the length of the working day, breaks, etc. Otherwise, the reference can only be to the exclusion of women from branches of labour which are specifically unhealthy for the female body or morally objectionable to the female sex. If this is what was meant, it should have been stated.

'Prohibition of child labour'! It was absolutely essential to give an *age-limit* here.

The *general prohibition* of child labour is incompatible with the existence of large-scale industry. It is thus only an empty, pious wish.

Its implementation – if possible – would be a reactionary step. With strict regulation of working hours according to age and with other precautionary measures to protect the children, the early combination of productive labour with education is one of the most powerful means for the transformation of present society.

16. The 'cultural struggle' was Bismarck's drive in the 1870s against the Catholic church and the Catholic Centre party.

4. State supervision of industry in the factory, workshop and home.

In the case of the Prusso-German state there should certainly have been a demand that inspectors be removable only by a court of law; that every worker should be able to take inspectors to court for neglect of duty; and that inspectors should only be recruited from the medical profession.

5. Regulation of prison labour.

A petty demand in a general workers' programme. In any case, it ought to have been made clear that there was no wish to see prisoners handled like animals for fear of competition, and especially no intention to deprive them of their only means of improvement, productive labour. Surely at least this much could have been expected from socialists.

6. An effective liability law.

What is meant by an 'effective' liability law should have been stated.

It could be noted in passing that, in speaking of the normal working day, the section of the factory laws relating to health regulations, safety measures, etc. has been overlooked. The liability law would only come into operation when these regulations were infringed.

In short, this appendix, too, is distinguished by its slovenly editing. *Dixi et salvavi animam meam.*[17]

17. I have spoken and saved my soul.

Circular Letter to Bebel, Liebknecht, Bracke, et al.[1]

Karl Marx and Frederick Engels

17–18 September 1879

Dear Bebel,

There has been a delay in replying to your letter of 29 August due on the one hand to the extended absence of Marx and on the other to several incidents: firstly the arrival of Richter's *Jahrbuch*[2] and then the arrival of Hirsch[3] himself.

I must assume that Liebknecht has not shown you my last letter to him, although I expressly requested him to do so. Otherwise you would certainly not have presented the same reasons which Liebknecht put forward and which I have already *answered* in that letter.[4]

Let us now go through the individual points at issue here.

I. The Negotiations with Karl Hirsch.

Liebknecht inquires whether Hirsch wants to take over the editorship of the newly founded party organ in Zurich.[5] Hirsch requests information about the founding of the paper: what funds are available and who is supplying them – the first question, in order to find out whether the paper will not have to cease publication after a few months; the other, in order to make sure who has his

1. This letter to the leadership of the German Social-Democratic Workers' Party was drafted by Engels and sent out over both Marx's and Engels's signatures after they had jointly revised it. It is translated here from the text printed in *MEW* 19.

2. The *Jahrbuch für Sozialwissenschaft und Sozialpolitik* was published in Zurich by Karl Höchberg, a philanthropist and reformist member of the SAPD, under the pseudonym Dr Ludwig Richter.

3. Karl Hirsch was a Social-Democratic publicist.

4. This interchange of letters has apparently not survived.

5. This was *Der Sozial-Demokrat*, the central organ of the SAPD published in Zurich from September 1879, and distributed clandestinely in Germany until the Anti-Socialist Law was repealed in 1890.

hand on the purse-strings and thus who has final control over the position of the paper. Liebknecht's answer to Hirsch: 'Everything in order, further information from Zurich' (Liebknecht to Hirsch, 28 July) does not arrive. But a letter from Bernstein to Hirsch does arrive from Zurich (24 July); Bernstein informs him that '*we* have been charged with the production and *supervision*' of the paper. He says a discussion has taken place 'between Viereck[6] and *us*' in which it was found, 'that your position would be made somewhat difficult by the differences of opinion which you had, as a *"Laterne"*[7] man, with individual comrades; however, *I* consider these reservations of no great importance'.

About the founding of the paper, not a word.

Hirsch answers on 26 July by return of post inquiring as to the financial position of the paper. Which comrades have pledged themselves to cover the deficit? Up to what amount and for how long a period? – The question of the editor's salary is of absolutely no importance in this connection; Hirsch merely wishes to know whether 'funds have been secured to guarantee the existence of the paper for at least one year'.

Bernstein answers on 31 July: Any potential deficit will be covered by voluntary contributions, of which *some* (!) have already been subscribed. In response to Hirsch's comments on the direction he intends to give the paper (of which more below), disapproving comments and *directives* are forthcoming:

> The *supervisory commission* must insist on this all the more, as it is itself subject to supervision, that is, is responsible. On this point, therefore, you would have to come to an agreement with the supervisory commission.

An immediate reply, if possible by telegraph, is requested.

Thus, instead of any answer to his justified questions Hirsch receives news that he is to carry on his editorial work under a *supervisory* commission with its seat in Zurich, a commission whose views differ very considerably from his own and whose members are not even named to him!

Hirsch, quite justifiably outraged at this treatment, prefers to come to an arrangement with the Leipzig people. You must be familiar with his letter of 2 August to Liebknecht, as Hirsch

6. Ludwig Viereck was a leader of the right wing of the SAPD.

7. *Die Laterne* was an anti-opportunist Social-Democratic satirical weekly, published by Karl Hirsch in Brussels from December 1878 to June 1879.

expressly demanded that you and Viereck be informed. Hirsch is even willing to place himself under a Zurich supervisory commission provided it makes comments to the editor in writing and is responsible to the Leipzig control commission.

Meanwhile Liebknecht writes to Hirsch on 28 July:

> *Of course* the undertaking has financial backing, as the whole party + (including) Höchberg are behind it. But I am not bothering about the details.

The next letter contains nothing about the financial backing either; on the other hand it contains the assurance that the Zurich commission is not an editorial commission but is only entrusted with *administration* and financial matters. On 14 August Liebknecht writes the same to me and demands that we persuade Hirsch to accept. On 29 August you yourself are so little informed about the true state of affairs that you write to me:

> In the editorial work of the newspaper he (Höchberg) has no more say than *any other prominent party comrade*.

Finally Hirsch receives a letter from Viereck on 11 August, in which he admits that

> ... the three men resident in Zurich were to tackle the founding of the paper as an *editorial commission* and to select an editor with the endorsement of the three Leipzig people ... *as far as I remember* it was also declared in the resolutions which were issued that the (Zurich) founding committee mentioned in clause 2 was to assume *the political as well as* the financial responsibility to the party ... Now this state of affairs seems to me to indicate that ... without the participation of the three men resident in Zurich, who have been charged by the party with the founding of the paper, an acceptance of the editorship cannot be considered.

Here Hirsch now has *something* definite at last, if only the information about the editor's position with regard to the Zurich people. They are an *editorial* commission; they also carry the *political* responsibility; it is not possible to take over the editorship without their participation. In short, Hirsch is simply directed to come to an arrangement with three people in Zurich whose names he has still not been given.

But so that the confusion is complete, Liebknecht writes a postscript to Viereck's letter:

Singer[8] has just been here from Berlin and has *reported*: The supervisory commission in Zurich is *not*, as Viereck thinks, an *editorial* commission but essentially an administrative commission, which is financially answerable to the party, i.e. to us, for the paper; of course the members have the right and the duty to discuss editorial matters with you (a right and a duty which, by the way, *every* party comrade has); they are *not* empowered to place you under *committee supervision*.

The three Zurich people and a member of the Leipzig executive – the only one who was present at the negotiations – insist that Hirsch is to be placed under the official direction of the Zurich commission; a second Leipzig member flatly denies this. And Hirsch is supposed to make up his mind before the gentlemen have reached an agreement among themselves? It does not seem to have occurred to anyone that Hirsch was entitled to be informed of the resolutions which had been passed containing the conditions which he was expected to comply with, the less so as it did not even occur to the Leipzig people to inform *themselves* reliably about those resolutions. Otherwise, how was the contradiction mentioned above possible?

Although the Leipzig people cannot agree on the powers delegated to the Zurich commission, the Zurich people are in absolutely no doubt.

Schramm[9] to Hirsch, 14 August:

If at that time you had not written that in the same case [as that of Kayser[10]] you would proceed in a similar fashion again, and if you had not thus held out the prospect of writing in the same manner, we would not consider the matter worth mentioning. But in view of your statement, we must reserve the right to cast a deciding vote on the acceptance of articles in the new journal.

The letter to Bernstein in which Hirsch is supposed to have said this is dated 26 July, *long* after the conference in Zurich in which the powers of the three Zurich people had been fixed. But in Zurich they are already revelling so much in the feeling of bureaucratic omnipotence that in reply to this later letter from Hirsch they are already laying claim to the new power to *decide* on the

8. Paul Singer was a leading Social-Democrat.

9. Karl Schramm, an economist and reformist Social-Democrat, edited the *Jahrbuch*.

10. Max Kayser was a right-wing Social-Democrat and Reichstag deputy; for his 'case' see below, pp. 365–7.

acceptance of articles. The editorial commission has already become a commission of *censorship*.

Not until Höchberg came to Paris did Hirsch learn from him the *names* of the members of the two commissions.

What were the reasons that the negotiations with Hirsch came to nothing?

1. The obstinate refusal not only of the Leipzigers but also of the Zurichers to give him any substantive information about the financial basis and thus about the possibility of keeping the paper alive, if only for a year. He only learned of the amount subscribed from me here (after your communication to me). Thus it was scarcely possible to draw any other conclusion from the earlier information (the party + Höchberg) than that the paper either is already predominantly financed by Höchberg or will soon be completely dependent upon his contributions. And this latter possibility is even now still far from excluded. The sum of – if I read it correctly – 800 marks is *exactly* the same (£40 sterling) which the *Freiheit*[11] association here lost in the first *half-year*.

2. The repeated assurance by Liebknecht, which has since been proved to be totally inaccurate, that the Zurich people were not to exercise official supervision over the editor and the resultant comedy of errors.

3. Finally, the certainty that the Zurich commission was not only to supervise but actually to censor the editor and that all that fell to Hirsch was the role of a figurehead.

We can only agree with his decision thereupon to refuse. The Leipzig executive, as we have heard from Höchberg, has been augmented by two members who do not live in Leipzig and therefore it can only intervene when the three Leipzig members are in agreement. As a result, the real centre of gravity is transferred completely to Zurich; and Hirsch would not have been able to work with them in the long run any more than would any other real revolutionary editor with proletarian loyalties. More of that later.

II. The Intended Position of the Paper.

Straightaway, on 24 July, Bernstein informs Hirsch that the prob-

---

11. *Freiheit* was published by Johann Most from the beginning of 1879, first in London, later in New York. Most was already veering towards anarchism, and was expelled from the SAPD in 1880.

lems which he, as a *'Laterne'* man, has had with individual comrades, would make his position difficult.

Hirsch answers that in his judgement the attitude of the paper will have to be the same, in general, as that of the *'Laterne'*, i.e. such as to avoid legal proceedings in Switzerland and not to cause too much alarm in Germany. He asks who the comrades are and continues:

I know only one and I promise you that in a similar case involving a *violation of discipline* I shall treat him again in just the same way.

Bernstein replies in the dignified spirit befitting his new office of censor:

As far as the attitude of the paper is concerned, however, it is the view of the supervisory commission that it should not take the *'Laterne'* as its model; the paper is, in our opinion, to be less totally taken up with political radicalism and to be kept fundamentally socialist. Cases such as the attack on Kayser, which was disapproved of by all comrades without exception [!], must be avoided at all costs.

Etcetera, etcetera. Liebknecht calls the attack on Kayser 'a blunder' and Schramm considers it so dangerous that he proceeds to impose censorship on Hirsch.

Hirsch writes once again to Höchberg that a case such as that of Kayser

cannot occur if an official party organ exists whose clear explanations and well-meaning hints *cannot* be so boldly disregarded by a deputy.

Viereck, too, writes that the new paper is 'directed to adopt a dispassionate attitude and, as much as possible, to ignore all differences of opinion which have occurred hitherto'; it is not to be an 'expanded *Laterne*' and Bernstein 'could be reproached at most with having too moderate a position, if that is a reproach at a time when, of course, we cannot proceed under full sail'.

Now, what is this Kayser affair, this unforgivable crime which Hirsch is supposed to have committed? Kayser is the only Social-Democratic deputy who speaks and votes in the Reichstag in favour of protective tariffs. Hirsch accuses him of having violated party discipline.

1. By voting for direct taxation, the abolition of which the party programme expressly demands;

2. By voting monies to Bismarck and thus infringing the first basic rule of our party tactics: Not a farthing for this government.

In both points Hirsch is undoubtedly right. And after Kayser had trampled, on the one hand, upon the party programme, to which the deputies, as it were, took an oath in the form of a congress resolution, and, on the other, upon the most imperative, most fundamental rule of party tactics, and had *voted* Bismarck *monies as thanks for the Anti-Socialist Law*, Hirsch was equally right, in our opinion, to attack him as roughly as he did.

We have never been able to understand why people in Germany have become so furious about this attack on Kayser. Now Höchberg tells me the 'parliamentary party' gave Kayser *permission* to act as he did and as a result of this permission Kayser is considered covered.

If this is the case, it is really a bit much. Firstly, Hirsch could not know of this secret resolution any more than could the rest of the world.[12]

Furthermore, the disgrace for the party, which before could have been laid on Kayser alone, becomes even greater as a result of this affair, as does Hirsch's merit, too, in having exposed to all the world these absurd turns of phrase and even more absurd votes of Kayser's and thus in having saved the party's honour. Or has German Social Democracy indeed been infected by the parliamentary disease and does it really believe that with the popular vote the Holy Ghost is poured out over the elect, that meetings of the parliamentary party are transformed into infallible councils and party decisions into inviolable dogmas?

A blunder has indeed been committed, but however not by Hirsch but by the deputies who covered Kayser with their decision. And if those whose task it is above all others to attend to party discipline, violate this party discipline themselves so outrageously, so much the worse. But it is worse still to go so far as to believe that it was not Kayser, with his speech and vote, and the other deputies, with their resolution, who have violated party discipline, but Hirsch, with his attack on Kayser – despite this resolution, which was still unknown to him anyway.

By the way, it is certain that the party has adopted the same unclear and indecisive attitude on the protective tariff system as it

12. Crossed out in the manuscript: 'Supposing, also, two or three other Social-Democratic deputies (for there could hardly have been more there) had been tempted to allow Kayser to produce his bilge in public and to vote monies for Bismarck, they would have been obliged to assume the responsibility in public and to wait and see what Hirsch would say about it.'

has done hitherto on almost all economic questions which have assumed practical importance, e.g. the question of the state railways. This happens because the party organs, in particular *Vorwärts*,[13] instead of discussing this question thoroughly have preferred to apply themselves to the construction of a social order for the future. When the protective tariff question suddenly became a practical problem *after* the Anti-Socialist Law, the views expressed diverged in the most various ways and not one was to be found which possessed the prerequisites for the formation of a clear and correct judgement: knowledge of the condition of German industry and its position on the world market. Groups in favour of protective tariffs could not, then, be avoided here and there among the voters, and the party wanted, of course, to make allowance for these people. They failed to act decisively and take the only way out of this confusion by reaching a purely political understanding of the question (such was offered in the *Laterne*). It was inevitable, therefore, that in this debate the party appeared for the first time hesitant, uncertain and confused, and that it finally thoroughly disgraced itself in the person and in the case of Kayser.

The attack on Kayser is now taken as an excuse to preach to Hirsch in all tones of voice that the new paper is under no circumstances to imitate the excesses of the *Laterne*; it is to be less taken up with political radicalism and rather to be kept fundamentally socialist and dispassionate – by Viereck no less than by Bernstein, who seems to Viereck to be the right man precisely because he is too moderate, because it is not possible to proceed under full sail at the present time.

But why does one go abroad at all if not to proceed under full sail? Abroad nothing stands in the way. In Switzerland the German press laws, laws of association and penal laws do not apply. It is not only possible, therefore, to say the things there that it was not possible to say at home even before the Anti-Socialist Law, on account of the ordinary German laws; one has a *duty* to do so. For one stands here not only before Germany but before Europe; one has the duty, so far as the Swiss laws allow it, to demonstrate to Europe with all frankness the tendencies and aims of the German party. Anyone who wants to bind himself to *German* laws in

13. *Vorwärts* was the central organ of the SAPD after its foundation at Gotha in 1875. In October 1878, after the passage of the Anti-Socialist Law, it was forced to cease publication and did not reappear until 1890.

Switzerland merely proves that he is worthy of these German laws and in fact has nothing to say other than what was allowed in Germany before the emergency law.[14] No regard must be paid either to the possibility of temporarily cutting off the return of the editor to Germany. Anyone who is not prepared to take this risk is not suitable for an honorary office which is so exposed.

Furthermore, the emergency law has outlawed the German party precisely because it was the only serious opposition party in Germany. If in a foreign journal it renders thanks to Bismarck by giving up this role of the only serious opposition party, by behaving nice and tamely, and if it puts up with the kick and shows no passion, it only proves that it has deserved the kick. Of all the German emigrant newspapers which have appeared abroad since 1830, the *Laterne* is certainly one of the most moderate. But if even the *Laterne* was too impudent – then the new organ can only compromise the party in the eyes of the supporters in non-German countries.

III. The Manifesto of the Three Zurichers.

In the meantime Höchberg's *Jahrbuch* has reached us and it contains an article: 'The Socialist Movement in Germany in Retrospect',[15] which, as Höchberg has told me himself, has been written by the three members of this same Zurich commission. We have here their authentic criticism of the movement so far and hence their authentic programme for the position of the new organ in so far as this attitude depends on them.

At the very beginning they say:

> The movement, which Lassalle regarded as an eminently political one, to which he summoned not only workers but all honourable democrats and *at whose head* the independent representatives of science and *all men filled with true love of humanity* were to march, was reduced under the presidency of J. B. von Schweitzer to a *one-sided struggle for the interests of the industrial workers*.

I will not investigate whether and to what extent this is historically the case. The special reproach which is directed at Schweitzer here consists in Schweitzer's having *reduced* Lassalleanism, which is understood here as a bourgeois democratic-philanthropic

14. I.e. the Anti-Socialist Law.
15. This article, signed with three asterisks, was the work of Höchberg, Schramm and Bernstein.

movement, to a one-sided struggle for the interests of the workers, whereas he *deepened* its character by making it a class struggle of the industrial workers against the bourgeoisie. He is further reproached with having 'rejected bourgeois democracy'. But what place has bourgeois democracy within the Social-Democratic Party? If it consists of 'honest men' it cannot want to be admitted, and if it nevertheless wishes to be admitted then this is only to cause trouble.

The Lassalle party 'preferred to conduct itself in a most *one-sided* fashion as a *workers' party*'. The gentlemen who wrote this are themselves members of a party which conducts itself in a most one-sided fashion as a workers' party; they now hold office and honour in it. This is an absolute incompatibility. If they mean what they write then they must leave the party, or at least resign from office and dignities. If they do not, then they admit that they intend to use their official position to combat the proletarian character of the party. The party, therefore, will betray itself if it leaves them their office and dignities.

In the view of these gentlemen, then, the Social-Democratic Party is *not* to be a one-sided workers' party but a party open on all sides 'for all men filled with true love of humanity'. It is to prove this, above all, by divesting itself of rough proletarian passions and by placing itself under the leadership of educated, philanthropic bourgeois in order to 'develop good taste' and 'to learn good form'. Then the 'disreputable behaviour' of many of its leaders will give way to an exemplary 'bourgeois behaviour'. (As if the superficially disreputable behaviour of those referred to were not the least they can be reproached with!) Then, too, '*numerous* supporters from the circles of the *educated* and *propertied* classes will join. But *these* must first be won, if the . . . agitation which is conducted is to achieve *tangible* successes'. German socialism has 'attached too much importance to winning the *masses* and has failed to conduct energetic (!) propaganda in the so-called upper strata of society'. For 'the party still lacks men who are fitted to represent it in the Reichstag'. But it is 'desirable and necessary to entrust mandates to men who have had opportunity and time enough to acquaint themselves with the relevant material. The simple worker and small craftsman . . . have the necessary leisure for this only in the most exceptional cases.'

So vote bourgeois!

In short, the working class is incapable of liberating itself by its own efforts. For this purpose it must first accept the leadership of 'educated and propertied' bourgeois, who alone have 'opportunity and time' to acquaint themselves with what is good for the workers. And secondly, the bourgeoisie is on no account to be combated, but to be *won* by energetic propaganda.

But if the upper strata of society, or even only their well-meaning elements are to be won, they must on no account be alarmed. And here the three Zurich people believe they have made a reassuring discovery:

The party is showing precisely at the present time, under the pressure of the Anti-Socialist Law, that it *does not desire* to follow the path of violent, bloody revolution, but is determined . . . to pursue the path of legality, i.e. of *reform*.

Thus, if 500,000–600,000 Social-Democratic voters, one tenth to one eighth of the whole electorate, dispersed, furthermore, far and wide across the whole country, are sensible enough not to run their heads against a wall and to attempt a 'bloody revolution', one against ten, this proves that they for ever exclude the possibility of making use of a tremendous external event, of a sudden revolutionary upsurge which might result from it, indeed of a *victory* gained by the people in a conflict arising from it! If Berlin should be again so uneducated as to have another 18 March,[16] the Social Democrats, instead of taking part in the struggle as 'rabble with a mania for barricades', must rather 'pursue the path of legality', curb the movement, clear away the barricades and, if necessary, march with the splendid army against the rough, one-sided, uneducated masses. If the gentlemen maintain that this is not what they meant, then what did they mean?

It becomes even better. 'Hence, the more calm, objective and deliberate it' (the party) 'is in its criticism of existing conditions and in its proposals for changing them, the less it will be possible to repeat the present successful move' (at the time of the introduction of the Anti-Socialist Law) 'with which the conscious forces of reaction have intimidated the bourgeoisie with their fear of the red bogey' (p. 88).

In order to dissolve the last trace of fear on the part of the bourgeoisie it must be shown clearly and convincingly that the red bogey is really only a phantom and does not exist. But what is the

16. 18 March 1848 saw the erection of barricades, as the German revolution reached Berlin.

secret of the red bogey if not the fear felt by the bourgeoisie of the inevitable life-and-death struggle between itself and the proletariat? The fear of the inevitable decision in the modern class struggle? Abolish the class struggle, and the bourgeoisie and 'all independent men' will 'not hesitate to go hand in hand with the proletarians'! And who would then be cheated if not precisely the proletarians?

Let the party demonstrate, therefore, by its humble and sorrowful demeanour that it has once and for all laid aside the 'improprieties and excesses' which gave rise to the Anti-Socialist Law. If it promises voluntarily that it intends only to operate within the limits of the Anti-Socialist Law, Bismarck and the bourgeoisie will then surely have the goodness to repeal this law, which will then be superfluous! 'Let no one misunderstand us!'

We do not want to give up our party and our programme, but we are of the opinion that we have enough to do for years to come if we direct our whole strength, our whole energy to the achievement of certain immediate goals, which must be achieved in any case before there can be any thought of fulfilling the more far-reaching aspirations.

Bourgeois, petty bourgeois, and workers who 'are now deterred by the far-reaching demands', will then join us in masses too.

The programme is not to be *abandoned* but only *postponed* – for an indefinite period. It is accepted, but not actually for oneself and for one's own lifetime, but posthumously, as an heirloom for one's children and one's children's children. In the meantime one applies 'all one's strength and energy' to all sorts of petty trifles and to patching up the capitalist social order, so that at least it looks as if something is happening and so that at the same time the bourgeoisie is not alarmed. Compared with that I would much prefer the communist Miquel, who proves his unshakeable belief in the inevitable overthrow of capitalist society in a few hundred years by indulging in swindles for all he is worth, making an honest contribution to the crash of 1873 and thus *really* doing something to bring about the collapse of the existing order.

Another offence against form was evident in the 'exaggerated attacks on the "founders" ',[17] who, of course, were 'only children

---

17. The 'founders' (*Gründer*) were the entrepreneurs who enriched themselves from the boom of the early 1870s, based on French reparations payments and the stimulus given by German unification. Bethel Strousberg, a railway magnate who was bankrupted by the 1873 crash, was a typical *Gründer*.

of the age'; 'it would have been better to abstain from the abuse of Strousberg and such people'. Unfortunately all people are 'only children of the age', and if this is an adequate excuse nobody may be attacked anymore and all polemics and all struggle on our part must come to an end; we simply put up with all the kicks from our opponents because we, in our wisdom, know of course that they are 'only children of the age' and cannot act any other way. Instead of repaying their kicks with interest we should rather feel pity for the poor souls.

Similarly, the support for the Commune, of course, had the disadvantage that 'people otherwise well disposed towards us were repelled and in general the *hatred felt by the bourgeoisie* towards us became greater'. And, furthermore, the party is 'not wholly blameless as far as the passing of the October law[18] was concerned, for it increased the *hatred of the bourgeoisie* unnecessarily'.

There you have the programme of the three Zurich censors. In clarity it leaves nothing to be desired. Least of all for us, as we know all these phrases very well from 1848. They are the representatives of the petty bourgeoisie who are making their presence felt, full of fear that the proletariat, under the pressure of its revolutionary position, may 'go too far'. Instead of a determined political opposition – general mediation; instead of the struggle against government and bourgeoisie – the attempt to win them over and persuade them; instead of defiant resistance to mistreatment from above – humble submissiveness and the admission that the punishment is deserved. All historically necessary conflicts are reinterpreted as misunderstandings and all discussions are brought to an end with the protestation that ultimately we are all agreed on the main points. The people who appeared as bourgeois democrats in 1848 can now just as well call themselves Social Democrats. Just as for the former the democratic republic was unattainably remote so, too, is the overthrow of the capitalist order for the latter, and it has therefore absolutely no significance for the political practice of the present day; one can mediate, compromise and philanthropize to one's heart's content. And it is just the same with the class struggle between the proletariat and the bourgeoisie. On paper it is acknowledged because its existence can no longer be denied; but in practice it is hushed up, watered down, attenuated. The Social-Democratic Party *is not* to be a

18. I.e. the Anti-Socialist Law, which had been passed the previous October.

workers' party; it is not to incur the hatred of the bourgeoisie or of anyone; above all it should conduct energetic propaganda among the bourgeoisie; instead of stressing far-reaching goals which deter the bourgeoisie and are unattainable in our generation anyway, it should rather devote its whole strength and energy to those petty-bourgeois patchwork reforms which could provide the old social order with new supports and hence perhaps transform the final catastrophe into a gradual, piecemeal and, as far as possible, peaceful process of dissolution. These are the same people who, under the guise of unflagging activity, not only do nothing but also try to prevent anything happening at all, except – chatter; the same people whose fear of every action in 1848 and 1849 obstructed the movement at every step and finally caused its downfall; the same people who never see reaction and are then quite amazed to find themselves in a blind alley, where neither resistance nor flight is possible, the same people who want to banish history to the confines of their own narrow philistine horizon and over whose heads history always proceeds to the real business on the agenda.

As far as their socialist substance is concerned this has already been adequately criticized in the 'Manifesto', in the section on 'German or "True" Socialism'.[19] When the class struggle is rejected as a disagreeable 'coarse' phenomenon, nothing remains as the basis of socialism other than 'true love of humanity' and empty phrases about 'justice'.

It is an inevitable phenomenon which is rooted in the course of the development that people from the hitherto ruling class join the struggling proletariat and supply it with educative elements. We have already stated this clearly in the Manifesto. But two points must be noted here:

Firstly, in order to be of use to the proletarian movement these people must bring real educative elements with them. But this is not the case with the great majority of the German bourgeois converts. Neither the *Zukunft* nor the *Neue Gesellschaft*[20] have contributed anything which has advanced the movement one step. Here there is an absolute lack of real educative material, factual or theoretical. Instead, attempts to harmonize superficially acquired socialist thoughts with the most varying theoretical stand-

19. See *The Revolutions of 1848*, pp. 90–93.

20. The *Zukunft* and the *Neue Gesellschaft* were both short-lived journals of the reformist intellectuals who gravitated around the SAPD.

points which the gentlemen have brought with them from the university or elsewhere and of which each is more confused than the one before, thanks to the process of decomposition which the remnants of German philosophy are undergoing today. Instead of first thoroughly studying the new science himself, each of them preferred to trim it according to the standpoint which he had brought with him, made forthwith his own private science, and came forward with the pretension of wanting to teach it. That is why among these gentlemen there are almost as many standpoints as heads; instead of bringing clarity anywhere they have only created dire confusion – fortunately almost exclusively among themselves. Such educative elements, whose first principle it is to teach what they have not learnt, the party can very well do without.

Secondly, when such people from other classes join the proletarian party the first requirement is that they do not bring any remnants of bourgeois, petty-bourgeois etc. prejudices with them, but that they adopt the proletarian outlook without prevarication. These gentlemen, however, as has been demonstrated, are chock full of bourgeois and petty-bourgeois ideas. In such a petty-bourgeois country as Germany these ideas certainly have their justification. But only *outside* the Social-Democratic Workers' Party. If these gentlemen constitute themselves as a social-democratic petty-bourgeois party they have a perfect right to do so; it would be possible, then, to negotiate with them and to form a common front with them under certain circumstances. But in a workers' party they are an adulterating element. If there are reasons for tolerating them in it for the present then it is our duty *only* to tolerate them, to allow them no influence on the party leadership and to remain conscious of the fact that the break with them is only a matter of time. The time, moreover, seems to have come. It seems to us incomprehensible that the party can allow the authors of this article in its midst any longer. But if the party leadership should fall more or less into their hands, then the party will simply be castrated and that would be the end of its proletarian drive.

As far as we are concerned, after our whole past only one way is open to us. For almost forty years we have stressed the class struggle as the most immediate driving power in history and, in particular, the class struggle between the bourgeoisie and the pro-

letariat as the great lever of the modern social upheaval; therefore it is impossible for us to ally ourselves with people who
want to eliminate this class struggle from the movement. When
the International was formed, we expressly formulated the battle-
cry: the emancipation of the working class must be the work of
the working class itself. We cannot ally ourselves, therefore, with
people who openly declare that the workers are too uneducated to
free themselves and must first be liberated from above by philanthropic big bourgeois and petty bourgeois. If the new party organ
assumes a position which corresponds to the opinions of those
gentlemen, which is bourgeois and not proletarian, then nothing
remains, much though we should regret it, but to declare publicly
our opposition to it and to abandon the solidarity with which we
have hitherto represented the German party abroad. We hope,
however, that it will not come to *this*.

This letter is intended for communication to all five members of
the executive in Germany and to Bracke . . .

As far as we are concerned nothing stands in the way of its
communication to the members of the Zurich commission.

Introduction to the Programme of the French Workers' Party[1]

Considering,

That the emancipation of the class of producers is that of all human beings, without distinction of sex or race;

That the producers can only be free when they are in possession of the means of production;

That there are only two forms in which the means of production can belong to them:

1. The individual form, which was never a universal phenomenon and is being ever more superseded by the progress of industry,

2. The collective form, the material and mental elements for which are created by the very development of capitalist society;

Considering,

That collective appropriation can only proceed from the revolutionary action of the class of producers – the proletariat – organized in an independent political party;

That such an organization must be pursued by all means that are available to the proletariat, especially including universal suffrage,

1. The Parti Ouvrier was founded in 1879 at Marseilles. It was federal in structure and contained anarchist and reformist components as well as socialist, and it was not long before the French workers' movement was again fragmented. Jules Guesde, the leading Marxist activist in the French workers' movement, visited London in May 1880 to draw up a programme for the new party in time for the forthcoming elections, in conjunction with Lafargue, Engels and Marx. Marx dictated to Guesde this theoretical introduction. The whole programme was published in *Égalité*, the journal of Guesde's group, on 30 June 1880, and it was adopted, against anarchist opposition, at the 'revolutionary workers' congress' at Le Havre in September 1880, after socialists and anarchists had walked out of the Parti Ouvrier congress at which the reformists were in a majority. It is translated here from the French text reproduced in Marx–Engels *Gesamtausgabe*, I/25, Berlin, 1985, p. 280.

which will thus be transformed from the instrument of fraud that it has been up till now into an instrument of emancipation;

The French socialist workers, who have set themselves in the economic arena the goal of the return of all means of production to collective ownership, have decided, as the means of organization and struggle, to enter the elections with the following minimum programme.[2]

2. This minimum programme demanded an extension of democratic liberties, including the general arming of the people, also economic reforms such as the eight-hour day, progressive income tax, and equal pay for men and women.

On Poland and Russia

WHAT HAVE THE WORKING CLASSES TO DO WITH POLAND?[1]

Frederick Engels

I *Commonwealth*, 24 March 1866

Wherever the working classes have taken a part of their own in political movements, there, from the very beginning, their foreign policy was expressed in the few words – restoration of Poland. This was the case with the Chartist movement so long as it existed; this was the case with the French working men long before 1848, as well as during that memorable year, when on 15 May they marched on to the National Assembly to the cry of *'Vive la Pologne!'* – Poland for ever![2] This was the case in Germany, when, in 1848 and 1849, the organs of the working class demanded war with Russia for the restoration of Poland.[3] It is the case even now; with one exception – of which more anon – the working men of Europe unanimously proclaim the restoration of Poland as a part and parcel of their political programme, as the most comprehensive expression of their foreign policy. The middle class, too, have had, and have still, 'sympathies' with the Poles; which sympathies have not prevented them from leaving the Poles in the lurch in 1831, in 1846, in 1863, nay, have not even prevented

1. This series of articles was written by Engels at Marx's explicit request for the *Commonwealth*, a London workers' paper. It was directed against the position of the French and Belgian Proudhonists, as expressed particularly by Hector Denis in *Le Tribune du Peuple* of Brussels and by the Proudhonist delegates at the 1865 London Conference of the International.

2. On 15 May 1848 150,000 demonstrators, led by Auguste Blanqui, marched on the French National Assembly, which was debating Poland, and demanded military help for the Polish struggle. When this was refused, they attempted to overthrow the National Assembly, but were defeated by the bourgeois National Guard (see 'The Class Struggles in France', *Surveys from Exile*, p. 58).

3. This refers in particular to the *Neue Rheinische Zeitung* which Marx and Engels edited in 1848. See *The Revolutions of 1848*, pp. 48–52.

them from leaving the worst enemies of Poland, such as Lord Palmerston, to manage matters so as to actually assist Russia while they talked in favour of Poland. But with the working classes it is different. They mean intervention, not non-intervention; they mean war with Russia while Russia meddles with Poland; and they have proved it every time the Poles rose against their oppressors. And recently, the International Working Men's Association has given a fuller expression to this universal instinctive feeling of the body it claims to represent, by inscribing on its banner, 'Resistance to Russian encroachments upon Europe – Restoration of Poland'.[4]

This programme of the foreign policy of the working men of western and central Europe has found a unanimous consent among the class to whom it was addressed, with one exception, as we said before. There are among the working men of France a small minority who belong to the school of the late P. J. Proudhon. This school differs *in toto* from the generality of the advanced and thinking working men: it declares them to be ignorant fools, and maintains on most points opinions quite contrary to theirs. This holds good in their foreign policy also. The Proudhonists, sitting in judgement on oppressed Poland, find the verdict of the Staleybridge jury, 'serves her right'. They admire Russia as the great land of the future, as the most progressive nation upon the face of the earth, at the side of which such a paltry country as the United States is not worthy of being named. They have charged the [General] Council of the International Association with setting up the Bonapartist principle of nationalities, and with declaring that magnanimous Russian people without the pale of civilized Europe, such being a grievous sin against the principles of universal democracy and the fraternity of all nations. These are the charges. Barring the democratic phraseology at the wind-up, they coincide, it will be seen at once, verbally and literally with what the extreme Tories of all countries have to say about Poland and Russia. Such charges are not worth refuting; but, as they come from a fraction of the working classes, be it ever so small a one, they may

4. The London Conference of September 1865 had carried the resolution, 'That it is imperative to annihilate the invading influence of Russia by applying to Poland "the right of every people to dispose of itself", and re-establishing that country on a social and democratic basis' (*IWMA* I, pp. 246–7). However, the resolutions on Poland which the General Council submitted to the Geneva Congress of September 1866 (see 'Instructions for Delegates', above, pp. 93–4) were defeated by the opposition of the Proudhonists.

render it desirable to state again the case of Poland and Russia, and to vindicate what we may henceforth call the foreign policy of the united working men of Europe.

But why do we always name Russia alone in connection with Poland? Have not two German powers, Austria and Prussia, shared in the plunder? Do not they, too, hold parts of Poland in bondage, and, in connection with Russia, do they not work to keep down every national Polish movement?

It is well known how hard Austria has struggled to keep out of the Polish business; how long she resisted the plans of Russia and Prussia for partition. Poland was a natural ally of Austria against Russia. When Russia once became formidable, nothing could be more in the interest of Austria than to keep Poland alive between herself and the newly rising empire. It was only when Austria saw that Poland's fate was settled, that with or without her, the other two powers were determined to annihilate her, it was only then that in self-protection she went in for a share of the territory. But as early as 1815 she held out for the restoration of an independent Poland; in 1831 and in 1863 she was ready to go to war for that object, and give up her own share of Poland provided England and France were prepared to join her. The same during the Crimean War. This is not said in justification of the general policy of the Austrian government. Austria has shown often enough that to oppress a weaker nation is congenial work to her rulers. But in the case of Poland the instinct of self-preservation was stronger than the desire for new territory or the habits of government. And this puts Austria out of court for the present.

As to Prussia, her share of Poland is too trifling to weigh much on the scale. Her friend and ally, Russia, has managed to ease her of nine tenths of what she got during the three partitions.[5] But what little is left to her weighs as an incubus upon her. It has chained her to the triumphal car of Russia, it has been the means of enabling her government, even in 1863–4, to practise unchallenged in Prussian Poland those breaches of the law, those infractions of individual liberty, of the right of meeting, of the liberty of the press, which were so soon afterwards to be applied to

5. The Congress of Vienna of 1814–15 left Prussia with a considerably smaller share of Poland than she had acquired by the earlier partitions, as the greater part of Poland was now constituted into the 'Kingdom of Poland', and placed under tsarist rule. By way of compensation, Prussia received the Rhineland. 'Nine tenths', however, is a bit of an exaggeration.

the rest of the country; it has falsified the whole middle-class liberal movement which, from fear of risking the loss of a few square miles of land on the eastern frontier, allowed the government to set all law aside with regard to the Poles. The working men, not only of Prussia, but of all Germany, have a greater interest than those of any other country in the restoration of Poland, and they have shown in every revolutionary movement that they know it. Restoration of Poland, to them, is emancipation of their own country from Russian vassalage. And this we think puts Prussia out of court too. Whenever the working classes of Russia (if there is such a thing in that country, in the sense it is understood in western Europe) form a political programme, and that programme contains the liberation of Poland – then, but not till then, Russia as a nation will be out of court too, and the government of the tsar will remain alone under indictment.

II *Commonwealth*, 31 March 1866

It is said that to claim independence for Poland is to acknowledge the 'principle of nationalities', and that the principle of nationalities is a Bonapartist invention concocted to prop up the Napoleonic despotism in France. Now what is this 'principle of nationalities'?

By the treaties of 1815 the boundaries of the various states of Europe were drawn merely to suit diplomatic convenience, and especially to suit the convenience of the then strongest continental power – Russia. No account was taken either of the wishes, the interests, or the national diversities of the populations. Thus, Poland was divided, Germany was divided, Italy was divided, not to speak of the many smaller nationalities inhabiting south-eastern Europe, and of which few people at that time knew anything. The consequence was that for Poland, Germany, and Italy, the very first step in every political movement was to attempt the restoration of that national unity without which national life was but a shadow. And when, after the suppression of the revolutionary attempts in Italy and Spain, 1821–3,[6] and again, after the

6. In January 1820 a military rising in Madrid forced the Spanish monarchy to revive the democratic constitution of 1812. In the summer of 1820 revolutions inspired by the Spanish example broke out in Naples and Piedmont. In March 1821 Austrian troops moved in to crush the Italian revolutions, and in April 1823 France invaded Spain in order to abolish the constitution and restore King Ferdinand.

revolution of July 1830 in France, the extreme politicians of the greater part of civilized Europe came into contact with each other,[7] and attempted to mark out a kind of common programme, the liberation and unification of the oppressed and subdivided nations became a watchword common to all of them. So it was again in 1848, when the number of oppressed nations was increased by a fresh one, viz., Hungary. There could, indeed, be no two opinions as to the right of every one of the great national subdivisions of Europe to dispose of itself, independently of its neighbours, in all internal matters, so long as it did not encroach upon the liberty of the others. This right was, in fact, one of the fundamental conditions of the internal liberty of all. How could, for instance, Germany aspire to liberty and unity, if at the same time she assisted Austria to keep Italy in bondage, either directly or by her vassals? Why, the total breaking-up of the Austrian monarchy is the very first condition of the unification of Germany!

This right of the great national subdivisions of Europe to political independence, acknowledged as it was by the European democracy, could not but find the same acknowledgement with the working classes especially. It was, in fact, nothing more than to recognize in other large national bodies of undoubted vitality the same right of individual national existence which the working men of each separate country claimed for themselves. But this recognition, and the sympathy with these national aspirations, were restricted to the large and well-defined historical nations of Europe; there was Italy, Poland, Germany, Hungary. France, Spain, England, Scandinavia were neither subdivided nor under foreign control, and therefore but indirectly interested in the matter; and as to Russia, she could only be mentioned as the detainer of an immense amount of stolen property, which would have to be disgorged on the day of reckoning.

After the coup d'état of 1851, Louis Napoleon, the emperor 'by the grace of God and the national will',[8] had to find a democrati-cized and popular sounding name for his foreign policy. What could be better than to inscribe upon his banners the 'principle

7. Engels is alluding here to Mazzini's secret organization Young Europe, which was formed in 1834 by the federation of Young Italy, Young Germany, and the Polish nationalist organization.

8. This phrase was used to justify the installation of Louis Philippe as the French king in 1830.

of nationalities'? Every nationality to be the arbiter of its own fate – every detached fraction of any nationality to be allowed to annex itself to its great mother-country – what could be more liberal? Only, mark, there was not, now, any more question of *nations*, but of *nationalities*.

There is no country in Europe where there are not different nationalities under the same government. The Highland Gaels and the Welsh are undoubtedly of different nationalities to what the English are, although nobody will give to these remnants of peoples long gone by the title of nations, any more than to the Celtic inhabitants of Brittany in France. Moreover, no state boundary coincides with the natural boundary of nationality, that of language. There are plenty of people out of France whose mother tongue is French, same as there are plenty of people of German language out of Germany; and in all probability it will ever remain so. It is a natural consequence of the confused and slow-working historical development through which Europe has passed during the last thousand years, that almost every great nation has parted with some outlying portions of its own body, which have become separated from the national life, and in most cases participated in the national life of some other people; so much so, that they do not wish to rejoin their own main stock. The Germans in Switzerland and Alsace do not desire to be reunited to Germany, any more than the French in Belgium and Switzerland wish to become attached politically to France. And after all, it is no slight advantage that various nations, as politically constituted, have most of them some foreign elements within themselves, which form connecting links with their neighbours, and vary the otherwise too monotonous uniformity of the national character.

Here, then, we perceive the difference between the 'principle of *nationalities*' and the old democratic and working-class tenet as to the right of the great European *nations* to separate and independent existence. The 'principle of nationalities' leaves entirely untouched the great question of the right of national existence for the historic peoples of Europe; nay, if it touches it, it is merely to disturb it. The principle of nationalities raises two sorts of questions; first of all, questions of boundary between these great historic peoples; and secondly, questions as to the right to independent national existence of those numerous small relics of peoples which, after having figured for a longer or shorter period on the stage of history, were finally absorbed as integral portions into one or the other of those more powerful nations whose greater vitality enabled them to overcome greater obstacles. The European importance, the vitality of a people is as nothing in the eyes of the principle of nationalities; before it, the Roumans of Wallachia, who never had a history[9] nor the energy required to have one, are of equal importance to the Italians who have a history of 2,000 years, and an unimpaired national vitality; the Welsh and Manxmen, if they desired it, would have an equal right to independent political existence, absurd though it would be, with the English. The whole thing is an absurdity, got up in a popular dress in order to throw dust in shallow people's eyes, and to be used as a convenient phrase, or to be laid aside if the occasion requires it.

Shallow as the thing is, it required cleverer brains than Louis Napoleon's to invent it. The principle of nationalities, so far from being a Bonapartist invention to favour a resurrection of Poland, is nothing but a *Russian invention concocted to destroy Poland*. Russia has absorbed the greater part of ancient Poland on the plea of the principle of nationalities, as we shall see hereafter. The idea is more than a hundred years old, and Russia uses it now every day. What is pan-Slavism but the application, by Russia and Russian interest, of the principle of nationalities to the Serbians, Croats, Ruthenes, Slovaks, Czechs, and other remnants of bygone Slavonian peoples in Turkey, Hungary, and Germany? Even at this present moment, the Russian government have agents travelling among the Lapponians in northern Norway and Sweden, trying to agitate among these nomadic savages the idea of a 'great Finnic nationality', which is to be restored in the extreme north of Europe, under Russian protection, of course. The 'cry of anguish' of the oppressed Laplanders is raised very loud in the Russian papers – not by those same oppressed nomads, but by the Russian agents – and indeed it is a frightful oppression, to induce these poor Laplanders to learn the civilized Norwegian or Swedish language, instead of confining themselves to their own barbaric, half Eskimo idiom! The principle of nationalities, indeed, could be invented in eastern Europe alone, where the tide of Asiatic invasion, for a thousand years, recurred again and again, and left on the shore those heaps of intermingled ruins of nations which even now the ethnologist can scarcely disentangle,

9. On Engels's mistaken conception that the smaller Slav peoples 'never had a history', see the Introduction to *The Revolutions of 1848*, p. 51.

and where the Turk, the Finnic Magyar, the Rouman, the Jew, and about a dozen Slavonic tribes, live intermixed in interminable confusion. That was the ground to work the principle of nationalities, and how Russia has worked it there, we shall see by-and-by in the example of Poland.

III *Commonwealth*, 5 May 1866

The doctrine of nationality applied to Poland.

Poland, like almost all other European countries, is inhabited by people of different nationalities. The mass of the population, the nucleus of its strength, is no doubt formed by the Poles proper, who speak the Polish language. But ever since 1390[10] Poland proper has been united to the Grand Duchy of Lithuania, which has formed, up to the last partition in 1795, an integral portion of the Polish republic. This Grand Duchy of Lithuania was inhabited by a great variety of races. The northern provinces, on the Baltic, were in possession of *Lithuanians* proper, people speaking a language distinct from that of their Slavonic neighbours; these Lithuanians had been, to a great extent, conquered by German immigrants, who again found it hard to hold their own against the Lithuanian Grand Dukes. Further south, and east of the present Kingdom of Poland, were the *White Russians*, speaking a language betwixt Polish and Russian, but nearer the latter; and finally the southern provinces were inhabited by the so-called *Little Russians*, whose language is now by best authorities considered as perfectly distinct from the Great Russian (the language we commonly call Russian). Therefore, if people say that to demand the restoration of Poland is to appeal to the principle of nationalities, they merely prove that they do not know what they are talking about, for the restoration of Poland means the re-establishment of a state composed of at least four different nationalities.

When the old Polish state was thus being formed by the union with Lithuania, where was then Russia? Under the heel of the Mongolian conqueror, whom the Poles and Germans combined, 150 years before, had driven back east of the Dnieper. It took a long struggle until the Grand Dukes of Moscow finally shook off the Mongol yoke, and set about combining the many different principalities of Great Russia into one state. But this success seems only to have increased their ambition. No sooner had Constantinople

10. This union in fact dates from 1386, when Jagiello of Lithuania married Jadviga of Poland.

fallen to the Turks, than the Muscovite Grand Duke placed in his coat-of-arms the double-headed eagle of the Byzantine emperors, thereby setting up his claim as successor and future avenger, and ever since, it is well known, the Russians worked to conquer Tsarigrad, the town of the tsar, as they call Constantinople in their language. Then, the rich plains of Little Russia excited their lust of annexation; but the Poles were then a strong, and always a brave people, and not only knew how to fight for their own, but also how to retaliate; in the beginning of the seventeenth century they even held Moscow for a few years.[11]

The gradual demoralization of the ruling aristocracy, the want of power to develop a middle class, and the constant wars devastating the country, at last broke the strength of Poland. A country which persisted in maintaining unimpaired the feudal system of society, while all its neighbours progressed, formed a middle class, developed commerce and industry, and created large towns – such a country was doomed to ruin. No doubt the aristocracy did ruin Poland, and ruin her thoroughly; and after ruining her, they upbraided each other for having done so, and sold themselves and their country to the foreigner. Polish history, from 1700 to 1772, is nothing but a record of Russian usurpation of dominion in Poland, rendered possible by the corruptibility of the nobles. Russian soldiers were almost constantly occupying the country, and the kings of Poland, if not willing traitors themselves, were placed more and more under the thumb of the Russian ambassador. So well had this game succeeded, and so long had it been played, that, when Poland at last was annihilated, there was no outcry at all in Europe, and, indeed, people were astonished at this only, that Russia should have the generosity of giving such a large slice of the territory to Austria and Prussia.

The way in which this partition was brought about is particularly interesting. There was, at that time, already an enlightened 'public opinion' in Europe. Although *The Times* newspaper had not yet begun to manufacture that article, there was that kind of public opinion which had been created by the immense influence of Diderot, Voltaire, Rousseau, and the other French writers of the eighteenth century. Russia always knew that it is important to have public opinion on one's side, if possible, and Russia took care to have it, too. The court of Catherine II was made the

11. In 1605–6, and again in September 1610, the Poles occupied Moscow. The city was finally freed by a popular uprising under Minin and Pozharski.

headquarters of the enlightened men of the day, especially Frenchmen; the most enlightened principles were professed by the empress and her court, and so well did she succeed in deceiving them that Voltaire and many others sang the praise of the 'Semiramis of the North', and proclaimed Russia the most progressive country in the world, the home of liberal principles, the champion of religious toleration.

Religious toleration – that was the word wanted to put down Poland. Poland had always been extremely liberal in religious matters; witness the asylum the Jews found there while they were persecuted in all other parts of Europe. The greater portion of the people in the eastern provinces belonged to the Greek faith, while the Poles proper were Roman Catholics. A considerable portion of these Greek Catholics had been induced, during the sixteenth century, to acknowledge the supremacy of the Pope, and were called United Greeks; but a great many continued true to their old Greek religion in all respects. They were principally the serfs, their noble masters being almost all Roman Catholics; they were Little Russians by nationality. Now, this Russian government, which did not tolerate at home any other religion but the Greek, and punished apostasy as a crime; which was conquering foreign nations and annexing foreign provinces right and left; and which was at that time engaged in riveting still firmer the fetters of the Russian serf – this same Russian government came soon upon Poland in the name of religious toleration, because Poland was said to oppress the Greek Catholics; in the name of the principle of nationalities, because the inhabitants of these eastern provinces were *Little* Russians, and ought, therefore, to be annexed to *Great* Russia; and in the name of the right of revolution arming the serfs against their masters. Russia is not at all scrupulous in the selection of her means. Talk about a war of class against class as something extremely revolutionary; – why, Russia set such a war on foot in Poland nearly 100 years ago, and a fine specimen of a class war it was, when Russian soldiers and Little Russian serfs went in company to burn down the castles of Polish lords, merely to prepare Russian annexation, which being once accomplished the same Russian soldiers put the serfs back again under the yoke of their lords.

All this was done in the cause of religious toleration, because the principle of nationalities was not then fashionable in western Europe. But it was held up before the eyes of the Little Russian peasants at the time, and has played an important part since in Polish affairs. The first and foremost ambition of Russia is the union of all Russian tribes under the tsar, who calls himself the autocrat of all Russias, and among these she includes White and Little Russia. And in order to prove that her ambition went no further, she took very good care, during the three partitions, to annex none but White and Little Russian provinces; leaving the country inhabited by Poles, and even a portion of Little Russia (eastern Galicia) to her accomplices. But how do matters stand now? The greater portion of the provinces annexed in 1793 and 1795 by Austria and Prussia are now under Russian dominion, under the name of the Kingdom of Poland, and from time to time hopes are raised among the Poles, that if they will only submit to Russian supremacy, and renounce all claims to the ancient Lithuanian provinces, they may expect a reunion of all other Polish provinces and a restoration of Poland, with the Russian emperor for a king. And if at the present juncture Prussia and Austria come to blows, it is more than probable that the war will not be, ultimately, for the annexation of Schleswig-Holstein to Prussia, or of Venice to Italy, but rather of Austrian, and at least a portion of Prussian, Poland to Russia.

So much for the principle of nationalities in Polish affairs.

FOR POLAND[12]

Karl Marx and Frederick Engels

Der Volksstaat, 24 March 1875

This year, too, a meeting took place to commemorate the Polish uprising of 22 January 1863. Our German party comrades took part in this commemoration in large numbers; many of them made speeches, among them Engels and Marx.

'We have spoken here,' said Engels, 'of the reasons why the revolutionaries of all countries are bound to sympathize with

12. The following speeches were delivered by Marx and Engels at an international meeting held in London to commemorate the twelfth anniversary of the Polish uprising of 22 January 1863. Engels himself wrote up the report of his and Marx's speeches for *Der Volksstaat*, the organ of the SDAP, and they are translated here from the texts reproduced in *MEW* 18.

and stand up for the cause of Poland. Only one point has been forgotten and it is this: the political situation into which Poland has been brought is a thoroughly revolutionary one, and it leaves Poland with no other choice but to be revolutionary or perish. This was evident even after the First Partition,[13] which was brought about by the efforts of the Polish nobility to preserve a constitution and privileges which had forfeited their right to exist and were detrimental to the country and to general order instead of preserving the peace and securing progress. Even after the First Partition a section of the aristocracy recognized their mistake and became convinced that Poland could only be restored by means of a revolution; – and ten years later we saw Poland fighting for freedom in America. The French revolution of 1789 found an immediate echo in Poland. The constitution of 1791, embodying the rights of man, became the banner of the revolution on the banks of the Vistula and made Poland the vanguard of revolutionary France, and that at a moment when the three powers which had already plundered Poland were uniting to march on Paris and to stifle the revolution there. Could they allow revolution to nestle at the centre of the Coalition? Impossible! Again they threw themselves upon Poland, this time intending to rob it completely of its national existence. The unfurling of the revolutionary banner was one of the main reasons for the subjugation of Poland. A land which has been fragmented and struck off the list of nations because it has been revolutionary can seek its salvation nowhere but in revolution. And thus we find Poland taking part in all revolutionary struggles. Poland understood this in 1863 and during the uprising whose anniversary we are celebrating today it published the most radical revolutionary programme which has ever been laid down in eastern Europe. It would be ridiculous, because of the existence of a Polish aristocratic party, to regard the Polish revolutionaries as aristocrats who want to restore the aristocratic Poland of 1772. The Poland of 1772 is lost for ever. No power on earth will be able to raise it up from the grave. The new Poland to which the revolution will give birth differs, from a social and political point of view, just as fundamentally from the Poland of 1772 as does the new society which we are rapidly approaching from present society.

'Another word. No one can enslave a nation with impunity.

13. Of 1772.

The three powers which murdered Poland have been severely punished. Let us look at my own fatherland, Prussia–Germany. In the name of national unification we have annexed Poles, Danes and Frenchmen – and we now have *a Venice three times over*;[14] we have enemies everywhere, we burden ourselves with debts and taxes in order to pay for countless masses of soldiers, who, at the same time, are used to oppress German workers. Austria – even official Austria – knows all too well what a burden its bit of Poland is. At the time of the Crimean War Austria was ready to march against Prussia on condition that Russian Poland was occupied and liberated. This, however, did not enter into the plans of Louis Napoleon and even less into the plans of Palmerston. And as far as Russia is concerned, we can see that in 1861 the first significant movement broke out among the students, which was all the more dangerous because the people everywhere were in a state of great agitation following the emancipation of the serfs; and what did the Russian government do, seeing, as it did, the danger? – *It provoked the uprising of 1863 in Poland*; for it has been *proved* that this uprising was its work. The movement among the students, the deep agitation among the people disappeared immediately and their place was taken by Russian chauvinism, which poured over Poland once the preservation of Russian rule in Poland was at stake. Thus, the first significant movement in Russia came to an end as a result of the pernicious struggle against Poland. Indeed, the reunification of Poland lies in the interests of revolutionary Russia and it is with pleasure that I learn this evening that this view corresponds with the convictions of the Russian revolutionaries' (who had expressed a similar view at the meeting).[15]

Marx spoke to this effect: 'The workers' party of Europe takes the most decisive interest in the emancipation of Poland and the original programme of the International Working Men's Association expresses the reunification of Poland as a working-class

14. In the province of Venice, under Austrian rule from 1798 to 1805 and from 1814 to 1866, the Italian national movement could only be kept down by a large and expensive military presence.

15. W. Smirnov, the editor of the Russian democratic newspaper *Vperiod (Forward)*, had stressed the common interest of the Russian and Polish workers.

political aim.[16] What are the reasons for this special interest of the workers' party in the fate of Poland?

'First of all, of course, sympathy for a subjugated people which, with its incessant and heroic struggle against its oppressors, has proven its historic right to national autonomy and self-determination. It is not in the least a contradiction that the *international* workers' party strives for the creation of the Polish nation. On the contrary; only after Poland has won its independence again, only after it is able to govern itself again as a free people, only then can its inner development begin again and can it cooperate as an independent force in the social transformation of Europe. As long as the independent life of a nation is suppressed by a foreign conqueror it inevitably directs all its strength, all its efforts and all its energy against the external enemy; during this time, therefore, its inner life remains paralysed; it is incapable of working for social emancipation. Ireland, and Russia under Mongol rule, provide striking proof of this.

'Another reason for the sympathy felt by the workers' party for the Polish uprising is its particular geographic, military and historical position. The partition of Poland is the cement which holds together the three great military despots: Russia, Prussia and Austria. Only the rebirth of Poland can tear these bonds apart and thereby remove the greatest obstacle in the way to the social emancipation of the European peoples.

'The main reason for the sympathy felt by the working class for Poland is, however, this: Poland is not only the only Slav race which has fought and is fighting as a *cosmopolitan soldier of the revolution*. Poland spilt its blood in the American War of Independence; its legions fought under the banner of the first French republic; with its revolution of 1830 it prevented the invasion of France, which had been decided upon by the partitioners of Poland; in 1846 in Cracow it was the first to plant the banner of revolution in Europe, in 1848 it had a glorious share in the revolutionary struggles in Hungary, Germany and Italy; finally, in 1871 it provided the Paris Commune with the best generals and the most heroic soldiers.

'In the brief moments when the popular masses in Europe have been able to move freely they have remembered what they owe to Poland. After the victorious March revolution of 1848 in Berlin

16. See 'Inaugural Address of the International Working Men's Association', above, p. 81.

the first act of the people was to set free the Polish prisoners, Mieroslawski and his fellow sufferers, and to proclaim the restoration of Poland;[17] in Paris in May 1848 Blanqui marched at the head of the workers against the reactionary National Assembly to force it into armed intervention on behalf of Poland; finally in 1871, when the French workers had constituted themselves as a government, they honoured Poland by giving its sons the leadership of its armed forces.[18]

'And at this moment, too, the German workers' party will not in the least be misled by the reactionary behaviour of the Polish deputies in the German Reichstag; it knows that these gentlemen are not acting for Poland but in their private interests; it knows that the Polish peasant, worker, in short, every Pole not blinded by the interests of social status, is bound to recognize that *Poland has and can only have one ally in Europe – the workers' party*.

'*Long live Poland!*'

17. Ludwig Mieroslawski was a leader of the 1846 Cracow uprising.
18. See p. 217, n. 71.

The Curtain Raised[1]

World, 18 JULY 1871

From our Special Correspondent
London, 1 July

. . . I went straight to my business. The world, I said, seemed to be in the dark about the International, hating it very much, but not able to say clearly what thing it hated. Some, who professed to have peered further into the gloom than their neighbours, declared that they had made out a sort of Janus figure with a fair, honest workman's smile on one of the faces, and on the other a murderous conspirator's scowl. Would he light up the case of mystery in which the theory dwelt?

The professor [*sic*] laughed, chuckled a little I fancied, at the thought that we were so frightened of him.

'There is no mystery to clear up, dear sir,' he began, in a very polished form of the Hans Breitmann dialect,[2] 'except perhaps the mystery of human stupidity in those who perpetually ignore the fact that our Association is a public one and that the fullest reports of its proceedings are published for all who care to read them. You may buy our rules for a penny, and a shilling laid out in pamphlets will teach you almost as much about us as we know ourselves.'

REPORTER: Almost – yes, perhaps so: but will not the something I shall not know constitute the all-important reservation? To be quite frank with you, and to put the case as it strikes an outside observer, this general claim of depreciation of yours must mean something more than the ignorant ill-will of the multitude.

---

1. This interview was conducted at Marx's home in Hampstead by the New York *World*'s reporter R. Landor. The reporter's introduction and conclusion have been omitted.

2. After the 'Breitmann ballads' of Charles Godfrey Leland, which parodied the speech of the German settlers in America.

And it is still pertinent to ask even after what you have told me, what is the International Society?

DR MARX: You have only to look at the individuals of which it is composed – workmen.

REPORTER: Yes, but the soldier need be no exponent of the statecraft that sets him in motion. I know some of your members, and I can believe that they are not the stuff of which conspirators are made. Besides, a secret shared by a million men would be no secret at all. But what if these were only the instruments in the hands of a bold, and I hope you will forgive me for adding, not over scrupulous conclave.

DR MARX: There is nothing to prove it.

REPORTER: The last Paris insurrection?[3]

DR MARX: I demand firstly the proof that there was any plot at all – that anything happened that was not the legitimate effect of the circumstances of the moment; or the plot granted, I demand the proofs of the participation in it of the International Association.

REPORTER: The presence in the Communal body of so many members of the Association.

DR MARX: Then it was a plot of the Freemasons, too, for their share in the work as individuals was by no means a slight one. I should not be surprised, indeed, to find the pope setting down the whole insurrection to their account. But try another explanation. The insurrection in Paris was made by the workmen of Paris. The ablest of the workmen must necessarily have been its leaders and administrators; but the ablest of the workmen happen also to be members of the International Association. Yet the Association as such may be in no way responsible for their action.

REPORTER: It will still seem otherwise to the world. People talk of secret instructions from London, and even grants of money. Can it be affirmed that the alleged openness of the Association's proceedings precludes all secrecy of communication?

DR MARX: What association ever formed carried on its work without private as well as public agencies? But to talk of secret instructions from London, as of decrees in the matter of faith and morals from some centre of papal domination and intrigue, is wholly to misconceive the nature of the International. This would imply a centralized form of government for the Inter-

3. I.e. the Paris Commune.

national, whereas the real form is designedly that which gives the greatest play to local energy and independence. In fact, the International is not properly a government for the working class at all. It is a bond of union rather than a controlling force.

REPORTER: And of union to what end?

DR MARX: The economical emancipation of the working class by the conquest of political power. The use of that political power to the attainment of social ends. It is necessary that our aims should be thus comprehensive to include every form of working-class activity. To have made them of a special character would have been to adapt them to the needs of one section – one nation of workmen alone. To have done that the Association must have forfeited its title of International. The Association does not dictate the form of political movements; it only requires a pledge as to their end. It is a network of affiliated societies spreading all over the world of labour. In each part of the world some special aspect of the problem presents itself, and the workmen there address themselves to its consideration in their own way. Combinations among workmen cannot be absolutely identical in Newcastle and in Barcelona, in London and in Berlin. In England, for instance, the way to show political power lies open to the working class. Insurrection would be madness where peaceful agitation would more swiftly and surely do the work. In France a hundred laws of repression and a mortal antagonism between classes seem to necessitate the violent solution of social war. The choice of that solution is the affair of the working classes of that country. The International does not presume to dictate in the matter and hardly to advise. But to every movement it accords its sympathy and its aid within the limits assigned by its own laws.

REPORTER: And what is the nature of that aid?

DR MARX: To give an example, one of the commonest forms of the movement for emancipation is that of strikes. Formerly, when a strike took place in one country it was defeated by the importation of workers from another. The International has nearly stopped all that. It receives information of the intended strike, it spreads that information among its members, who at once see that for them the seat of the struggle must be forbidden ground. The masters are thus left alone to reckon with their men. In most cases the men require no other aid than that. Their own subscriptions or those of the societies to which they are more immediately affiliated supply them with funds, but should the pressure upon them become too heavy and the strike be one of which the Association approves, their necessities are supplied out of the common purse. By these means a strike of the cigar-makers of Barcelona was brought to a victorious issue the other day.[4] But the society has no interest in strikes, though it supports them under certain conditions. It cannot possibly gain by them in a pecuniary point of view, but it may easily lose. Let us sum it all up in a word. The working classes remain poor amid the increase of wealth, wretched amid the increase of luxury. Their material privation dwarfs their moral as well as their physical stature. They cannot rely on others for a remedy. It has become then with them an imperative necessity to take their own case in hand. They must revise the relations between themselves and the capitalists and landlords, and that means they must transform society. This is the general end of every known workmen's organization; land and labour leagues,[5] trade and friendly societies, cooperative stores and cooperative production are but means towards it. To establish a perfect solidarity between these organizations is the business of the International Association. Its influence is beginning to be felt everywhere. Two papers spread its views in Spain, three in Germany, the same number in Austria and in Holland, six in Belgium, and six in Switzerland. And now that I have told you what the International is, you may, perhaps, be in a position to form your own opinion as to its pretended plots.

REPORTER: I do not quite understand you.

DR MARX: Do you not see that the old society, wanting the strength to meet it with its own weapons of discussion and combination, is obliged to resort to the fraud of fixing upon it the imputation of conspiracy?

REPORTER: But the French police declare that they are in a position to prove its complicity in the late affair, to say nothing of preceding attempts.

DR MARX: But we will say something of those attempts, if you please, because they best serve to test the gravity of all the

4. Either Marx or the reporter is in error here. The spring 1871 strike in Barcelona was of textile workers, while the strike of cigar workers in which the International intervened was in Belgium.

5. On the Land and Labour League, see the Introduction to this volume, p. 29, n. 47.

charges of conspiracy brought against the International. You remember the last 'plot' but one.[6] A plebiscite had been announced. Many of the electors were known to be wavering. They had no longer a keen sense of the value of the Imperial rule, having come to disbelieve in those threatened dangers from which it was supposed to have saved them. A new bugbear was wanted. The police undertook to find one. All combinations of workmen being hateful to them, they naturally owed to the International an ill turn. A happy thought inspired them. What if they should select the International for their bugbear, and thus at one stroke discredit that society and curry favour for the Imperial cause? Out of that happy thought came the ridiculous 'plot' against the emperor's life – as if we wanted to kill the wretched old fellow. They seized the leading members of the International. They manufactured evidence. They prepared their case for trial, and in the meantime they had their plebiscite. But the intended comedy was too obviously but a broad, coarse farce. Intelligent Europe, which witnessed the spectacle, was not deceived for a moment as to its character, and only the French peasant elector was befooled. Your English papers reported the beginnings of the miserable affair; they forgot to notice the end. The French judges, admitting the existence of the plot by official courtesy, were obliged to declare that there was nothing to show the complicity of the International. Believe me, the second plot is like the first. The French functionary is again in business. He is called in to account for the biggest civil movement the world has ever seen. A hundred signs of the times ought to suggest the right explanation – the growth of intelligence among the workmen, of luxury and incompetence among their rulers, the historical process now going on of that final transfer of power from a class to the people, the apparent fitness of time, place and circumstance for the great movement of emancipation. But to have seen these the functionary must have been a philosopher, and he is only a *mouchard*.[7] By the law of his being, therefore, he has fallen back upon the *mouchard*'s explanation – a 'conspiracy'. His old portfolio of forged documents will supply him with the proofs, and this time Europe in its scare will believe the tale.

6. On the summer 1870 trial of the Paris Internationalists, see p. 173, n. 3.
7. Police spy.

REPORTER: Europe can scarcely help itself, seeing that every French newspaper spreads the report.

DR MARX: Every French newspaper! See, here is one of them [taking up *La Situation*], and judge for yourself of the value of its evidence as to a matter of fact, [reads:] 'Dr Karl Marx, of the International, has been arrested in Belgium, trying to make his way to France. The police of London have long had their eye on the society with which he is connected, and are now taking active measures for its suppression.' Two sentences and two lies. You can test the truth of one story by the evidence of your own senses. You see that instead of being in prison in Belgium I am at home in England. You must also know that the police in England are as powerless to interfere with the International society as the society with them. Yet what is most regular in all this is that the report will go the round of the continental press without a contradiction, and could continue to do so if I were to circularize every journal in Europe from this place.

REPORTER: Have you attempted to contradict many of these false reports?

DR MARX: I have done so till I have grown weary of the labour. To show the gross curiousness with which they are concocted I may mention that in one of them I saw Félix Pyat set down as a member of the International.

REPORTER: And he is not so?

DR MARX: The Association could hardly have room for such a wild man. He was once presumptuous enough to issue a rash proclamation in our name, but it was instantly disavowed, though to do them justice, the press of course ignored the disavowal.[8]

REPORTER: And Mazzini, is he a member of your body?

DR MARX [laughing]: Ah, no. We should have made but little progress if we had not got beyond the range of his ideas.

REPORTER: You surprise me. I should certainly have thought that he represented the most advanced views.

DR MARX: He represents nothing better than the old idea of a middle-class republic. We seek no part with the middle class. He has fallen as far to the rear of the modern movement as the

8. Félix Pyat, who dominated the London French branch of the International, compromised the Association by calling for the assassination of Louis Napoleon. See *IWMA* II, p. 224.

German professors, who, nevertheless, are still considered in Europe as the apostles of the cultured democratism of the future. They were so at one time – before '48, perhaps, when the German middle class, in the English sense, had scarcely attained its proper development. But now they have gone over bodily to the reaction, and the proletariat knows them no more.

REPORTER: Some people have thought they saw signs of a Positivist[9] element in your organization.

DR MARX: No such thing. We have Positivists among us, and others not of our body who work as well. But this is not by virtue of their philosophy, which will have nothing to do with popular government, as we understand it, and which seeks only to put a new hierarchy in place of the old one.

REPORTER: It seems to me, then, that the leaders of the new international movement have had to form a philosophy as well as an association for themselves.

DR MARX: Precisely. It is hardly likely, for instance, that we could hope to prosper in our way against capital if we derived our tactics, say, from the political economy of Mill. He has traced one kind of relationship between labour and capital. We hope to show that it is possible to establish another.

REPORTER: And as to religion?

DR MARX: On that point I cannot speak in the name of the society. I myself am an atheist. It is startling, no doubt, to hear such an avowal in England, but there is some comfort in the thought that it need not be made in a whisper in either Germany or France.

REPORTER: And yet you make your headquarters in this country?

DR MARX: For obvious reasons: the right of association is here an established thing. It exists, indeed, in Germany, but it is beset with innumerable difficulties: in France for many years it has not existed at all.

REPORTER: And the United States?

DR MARX: The chief centres of our activity are for the present among the old societies of Europe. Many circumstances have hitherto tended to prevent the labour problem from assuming an all-absorbing importance in the United States. But they are

9. The disciples of Auguste Comte. Edward Beesly, a London University professor and a leading figure of English Positivism, collaborated with Marx at this time in defending the Paris Commune. In this he was virtually unique among the British intelligentsia.

rapidly disappearing, and it is rapidly coming to the front there with the growth as in Europe of a labouring class distinct from the rest of the community and divorced from capital.

REPORTER: It would seem that in this country the hoped-for solution, whatever it may be, will be attained without the violent means of revolution. The English system of agitating by platform and press until minorities become converted into majorities is a hopeful sign.

DR MARX: I am not so sanguine on that point as you. The English middle class has always shown itself willing enough to accept the verdict of the majority so long as it enjoyed the monopoly of the voting power. But mark me, as soon as it finds itself outvoted on what it considers vital questions we shall see here a new slave-owners' war . . .[10]

R. LANDOR

10. Marx's reference here is to the North American civil war.

Index